BOYD'S COMMENTARY

for the

Sunday School

2017–2018

VOLUME ONE HUNDRED TWELVE
STRICTLY ORTHODOX AND
PURELY BAPTISTIC

These commentaries are based on the International Uniform Sunday School Lesson Outlines, copyrighted by the Division of Christian Education, the National Council of the Churches of Christ in the U.S.A., and used by permission.

Entered according to Act of Congress in the Office of Librarian of Congress in the year 1903 at Washington, D.C. by R.H. Boyd, D.D., LL.D.

R. H. Boyd, D.D., LL.D., Founder (1896–1922)

H. A. Boyd, D.D. (1922–1959)

T. B. Boyd, Jr., D.D. (1959–1979)

Dr. T. B. Boyd III
President/CEO (1979–Present)

A GLOBAL NAME IN PUBLISHING FOR OVER 100 YEARS

ᴬⁿ R.H.Boyd company

www.rhboydpublishing.com

President/CEO

LaDonna Boyd, MBA
Chief Operating Officer

David Groves, D.Min., Ph.D.
Director of Publications

Heather Sanders, M.Ed.
Director of Marketing

Steven Puckett, AAS
Director of Operations

EDITORIAL STAFF:
Tia Ferrell, M.S.
(Coordinator)
Olivia M. Cloud, M.R.E.
(Associate Editor)
Christopher R. Cotten, M.A., M.Div.
Landon Dickerson, B.A.
Jane Ann Kenney, M.Div.
Lee Perkins, M.Div.
Kaitlyn Phillips, B.A.
Vanessa Lewis, B.A.
LaKeva Lewis, B.S.
Lauren Oldham, B.A.
Freida Crawley, B.S.
Carla Davis, B.A.
Yoni Limor, B.A.

Rev. Richard Montgomery

Dr. Barry Johnson
Writers

Melissa Phillips
Cover Design

• • • • • • • • • • • • • • • • • • • •

R.H. Boyd Publishing Corporation
6717 Centennial Blvd.
Nashville, Tennessee 37209-1017

**For Customer Service
and Toll-Free Ordering, Call**
1–877–4RHBOYD (474–2693)
Monday–Friday
8 a.m.–5 p.m. Central Time or
Fax Toll-Free (800) 615–1815

A WORD FROM THE PUBLISHER

Welcome to the 2017–2018 edition of the Boyd's Commentary for the Sunday School.

We humbly present for your consideration another edition of Boyd's Commentary for the Sunday School, our most scholarly and in-depth resource for use by pastors, deacons, Sunday school teachers, and laypersons. This year's edition is packed with cogent and penetrating Scriptural exposition and theological analysis. For those who seek a deeper understanding of God's Word, there is simply no better resource on the market today. Pastors who labor to prepare sermons and Sunday school teachers and work diligently to explain the Word to their students will find this to be a valuable, time-saving resource. So, too, will laypersons who simply want to develop a closer relationship with God.

R.H. Boyd Publishing Corporation is committed to selecting the finest and most qualified scholars to prepare the material you now hold in your hands. Not only do they possess the appropriate academic credentials, but they are also men and women who bring essential ministry experience to the task at hand. In conjunction with them, our highly skilled and conscientious editorial staff has also worked to ensure the reliability and readability of every single lesson. Truly, this is a labor of love for our entire staff.

We pray God's richest blessings upon each and every one of you in your journey of faith, that you will use these lessons to further your understanding of His Word and your growth in Christian discipleship.

Grace and peace to you,

Dr. T. B. Boyd III, *President/CEO*

A WORD FROM THE DIRECTOR

It is with great pleasure that I present to you the 2017–2018 edition of Boyd's Commentary for the Sunday School. Now in its 113th year, Boyd's Commentary has an enduring reputation for providing sound biblical commentary that is committed to revealing the truth of God's Word and to the value of that Word in addressing the problems of human existence. Each lesson in this commentary seeks to strike a balance between deeply delving into the biblical text for the week and emphasizing an exploration for how to better embody the teachings of Scripture in everyday life. Throughout this commentary, the writers and editors have given attention to the myriad ways in which the Bible informs the social and ethical difficulties that characterize the complex national and international environment in which we live.

Designed, written, and edited especially for the needs of busy pastors, deacons, Sunday school teachers, and lay Bible students, Boyd's Commentary allows the reader to probe the surface reading of the biblical text to discover previously unknown wonders of exegetical and theological insight. Indeed, the commentary has been designed to be a holistic resource for help with both sermon and class preparation. It is my hope, as we place this resource in your hands, that it will do much good for the Kingdom of God. May your ministry be blessed by the Lord as you seek His face and lead others in that quest.

Yours in Christ,

Rev. David Groves, D.Min., Ph.D.

NOTE FROM THE EDITOR

The layout of the *2017–2018 Commentary* has been formatted for easy use in the classroom. In keeping with our rich history of publishing quality Christian literature, we have added the "Unifying Principle" as a feature that will enhance our commentary. Listed below is an explanation of each feature and its intended use.

Lesson Setting: Gives the basic timeline and place for the events in the lesson.

Lesson Outline: Provides the topics used in the exposition of the lesson.

Unifying Principle: States the main idea for the lesson across age groups. This feature allows the teacher to understand exactly what each lesson is about.

Introduction: Gives the thesis and also any background information that will be useful in the study of the lesson.

Exposition: Provides the exegetical study done by the writer, breaking down the text for discussion.

The Lesson Applied: Provides possible life applications of the biblical text for today's learners.

Let's Talk About It: Highlights ideas from the text in a question-and-answer format.

Home Daily Devotional Readings: Located at the end of each lesson, the topics are designed to lead into the following lesson.

Know Your Writers

Rev. Richard Montgomery

Rev. Richard Montgomery lives in Pittsburgh, Pennsylvania with his wife, Racquel, and their children. Rick is a graduate of Southwestern Baptist Theological Seminary in Ft. Worth, Texas, and has served as a pastor and director of a community service non-profit organization.

He served in Vietnam with the 2nd Battalion, 506th Infantry of the 101st Airborne Division, and was awarded the Purple Heart for wounds sustained in combat. God led him, from his experience as a combat soldier, to write the book, *Kingdom Soldiers: A Warrior's Guide to Winning Life's Battles*, dealing with the spiritual warfare Christians face every day of our lives.

Rick is now retired, but continues to volunteer as an administrator with the Pittsburgh Experiment, an evangelistic workplace ministry serving the men and women of Pittsburgh.

Barry C. Johnson, Sr., D.M.A., D.Min.

Dr. Barry C. Johnson, Sr., is a native of and resides in Louisville, Kentucky. Dr. Johnson earned a Bachelor of Music Composition (B.M.) and Master of Music Composition (M.M.) from the University of Louisville, and a Doctor of Musical Arts (D.M.A.) from the University of Kentucky. In addition, Dr. Johnson earned a Master of Divinity (M.Div.) and Doctor of Ministry (D.Min.) from the Southern Baptist Theological Seminary in Louisville, Kentucky.

Dr. Johnson serves as a tenured, Associate Professor of Music Composition and Theory in the Division of Fine Arts at Kentucky State University in Frankfort, Kentucky. In addition, Dr. Johnson serves as Pastor of the Evergreen Baptist Church, located in Lawrenceburg, Kentucky. He is an avid scholar and his interests encompass the spectrum of music, history, and religion. Among his many interests is the integration and relationship of the music of the Black Church and the streets, influenced by urban contemporary and gospel sounds, as well as, the relationship of commercial music and its position in academe and the local church.

Dr. Johnson, a prolific composer, arranger, preacher, and civic activist, continues to be an active performer in shows, plays, and musicals, and is an active clinician for Gospel Choral Festivals and Workshops.

2017–2018 LESSON OVERVIEW

Four major themes are explored in this year's commentary. The first theme is "Covenants with God" (September–November 2017), which explores several Old Testament texts as well as a pair of texts from the New Testament. These lessons focus on covenants that the Lord has made with His people to explore the confidence that His people can have today in His faithfulness to covenant promises. "Faith in Action," the second theme (December 2017–February 2018), considers texts from the New Testament as well as the book of Daniel. In all of these texts, various examples and blessings of faith are explored. The third theme is "Acknowledging God" (March–May 2018). Texts span the entire Bible, from Genesis to Revelation, with a focus on the sort of life that God's great work calls believers to live. The final theme, "Justice in the New Testament" (June–August 2018), focuses on the Gospels and Paul's letters to paint a picture of God's justice at work in Jesus' ministry and the Church.

• •

BOYD'S Commentary for the Sunday School (2017–2018)

Copyright © 2017 by R.H. Boyd Publishing Corporation
6717 Centennial Blvd.
Nashville, TN 37209–1017

PREFACE

The *2017–2018 Boyd's Commentary* has been formatted and written with you in mind. This format is to help you further your preparation and study of the Sunday school lessons.

We have presented a parallel Scripture lesson passage with the *New Revised Standard Version* alongside the *King James Version*. This allows you to have a clearer and more contemporary approach to the Scripture. This version is very reliable and reputable. It will bless you as you "rightly [divide] the word of truth" (2 Tim. 2:15, KJV).

These lessons have a new look, but they still have the same accurate interpretation, concise Christian doctrine, and competent, skilled scholarship.

The abbreviations used throughout the commentary are as follows:

KJV — King James Version
NIV — New International Version
NKJV — New King James Version
NLT — New Living Translation
NRSV — New Revised Standard Version
RSV — Revised Standard Version
TLB — The Living Bible
NEB — New English Bible
JB — Jerusalem Bible
ESV — English Standard Version

To the pastor: It is our hope that this commentary will provide context and insight for your sermons. Also, we hope this commentary will serve as a preparatory aid for the message of God. To the Bible teacher: This commentary also has you in mind. It can be used as a ready reference to the background of the text and difficult terms that are used in the Bible. To be sure, this commentary will provide your lesson study with the historical context that will enable you to better interpret the text for your students.

Lastly, this text is for anyone who wants to get a glimpse at the glory of God. This commentary seeks to highlight and lift the workings of God with His people and to make God's history with humanity ever present.

We hope and pray that God will bless you and keep you as you diligently study His mighty and majestic Word. Remain ever steadfast to our one eternal God. Keep the faith and pray always.

CONTENTS

FIRST QUARTER

CONTENTS

CONTENTS

CONTENTS

FOURTH QUARTER

UNIT THEME: GOD IS JUST AND MERCIFUL

UNIT THEME: JESUS CALLS FOR JUSTICE AND MERCY

UNIT THEME: PAUL TEACHES ABOUT NEW LIFE IN CHRIST

An Approach to God's Word

The Bible is a book of revelation wherein God discloses Himself and His thoughts to His beloved creation. The Bible accurately communicates the messages and revelations about God that He intends for His people to have. Inspired by the Holy Spirit, the components that make up Scripture are fully authoritative, a trustworthy means to bring us to salvation and guide us in a life of faith.

God did not share His Word with us simply to give us information or simply so we may believe correctly. Rather, God gave us His Word to draw us into a transformative relationship with Him.

The Bible is a book we can experience. So, how can we approach the Word of God so that it will shape and enrich our experience?

1. *Read with faith.* The Bible is deeply personal. We can approach Scripture with the confidence that God is, that God loves us, and that in Jesus Christ God has called us into a personal, saving relationship with Him. We can never have a full understanding of the Bible until we come to Jesus by faith and invite Him into our lives as Savior and Lord.

2. *Read with an open mind and heart.* As we read Scripture, we ask God to speak to us through His Word. We consciously seek to relate what we read to our daily living. We must be willing to let God's Word touch and inform our joys and sorrows, our strengths and weaknesses. God's Word is not only a record of history—but God's Word is still alive today. The Bible becomes active in the lives of believers who run to it seeking solace. Moreover, constant meditation on God's Word empowers us with a source of strength, even when the Word is not at our fingertips. If we often meditate on God's Word, we will have a constant source of encouragement on which to depend. The psalmist said, "Thy word have I hid in mine heart, that I might not sin against thee" (Psalm 119:11, KJV). When Scripture abides in our hearts and minds, we will not face our trials without a defense but come to them with the power of God's Word.

3. *Read with readiness to respond.* The Bible is a relational book. Through it, God speaks to us individually and personally. When we read the Bible with open hearts, we hear Him speaking to us. It is then that our response is vital. Both the Old and New Testaments emphasize the importance of an obedient response to God. We are called by Scripture to pattern our lives on the moral and spiritual teachings of the Bible, and to be responsive to the voice of God when He speaks to us with personal applications. Our obedient response to God's Word flows out of our love for Him. This response should be natural. It should be as natural as flipping a switch and a light coming on, or turning a faucet and seeing water come out. In a typical family setting, children are expected to follow the instructions of their parents. All of these examples have command–response scenarios. Likewise, Christians are to respond to the commands (or instructions) found in Scripture. Jesus said, "If ye love me, keep my commandments" (John 14:15, KJV).If we confess Christ, a sign of our love for Him is our obedience to His commands.

FIRST QUARTER

Lesson material is based on International Sunday School Lessons and International Bible Lessons for Christian Teaching. Copyrighted by the International Council of Religious Education and is used by its permission.

SEPTEMBER, OCTOBER, NOVEMBER 2017

WRITER: REV. RICHARD MONTGOMERY

SUGGESTED OPENING EXERCISES

1. **Usual Signal for Beginning**
2. **Prayer (Closing with the Lord's Prayer)**
3. **Singing (Song to Be Selected)**
4. **Scripture Reading:**
   Psalm 1:1–6 (KJV)

Director: Blessed is the man that walketh not in the counsel of the ungodly, nor standeth in the way of sinners, nor sitteth in the seat of the scornful.

School: But his delight is in the law of the LORD; and in his law doth he meditate day and night.

Director: And he shall be like a tree planted by the rivers of water, that bringeth forth his fruit in his season; his leaf also shall not wither; and whatsoever he doeth shall prosper.

School: The ungodly are not so: but are like the chaff which the wind driveth away.

Director: Therefore the ungodly shall not stand in the judgment, nor sinners in the congregation of the righteous.

All: For the LORD knoweth the way of the righteous: but the way of the ungodly shall perish.

Recitation in Concert:
Joshua 1:6–8 (KJV)

6 Be strong and of a good courage: for unto this people shalt thou divide for an inheritance the land, which I sware unto their fathers to give them.

7 Only be thou strong and very courageous, that thou mayest observe to do according to all the law, which Moses my servant commanded thee: turn not from it to the right hand or to the left, that thou mayest prosper withersoever thou goest.

8 This book of the law shall not depart out of thy mouth; but thou shalt meditate therein day and night, that thou mayest observe to do according to all that is written therein: for then thou shalt make thy way prosperous, and then thou shalt have good success.

CLOSING WORK

1. **Singing**
2. **Sentences:**
   James 4:6–10 (KJV)

6 But he giveth more grace. Wherefore he saith, God resisteth the proud, but giveth grace unto the humble.

7 Submit yourselves therefore to God. Resist the devil, and he will flee from you.

8 Draw nigh to God, and he will draw nigh to you. Cleanse your hands, ye sinners; and purify your hearts, ye double minded.

9 Be afflicted, and mourn, and weep: let your laughter be turned to mourning, and your joy to heaviness.

10 Humble yourselves in the sight of the Lord, and he shall lift you up.

3. **Dismissal with Prayer**

MAKING A PROMISE

ADULT TOPIC: THE RAINBOW	BACKGROUND SCRIPTURES: GENESIS 8:20–9:17

GENESIS 8:20–22; 9:8–17

King James Version

AND Noah builded an altar unto the LORD; and took of every clean beast, and of every clean fowl, and offered burnt offerings on the altar.

21 And the LORD smelled a sweet savour; and the LORD said in his heart, I will not again curse the ground any more for man's sake; for the imagination of man's heart is evil from his youth; neither will I again smite any more every thing living, as I have done.

22 While the earth remaineth, seedtime and harvest, and cold and heat, and summer and winter, and day and night shall not cease.

• • • Genesis 9:8–17 • • •

8 And God spake unto Noah, and to his sons with him, saying,

9 And I, behold, I establish my covenant with you, and with your seed after you;

10 And with every living creature that is with you, of the fowl, of the cattle, and of every beast of the earth with you; from all that go out of the ark, to every beast of the earth.

11 And I will establish my covenant with you, neither shall all flesh be cut off any more by the waters of a flood; neither shall there any more be a flood to destroy the earth.

12 And God said, This is the token of the covenant which I make between me and you and every living creature that is with you, for perpetual generations:

13 I do set my bow in the cloud, and it shall be for a token of a covenant between me and the earth.

New Revised Standard Version

THEN Noah built an altar to the LORD, and took of every clean animal and of every clean bird, and offered burnt offerings on the altar.

21 And when the LORD smelled the pleasing odor, the LORD said in his heart, "I will never again curse the ground because of humankind, for the inclination of the human heart is evil from youth; nor will I ever again destroy every living creature as I have done.

22 As long as the earth endures, seedtime and harvest, cold and heat, summer and winter, day and night, shall not cease."

• • • Genesis 9:8–17 • • •

8 Then God said to Noah and to his sons with him,

9 "As for me, I am establishing my covenant with you and your descendants after you,

10 and with every living creature that is with you, the birds, the domestic animals, and every animal of the earth with you, as many as came out of the ark.

11 I establish my covenant with you, that never again shall all flesh be cut off by the waters of a flood, and never again shall there be a flood to destroy the earth."

12 God said, "This is the sign of the covenant that I make between me and you and every living creature that is with you, for all future generations:

13 I have set my bow in the clouds, and it shall be a sign of the covenant between me and the earth.

MAIN THOUGHT: And I will establish my covenant with you, neither shall all flesh be cut off any more by the waters of a flood; neither shall there any more be a flood to destroy the earth. (Genesis 9:11, KJV)

GENESIS 8:20–22; 9:8–17

King James Version	*New Revised Standard Version*
14 And it shall come to pass, when I bring a cloud over the earth, that the bow shall be seen in the cloud:	14 When I bring clouds over the earth and the bow is seen in the clouds,
15 And I will remember my covenant, which is between me and you and every living creature of all flesh; and the waters shall no more become a flood to destroy all flesh.	15 I will remember my covenant that is between me and you and every living creature of all flesh; and the waters shall never again become a flood to destroy all flesh.
16 And the bow shall be in the cloud; and I will look upon it, that I may remember the everlasting covenant between God and every living creature of all flesh that is upon the earth.	16 When the bow is in the clouds, I will see it and remember the everlasting covenant between God and every living creature of all flesh that is on the earth."
17 And God said unto Noah, This is the token of the covenant, which I have established between me and all flesh that is upon the earth.	17 God said to Noah, "This is the sign of the covenant that I have established between me and all flesh that is on the earth."

LESSON SETTING
    Time: Unknown
    Place: Mount Ararat

LESSON OUTLINE
  I. **A Test Passed
     (Genesis 8:20–22)**
  II. **A Covenant Enacted
     (Genesis 9:8–11)**
  III. **A Sign Given
     (Genesis 9:12–17)**

UNIFYING PRINCIPLE

After tragedy strikes, there are possibilities for people to seek renewed hope and strength to rebuild their lives. Is there a reliable source humans can turn to for rebuilding and protecting their lives? As an act of benevolence, God used the rainbow to assure Noah that neither humankind nor the earth would ever again be destroyed by water.

INTRODUCTION

The book of Genesis is aptly called a book of beginnings. The various writers and editors who worked faithfully to record the works of their Lord spanned a wide swath of time and Israelite tradition.

Scholars today commonly divide Genesis into two unequal halves. The first eleven chapters compose the first half while the remaining chapters are the second half. Genesis 12 and following chapters introduces Abram and Sarai, their promised son Isaac, and finally Jacob, who would be called Israel, along with his twelve sons. Thus, the beginning of Israel is recounted. In contrast to this very specific origin story of God's people, Genesis 1–11 is concerned largely with God's interaction with His entire creation, not just one people or region. The narrative of the flood and its aftermath belongs in this section. In it, God did what He needed to do in order to cleanse the world of the evil that had overtaken it, but He also made provision so that life could go on. This provision came in the form of Noah, his family, and all the many animals who were saved in the ark.

Noah was both blessed and sorely tested. His immediate family was the only group of humans to be spared death by the great flood. That was a blessing. But, once the flood waters receded, Noah and his family were the only people left on earth. Genesis does not say where Noah was living at the time of the flood, but many scholars believe that he lived in Urartu, located in what is today southeastern Turkey. If that is true, then the ark did not travel far since the Ararat Mountains are in the same general area. But it was an entirely different world into which Noah and his family disembarked from the ark.

EXPOSITION

I. A TEST PASSED
(GENESIS 8:20–22)

Before doing any of the myriad chores necessary to start life over from scratch, Noah made sacrifices to God. God had instructed Noah to fill the ark with seven pairs of clean animals and one pair of unclean animals (see Gen. 7:2). What characteristics made an animal clean or unclean is not defined, but it is generally assumed that the people of Noah's day already understood that some animals were acceptable for sacrifice to God while others were not, a distinction later codified (see Lev. 11). From the seven pairs of clean animals that remained to repopulate the earth, Noah took one clean animal of each kind and sacrificed it to God. It was a demonstration of faith on Noah's part that indicates he was willing to kill off nearly 15 percent of his available stock of animals.

The aroma that rose from Noah's sacrifice was pleasing to God. Psalm 51:16–17 says, "For you have no delight in sacrifice; if I were to give a burnt offering, you would not be pleased. The sacrifice acceptable to God is a broken spirit; a broken and contrite heart, O God, you will not despise" (NRSV). It is not the aroma of roasting meat that pleased God. Noah's contrite heart put sacrificing to God ahead of finding food, building a new home, or figuring out what the family was to wear and that pleased God.

The Hebrew word translated "aroma" is *reyach*. In the Septuagint, which was the Old Testament that most Jews in Christ's time knew, the Greek word chosen to translate *reyach* is *hosmē*. The Greek word is interesting because it appears three times in the New Testament. In 2 Corinthians 2:14, one learns that those who know Christ give off an aroma. In Ephesians 5:2, Paul says that Christ, as He hung dying on the cross, gave off a fragrant aroma. Paul recounts, in Philippians 4:18, that the monetary offering sent to him by Epaphroditus was a fragrant aroma that pleased God.

Noah was being put to the test by God to see how he would handle the responsibility of rebuilding the earth. When Noah put God first, offering a valuable portion of what had been left to him for rebuilding, God smelled the aroma of faith and found it pleasing. God had tested Noah and Noah passed the test. The creation could continue safe in the knowledge that no more cataclysmic floods would come.

This in no way suggests that God expected Noah to be perfect. Genesis 8:21 clearly states God's recognition that "'the inclination of the human heart is evil from youth'" (NRSV). Noah was no exception. Don Fleming writes, "God's promise not to destroy the earth by a flood again was not because he expected people to improve. He knew they would be as sinful as ever. If God always dealt with people as they deserved, such floods would occur constantly" (*Bridgeway Bible Commentary*. https://www.studylight.org/commentaries/bbc/genesis-8.html). What God saw in Noah was a hopeful sign that faith was present in the human heart. This somber reflection on the state of human hearts excludes optimism about the direction of human history or the improvement of people over the generations. Though each generation would like to believe that they are more righteous than those who came before, it remains true that human hearts are bent toward evil from birth. Only few turn from this path when God is allowed to change those hearts as part of His recreating of His world.

II. A COVENANT ENACTED (GENESIS 9:8–11)

Noah needed help from God, and God came through. While the creatures that had previously viewed people as their caretaker would now regard people with fear and dread (see Gen. 2:9–20; 9:2–3), God placed these creatures into Noah's hand. They would be his to use as he required, including sustenance.

God required only one thing of Noah, just as he had only one requirement of Adam. Adam was to leave the Tree of the Knowledge of Good and Evil alone. Now, Noah was to leave the blood of the animals alone. Israel was also prohibited from eating animals with their blood as recorded in Leviticus 17:10. The Church is still prohibited from eating blood by the decision of the Apostles recorded in Acts 15:28–29. The reason God gave to Noah for the prohibition about eating blood was that the blood represents the life of the creature (see Gen. 9:4–5). Adam Clarke observes, "No blood was eaten under the law, because the blood was to be shed for the sin of the world; and under the Gospel it should not be eaten, because it should ever be considered as representing the blood which has been shed for the remission of sins" (*Adam Clarke's Commentary*. https://www.studylight.org/commentaries/acc/genesis-9.html).

As Noah and his family left the ark and began the process of starting humanity all over again, God gave them a gift. He offered them a covenant that would bind Him to His promise that He would never again destroy the earth by flood. The Hebrew word *berit* is translated *covenant*. A covenant is, in general terms, simply a contract between two; marriage is such a contract and is illustrative of what a covenant entails. The marriage covenant involves promises given from a man to his betrothed and from the woman to her betrothed. Each typically promises to love, cherish, and honor the other. Blessings come in the form of a happy marriage when those promises are kept. Curses, in the form of discord, strife, and, ultimately perhaps, divorce, come when the promises are broken. The covenant is symbolized by the exchange of rings that are said to represent the unbreakable bond between the new husband and wife.

A covenant between God and humanity is slightly different. In covenants between two people, both may give blessings and both may receive blessings. In God's covenants, only God is the Giver. He, alone, offers the blessings and He, alone, threatens the curses. It is left to people to choose whether or not they will obey the terms of the covenant. When Joshua gave his speech in preparation for the people of Israel to cross into the Promised Land, he asked them to choose whether or not they would obey God (see Josh. 24:15). Their continued obedience was by no means a foregone conclusion. The power imbalance between God and His people reflects the dynamic of many ancient Near Eastern covenants in which a more powerful figure or nation would enter into a covenant with a less powerful individual or group. In exchange for the loyalty of the less powerful party, the more powerful party would provide protections of various kinds and other incentives. Israel's obedience to covenants with God would result in His showers of blessings and through them blessing the whole world.

God's covenant with Noah was to be applied to all flesh. The animals had been given into Noah's hand, and they were to receive the blessing of the covenant just the same as the people were. All living things were blessed as a result of God's graciousness and Noah's humble submission.

III. A Sign Given
   ## (Genesis 9:12–17)

The rainbow was God's symbol given to all creation as a reminder of His promise to them. God, of course, does not forget, but the Hebrew word *zakar* translated as *remember* implies having something brought to the forefront of one's thought (Gen. 9:16, NRSV). A person might place a note on the bathroom mirror to remind himself to pay a bill, for example. It is not that the person will simply forget, but rather, that the note serves to bring the payment back to his attention. Every time there is a rainbow, God's promise is

returned to the forefront of His mind and He thinks of His promise to Noah. God's remembrance is not just a mental process; it is an action. When God remembers, He acts on His memory. Remembering His promise to Noah, He would act by refraining from sending a flood to destroy the world in water.

The words of God's promise to Noah emphasize that the promise is not actually just for Noah, or his family or the people who would come to repopulate the world. The promise is for every single creature in the world. The covenant was made between God, Noah, and "every living creature…for all future generations" (v. 12, NRSV). "The involvement of the nonhuman in the promise parallels their presence in the expectations of vv. 1–7 (see also 6:11–13)…. The bow thus suggests restraint in the midst of deserved judgment. It therefore seems best to retain the bow as a symbol of peace and divine good will toward creation. In either case, the bow serves as an important sign of God's deep, ongoing commitment to the life of the creation" (Terence E. Fretheim, *Genesis* in *The New Interpreter's Bible Vol. I* [Nashville, TN: Abingdon Press, 1994], 400).

God's concern was for all of His creation, just as it is today. Though the bow reminds believers that God would not destroy the world again in water, the reminder was primarily to the Lord to see and remember all of His beloved creation. For this reason, God repeated Himself to Noah and said "'This is the sign of the covenant that I have established between me and all flesh that is on the earth'" (v. 17, NRSV).

The Lesson Applied

Noah was tested, and he passed by making submission to God a priority in the aftermath of his ordeal. Because he humbly acknowledged God first, God blessed Noah. All people have the same opportunity whenever we face the trials and tests of life. When what seems like a tragedy strikes, we have the choice of either accepting it in faith that God knows what He is doing, or grumbling and complaining in rebellion against the will of God, who allowed it. When something that seems wonderful happens, people face a similar choice as to how to react. We may choose to congratulate ourselves and use the blessing for our own desires, or we may choose to gratefully offer the blessing back to the God who sent it to be used in service to His Kingdom. James wrote about this truth: those who petition God's blessings for personal comfort and pleasure will not be heard (see James 4:3).

It all comes down to the aroma of our lives, just as it did with Noah. Those of us who spread around an aroma of faith, obedience, humility, and surrender will pass the tests of life and find from God what we need to overcome. He has told us what the fruits of the Spirit are and he has been just as clear about what are the fruits of the flesh (see Gal. 5:16–26). We cannot claim that God has not told us what He desires from us. If a person wishes to triumph over all that life can throw, she should strive to be like Noah and offer to God the fragrance of a surrendered life.

Let's Talk About It

1. Are covenant and contract the same?

The words contract and covenant are often thought of as being synonymous, but these two forms of agreement are not parallel.

Contract signers agree to uphold up their end as long as the other signatories uphold theirs. If one party violates the terms of the agreement, the contract is broken in the eyes of the law, often rendering the contract null and void.

A covenantal agreement is more binding, such as the bond within a matrimonial relationship. It has often been observed that marriage is not a 50-50 arrangement; but rather, a 100-100 partnership. Each party commits to giving 100 percent of themselves to the marriage, regardless of the marital partner's actions.

When parties enter into covenant, both are bound to the agreement, regardless of whether the other party keeps honors the terms. One party's violation of the covenant does not release the other party from the alliance. The other violated party still has a responsibility to faithfully honor the covenant.

Home Daily Devotional Readings
September 4–10, 2017

Monday	Tuesday	Wednesday	Thursday	Friday	Saturday	Sunday
Sarai (Sarah), Mother of Many Nations	Ishmael, Father of a Nation	All Males of Abraham's Household Circumcised	Circumcision Event Remembered	God's Promise Realized Through Faith	Jesus, Mediator of Better Covenant	God's Covenant with Abraham Reaffirmed
Genesis 17:15–17	Genesis 17:20–22	Genesis 17:23–27	Acts 7:1–8	Romans 4:13–25	Hebrews 8:1–8	Genesis 17:1–14

A SIGN OF AGREEMENT

ADULT TOPIC: CIRCUMCISION	BACKGROUND SCRIPTURE: GENESIS 17

GENESIS 17:1–14

King James Version

AND when Abram was ninety years old and nine, the LORD appeared to Abram, and said unto him, I am the Almighty God; walk before me, and be thou perfect.

2 And I will make my covenant between me and thee, and will multiply thee exceedingly.

3 And Abram fell on his face: and God talked with him, saying,

4 As for me, behold, my covenant is with thee, and thou shalt be a father of many nations.

5 Neither shall thy name any more be called Abram, but thy name shall be Abraham; for a father of many nations have I made thee.

6 And I will make thee exceeding fruitful, and I will make nations of thee, and kings shall come out of thee.

7 And I will establish my covenant between me and thee and thy seed after thee in their generations for an everlasting covenant, to be a God unto thee, and to thy seed after thee.

8 And I will give unto thee, and to thy seed after thee, the land wherein thou art a stranger, all the land of Canaan, for an everlasting possession; and I will be their God.

9 And God said unto Abraham, Thou shalt keep my covenant therefore, thou, and thy seed after thee in their generations.

10 This is my covenant, which ye shall keep, between me and you and thy seed after thee; Every man child among you shall be circumcised.

New Revised Standard Version

WHEN Abram was ninety-nine years old, the LORD appeared to Abram, and said to him, "I am God Almighty; walk before me, and be blameless.

2 And I will make my covenant between me and you, and will make you exceedingly numerous."

3 Then Abram fell on his face; and God said to him,

4 "As for me, this is my covenant with you: You shall be the ancestor of a multitude of nations.

5 No longer shall your name be Abram, but your name shall be Abraham; for I have made you the ancestor of a multitude of nations.

6 I will make you exceedingly fruitful; and I will make nations of you, and kings shall come from you.

7 I will establish my covenant between me and you, and your offspring after you throughout their generations, for an everlasting covenant, to be God to you and to your offspring after you.

8 And I will give to you, and to your offspring after you, the land where you are now an alien, all the land of Canaan, for a perpetual holding; and I will be their God."

9 God said to Abraham, "As for you, you shall keep my covenant, you and your offspring after you throughout their generations.

10 This is my covenant, which you shall keep, between me and you and your offspring after you: Every male among you shall be circumcised.

MAIN THOUGHT: This is my covenant, which ye shall keep, between me and you and thy seed after thee; Every man child among you shall be circumcised. (Genesis 17:10, KJV)

King James Version	New Revised Standard Version
11 And ye shall circumcise the flesh of your foreskin; and it shall be a token of the covenant betwixt me and you.	11 You shall circumcise the flesh of your foreskins, and it shall be a sign of the covenant between me and you.
12 And he that is eight days old shall be circumcised among you, every man child in your generations, he that is born in the house, or bought with money of any stranger, which is not of thy seed.	12 Throughout your generations every male among you shall be circumcised when he is eight days old, including the slave born in your house and the one bought with your money from any foreigner who is not of your offspring.
13 He that is born in thy house, and he that is bought with thy money, must needs be circumcised: and my covenant shall be in your flesh for an everlasting covenant.	13 Both the slave born in your house and the one bought with your money must be circumcised. So shall my covenant be in your flesh an everlasting covenant.
14 And the uncircumcised man child whose flesh of his foreskin is not circumcised, that soul shall be cut off from his people; he hath broken my covenant.	14 Any uncircumcised male who is not circumcised in the flesh of his foreskin shall be cut off from his people; he has broken my covenant."

LESSON SETTING
Time: Third Millennium B.C.
Place: Canaan

LESSON OUTLINE
I. **Covenant from God (Genesis 17:1–2)**
II. **Covenant Promises (Genesis 17:3–8)**
III. **Covenant Requirements (Genesis 17:9–14)**

UNIFYING PRINCIPLE

Humans have an innate desire to support their children and ensure their future. What is required to make this possible? God used circumcision to ratify an everlasting covenant between God and Abram to make him and his descendants prosperous, provided they walk with God and live blameless lives.

INTRODUCTION

It is difficult to date with any certainty when Abraham and Sarah may have been alive. "The earliest surviving reference to Abraham may be in a 10th century Egyptian text, which refers to a place in the Negeb called 'the Fortress of Abraham,' listed among places conquered by the 22nd-Dynasty king Sheshonq (Shishak) in his incursion into Palestine during the reign of Rehoboam" (P. Kyle McCarter, Jr, "Abraham" in *Eerdman's Dictionary of the Bible* [Grand Rapids, MI: Eerdmans, 2000], 8). Scholars generally date Abraham's lifetime to the third millennium B.C. during the Middle Bronze Age. However, more important to Christians than when exactly Abraham lived are the promises that God made to Abraham and how they have been fulfilled in the span of human history.

It should come as no surprise to Christians that God offers similar agreements. One of the earliest examples in Scripture of a conditional covenant between God and humanity is the agreement God made with Abram, as recorded in Genesis 17. One can learn much about God and His dealings with people by examining who the participants were in God's covenant with Abram, what the requirements were that Abram and other participants had to meet, and what they would earn if they met the requirements.

EXPOSITION

I. COVENANT FROM GOD (GENESIS 17:1–2)

In Genesis 17:1, God initiated the covenant of circumcision with Abram. It is not a covenant between equals. Had God not approached Abram, introducing himself as the almighty God, the covenant would never have been offered. Agreements between people and God always begin with God. While God, in His infinite grace and mercy, may do what His people seek, He does it out of His love, not because anyone can bind him into an agreement that He did not initiate. Abram needed to clearly understand that this is the God above all other gods. Abram was living at the time in Canaan, where there was a multitude of local deities. It was not a local god who spoke to Abram, however. This was the God whose power and glory transcended anything that anyone might claim on behalf of another god. Abram prostrated himself in total submission.

Abram had a history with God. God had called Abram to leave his family and his home in Haran and journey to some unknown land (see Gen. 12:1–3). Leaving and unsure of his destination, Abram next encountered God when God promised that a land of Abram's own awaited him (see Gen. 13:14–18). In those days, land was everything. To have land was to have an identity, to have stature and honor among the various groups of people. Land provided security for entire families, extended relations included. Abram's next encounter with God came in the aftermath of the promise of land. Having land was important, but Abram also needed offspring to whom he could bequeath the land God would give. He cried out to God for a son (see Gen. 15:1–6). God heard Abram's cry and promised him an heir, despite Abram's advanced age.

In short, Abram had a history of encounters with God and had responded with obedience. He had journeyed forward from Haran (Gen. 12) in the face of a promise that someday, somewhere, a new home awaited. Then he accepted God's promise that a childless couple would produce an heir in their old age. Abram was a man of faith, though that faith was not always perfect (see Gen. 16). Abram had a track record of trust in God's commands.

In a covenant between God and humanity, the only requirement with which God binds Himself is to honor the terms of the covenant by providing the blessings for obedience. People, however, have requirements that must be met to remain inside the bounds of the covenant. Two requirements were presented to Abram from the start. God told Abram and all who would come after him through faith, to "walk before me" (Gen. 17:1, NRSV). To walk before God did not mean, as it did with many of the local gods in Canaan, to physically present oneself at a specific location. Canaanite peoples had their baals and their Ashtoreth images before which the believers would bow in worship and supplication. Stephen, in his speech before the Sanhedrin, said, "'The Most High does not dwell in houses made with human hands'" (Acts 7:48, NRSV). God dwells in the hearts of people whose faith opens them to His presence. That has always been the case, despite the focus in Israel on building temples of stone. God walked in the Garden of Eden as a companion to Adam and Eve (see Gen. 3:8). It was an intimate personal relationship between a loving God and the crown of His creation. Therefore, walking before God has nothing to do with one's location or any building or statue. Walking before God is a matter of the heart, where God dwells.

The second requirement God placed on Abram—and Abram's seed as people of faith—is to be "blameless" (Gen. 17:1, NRSV). God never expected that Abram or anyone else would be sinless; therefore, God's instruction to be blameless should not be misinterpreted as a requirement to live without committing sin. To understand what God was requiring necessitates an examination of sin. There are two basic ways in which a person might sin. One is unintentional. Through negligence, absent-mindedness, or otherwise distractedness, a person can sin without meaning to do so. The other means is intentional. People can choose to do wrong—whether by omission or comission—and frequently decide to sin rather than walking in righteousness.

God knows that human hearts are inclined to evil, but He takes great delight in those who earnestly endeavor to set aside fleshly desires and strive to obey His laws. God did not require Abram to be sinless and perfect to receive His promises. He simply required that Abram's life be characterized by a willingness to do as God instructed him.

II. Covenant Promises (Genesis 17:3–8)

Another participant in the covenant of circumcision was not an individual, but the seed that would come from Abram and Sarai. The Hebrew word used describes any source of life, from the seed of a plant to the life-carrying seed of human beings. The natural tendency, and the one which Israel chose, was to consider the "seed" of Abram the biological descendants of the union between Abram and Sarai. Jews took pride in their heritage as the literal descendants of Abram in Jesus' days. John the Baptist warned the Jews not to think that being descendants of Abraham would excuse their lack of repentance (see Luke 3:8). It took Paul to straighten out and elaborate the misunderstanding of exactly who were the "seeds" of Abram. Romans 4 explains in great detail that the descendants of Abram's faith, as exemplified in Isaac, are the actual participants in the covenant of circumcision, not the literal biological descendants.

This in no way means that God did not intend to bless Abraham's biological descendants. He blessed Ishmael, despite him not being the promised heir. He blessed the people of Israel as well, though it was their faith in God's promises that God honored, not the biological connection. This understanding that it is Abram's faith, not Abram's biology, that God is primarily focused on changes the understanding of the covenant He made with Abram.

III. Covenant Requirements (Genesis 17:9–14)

A final requirement was the covenant is circumcision. God clearly described this rite as a symbol (see 17:11). Symbols are outward indicators of an inward reality. While God expected Abram to physically circumcise all the males living under his protection, whether family or servants, the act of circumcision was to symbolize the cutting away of the world and the turning of the heart to God. Paul makes this clear in Romans 2:28–29: "For a person is not a Jew who is one outwardly, nor is true circumcision something external and physical. Rather, a person is a Jew who is one inwardly, and real circumcision is a matter of the heart—it is spiritual and not literal" (NRSV). Both the outer symbol and the inner reality were important to God's covenant.

God promised that the covenant with Abram—now called Abraham—would be everlasting. There will come a day when the sky is rolled up like a scroll, and yet the covenant with Abraham will continue. Jerusalem may vanish in the fire of God's judgment, yet a new Jerusalem will descend from heaven to be the home of all those who keep the covenant (see Rev. 21:1–2). This promise awaits all who, by faith, keep the requirements. Though believers may only dimly understand the true glory of what God has planned.

God promised a land, which represented security, identity, stature, and honor. While Abraham was certain to gain a worldly home, God also had in view something much more significant.

God introduced Himself by using a name humanity had never before heard—*El Shaddai*, or "Almighty God." He was not the only one to get a new name that day. Abram became Abraham, and Sarai became Sarah. New names signify new realities. Abram signified a great

father, Abraham a father of multitudes. Through covenant participation in the faith of Abraham, people can be included in that multitude today.

The final promise to Abraham was more of a warning. It is possible to be cut off from the promises. An individual who has the opportunity to join the covenant family of faith but refuses to circumcise his or her heart will have no place among the multitude of Abraham's offspring. This should be a sobering warning to those who believe that simply walking down an aisle and praying a quick prayer is enough to guarantee them inclusion among Abraham's covenant family.

While God spoke to Abram at first, Sarai was one flesh with Abram in God's sight and so, what God would do for Abram, he would do for Sarai as well. She, like Abram, had demonstrated faith by accompanying Abram as he left behind all they had ever known in life. Sarai, too, left behind family, friends, a community, and the security of a homeland, trusting both in God and in her spouse. In some ways, her faith might be considered stronger than Abram's because none of the promises were made directly to her. Despite her pushing Abram to produce an heir through Hagar, Sarai found favor in God's sight and would be blessed by God's covenant.

Faith was the key for Abraham and Sarah. It was not to be the first son, Ishmael, through whom the covenant would be fulfilled, but through the child of promise, Isaac. The promise to Abraham was given prior to physical circumcision and is for those who carry on Abraham's faith, not for those who are biological descendants.

THE LESSON APPLIED

Sometimes, American Christians seem to be very much interested in what we get by being children of God. We want salvation for ourselves and for those we love. We want blessings of health, wealth, and happiness all the time. We often expect God to come through for us in myriad of ways. Before we can expect the blessings, we must meet the requirements. The covenant between God and Abraham makes clear that God expects His people to have hearts that are completely inclined to Him at all times. Proverbs 4:23 warns believers to "keep your heart with all vigilance" (NRSV).

Directly speaking to those awaiting the coming of the day of the Lord, Jesus warned, "Be on guard so that your hearts are not weighed down with dissipation and drunkenness and the worries of this life, and that day does not catch you unexpectedly, like a trap" (Luke 21:34–35, NRSV). To guard our hearts, we must be on high alert as we maneuver through our daily lives, aware that the deceiver prowls like a lion seeking our total destruction. We do well to humbly examine ourselves at the close of each day, asking God to alert our awareness any and every time our hearts have turned away from him, so that we might repent and be restored before our stumbling turns into something deadly.

LET'S TALK ABOUT IT

1. Does God promise material prosperity to His children?

Being a Christian brings no guarantee of material prosperity, yet the television is replete with clergy who try to convince us otherwise. Prosperity is, in a sense, about attaining one's desired outcome and moving steadily toward that goal. When a person walks before God blamelessly, that person can expect to steadily move toward the goal of salvation and eternity with God, whether they are rich or poor or somewhere in between. This is the spiritual reality we receive as a promise from God if we keep the requirements of the covenant. Paul shouts in Romans 8, "Who will separate us from the love of Christ?" (v. 35, NRSV). It is a rhetorical question to which the answer is "nothing!"

God needs nothing from His people. He offers us a covenant agreement only because He loves His creation and desires to see it redeemed from the mess that sin has made of it. God desires that today's people walk before Him just as he commanded Abram to do. God is not some distant, unapproachable deity dwelling behind a curtain in a stone temple. He desires to be our intimate companion, dwelling daily in our hearts through our faith in Him.

HOME DAILY DEVOTIONAL READINGS
SEPTEMBER 11–17, 2017

MONDAY	TUESDAY	WEDNESDAY	THURSDAY	FRIDAY	SATURDAY	SUNDAY
The Sabbath Commandment	Recall God's Deliverance on the Sabbath	Healing on the Sabbath	Teaching on the Sabbath	Worship on the Sabbath	A Psalm for the Sabbath	The Sabbath, Sign of the Covenant
Exodus 20:8–11	Deuteronomy 5:12–15	Matthew 12:9–14	Mark 6:1–5	Acts 16:11–15	Psalm 92	Exodus 31:12–18

TAKING TIME TO REST AND RENEW

ADULT TOPIC:	BACKGROUND SCRIPTURES:
SABBATH OBSERVANCE	GENESIS 2:1–3; EXODUS 31:12–18; ISAIAH 56:1–8

EXODUS 31:12—18

King James Version

AND the LORD spake unto Moses, saying,

13 Speak thou also unto the children of Israel, saying, Verily my sabbaths ye shall keep: for it is a sign between me and you throughout your generations; that ye may know that I am the LORD that doth sanctify you.

14 Ye shall keep the sabbath therefore; for it is holy unto you: every one that defileth it shall surely be put to death: for whosoever doeth any work therein, that soul shall be cut off from among his people.

15 Six days may work be done; but in the seventh is the sabbath of rest, holy to the LORD: whosoever doeth any work in the sabbath day, he shall surely be put to death.

16 Wherefore the children of Israel shall keep the sabbath, to observe the sabbath throughout their generations, for a perpetual covenant.

17 It is a sign between me and the children of Israel for ever: for in six days the LORD made heaven and earth, and on the seventh day he rested, and was refreshed.

18 And he gave unto Moses, when he had made an end of communing with him upon mount Sinai, two tables of testimony, tables of stone, written with the finger of God.

New Revised Standard Version

THE LORD said to Moses:

13 You yourself are to speak to the Israelites: "You shall keep my sabbaths, for this is a sign between me and you throughout your generations, given in order that you may know that I, the LORD, sanctify you.

14 You shall keep the sabbath, because it is holy for you; everyone who profanes it shall be put to death; whoever does any work on it shall be cut off from among the people.

15 Six days shall work be done, but the seventh day is a sabbath of solemn rest, holy to the LORD; whoever does any work on the sabbath day shall be put to death.

16 Therefore the Israelites shall keep the sabbath, observing the sabbath throughout their generations, as a perpetual covenant.

17 It is a sign forever between me and the people of Israel that in six days the LORD made heaven and earth, and on the seventh day he rested, and was refreshed."

18 When God finished speaking with Moses on Mount Sinai, he gave him the two tablets of the covenant, tablets of stone, written with the finger of God.

MAIN THOUGHT: Speak thou also unto the children of Israel, saying, Verily my sabbaths ye shall keep: for it is a sign between me and you throughout your generations; that ye may know that I am the LORD that doth sanctify you. Ye shall keep the sabbath therefore; for it is holy unto you: every one that defileth it shall surely be put to death: for whosoever doeth any work therein, that soul shall be cut off from among his people. (Exodus 31:13–14, KJV)

LESSON SETTING

Time: **Thirteenth Century** B.C.
Place: **Mt. Sinai**

LESSON OUTLINE

I. **Why Have a Sabbath?**
(Exodus: 31:12–14)

II. **Keeping the Sabbath**
(Exodus: 31:15–17)

III. **Two Stone Tablets**
(Exodus: 31:18)

UNIFYING PRINCIPLE

Multitasking, complex job responsibilities, and diverse family structures and commitments may make persons feel overwhelmed. How can one find relief from the tedious and mundane? God commanded Moses and the Israelites to rest on the sabbath and keep it holy as a sign of their reverence to God who created the earth in six days and who rested and was refreshed on the seventh day.

INTRODUCTION

From the earliest days of recorded human history, a day of rest has been common place. The biblical creation account says that observance of Sabbath rest began at creation when God rested on the seventh day (see Gen. 2:2). From that example, humanity dispersed across the earth, as they migrated taking with them the habit of doing as God had done. M.G. Easton writes, "The ancient Babylonian calendar, as seen from recently recovered inscriptions on the bricks among the ruins of the royal palace, was based on the division of time into weeks of seven days. The Sabbath is in these inscriptions designated *Sabattu*, and defined as 'a day of rest for the heart' and 'a day of completion of labour [sic]'" (*Illustrated Bible Dictionary* [New York City, NY: Cosimo Classics, 2005], 591). However, not all cultures permitted everyone to have the day of rest. The biblical account suggests that the Egyptians worked their Hebrew slaves without a day off (see Exod. 1:11–14).

As the Hebrew people left the tyranny of Egypt and journeyed into the Negev desert to Mt. Sinai, they turned to God for guidance in putting their culture back together after centuries of enslavement. Moses, as recorded in Exodus 19:3, climbed Mt. Sinai to hear from God. One of the things God presented to Moses was a detailed set of instructions for the construction of the tabernacle and the accompanying priestly vestments (see Exod. 25:8ff). These instructions were given to establish the ongoing worship patterns for the people of Israel. As part of the tabernacle instructions, God commanded the Israelites to observe a day of Sabbath rest.

EXPOSITION

I. WHY HAVE A SABBATH? (EXODUS 31:12–14)

God created humanity in His own image. Part of what that suggests is that, to some degree, human beings share God's nature. If God took the seventh day off from His creative work, it is reasonable to believe that rest is important to humans also. Studies are increasingly emphasizing the importance of detaching from the rigors of daily living to give body, mind, and spirit an opportunity to be rested and refreshed. People need rest. No matter whether one is a laborer, a farmer, an office worker, or a young student, no person functions properly without rest. Even given sufficient sleep, people eventually wear down if all they do is work, work, and work some more. People need Sabbath because God has built that need into humans as a reflection of His own divine nature.

If one imagines what it must have been like when Moses brought God's tabernacle instructions back to the people, another reason for Sabbath suggests itself. The people of Israel had just been rescued miraculously by God from generations of bondage in Egypt. Those with Moses at Mt. Sinai had never known freedom. Now, thanks to God, they were free. They pledged several times that they would remain obedient to everything God told them (see Exod. 19:8; 24:3, 7). Meanwhile, they rebelled against eating manna and built a golden calf, but as Moses presented the instructions for the tabernacle the people were ready to get to work.

God commanded them to honor the Sabbath and keep it holy (see Exod. 20:8–11), but the people then were like people are now. Get people excited about a blessing, like God's presence in the tabernacle, give them instructions about how to go about receiving this blessing, and the danger arises when the people will work themselves beyond the point of exhaustion, without taking a break. "The reason for the fresh inculcation of the fourth commandment at this particular period was, that the great ardor and eagerness, with which all classes betook themselves to the construction of the tabernacle, exposed them to the temptation of encroaching on the sanctity of the appointed day of rest" (Robert Jamieson, A.R. Fausset, & David Brown. *Commentary Critical & Explanatory on the Whole Bible.* http://www.biblestudytools.com/commentaries/jamieson-fausset-brown/exodus/exodus-31.html). Don Fleming agrees: "People might have thought that, because the tabernacle was a sacred structure, they could work on it on the Sabbath day" (*Bridgeway Bible Commentary.* https://www.studylight.org/commentaries/bbc/exodus-31.html).

Another reason for keeping Sabbath is to protect spiritual health. At times it can seem as if God has moved away from His people. At such times His people may be discouraged, sorely tempted by the flesh, and without the resources to stand against the wiles of the enemy. At such times, the Sabbath can make the difference between spiritual triumph and defeat. Adam Clarke notes, "If a man religiously rests on the Sabbath, both his body and soul shall be refreshed; he shall acquire new light and life" (*Adam Clarke's Commentary.* https://www.studylight.org/commentaries/acc/exodus-31.html).

There are many legitimate reasons why the people of God are wise to observe the Sabbath. The best and ultimate reason is simply that God commanded it. Israel may not have believed or felt that they needed one day off a week because much more could be accomplished by working one more day, but God instructed them to take a day off whether they thought it was necessary or not.

II. KEEPING THE SABBATH (EXODUS 31:15–17)

From Mt. Sinai Moses brought down with him three specific instructions about keeping the Sabbath. Many centuries later, Isaiah noted a fourth. First of all, God's Sabbath instruction must be kept because through Sabbath observance God would sanctify His people (see Exod. 31:13). By this, He meant that Sabbath observance would both set the people apart from the nations around them and would mark them as God's own people. The Sabbath observance was a key to people growing in grace. To those ends, God forbade anyone to profane the Sabbath. The word "profane" is not limited to that which is vulgar, but more generally means that which is common or irreligious. Not only would sexual immorality be profane, but also everyday activities like cooking or farming. The Sabbath was to be a day sacredly devoted to God, not simply another day of the week to accomplish the normal, everyday tasks of life. God was not fooling around about this; those who profaned the Sabbath were to be put to death.

There is little evidence that the people of Israel regularly executed Sabbath-breakers. Rather, they were typically ostracized or whipped publicly as examples for everyone else. There is no specific explanation given in Scripture, but the death penalty seems to be connected to ridding God's people of those who had no willingness to obey God at all, rather than punishing an individual who may have broken a rule through necessity or ignorance.

The Pharisees' encounter with Jesus makes it clear that the guardians of Jewish legal observance in His lifetime took the Sabbath very seriously, according to their understanding of what the Sabbath was to be (see Mark 2:23–28). The Pharisees seemed clearly to want to have Jesus stoned for His perceived Sabbath-breaking.

Work was forbidden with the same death penalty attached for profaning the Sabbath. This prohibition was deemed immediately important to restrain any tendency the people might have had to work on the tabernacle, but it was not simply for that reason. God reminded Moses and the people through him, that God had only worked on creation for six of the seven days of the week, and He commanded His people to follow His lead. The pursuit of any occupational work, including the normal routine work around the home,

was to give way on the Sabbath to rest and spiritual renewal.

The people were not to work, and were not to treat the Sabbath as just another day, and, finally, according to the instructions Moses brought from Sinai, they were not to cease honoring the Sabbath. It was to be observed "throughout their generations, as a perpetual covenant" (Exod. 31:16, NRSV). While it was immediately important that the people took a break from the work of building the tabernacle, the Sabbath was to remain a vital part of the life of God's people forever. As such, it referred to the final Sabbath rest awaiting the people of God in heaven.

During their enslavement in Egypt, the Hebrews had been worked seven days a week. Isaiah noted many generations later that the Sabbath was a blessing to those who found themselves outsiders among the people of Israel. Specifically, Isaiah 56:3 speaks of inclusiveness to people who were foreigners among God's people and to those who had been made eunuchs in service to others. These were people who were likely to feel as if they were less than the Israelites among whom they dwelt. Including such people in the observance of the Sabbath brought them into the fold and made the manifold blessings of God available to them (56:5–7, NRSV). Of this, Fleming says, "The law of Moses made it plain that eunuchs were to be excluded from the tabernacle worship, probably to discourage the Israelites from making their own people eunuchs (Deut. 23:1). But in the new Jerusalem all foreigners, eunuchs or otherwise, who honour [sic] God and keep his law should be allowed to worship in the temple along with godly Israelites

(3–5). Love and obedience towards God, not physical or national characteristics, are the important things in God's sight. The temple is for the use of all people, not just Jews, because God's mercy is for all people (6–8)" (https://www.studylight.org/commentaries/bbc/isaiah-56.html?print=yes).

III. Two Stone Tablets (Exodus 31:18)

Although God's speech preceding verse eighteen was concerned with the Sabbath, here, His words offer a summation of His laws and highlight which of His commands Israel needed to consider the most important guiding laws the Lord chose to give them. "When God finished speaking with Moses on Mount Sinai, he gave him the two tablets of the covenant, tablets of stone, written with the finger of God" (Exod. 31:18, NRSV). God's instructions, which had begun in Exodus 20, concluded here. Moses came down from the mountain bearing the only document that was written on two stone tablets, a testament to their lasting importance for Israel. Other laws would spring from these, but with His own finger God wrote the most important commands on stone. "This verse creates something of a 'canon within the canon,' instructing the community in what counts most. And what counts the most, so that it is formalized and transmitted in writing, is not tabernacle provisions but the commandments" (Walter Brueggemann, *Exodus* in *The New Interpreter's Bible Vol. I* [Nashville, TN: Abingdon Press, 1995], 924). Written by God's finger in stone, these words would be stored in the Ark of the Covenant, arguably, the most holy object in Israel and a symbol of God's presence with the people.

THE LESSON APPLIED

In the immediate aftermath of the crucifixion and resurrection of Jesus, His followers continued to observe the Jewish Sabbath. Beginning at sundown on Friday, all normal activity ceased. Rising early on Saturday, they went to their local synagogue, and they gathered with all the other observant Jews for worship and the reading of Scripture. Later that day, they relaxed at home, and shunned work or anything that might profane the holiness of the day as known as the Sabbath.

Very quickly, however, the followers of Jesus began to meet on the first day of the new week, Sunday, to celebrate the resurrection of their Lord. They shared a meal and encouraged one another to remain steadfast in the face of growing opposition from the other Jews. When the persecution became so intense that the followers of Jesus were forced to leave the synagogue, the Christian Sabbath became standardized on Sunday and was known as the Lord's Day. While looking to Jesus' teaching and His example of elevating the spirit of the Sabbath over the rigorous Jewish legal structure (see Mark 2:23–28), the early Church emphasized keeping the Sabbath holy to God and God only, and refraining from unnecessary work and frivolous entertainment and doing the good works commanded by Jesus. Rather than the burden of an impossibly long and stringent set of rules, the Church sought to honor God and obey His Sabbath command by devoting themselves to God and to the advancement of the Kingdom. As Jesus made it very clear, the Sabbath was made as a blessing for all of humanity.

Let's Talk About It

1. How might Sabbath observance serve as a sign of our devotion to God?

The rules for keeping the Sabbath were simple. Do not disrespect it. Do not do work on it. Do not stop doing it, and do not exclude anyone from keeping it. Yet by the time of Jesus, the Jews had developed a set of regulations that would rival the United States Income Tax Code in complexity. One could walk 3000 paces, but the 3001st pace would break the Sabbath. Cities like Jerusalem were divided into sectors and one's "home" was defined as being a sector to enable people to venture further on the Sabbath. The blind man healed by Jesus was condemned by the Jewish leaders for carrying his mat on the Sabbath (see John 5). What had been intended by God as a blessing and a way to be refreshed had become a burden among the people who feared that somehow they would inadvertently break a rule.

So, what is a Christian to do? Such questions can spark disagreement among devout Christians, but they also grow out of the same sort of legalistic view of the Sabbath that Jesus condemned. Rather than try to obey a lengthy and debatable set of rules, keep God central in your heart and your attention on Sunday, devote the most time possible to worship, prayer, and fellow Christians, and then do what must be done if a genuine need arises. Remember the heart of the Sabbath is to refresh God's people physically, mentally, and spiritually and to honor God, who Himself rested on the seventh day of creation. The Sabbath day was made as a blessing. By limiting our activities to what is essential, devoting ourselves to worship, prayer, reading of the Scriptures, to the welfare of both our biological and spiritual families, and to doing good for those around us who are in need, we can restore the rest of Sabbath to the time of relaxation, restoration, and devotion for which God gave it to us.

Because we often neglect Sabbath rest, we have lost the awareness of what a blessing it can be to our spiritual vigor to spend one day each week quietly basking in the presence of God. The nations surrounding Israel did not typically recognize a Sabbath or at least did not treat it very observantly. If we Christians honor the Sabbath rest by not engaging in business and by limiting our other activities as much as possible to only those which are truly necessary, we will open up for ourselves opportunities to explain to unbelievers why we do so, and to call those around us toward God.

HOME DAILY DEVOTIONAL READINGS
SEPTEMBER 18–24, 2017

MONDAY	TUESDAY	WEDNESDAY	THURSDAY	FRIDAY	SATURDAY	SUNDAY
A New Covenant of the Heart	Nations Will Know the Lord	The Lord Will Restore Israel	Restored as One People	Making a Covenant of Peace	Profitable Actions for Everyone	I Will Restore My Holy Name
Jeremiah 31:31–34	Ezekiel 36:33–38	Ezekiel 37:11–14	Ezekiel 37:15–23	Ezekiel 37:24–28	Titus 3:8–11	Ezekiel 36:22–32

A Change of Heart

Adult Topic: Spirit-Filled Heart	Background Scriptures: Ezekiel 36–37; Titus 3:1–11

Ezekiel 36:22–32

King James Version

THEREFORE say unto the house of Israel, thus saith the Lord God; I do not this for your sakes, O house of Israel, but for mine holy name's sake, which ye have profaned among the heathen, whither ye went.

23 And I will sanctify my great name, which was profaned among the heathen, which ye have profaned in the midst of them; and the heathen shall know that I am the Lord, saith the Lord God, when I shall be sanctified in you before their eyes.

24 For I will take you from among the heathen, and gather you out of all countries, and will bring you into your own land.

25 Then will I sprinkle clean water upon you, and ye shall be clean: from all your filthiness, and from all your idols, will I cleanse you.

26 A new heart also will I give you, and a new spirit will I put within you: and I will take away the stony heart out of your flesh, and I will give you an heart of flesh.

27 And I will put my spirit within you, and cause you to walk in my statutes, and ye shall keep my judgments, and do them.

28 And ye shall dwell in the land that I gave to your fathers; and ye shall be my people, and I will be your God.

29 I will also save you from all your uncleannesses: and I will call for the corn, and will increase it, and lay no famine upon you.

30 And I will multiply the fruit of the tree, and the increase of the field, that ye shall receive no more reproach of famine among the heathen.

New Revised Standard Version

THEREFORE say to the house of Israel, Thus says the Lord God: It is not for your sake, O house of Israel, that I am about to act, but for the sake of my holy name, which you have profaned among the nations to which you came.

23 I will sanctify my great name, which has been profaned among the nations, and which you have profaned among them; and the nations shall know that I am the Lord, says the Lord God, when through you I display my holiness before their eyes.

24 I will take you from the nations, and gather you from all the countries, and bring you into your own land.

25 I will sprinkle clean water upon you, and you shall be clean from all your uncleannesses, and from all your idols I will cleanse you.

26 A new heart I will give you, and a new spirit I will put within you; and I will remove from your body the heart of stone and give you a heart of flesh.

27 I will put my spirit within you, and make you follow my statutes and be careful to observe my ordinances.

28 Then you shall live in the land that I gave to your ancestors; and you shall be my people, and I will be your God.

29 I will save you from all your uncleannesses, and I will summon the grain and make it abundant and lay no famine upon you.

30 I will make the fruit of the tree and the produce of the field abundant, so that you may never again suffer the disgrace of famine among the nations.

MAIN THOUGHT: A new heart also will I give you, and a new spirit will I put within you: and I will take away the stony heart out of your flesh, and I will give you an heart of flesh. (Ezekiel 36:26, KJV)

EZEKIEL 36:22–32

King James Version	*New Revised Standard Version*
31 Then shall ye remember your own evil ways, and your doings that were not good, and shall lothe yourselves in your own sight for your iniquities and for your abominations.	31 Then you shall remember your evil ways, and your dealings that were not good; and you shall loathe yourselves for your iniquities and your abominable deeds.
32 Not for your sakes do I this, saith the Lord GOD, be it known unto you: be ashamed and confounded for your own ways, O house of Israel.	32 It is not for your sake that I will act, says the Lord GOD; let that be known to you. Be ashamed and dismayed for your ways, O house of Israel.

LESSON SETTING
Time: Circa 590 B.C.
Place: Babylonia

LESSON OUTLINE
I. **God Defends His Name (Ezekiel 36:22–27)**
II. **God's People Benefit (Ezekiel 36:28–30)**
III. **God's People Must Respond (Ezekiel 36:31–32)**

UNIFYING PRINCIPLE
People stubbornly follow their own agendas without regard to the impact of their actions on those they respect and admire. What will motivate these persons to change? God will give them new hearts and put a new spirit in their hearts.

INTRODUCTION
Time and time again, Israel corrupted their purity as God's chosen nation by adopting the gods and practices of the nations that surrounded them. It was undoubtedly easier to get along by giving in to social pressure than to stand in opposition to the customs of their neighbors. Finally, God had enough. First, the Assyrians seized the northern kingdom of Israel and then the Babylonians took over the southern kingdom of Judah. The people of Judah and Israel were transplanted from their God-given Promised Land and resettled in small, manageable groups in the various cities and towns of the Assyrian and Babylonian empires. One group, from which the prophet, Ezekiel, arose, was moved to the town we now know as Tel-Abib, near the capitol of Babylon. The Promised Land was left desolate of God's people and the people of God were often mocked by their captors because their God had failed to protect them (see Ezek. 36:2–4). The holiness of God's name was being blasphemed. Ezekiel 36:17 tells us why God allowed this to happen: "When the house of Israel lived on their own soil, they defiled it with their ways and their deeds" (NRSV). Yet God was not done with His people.

And so, the word of the Lord came to the prophet Ezekiel. "Jerome calls the book [of Ezekiel] 'a labyrinth of the mysteries of God.' It was because of this obscurity that the Jews forbade any one to read it till he had attained the age of thirty" (M.G. Easton, *Illustrated Bible Dictionary* [New York City, NY: Cosimo Classics, 2005], 247). Ezekiel was a priest or a priest-in-training when he and a wave of professionals and scholars were taken from Judah into captivity in Babylon in

597 B.C. His calling to ministry came a few years later in 593 B.C. during which "he engaged in the harsh task of dismantling the orthodox Yahwistic theology of his day. That theology emphasized Yahweh's promises to the Israelites—e.g., the blessings attending the covenant forged at Sinai, God's absolute commitment to the Davidic dynasty, and the inviolability of Jerusalem, site of Yahweh's Temple" (Katheryn Pfisterer Darr, *The Book of Ezekiel* in *The New Interpreter's Bible Vol. VI* [Nashville, TN: Abingdon Press, 2001], 1075–1076). The exile to Babylon caused a crisis for those who believed these things because the destruction of the temple and the fall of the Davidic dynasty suggested that God was not faithful any longer to the covenant He had given at Sinai. They failed to realize that the flipside of covenant blessings were covenant curses that would result if the people were unfaithful to the Lord. In his ministry, Ezekiel was tasked with reminding them of their faithlessness and eventually assuring them that the Lord had not forgotten them or abandoned them and would restore them.

EXPOSITION

I. GOD DEFENDS HIS NAME (EZEKIEL 36:22–27)

The holy name of God was being disrespected. The Jews would not even so much as pronounce this name, but the nations into which they had been led captive had no such hesitancy. Yahweh was, in their sight, just another god, and not a particularly great one at that. Furthermore, the people of God had defiled God's name by failing to keep His covenant and by mixing a little of this custom and a bit of that religious practice into their culture. They intermarried with idolatrous people and brought those people's gods into their homes alongside Yahweh. Now God would sanctify what they had polluted.

To sanctify means to set something apart as completely different or special from anything else. God would show Himself different from the other gods to which He was now being unfavorably compared, as a result of the practices of His children. The people of Israel and Judah did not deserve God's saving intervention, but God was not going to allow His holy name to be dragged through the mud, or treated as if He were another of the myriad deities to which various groups prayed. His intervention was to be "not for your sake … but for the sake of my holy name" (Ezek. 36:22, NRSV).

Through Ezekiel, God listed four specific actions He was to take that would "display [His] holiness" (36:23, NRSV) before the people who were scoffing at Him. First, God would remove His children from the nations to which they had been abducted. Babylon was the great power of the earth at this time. They had conquered Assyria, and they had captured the people of Judah. Captive people were expected to blend in, to become new members of the conquering society, adopting their customs and learning their language. Babylon had every expectation that the children of God would simply cease to exist separately from the rest of the Babylonians. God would have to be powerful, indeed, to take these captives away from Babylon and its gods. That is exactly what Yahweh was going to do. God's power would be vindicated.

Along with removing His children from Babylon, God said He would return them to the land He had given them. The people of God may have been questioning God's faithfulness. God had promised that the land would be theirs forever, but they remained captive in Babylon while the surrounding nations moved into their land and desecrated it with idolatry and uncleanness. However, God would demonstrate that He was faithful to the covenant He forged with Moses on Mt. Sinai. The nation of Israel would rise from the ashes of Babylonian captivity and live on the land God had given their forebears centuries before.

Having taken His people away from Babylon and returned them to their homeland, God next said that He would change those same people. God was not about to tolerate another defilement of His holy name, and that meant the people must be different. God told them he would "sprinkle clean water" on them to remove the uncleanness that they had brought upon themselves by profaning God's name (36:25, NRSV). Once cleansed, they would receive from God a new heart and a new spirit. These two statements together indicate a radical and total transformation. The new spirit indicates that God intended to change the intentions and worship the people gave to God. One can see the beginnings of this transformation in the books of Ezra and Nehemiah. Once this was done, the people would follow God's statutes and observe His ordinances. God was going to defend the holiness of His name by not simply bringing the people back home, but by also changing them to become the obedient, worshipful, grateful people He desired.

II. God's People Benefit (Ezekiel 36:28–30)

All that God said He would do was primarily for the sake of demonstrating to a skeptical world that He was, indeed, the one supreme God above all the surrounding deities—transcendent in power and faithful to His covenants. However, the children of this transcendent God would benefit at that same time God defended His name. Having been removed from captivity, restored to their land, cleansed, and given new hearts and spirits, the scattered people would again be called God's people. Here, the emphasis is not on the people becoming something they had ceased to be, but rather on the restoration of their position in the eyes of the nations around them. God had not abandoned them nor disowned them during their captivity in Babylon, but it certainly looked that way. Foreign nations had taunted the people of Judah with "Where is your god now?" as if the captivity had proven that Yahweh was incapable of defending His people. It proved the people foolish for believing He would. The scoffing nations soon saw who the fools truly were.

God would, again, be Israel's God. This statement reflects the sad reality that many of God's people had come to believe the taunts of their captives. They wondered how it could be that God would allow the captivity. Perhaps, they mused, He was not truly all-powerful and was only one of the myriad local gods. Many of the captives had brought idols into their homes and worshipped them alongside Yahweh. All that syncretism eventually came to an end. Never again would God's people set any other deity alongside Yahweh. The

God who had given them the land, according to His covenant promise to Moses, would alone be their God.

Once their homeland and their reputation was restored, the people would also find that God had made provision for them to deal again with their uncleanness. This uncleanness was the ceremonial uncleanness delineated in the Levitical codes. Such filth could only be cleansed by making the proper sacrifices, but for the captives such sacrifices had not been possible. There was no longer a temple; the priestly activities ceased. If a captive was fortunate enough to own an unblemished lamb or a pair of turtledoves, there was no place to go, no one available to perform the sacrifice, and no altar upon which to offer the blood. This ceremonial denial was under development, as well. Once the people got back to their homeland, rebuilding the temple, reinstituting the sacrifices and the Levitical priesthood, and cleansing themselves ritually from sin would again be possible (see Ezra 6:16–22).

God promised to provide abundantly for His people. Their homeland had become desolate during the absence of God's people through neglect and invading armies that trampled the fields and gardens. Famine often accompanies war, as it had when Babylon invaded. However, when the people returned, grain would be abundant, the trees would hang heavy with fruit, and the people would not be faced with famine. No prayers to false gods for abundant harvests would be uttered because the God of the people would give them all they needed to sustain life and for them to prosper in the eyes of the surrounding nations.

All of this yielded something that cannot be overlooked. Ezekiel 36:30 speaks of the disgrace suffered by the people who had been taken into captivity. The Hebrew word translated disgrace is *cherpāh*. The Greek word used in the Septuagint, *oneidismos,* is used several times in the New Testament, usually referring either to the abuse hurled at Christ as He hung on the cross (see Rom. 15:3) or to the reproaches hurled at those who seek to follow and emulate Christ (see Heb. 13:13).

Feelings of shame and worthlessness are devastating, and the people of God had endured many years of such abuse. The disgrace felt by the people of God in Babylon was ending. Once again, they could hold their heads high, and remain confident that the God whom they worshipped and served truly cared for them, and they would honor His promises.

III. God's People Must Respond (Ezekiel 36:31–32)

God asked of His people that they remember what they had done to get themselves carried away into captivity, to maintain a proper perspective on their sinful behavior, and to change the way they acted as a result. When God called upon the people to remember their evil ways, He was not asking them to occasionally recall what they had done. The Hebrew word translated remember is *zākar*, the same word used in Genesis 9:15–16, when God promised Noah that the rainbow would prompt God to remember his promise to never again destroy the world by flood. *Zākar* implies a deeper formal remembering which, in the case of His people, should be ritualized. Consider the difference between simply calling to mind, momentarily, that Christ died on the cross and the remembrance of communion. These are both remembering, but they are very different kinds of remembering. Here, Ezekiel is calling the people of God to the latter, more formal and more intense remembering. He wanted more than a quick flashback in time from them. He wanted them to think about what they had done, to again feel the weight of what it brought upon them, and to teach these realities to the generations to follow.

As they remembered, God asked of His people an attitude about what they remembered. He asked that they loathe their former behavior. Just as God was not seeking a quick momentary recall, He was also not seeking a quick feeling of dismay. He wanted His people to feel the pain and hate what they had done to bring it upon themselves. They were to be grieved in their new spirits, crying out again and again in misery for offending their God. This deep loathing was the key to ongoing repentance, which would maintain the resolve of God's people to never again allow themselves to lapse into such offensive behavior.

THE LESSON APPLIED

Ezekiel said that God would change the hearts and spirits of His people. Titus gave counsel about how those changed hearts and spirits should be manifest to the world. Christians are to be different. Perhaps the most challenging test of being different these days is in facing the increasing cultural tension all around us. Unbelievers need to see people who defuse rather than ignite, who speak gently rather than in anger and frustration. Titus wrote to "show every courtesy to everyone" (Titus 3:2, NRSV). God's people have an opportunity to prayerfully seek God's purposes. In so doing, we may find that we can bridge seemingly unbridgeable gaps and promote reconciliation and understanding.

LET'S TALK ABOUT IT

1. **Is it really good to "loathe" the way we were before we came to Christ?**

The primary reason that this command to "loathe" our former life seems strange is because we live in a culture that places a high value on self-esteem. Modern psychology tells us that we must learn to accept ourselves, warts and all, and feel good about what makes each of us unique. Christians should be careful about putting too much emphasis on feeling good about ourselves. We strive to live now in a way that pleases God and, to the extent that we succeed, we should feel good about it. But we must always loathe the sinful attitudes and behaviors that offend God.

HOME DAILY DEVOTIONAL READINGS
SEPTEMBER 25–OCTOBER 1, 2017

MONDAY	TUESDAY	WEDNESDAY	THURSDAY	FRIDAY	SATURDAY	SUNDAY
The Lord's Words Become Actions	Abram Called and Blessed	God Promises Abram Land and Descendents	Angel Will Lead Conquest of Canaan	Promises of Land and Posterity Fulfilled	Abraham, an Example of Righteous Faith	Abram Enters into Covenant with God
Psalm 33:1–9	Genesis 12:1–3	Genesis 13:14–17	Exodus 23:23–27	1 Kings 4:20–25	Romans 4:1–4	Genesis 15:1–6, 17–21

I WILL DO THIS

ADULT TOPIC:	BACKGROUND SCRIPTURE:
GOD'S COVENANT WITH ABRAM	GENESIS 15

GENESIS 15:1–6, 17–21

King James Version	New Revised Standard Version
AFTER these things the word of the LORD came unto Abram in a vision, saying, Fear not, Abram: I am thy shield, and thy exceeding great reward.	AFTER these things the word of the LORD came to Abram in a vision, "Do not be afraid, Abram, I am your shield; your reward shall be very great."
2 And Abram said, Lord GOD, what wilt thou give me, seeing I go childless, and the steward of my house is this Eliezer of Damascus?	2 But Abram said, "O Lord GOD, what will you give me, for I continue childless, and the heir of my house is Eliezer of Damascus?"
3 And Abram said, Behold, to me thou hast given no seed: and, lo, one born in my house is mine heir.	3 And Abram said, "You have given me no offspring, and so a slave born in my house is to be my heir."
4 And, behold, the word of the LORD came unto him, saying, This shall not be thine heir; but he that shall come forth out of thine own bowels shall be thine heir.	4 But the word of the LORD came to him, "This man shall not be your heir; no one but your very own issue shall be your heir."
5 And he brought him forth abroad, and said, Look now toward heaven, and tell the stars, if thou be able to number them: and he said unto him, So shall thy seed be.	5 He brought him outside and said, "Look toward heaven and count the stars, if you are able to count them." Then he said to him, "So shall your descendants be."
6 And he believed in the LORD; and he counted it to him for righteousness.	6 And he believed the LORD; and the LORD reckoned it to him as righteousness.
• • • • • •	• • • • • •
17 And it came to pass, that, when the sun went down, and it was dark, behold a smoking furnace, and a burning lamp that passed between those pieces.	17 When the sun had gone down and it was dark, a smoking fire pot and a flaming torch passed between these pieces.
18 In the same day the LORD made a covenant with Abram, saying, Unto thy seed have I given this land, from the river of Egypt unto the great river, the river Euphrates:	18 On that day the LORD made a covenant with Abram, saying, "To your descendants I give this land, from the river of Egypt to the great river, the river Euphrates,
19 The Kenites, and the Kenizzites, and the Kadmonites,	19 the land of the Kenites, the Kenizzites, the Kadmonites,
20 And the Hittites, and the Perizzites, and the Rephaims,	20 the Hittites, the Perizzites, the Rephaim,

MAIN THOUGHT: In the same day the LORD made a covenant with Abram, saying, Unto thy seed have I given this land, from the river of Egypt unto the great river, the river Euphrates. (Genesis 15:18, KJV)

GENESIS 15:1–6, 17–21

King James Version	*New Revised Standard Version*
21 And the Amorites, and the Canaanites, and the Girgashites, and the Jebusites.	21 the Amorites, the Canaanites, the Girgashites, and the Jebusites."

LESSON SETTING
Time: Third Millennium B.C.
Place: Canaan

LESSON OUTLINE
I. **Abram's Heir**
(Genesis 15:1–4)
II. **Like the Stars**
(Genesis 15:5–6)
III. **A Covenant for Land**
(Genesis 15:17–21)

UNIFYING PRINCIPLE

Desperate from past disappointments and failures, people fear a continued downward spiral of unfulfilled dreams and goals. How can people find hope to reach fulfillment in life? Although childless, Abram based his hope for descendants on the promises of his covenant with the faithful God.

INTRODUCTION

Things had been going well for Abram. After being told by God to leave behind his extended family and journey to a land he did not know, it appeared that Abram and his family had finally arrived. They had settled in Canaan, south of Salem on property belonging to one of the Amorite rulers, Mamre, at the city of Hebron (see Gen. 13:18). At the time, Abram had already journeyed to and from Egypt and had great wealth and 318 trained fighting men among his greater household (see Gen. 14:14). War broke out, as recorded in Genesis 14, between nine kings of the area. At that time, each city of any size would have had a king and, as political leaders are inclined to do, the various kings of the region mistrusted one another. During the war, Abram's nephew, Lot, was taken prisoner when Lot's city, Sodom, was defeated. Abram gathered his 318 men and defeated Chedorlaomer, king of Edom, and freed his nephew. Upon returning home, Melchizedek, king of Salem and "priest of God Most High" (Gen. 14:18, NRSV), blessed Abram.

And yet, despite all of this, Genesis 15:1 indicates that Abram was afraid. He was wealthy, powerful, had the blessing of God's priest, and had just been the hero coming to the rescue of his nephew. Still, Abram was fearful. Why would a man with seemingly everything going for him be afraid? Many people can identify with a man who mistrusted his success, and who, for whatever reason, feared it would not last. It was at this moment, at a time of Abram's need for assurance, that the word of the Lord came to him in a vision.

EXPOSITION

I. ABRAM'S HEIR
(GENESIS 15:1–4)

God made His will known to the personalities in the Old Testament narrative in several ways. Moses met God face-to-face. Jacob wrestled with God. Most people, however, were given dreams and visions. That is what happened with Abram as he slept by the oaks of Mamre. The source of Abram's fear is not explicitly stated in Genesis 15, but God addressed

Abram's fear with His very first words, "Do not be afraid, Abram" (15:1, NRSV).

God's next words gave a hint as to the nature of Abram's fear. God told Abram that He, God, was Abram's shield. The specific shield to which the Hebrew word *magen* refers is the smaller, personal defensive shield carried by men into battle to protect them against the thrusts of spears and daggers in close combat. The implication is that God, in His role as Abram's shield, would be very close to Abram, and was ready to handle anything that might try to do deadly harm to him. When God saw the need to tell Abram that He would be his shield suggests that Abram feared he had made enemies who might wish him harm and they had means to carry out their desires. Chedorlaomer probably topped that list since Abram had just defeated the king and taken from him what Abram himself had won from Sodom. This was not an unreasonable fear, and it was not some general sense of dread. It was specific and quite real.

Along with God's promise to be Abram's protection, God told Abram that the reward Abram would receive would be a great one. The language is not clear as to exactly what kind of reward Abram might have expected, but it is not likely God meant it as a material reward, since Abram had already amassed great riches. More likely the reward to which God hinted was one of stature and power. Abram was a newcomer to the area, had no land to give him status, and was vulnerable to all the various groups surrounding him. Kings had ganged up on Sodom, and they could start to target this upstart newcomer next, to ensure their own security. God addressed Abram's fearful vulnerability by assuring that he would reap all he needed to establish his position in his new home.

These initial promises from God sparked a question that unveiled something else that was gnawing at Abram. Whatever God might be planning to give to Abram was a great reward, though Abram could not see how it would change things much. To have stature and security among the people surrounding his family, he needed an heir. Without a son to whom he could bequeath his land and his wealth, Abram could simply be waited out. If he died without an heir, there would be no clear leader to be the spiritual head of Abram's home. Abram complained to God that God had not blessed him with such an heir. He considered whether he could adopt his servant, Eliezer of Damascus, but that would be a desperate attempt to provide for the future of his family. Abram had responsibility for those under his care. Having God as his personal shield would have to suffice for now, though when Abram died, those he left behind would be at the mercy of an adopted servant.

God responded to Abram's complaint with a promise that what Abram desired in life more than anything else would be granted. God gave Abram reassurance of divine protection and reward. The blessing received from Melchizedek was to be completely overcome by the gracious intervention of God. Abram would find security in spite of whatever might occur. Chedorlaomer had a vendetta against Abram, but God would protect him. He had no land to call his own or the security such land would bring, and he lacked a biological heir to whom the family could turn as Abram grew old and died, but God knew exactly what was bothering Abram and promised that it would all be resolved in his favor.

Abram was at a turning point in life. The circumstances in which he and his family were living were fraught with danger, both at that moment and for the foreseeable future. God, however, was promising in a dream to provide. Abram had to choose to believe the circumstances and live in ongoing fear, or trust the promises of God, even though he had little information about exactly how those promises might be met.

II. LIKE THE STARS (GENESIS 15:5–6)

Abram went outside on a clear night to spend time with the Lord. Looking up, the Lord told Abram, "'Look toward heaven and count the stars, if you are able to count them…. So shall your descendants be'" (v. 5, NRSV). As the Lord reminded Israel following the exodus, "It was not because you were more numerous than any other people that the LORD set his heart on you and chose you—for you were the fewest of all peoples. It was because the LORD loved you and kept the oath that he swore to your ancestors, that the LORD has brought you out with a mighty hand, and redeemed you from the house of slavery, from the hand of Pharaoh king of Egypt" (Deut. 7:7–8, NRSV). What the Lord promised to Abram remained true generations later when the people were so numerous that pharaohs feared them and enslaved them to keep them under control. The Lord remains faithful to this promise as He continues to add descendants to Abram each time a person chooses to follow his descendant,

Jesus. Just like stars in the sky, God's people can be found the whole world over. Though the number of Christians globally can be estimated today, who can know the number of faithful followers since Abram's days?

Genesis 15:6 is one of the most famous verses in Scripture: "And he believed the LORD; and the LORD reckoned it to him as righteousness" (NRSV). Adam Clarke says, "This I conceive to be one of the most important passages in the whole Old Testament. It properly contains and specifies [the] doctrine of justification by faith" (*Adam Clarke's Commentary.* https://www.studylight.org/commentaries/acc/genesis-15.html). Genesis 15:6 is quoted on three separate occasions in the New Testament: Romans 4:3, Galatians 3:6, and James 2:23. Paul uses Abram's response to God's promises as a springboard, in Romans 4, for one of the most detailed discussions of faith in the Bible.

There are three key concepts within this verse. The first is that Abram believed God. This belief was not simply agreeing that God was making a promise, but a firm acceptance that what God was promising would be delivered. Abram put his fear to rest. He might have enemies, but they would not conquer him, nor would they destroy the family. He might not yet have land to give him and his family security, but the land would come. He might not have a biological heir to which he could currently point to at the moment, but God had promised that he would have such heirs, and that they would be as numerous as the stars in heaven.

The second key concept is that Abram's belief satisfied God. That is what is meant by the term "reckoned" (Gen. 15:6, NRSV). It is a term used to refer to a judicial ruling. Disputes could be settled by appearing before the king. Both sides would present their arguments and the king, acting as judge, would reckon the right solution. It involved weighing the arguments made by both parties and coming to a conclusion as to the correct resolution for the situation. In this case, Abram's belief that God would do as He promised satisfied God the Judge so God decided in Abram's favor. The result of that decision was the granting of the status of righteousness to Abram. It does not mean that God declared Abram to be perfect or sinless. It means simply that Abram's decision to believe God's promises was the right decision. The result was that God viewed Abram as being a "friend of God" (James 2:23, NRSV).

III. A COVENANT FOR LAND (GENESIS 15:17–21)

When he made the right decision in favor of trusting God's promises, Abram now received confirmation and information about what God had promised. God would give Abram the land that he was now occupying and sealed that promise by a covenant ritual. This ritual was still part of Abram's vision, though the covenant ritual, itself, was a common ritual marking a solemn agreement between two parties—one with which Abram would have been familiar. In this ancient ritual, each party would bring an animal. The animals would be sliced and sacrificed. Then, the parties of the covenant agreement would pass between the parts, promising as they walked to honor the agreement and calling down on themselves curses should they fail to do so. A smoking torch would be passed between the chunks of flesh. In Abram's vision, only God passed between the animal pieces as a flaming torch since only God was making a promise. Abram did nothing other than accept and receive what God promised. The covenant details, which appear also in Ezekiel 1:13, are very vivid, yet they were simple details. They convey the ceremonial nature of the covenant. The covenant is important to understand, not the specifics that comprise the ceremony.

As God revealed more about the promise to Abram, it became clear that the fulfillment would not be quick in coming, nor would its coming to fruition be easy to attain. Ron Fleming says, "Abram felt a terrifying darkness upon him, for the covenant would be fulfilled amid opposition, bondage, judgment and oppression over a period of hundreds of years" (*Bridgeway Bible Commentary*. https://www.study-light.org/commentaries/bbc/genesis-15.html). Abram's descendants would be in bondage as slaves and would be sorely oppressed, but eventually they would be set free, bringing with them a great wealth of possessions. Abram himself would die peacefully at a ripe old age and be buried on the land that God promised to give.

THE LESSON APPLIED

Life is hard. People often spend much of their time praying and asking God to make easier routes or lives. When those prayers go unanswered, there is the temptation to think that, somehow, God has failed to come through. Abram appears to have faced this kind of doubt in the aftermath of God's covenant promise in Genesis 15. Some years had gone by, and

Abram and Sarai were still childless. They decided that maybe God was expecting them to help out, so Abram fathered Ishmael by Hagar, Sarah's servant. This son also became a great nation, but the consequences of trying to force God's promise to fruition more quickly are often disastrous. The children of Ishmael and the children of Isaac often clash to this day, killing one another over their religious identities, which began and solidified with Abram.

When God seems not to have heard our cries for relief from the difficulties of life, we must always remember that our short sojourn on earth is but the brief prelude to eternal life. When God waits to answer our prayers, He is not expecting us to take control of our situations and make things happen. We don't have that power or the foresight to know the consequences of our haste. He is looking for some eternal perspective from us and a quiet confidence that all the pain and anguish of life will have been worth it in the end, if we only will remain steadfast in our faith. Fulfillment in life comes from standing firm in trial, not from avoiding or escaping from under trial.

As we consider the promises of God, let us not grow weary as we await their fulfillment. We may experience trials, setbacks, crises and may not live to see them fully realized, but let us master the trust that earned Abram the status of righteousness. What God has promised, He will do.

LET'S TALK ABOUT IT

1. Why didn't Abram's descendants ever control all of the land that the Lord promised to Abram?

A look at a map of Palestine at the time of Abram shows that the land detailed in Genesis 15:18–20 has never fully belonged to the people of Israel. Even at the height of Solomon's power, Israel did not control land all the way to the Euphrates River. The fact that Israel never inhabited this land may have been, and likely was, interpreted as either God's faithlessness or powerlessness. Nevertheless, one must look to the covenant and consider whether Israel faithfully kept their promises to the Lord. If they had been faithful to Him, then surely He would have given them all the lands that were stipulated in the covenant. They were frequently faithless, choosing to associate with foreign people and adopting their gods and pagan practices, rather than being a special nation, uniquely chosen to be a light in the world.

God's covenant with Israel is ongoing and eternal. Nevertheless, since the coming of Christ, the Body of Christ enters into the promises of blessing given to those in Christ. It is to this extent that we are the spiritual children of Abraham.

HOME DAILY DEVOTIONAL READINGS
OCTOBER 2–8, 2017

MONDAY	TUESDAY	WEDNESDAY	THURSDAY	FRIDAY	SATURDAY	SUNDAY
You Are God's Choice	Prepare to Meet Your God	The Triumphant Glory of God	House of Israel, Praise the Lord	Revealed in a New Way	A Chosen Race, a Holy People	Worship God Through Obedience
Deuteronomy 10:12–22	Exodus 19:9–15	Isaiah 60:1–7	Psalm 135:1–9, 19–21	Luke 9:28–36	1 Peter 2:1–10	Exodus 19:16–25

BE READY

EXODUS 19:16–25

King James Version

AND it came to pass on the third day in the morning, that there were thunders and lightnings, and a thick cloud upon the mount, and the voice of the trumpet exceeding loud; so that all the people that was in the camp trembled.

17 And Moses brought forth the people out of the camp to meet with God; and they stood at the nether part of the mount.

18 And mount Sinai was altogether on a smoke, because the LORD descended upon it in fire: and the smoke thereof ascended as the smoke of a furnace, and the whole mount quaked greatly.

19 And when the voice of the trumpet sounded long, and waxed louder and louder, Moses spake, and God answered him by a voice.

20 And the LORD came down upon mount Sinai, on the top of the mount: and the LORD called Moses up to the top of the mount; and Moses went up.

21 And the LORD said unto Moses, Go down, charge the people, lest they break through unto the LORD to gaze, and many of them perish.

22 And let the priests also, which come near to the LORD, sanctify themselves, lest the LORD break forth upon them.

23 And Moses said unto the LORD, The people cannot come up to mount Sinai: for thou chargedst us, saying, Set bounds about the mount, and sanctify it.

24 And the LORD said unto him, Away, get thee down, and thou shalt come up, thou, and Aaron with thee: but let not the priests and

New Revised Standard Version

ON the morning of the third day there was thunder and lightning, as well as a thick cloud on the mountain, and a blast of a trumpet so loud that all the people who were in the camp trembled.

17 Moses brought the people out of the camp to meet God. They took their stand at the foot of the mountain.

18 Now Mount Sinai was wrapped in smoke, because the LORD had descended upon it in fire; the smoke went up like the smoke of a kiln, while the whole mountain shook violently.

19 As the blast of the trumpet grew louder and louder, Moses would speak and God would answer him in thunder.

20 When the LORD descended upon Mount Sinai, to the top of the mountain, the LORD summoned Moses to the top of the mountain, and Moses went up.

21 Then the LORD said to Moses, "Go down and warn the people not to break through to the LORD to look; otherwise many of them will perish.

22 Even the priests who approach the LORD must consecrate themselves or the LORD will break out against them."

23 Moses said to the LORD, "The people are not permitted to come up to Mount Sinai; for you yourself warned us, saying, 'Set limits around the mountain and keep it holy.'"

24 The LORD said to him, "Go down, and come up bringing Aaron with you; but do not let either the priests or the people break through

MAIN THOUGHT: And Moses brought forth the people out of the camp to meet with God; and they stood at the nether part of the mount. (Exodus 19:17, KJV)

EXODUS 19:16–25

King James Version	*New Revised Standard Version*
the people break through to come up unto the LORD, lest he break forth upon them. 25 So Moses went down unto the people, and spake unto them.	to come up to the LORD; otherwise he will break out against them." 25 So Moses went down to the people and told them.

LESSON SETTING

Time: Thirteenth Century B.C.

Place: Mt. Sinai

LESSON OUTLINE

I. **The Stage Is Set (Exodus 19:16–20)**

II. **The People Prepare (Exodus 19:21–23)**

III. **Meeting God (Exodus 19:24–25)**

UNIFYING PRINCIPLE

Because of their human weakness, people need help from beyond themselves. How do people engage a power stronger and different than they are? In making a covenant with the holy and powerful God, the people of Israel consecrated themselves to stand in God's awesome presence.

INTRODUCTION

Exodus 19 smoothly divides into three sections. The first section is comprised of verses 1–9. These verses reminded the Israelites of what God has already done for them, in not only delivering them from Egypt but defeating the Egyptian army so that they did not need to fear retaliation from that nation also. These people that God called to be "[His] priestly kingdom and a holy nation" promised Him that they would follow faithfully everything He would tell them to do (Exod. 19:6, NRSV). Section two runs from verses 10–15, with instructions about how the people should prepare for God's visiting the mountain. They were to consecrate themselves and take care to not touch the mountain. On the third day of their consecration, God would show up in a mighty way. The final section contains verses 16–25. This drama has one main message upon which the action focuses. That message details what it is like to come into the presence of God.

It had been three months since the Israelites had fled Egypt. Scholars disagree over what path the fleeing nation took and even about the exact location of Mt. Sinai. The Hebrew is unclear and could be translated as referring more to a general location than to a specific peak. Even so, many scholars are inclined to heed the ancient tradition of identifying Mt. Sinai as Jebel Mûsā. "Since the 4th century C.E. [sic] tradition has identified Mr. Sinai with Jebel Mûsā (Arab. "Mountain of Moses," 2300 m. [7486 ft.]) in the southern part of the [Sinai] peninsula.... For many scholars the most likely location of Sinai is still in the southern part of the peninsula. The reference in Deut. 1:2 to 'eleven days' journey' from Horeb to Kadesh-barnea by way of Mt. Seir fits that location, as does the ancient tradition linking Mt. Sinai to Jebel Mûsā" (Marilyn J. Lundberg, "Sinai" in *Eerdmans Dictionary of the Bible* [Grand Rapids, MI: Eerdmans, 2000], 1227). M.G. Easton suggests of the journey that "the Israelites advanced into the wilderness of Sinai (Ex. 19:1,2; Num. 22:14–16), marching probably through the two passes of the Wady Solaf and the Wady esh-Sheikh, which converge at the entrance to the plain er-Rahah, the 'desert of Sinai,' which is two miles long and about half a mile broad" (*Illustrated Bible Dictionary* [New York City, NY: Cosimo Classics, 2005], 580). Regardless of the exact peak, the people had arrived at a place of special significance chosen by God to reveal Himself to them. Exodus 19:3 indicates that Moses met God there and the people had journeyed to that location specifically for that purpose.

EXPOSITION

I. THE STAGE IS SET (EXODUS 19:16–20)

They arrived before the mountain; the people set up camp. The er-Rahah plain is large enough that the many thousands of people could easily have pitched their tents, leaving plenty of room between their camp and the edge of the mountain. Once camp was established, Moses "went up to God" (Exod. 19:3, NRSV). He could do so without all the conditions imposed upon the rest of the people, including the priests, only because God called to him specifically. He had been God's chosen spokesperson all along, and everyone knew his relationship with God was a special one. He was saved from the pharaoh's fear as a baby when his mother set him in the river rather than allow him to be killed. After forfeiting his role as a prince in Egypt, Moses was called by the Lord in a foreign land to return to Egypt and lead the people of Israel out of their slavery and into the Promised Land. Though Israel did not always trust him or obey him and with the assistance of Aaron, Moses was the unquestioned leader of the people.

God had two wonderful things to say. He reminded Moses of what He had already done to bring the people out of slavery in Egypt. Then He said that, if the people would obey what God had to say and keep the covenant that was soon to be made, then these former slaves would find themselves chosen as God's treasured possession. They were to be a holy, priestly nation, implying that it would be through the people of Israel that all nations and peoples of the world would come to know God. God then told Moses that God would appear to all the people as a dense cloud. To look upon God was to die (see Gen. 16:13; 32:30). It was God's gracious protection that necessitated the dense cloud, to protect the people from the consequences of gazing directly upon the unveiled glory of God.

Three days later, the morning stillness was shattered. A thick cloud descended upon the mountain and peals of thunder and flashes of lightning split the cloud. The description of this encounter with God sounds to some scholars like the description of a volcanic eruption. Smoke billowed forth, rising toward heaven. There was fire visible on the mountain, and the earth shook violently. From nowhere and everywhere the sound of a heavenly trumpet call was heard. It was so loud the people trembled in fear and awe. "This gave the scene the character of a miraculous transaction, in which other elements than those of nature were at work, and some other than material trumpet was blown by other means than human breath" (Robert Jamieson, A.R.

Fausset, & David Brown. *Commentary Critical & Explanatory on the Whole Bible.* http://www.biblestudytools.com/commentaries/jamieson-fausset-brown/exodus/exodus-19.html). At the sound of this trumpet, Moses called to the people and they slowly and reverently began to approach the mountain.

II. THE PEOPLE PREPARE (EXODUS 19:21–23)

God made it clear to Moses that the people were to consecrate themselves prior to coming into God's presence (see vv. 9–15). As per God's instructions, Moses consecrated the people. They were to make sure they did not come too close to the mountain. The death penalty was to be imposed on anyone who actually touched even so much as the edge of the mountain. The order by God not to so much as touch the edge is one of the points mentioned by those scholars who favored the site of Ras Sufsafeh as being Mt. Sinai. While Jebel Mûsā rises gradually at first out of the Sinai desert, making it difficult to tell where the "edge" might be, Ras Sufsafeh erupts nearly vertically as a cliff. One could stand on the plain and literally reach out and touch the cliff as it rises steeply. Moses told the people that once a trumpet sounded a long blast, it would be okay for the people to go up onto the mountain. This trumpet would be sounded by God or by one of His accompanying archangels.

The people were preparing to meet God. The normal routines and rhythms of daily life might continue, but over and above all of it a sense of importance loomed. The anticipation must have been palpable as they stood off and gazed at the mountain rising nearby. They had seen the hand of God in the plagues and the miraculous crossing through parted waters, but now they were to see the One from whom those signs came. Centuries later, the climax of Israel's journey to Mt. Sinai seems to have been the collection of the Ten Commandments. But to the people assembled before the mountain, the climax of their journey might have been coming on the morning of the third day. The consecration of the people had been finished.

As the trumpet continued to sound, louder and louder, Moses spoke with God. God had indicated that one of His purposes for this was to validate Moses in Israel's eyes so that he could lead the people without challenge. Moses climbed to the very top of the mountain, the point at which the very presence of God was focused. There, God ordered Moses to return to the people and warn them not to attempt to "break through" the defensive shield of smoke or they would perish (v. 21, NRSV). God warned the people through Moses that even the priests were to be consecrated if they wished to avoid God "breaking out" against them (v. 22, NRSV). These two commands about breaking both seem to refer to the screen of smoke which hid the glory of the Lord from the people.

The Lord had much more to say, as is recorded in Exodus 20 and elsewhere, yet the miracle of miracles had occurred. The people, fleeing for their lives from the greatest power on earth, had come to a sign of agreement. Under the leadership of Moses, they had prepared themselves according to God's command and had seen God descend upon the top of the mountain and speak with Moses. Three months earlier they had been slaves, cruelly oppressed in Egypt. Now, they watched in silence, awe-struck, as the God of creation called them to be His treasured possession, a priestly kingdom and a holy nation. Those who were there that day would not be perfect. Some would fall away and earn death for themselves by so doing. Others would invite sickness and tragedy into their lives by grumbling and disobedience.

III. MEETING GOD
(EXODUS 19:24–25)

The Lord sent Moses back down the mountain to the people with further instructions: "'Go down, and come up bringing Aaron with you; but do not let either the priests or the people break through to come up to the LORD; otherwise he will break out against them'" (v. 24, NRSV). Along with Moses and his sister Miriam, Aaron was a leader among the people. He was the first high priest in Israel as appointed by the Lord (see Exod. 28). The priesthood would be an inheritance of Aaron's descendants, leading to the Levitical priesthood in Israel (see Exod. 28:1, 43). This is not to say that Aaron always acted prudently. Indeed, he was guilty of fashioning the golden calf for Israel when they grew tired of waiting for Moses to return from the Lord's mountain (see Exod. 32). Even so, he was not removed from his role among the people. From its inception, God showed great mercy to the priesthood in Israel.

Even so, while Aaron and Moses went up the mountain to meet the Lord, none of the other priestly men in Israel were to approach to the mountain. The invitation to meet God on the mountain was not extended to all; it was specific to Aaron and Moses. This tension is found throughout the Bible. God calls entire groups of people for His purposes and makes Himself known to them, but He also calls individuals to specific tasks. Should a different person try to take up that task, only frustration and failure could follow. However, when the person called by the Lord lives in His calling, that person serves His people and the world in whatever capacity God has seen fit to bestow.

Consequences would follow if the people and priests did not obey the Lord and stay away from the mountain. The Lord would "'break out against them'" (Exod. 19:24, NRSV). "Twice the term 'break out'…is used (v. 22, 24), as though Yahweh is a contained poison, almost substantive, that will break out to contaminate, destroy, and kill" (Walter Brueggemann, Exodus in *The New Interpreter's Bible* Vol. I [Nashville, TN: Abingdon Press, 1994], 837). Though He was willing to reveal Himself to the people, these revelations would take place only on His terms. To approach the Lord casually would result in deadly consequences. Only Aaron and Moses were invited onto the mountain with the Lord; He would spare them in their obedience just as He would spare the people when they obeyed the opposite command given to them to maintain their distance from His holy presence.

THE LESSON APPLIED

To what extent are Christians in awe of the presence of our holy God on Sunday mornings? When was the last time the smoke of His presence was so powerful that His people were overcome? It is easy enough to dismiss the mundane nature of much of what we experience on Sunday mornings by pointing to the quality of the music that gladdens our hearts and the power of carefully crafted and artfully delivered sermons that appeal to our minds and emotions. Two popular answers to the question, "What do you like about church?" are the preaching and the music. These are not bad things to like but they do lend credence to the perception among the unchurched that going to church is not all that much different than going to a concert.

We settle for what is humanly possible because what is humanly impossible is so foreign that we no longer expect it. The problem may well be with our preparation. We rush into church, chatter with our neighbors and friends for a few moments, get our dose of worship, and rush off to the buffet line at our favorite restaurants. Sometimes, we give hardly a thought to consecration and holy preparation to meet the living God.

Let's Talk About It

1. Why did God specify that the priests must be consecrated?

Those who are called to positions of leadership in God's Kingdom always face the temptation to believe that they are leaders because of one or few extraordinary quality they possess that sets them above everyone else. With human nature being what it is, it may have been that the priests thought that their position as priests meant that they were somehow not required to do as the "regular" people had to do. Jesus Himself, many years later, would find the Jewish religious leaders to be undutifully arrogant in their self-righteousness.

No matter how godly a priest seemed, he was still a fallen, sinful man. No one other than Jesus, Himself, can stand before the throne of God and claim to be without sin. The nation of Israel was consecrated—or set apart—to be a nation of priests to the world. In the same way, the priests were consecrated to be an example God's own people of righteousness and justice. Only if the priests and the nation spoke and acted in accordance with their special status as God's chosen nation that could they be a light in the dark world. For this reason only, it was important for each person to understand the role he or she played or will have played. Priests needed to take extra precaution and be especially aware, and they were called out so they would understand the immense responsibility they had in Israel.

HOME DAILY DEVOTIONAL READINGS
OCTOBER 9–15, 2017

MONDAY	TUESDAY	WEDNESDAY	THURSDAY	FRIDAY	SATURDAY	SUNDAY
People Hear God Speak the Commandments	God's Exclusive Claim	Guide for Human Relationships	The Law Finds Fulfillment in Jesus	Anger Leads to Murder	Lust Leads to Adultery	People Hear God's Word from Moses
Deuteronomy 5:22–27	Exodus 20:1–12	Exodus 20:13–17	Matthew 5:17–20	Matthew 5:21–26	Matthew 5:27–32	Exodus 20:18–26

A COVENANT IS A SERIOUS THING

ADULT TOPIC: OBEYING GOD'S LAW	BACKGROUND SCRIPTURE: EXODUS 20

EXODUS 20:18–26

King James Version

AND all the people saw the thunderings, and the lightnings, and the noise of the trumpet, and the mountain smoking: and when the people saw it, they removed, and stood afar off.

19 And they said unto Moses, Speak thou with us, and we will hear: but let not God speak with us, lest we die.

20 And Moses said unto the people, Fear not: for God is come to prove you, and that his fear may be before your faces, that ye sin not.

21 And the people stood afar off, and Moses drew near unto the thick darkness where God was.

22 And the LORD said unto Moses, Thus thou shalt say unto the children of Israel, Ye have seen that I have talked with you from heaven.

23 Ye shall not make with me gods of silver, neither shall ye make unto you gods of gold.

24 An altar of earth thou shalt make unto me, and shalt sacrifice thereon thy burnt offerings, and thy peace offerings, thy sheep, and thine oxen: in all places where I record my name I will come unto thee, and I will bless thee.

25 And if thou wilt make me an altar of stone, thou shalt not build it of hewn stone: for if thou lift up thy tool upon it, thou hast polluted it.

26 Neither shalt thou go up by steps unto mine altar, that thy nakedness be not discovered thereon.

New Revised Standard Version

WHEN all the people witnessed the thunder and lightning, the sound of the trumpet, and the mountain smoking, they were afraid and trembled and stood at a distance,

19 and said to Moses, "You speak to us, and we will listen; but do not let God speak to us, or we will die."

20 Moses said to the people, "Do not be afraid; for God has come only to test you and to put the fear of him upon you so that you do not sin."

21 Then the people stood at a distance, while Moses drew near to the thick darkness where God was.

22 The LORD said to Moses: Thus you shall say to the Israelites: "You have seen for yourselves that I spoke with you from heaven.

23 You shall not make gods of silver alongside me, nor shall you make for yourselves gods of gold.

24 You need make for me only an altar of earth and sacrifice on it your burnt offerings and your offerings of well-being, your sheep and your oxen; in every place where I cause my name to be remembered I will come to you and bless you.

25 But if you make for me an altar of stone, do not build it of hewn stones; for if you use a chisel upon it you profane it.

26 You shall not go up by steps to my altar, so that your nakedness may not be exposed on it."

MAIN THOUGHT: An altar of earth thou shalt make unto me, and shalt sacrifice thereon thy burnt offerings, and thy peace offerings, thy sheep, and thine oxen: in all places where I record my name I will come unto thee, and I will bless thee. (Exodus 20:24, KJV)

LESSON SETTING

Time: Thirteenth Century B.C.
Place: Mt. Sinai

LESSON OUTLINE

I. **Israel's Fear**
(Exodus 20:18–21)
II. **An Altar of Earth**
(Exodus 20:22–24)
III. **Further Altar Instructions**
(Exodus 20:25–26)

UNIFYING PRINCIPLE

Without obedience to law, people live in chaos, hurting themselves, others, and their environment. Where can people get a law that they will obey? God delivered the commandments to the Israelites while showing divine and holy power that tested them to convince them to obey the laws of the covenant.

INTRODUCTION

The people knew about God. Although for more than 400 years their people had been in oppressive enslavement in Egypt, Israel knew that God had chosen Jacob and his sons. They had been told the story from childhood about how Joseph had been betrayed by his brothers and sold into slavery in Egypt, only to be used by the Lord to rise and become the most trusted advisor to the pharaoh. Even stories of the great flood, of Noah's ark, and how God had promised never again to destroy the earth by flood had been passed down from generation to generation.

They also knew about Moses' origin. The stories of his birth and miraculous rescue by the daughter of pharaoh, of his concern for his people, and his escape after having killed an overseer had been whispered among the slaves and their children. When Moses returned with Aaron at his side to confront the current pharaoh, the people had witnessed the power of their God on display. Frogs and locusts swarmed as Moses called down God's might on those who mocked and ignored God. Even thunder and lightning played across the sky as the plague of hail fell, destroying much of Egypt as God's fury poured out. The firstborn of Egypt died while the Hebrew children were spared because they had obeyed God and painted their doorposts with blood. These people had seen the waters part and had crossed the sea on dry land. The walls of water on either side of them were held off by the might of God and the raised staff of Moses. Then they had watched, struck silent in awe, as the waters came together again, washing away the most powerful army on earth. They knew God's power, and they recognized that Moses had been specially chosen by God to deliver them.

Some three months after fleeing Egypt, this nation stood before their God at the foot of Mt. Sinai. Once again the thunder and lightning echoed in the sky above the mountain. Fire and smoke poured forth to obscure their view, but they heard the trumpet sound, and they heard the voice of God calling out to Moses from the shrouded mountain. Their God was not a God to be toyed with. The people had made it clear to Moses and to God that whatever God commanded them to do, they would do.

Just in case the people had any doubt about the identity of the God who now spoke to them, God began His commands (which came to be called the Ten Commandments) by telling them He was the God who had delivered them from slavery. His first command to the people was to never let any other gods come before Him. He would tolerate no second-in-command god, a lesser, not-so-frightening deity. The Lord would not be portrayed as a creature, as well. He had created all living beings. Also, human beings were made in His image, but He could not be described by being portrayed as a creature. He would not be so limited in the minds of His chosen people. The next command from God was about using His name. The meaning of this prohibition goes far beyond using God's name as a curse word, though that is certainly included in the prohibition. God's name would not be used deceptively.

Having set the ground rules, God issued commandments about how the Israelites were to live as His chosen people. They were to keep the Sabbath holy and devoted only to God. The people were to honor their parents, they were not to murder, commit adultery, steal, or bear false witness. They were never to lust after a neighbor's blessings—such as nicer material things or a very attractive spouse. These commands, if obeyed, would provide a peaceful and just framework for the society in which the people would live.

EXPOSITION

I. ISRAEL'S FEAR (EXODUS 20:18–21)

Moses returned from the mountain to find that Israel "trembled and stood at a distance" (Exod. 20:18, NRSV). The image created is that of people gathered at the foot of the mountain, recoiling in terror at what likely reminded them of the terrifying plagues God had sent upon Egypt. "The phenomena of thunder and lightning had been one of the plagues so fatal to Egypt, and as they heard God speaking to them now, they were apprehensive of instant death also" (Robert Jamieson, A.R. Fausset, & David Brown. *Commentary Critical & Explanatory on the Whole Bible.* http://www.biblestudytools.com/commentaries/jamieson-fausset-brown/exodus/exodus-20.html). They told Moses that they wanted him to speak for them. They were not going to risk coming any closer to the Lord or His mountain, but they did promise to take heed and listen to whatever God said to Moses. The people needed to hear a message from God, but not one of them wanted to venture too close.

That they were afraid of God is clear from their next comment to Moses: "'Do not let God speak to us, or we will die'" (v. 19, NRSV). It is not clear from the language exactly why they thought they would die though it likely related to God's commands not to touch the mountain (see Exod. 19:11–13). This fear may have been exacerbated by the fact that the Lord had just spoken directly to the people. Notice that in verse twenty-two God spoke specifically to Moses, but when He began to speak the Ten Commandments God simply "spoke all these words" to the gathered people (v. 1, NRSV). The terrifying theophany convinced the people that they preferred to have an intermediary; Moses would continue to be that man.

Whatever their specific fear, Israel needed reassurance, and Moses gave them what they needed. He told them that there was no reason for them to fear that God might kill them. God had come to them in the way He had simply to test them and that it might help ensure that the people would obey God's commands and not sin by taking these commands too lightly. It may be that the fear of the people was lessened upon hearing that, but still they stood away at a distance while Moses alone drew near to the darkness which enveloped the presence of God. After all, fear of the Lord is a healthy and appropriate response to His power and glory. After all, "The fear of the LORD is the beginning of wisdom, and the knowledge of the Holy One is insight" (Prov. 9:10, NRSV). The question regarding fear was not whether the people would feel it or understand it, but instead, whether it would lead them to obedience and faithfulness. As the Teacher wrote in Ecclesiastes, "Fear God, and keep his commandments; for that is the whole duty of everyone" (12:13, NRSV).

II. AN ALTAR OF EARTH (EXODUS 20:22–24)

God recognized that the people were afraid, and so He gave Moses words of reassurance that He had the best interests of His people at heart. He did not intend to leave them stranded far from the only home they had known. First, He reminded the people that He had personally spoken to them from heaven. Priests in other nations usually spoke to the people for the gods, but Yahweh had spoken directly to His chosen people. This personal address was intended to make the people understand that their God was approachable and concerned for each and every one of them. If there were any lingering doubts that the Lord would deliver the people and keep them safe outside of Egypt, His words speaking to them and continued pres-

ence—though terrifying—should have served as reassurance that He continually had their interests in mind.

The people were not to make images out of gold or silver, as if their God could be somehow impressed or influenced by such things. Yahweh is a jealous God who tolerates no limitations on His power and authority. His people were not to make any such images, bow down in submission to such images, or worship them by serving what the people thought these images might require of them. The issue of an image of God is fraught. Of course, making an image of God was impossible because no one had seen Him (and even after Jesus' lifetime, it remains impossible—no one agrees what He looked like). Furthermore, "God created humankind in his image, in the image of God he created them; male and female he created them" (Gen. 1:27, NRSV). The image of God is thus seen in people who are meant to be the only image of God on earth. Making an image of God in stone or wood would diminish both the Lord and His beloved creatures. Sadly, the people would let their terror lead them, not to obedience, but rather, to desperation that would result in making a golden calf to worship before Moses returned from the mountain (see Exod. 32).

For Yahweh, a simple altar of earth would suffice for His people to make their sacrifices. This may have to do with God's forbidding extravagance and with the transient nature of the life that lay ahead of the people. They were not to construct permanent altars in the wilderness that would have to be quickly abandoned when it was time to move on toward their eventual homeland. Building something permanent could have led the people to believe that the Lord really didn't have a land flowing with milk and honey prepared for them or that they should just settle down where they were and make the best of it. They did not need the additional temptation of accepting less than God's intentions for them. Offering their sacrifices on altars made from materials that were convenient would be quite sufficient. With this instruction, God reveals that He cares more about the sincerity of worship than with all the fancy trappings of that worship. Did He only desire sacrifices of calves, rams, oil, or even one's own firstborn? Did He only care about how the acts of sacrifice would look to others? "He has told you, O mortal, what is good; and what does the LORD require of you but to do justice, and to love kindness, and to walk humbly with your God?" (Micah 6:8, NRSV).

As the people continued to journey from this point, God was going to require His name to be remembered, not only by the people of Israel, but also by the nations around them. At that time, most groups and nations believed that gods could be influenced by lavish structures and possessions. The pyramids in Egypt reached toward heaven to convince the gods to pay attention to those below. Gold, silver, precious gems, and jewels, intricately woven robes and the like were typical of religious observances, and the people of Israel would have such things at the proper time. For now, they were a nomadic nation, and God wanted them to understand that He would not neglect them or their worship simply because they did not possess the lavish accoutrements of neighboring groups. Rather, He would bless them in their simplicity.

III. FURTHER ALTAR INSTRUCTIONS (EXODUS 20:25–26)

God told Israel not to chisel stone for altars in the desert, which represented the idea of fashioning that which is natural into something fancier. They were also not to make steps going up to the altars that they constructed out of earth and unworked stone. Most nations had altars that were raised high above the level of the common people in order to worship their gods. In fact, the later mentions of "the high places" (see Lev. 26:30, for example) sometimes refers to altars that were constructed as so. "The heathens, who imitated the rites of the true God in their idolatrous worship, made their altars very high … which they built thus, partly through pride and vain glory, and partly that their gods might the better hear them" (*Adam Clarke's Commentary*. https://www.studylight.org/commentaries/acc/exodus-20.html).

The entire act of worship was to be regarded as sacred. Biblical comentators vary in their assessment of whether verse twenty-six refers to physical nakedness or to the uncovering of a sinful and impure soul before a holy God. In either case, worship rendered unto the God of Israel was to be reverent and holy in all of its ways. Israel's worship of God was to be chaste in both thought and behavior. Their worship practices were not to be confused with those offered to pagan dieties. All forms of immodesty and impurity were forbidden before the holy, incomparable God who had chosen them as his people.

God intended to care for His people, as He gave attention to even the smallest details about what kinds of altars are to be built and what kinds of representations the people could make. Israel's God was a personal God, an approachable God, and a God who intended to bless His people. Nevertheless, He was not a God to ignore. They had witnessed His power and they knew He had command even over the elements, yet they need not fear Him as long as they were diligent to obey His commands.

THE LESSON APPLIED

Christians believe our relationship with God is intimate and personal because of Christ, who has called us to be friends of God, sons and daughters in His family. That the God of creation, the Lord of the universe, should allow us to have this kind of relationship with Him is one of the mysteries of Christianity. It is a treasure for our hearts, and yet we must be careful. Having an intimate personal relationship with God in no way gives us license to be casual toward our God. We ought never to treat God as if He is our peer. We don't boss Him around based on the promises He has made to us nor insist that He act on our behalf.

The holy fear that the people of Israel exhibited is a good thing. He is, after all, the omnipotent, omniscient, and omnipresent Lord of hosts, not a drawing room god who is to be at our beck and call. He may call us friends and allow us the privilege of calling Him "Abba," but treating Him casually is a dangerous thing to do.

LET'S TALK ABOUT IT

1. Are the Ten Commandments unique?

Every ancient society appears to have had some sort of moral code upon which it based its laws and behavior. The Code of Hammurabi—the Babylonian law code of ancient Mesopotamia—is one of the oldest, predating the Ten Commandments by more than 300 years. Like the Decalogue, it was written on stone tablets, the most permanent way of preserving important writings at that point in human history. Such codes were essential to the development of social norms and laws upon which any civil society depends.

The Ten Commandments are unique among law codes. They established a covenant with the Lord and were laws, primarily meant to give direction on how to be God's faithful covenant people. The first four commands address the people's relationship with God because that relationship was, and still is, the basis of human thriving. Only by knowing and obeying the Creator can His creatures hope to establish a just and peaceful society in His creation.

HOME DAILY DEVOTIONAL READINGS
OCTOBER 16–22, 2017

MONDAY	TUESDAY	WEDNESDAY	THURSDAY	FRIDAY	SATURDAY	SUNDAY
Samuel Anoints David King of Israel	God to Build the House of David	Resources to Build the Temple	David Instructs Solomon About the Temple	Extolling the Majesty of the Lord	David, Prepared for Service	God's Covenant with David
1 Samuel 16:1, 11–13	1 Chronicles 17:9–15	1 Chronicles 22:2–5	1 Chronicles 22:6–16	Psalm 89:1–15	1 Samuel 16:19–23	2 Samuel 7:1–6, 8–10, 12–16

A MUCH BIGGER PLAN

ADULT TOPIC: GOD'S COVENANT WITH DAVID	BACKGROUND SCRIPTURES: 2 SAMUEL 7:1–16; PSALM 89; 1 CHRONICLES 22:6–8

2 SAMUEL 7:1–6, 8–10, 12–16

King James Version	*New Revised Standard Version*
AND it came to pass, when the king sat in his house, and the LORD had given him rest round about from all his enemies;	NOW when the king was settled in his house, and the LORD had given him rest from all his enemies around him,
2 That the king said unto Nathan the prophet, See now, I dwell in an house of cedar, but the ark of God dwelleth within curtains.	2 the king said to the prophet Nathan, "See now, I am living in a house of cedar, but the ark of God stays in a tent."
3 And Nathan said to the king, Go, do all that is in thine heart; for the LORD is with thee.	3 Nathan said to the king, "Go, do all that you have in mind; for the LORD is with you."
4 And it came to pass that night, that the word of the LORD came unto Nathan, saying,	4 But that same night the word of the LORD came to Nathan:
5 Go and tell my servant David, Thus saith the LORD, Shalt thou build me an house for me to dwell in?	5 Go and tell my servant David: Thus says the LORD: Are you the one to build me a house to live in?
6 Whereas I have not dwelt in any house since the time that I brought up the children of Israel out of Egypt, even to this day, but have walked in a tent and in a tabernacle.	6 I have not lived in a house since the day I brought up the people of Israel from Egypt to this day, but I have been moving about in a tent and a tabernacle.
• • • • • •	• • • • • •
8 Now therefore so shalt thou say unto my servant David, Thus saith the LORD of hosts, I took thee from the sheepcote, from following the sheep, to be ruler over my people, over Israel:	8 Now therefore thus you shall say to my servant David: Thus says the LORD of hosts: I took you from the pasture, from following the sheep to be prince over my people Israel;
9 And I was with thee whithersoever thou wentest, and have cut off all thine enemies out of thy sight, and have made thee a great name, like unto the name of the great men that are in the earth.	9 and I have been with you wherever you went, and have cut off all your enemies from before you; and I will make for you a great name, like the name of the great ones of the earth.
10 Moreover I will appoint a place for my people Israel, and will plant them, that they may dwell in a place of their own, and move no more; neither shall the children of wickedness afflict them any more, as beforetime.	10 And I will appoint a place for my people Israel and will plant them, so that they may live in their own place, and be disturbed no more; and evildoers shall afflict them no more, as formerly.
• • • • • •	• • • • • •

MAIN THOUGHT: And thine house and thy kingdom shall be established for ever before thee: thy throne shall be established for ever. (2 Samuel 7:16, KJV)

2 Samuel 7:1–6, 8–10, 12–16

King James Version	New Revised Standard Version
12 And when thy days be fulfilled, and thou shalt sleep with thy fathers, I will set up thy seed after thee, which shall proceed out of thy bowels, and I will establish his kingdom.	12 When your days are fulfilled and you lie down with your ancestors, I will raise up your offspring after you, who shall come forth from your body, and I will establish his kingdom.
13 He shall build an house for my name, and I will stablish the throne of his kingdom for ever.	13 He shall build a house for my name, and I will establish the throne of his kingdom forever.
14 I will be his father, and he shall be my son. If he commit iniquity, I will chasten him with the rod of men, and with the stripes of the children of men:	14 I will be a father to him, and he shall be a son to me. When he commits iniquity, I will punish him with a rod such as mortals use, with blows inflicted by human beings.
15 But my mercy shall not depart away from him, as I took it from Saul, whom I put away before thee.	15 But I will not take my steadfast love from him, as I took it from Saul, whom I put away from before you.
16 And thine house and thy kingdom shall be established for ever before thee: thy throne shall be established for ever.	16 Your house and your kingdom shall be made sure forever before me; your throne shall be established forever.

LESSON SETTING

Time: Circa 1000 B.C.
Place: Jerusalem

LESSON OUTLINE

I. **David Expresses a Desire**
   (2 Samuel 7:1–6)
II. **God Responds**
   (2 Samuel 7:8–10)
III. **The Unfolding of the Promise**
   (2 Samuel 7:12–16)

UNIFYING PRINCIPLE

When entering into relationships with others, people struggle to retain control of their plans and dreams. How can people sacrifice control in order to maintain vital relationships? God's covenant with David is a compromise between the eternal, omnipresent God and the time- and space-bound David by allowing a temple to be built, but beyond David's lifetime.

INTRODUCTION

The books of 1 and 2 Samuel record the calling of Samuel to be God's prophet and judge, the kingship of Saul, and finally the calling and kingship of David. These texts do not shy away from revealing the flaws of the kings, while drawing a sharp contrast at times between the leadership in Israel and the God who had led Israel exclusively in the past. Authorship is unknown, though it is likely the work of several writers and editors, a fact seen in the tension between certain parallel accounts within the books themselves. The books were likely written at a time of social and political upheaval in Judah with an eye toward, not just remembering Israel's history, but also interpreting that history in terms of God's ongoing faithfulness to the nation.

Relationships demand flexibility, compromise and reciprocity, if they are to last. One party's desires must allow room for the yearnings of the other party to maintain a healthy and ongoing relationship. What is amazing is that God desires a relationship with humanity so much that even He is willing to compromise in order to make and sustain those relationships.

When the people of Israel first arrived in the Promised Land, God gave them judges who were charged with overseeing the welfare of His people. Yet, as the people looked around them, every other group had a king. They felt inferior and began to cry out to God for their own king. Some of the judges had led Israel into sin. It is also true that, under the leadership of the judges, many of the nations surrounding Israel had attacked them. Yet God made it clear that the people's call for a king was an affront to God's leadership (see 1 Sam. 8:7). Despite all this, God gave the people what they desired, even knowing that the king they would get (Saul) would be no better than the worst of the judges.

God would have been perfectly within His rights to deny the people what they desired. He did not, however. He would work within the boundaries of what His people wanted because He truly loved them and was willing to compromise with their desires. This allowance for the desires of His people was to appear yet again when David expressed a desire to build God a house.

EXPOSITION

I. DAVID EXPRESSES A DESIRE (2 SAMUEL 7:1–6)

In 2 Samuel 5:11, we learn that King Hiram of Tyre, upon David's establishment of Jerusalem as the capitol city of Israel, had sent cedar trees and workmen to build a home for David using the cedar. These trees were the cedars from Lebanon, among the most valuable commodities in the ancient Near East at that time, prized for their beauty and sturdiness. While there is no physical description of the house, it was undoubtedly large, for the next verses,

in 2 Samuel 5, tell us that David added wives, concubines, and children to his family. The home would have been big enough to accommodate all these people, along with servants.

Having established his capitol and his palace, David brought the ark of the covenant from Hebron to Jerusalem. The dwelling place of God among His people, and the area between the outstretched wings of the cherubim on the cover of the ark, was placed in a "tent that David had pitched for it" (2 Sam. 6:17, NRSV). David lived in a lavish palace constructed from the finest cedar, but God dwelt in a tent. Something seemed wrong about this to David. Once his reign was secure, the Philistines were driven off, and his home completed, David approached Nathan, the prophet, and voiced his concern. Adam Clarke observes of Nathan's response, "He gave his judgment as a pious and prudent man, not as a prophet; for the prophets were not always under a Divine [inspiration]; it was only at select times they were thus honored" (*Adam Clarke's Commentary*. https://www.studylight.org/commentaries/acc/2-samuel-7.html). Scripture only records David's statement about the disparity of the two homes, but Nathan's response suggests that David made it clear to Nathan what he had in mind. God, David felt, needed a home befitting divinity; for God was greater than the new king of Israel.

On its surface, David's desire seems eminently reasonable. Why should a human king live in a home fancier than the King of the universe? David may well have feared that God would take offense at being required to dwell in what David considered substandard housing. Yet David's desire was at least partially built upon the human desire for status and image. Kings had palaces. If David was to be taken seriously as a king, he, too, must have a palace. Otherwise, the people surrounding Israel would look down upon Israel and regard them as a second-class nation. Furthermore, the gods of those people had lavish temples built to honor the gods and impress other people with how great their gods were. Could the God of Israel be given less than a god named baal? It does not appear that David stopped for very long to ask God if God wanted a temple.

David came to understand that God was not going to permit him to build a temple, yet it appears that David understood God's reluctance in reference to David's bloody past. In 1 Chronicles, David called his son, Solomon, to him and explained, "I had planned to build a house to the name of the Lord my God. But the word of the Lord came to me, saying, 'You have shed much blood and have waged great wars; you shall not build a house to my name, because you have shed so much blood in my sight on the earth. See, a son shall be born to you; he shall be a man of peace. I will give him peace from all his enemies on every side; for his name shall be Solomon, and I will give peace and quiet to Israel in his days. He shall build a house for my name. He shall be a son to me, and I will be a father to him, and I will establish his royal throne in Israel forever'" (22:7–10, NRSV).

The difference between God's words and David's quotation of His words certainly do not put the accounts into conflict. The writer of the books of Samuel emphasized throughout that the Lord was the true King in Israel and unlike any earthly king, even David. The Lord did not care about His accommodations; He simply wanted to live among His obedient people and bless them. The writer of Chronicles, however, recorded the history of the many kings of Israel and Judah, and in this passage emphasized the peace that the Lord willed for His people instead of the constant warring that was the usual mark of kings. Surely, the Lord was concerned with both the peaceful prosperity of His people and with His people recognizing that He was not like earthly kings and did not endorse everything an earthly king might desire or want to accomplish.

II. GOD RESPONDS (2 SAMUEL 7:8–10)

David needed to be told that his plan was not God's plan. Nathan introduced his vision with such words that left no doubt that God, Himself, was speaking. "Thus says the LORD" were words that typically led prophetic utterances (2 Sam. 7:5, NRSV). Where Nathan's earlier suggestion that David do as he wanted and build a temple came from the wise counsel of a trusted mentor, what followed came from the God who had ordained Nathan to speak on His behalf.

God wanted David to understand that David had presumed that God would be delighted to have a home as grand as David's cedar palace. The question in verse five could have been phrased, "Who told you that you should build me a house to live in?" No one had told David to do it. God expressed satisfaction with His current quarters, highlighting that all the time the people of Israel had been moving about to establish their homeland, God had been content with moving along with them in a tabernacle. God had never once questioned why Israel's leaders had failed to build him a permanent home. "God reminded him through the prophet Nathan that Israel's God, Yahweh, was not limited to one land or one place. For that reason his symbolic dwelling place had been a tent, something that was movable and could be set up in any place at all (7:1–7)" (Don Fleming, *Bridgeway Bible Commentary*. https://www.studylight.org/commentaries/bbc/2-samuel-7.html). For these reasons, God was not going to allow David to fulfill his ambition.

To make it evident to David that God was not weakened because He did not have a fancy home, God reminded David of all that God had done in leading the people to this position. He had been with David entirely, specifically through the trials David had endured as he rose from being a simple shepherd to being Israel's king. God was there when David slung the stone that killed Goliath. God was there as Saul turned against David and tried to have him killed. David defeated the Philistines, and God was with him, then. Now, God intended to elevate David's name above all the other kings of the earth and give His people a homeland where they might be safe and secure under the protection of their God. He had done all this and would do more while living humbly among the people in a tent.

III. THE UNFOLDING OF THE PROMISE (2 SAMUEL 7:12–16)

Following these statements of current sufficiency, God spoke of one of the most important promises in the Old Testament. In this passage, God spoke of Solomon and David, but also of the Messiah, Jesus Christ (see 2 Sam. 7:11–16). Solomon is used as a type, a theological term meaning that what applied to Solomon also applied to Christ. Through Solomon, we gain a glimpse of the Messiah. The first part of this prophecy is that God would make of David a "house" (vv. 11, 12, 16, NRSV). The tables were turned. God would not allow David to build God a house, but instead God would build a house out of David—not *for* David but *of* David. Solomon would be of the house of David. Christ, too, would arise from the house of David.

David thought that God was speaking of a physical descendant. Once it became clear that Solomon would reign after David, David set Solomon to the task of building the Temple (see 2 Chron. 22:6). He was still thinking of a house like the one of cedar in which he dwelt, but God also had a different kind of house in mind. Paul, writing many centuries later from the Body of Christ, said, "In him the whole structure is joined together and grows into a holy temple in the Lord; in whom you also are built together spiritually into a dwelling place for God" (Eph 2:21–22). This is the house of which God spoke to Nathan. Solomon would stem from David's body, but not "when your days are fulfilled and you lie down with your ancestors" (2 Sam. 7:12, NRSV). That statement, though it applies to Solomon as of David's lineage, applies best to the Messiah, Jesus Christ who would come from the direct lineage of King David and whose kingdom would be established forever. God had dealt with Solomon as a special son, and made him one of the most powerful and wealthiest kings of history. The wisdom God gave

Solomon is legendary and has given us the book of Proverbs. Yet Solomon was not without sin, and God made it clear that he would find himself suffering in this life as any other mortal might.

Psalm 89 extensively quotes from the prophecy given by Nathan to David as he recounts the glory of what God promised to David. God's steadfast love is mentioned throughout (see vv. 1, 2, 24, 28, 33, and 49). The key concept of the psalm is that once God promises His love, it will never be withdrawn. And yet, as the psalmist asked toward the end of the psalm, "Where is your steadfast love of old?" (v. 49). What seemed to be a clear promise of never ending power and glory somehow turned sour. The final chapters of 2 Samuel reveal some of the details (see 2 Sam. 18; 20; 21; 24). These acts of God brought David's reign to a bitter end. Thus Psalm 89 closes with a cry of "How long?" (v. 46, NRSV). The psalmist asked God to remember the covenant promises made to David. God had not forgotten; Israel had misunderstood. God's people only thought of life briefly. God acts with more than the present moments in consideration.

The Lesson Applied

Sometimes, love means giving another his or her desire at the expense one's own. To do such a thing is one of the greatest blessings of being in a relationship. This is especially true of one's personal relationship with God. His knowledge is far more complete than ours, and His wisdom and purposes are more excellent in every way. A wise person always prefers God's desires to personal desires, even though it means not receiving exactly what one wants. It may take time before seeing the wisdom of letting God's desires take precedence over our own, but we can trust that, in the end, we will always be better off when we show that love to our Lord.

Let's Talk About It

1. How could Jesus fulfill a prophecy about one who sinned?

The Hebrew language leaves room for 2 Samuel 7:14 to be translated, "when one commits iniquity *against* him." With that optional translation, the verse fits the Messiah perfectly. Even though Solomon and Christ were afflicted by blows from human hands, God's steadfast love remained. All along, these prophecies were intended to have greater implications than Solomon. That is made clear by the Hebrews writer, who quotes from Nathan's prophecy in Hebrews 1. David had received more than he bargained for as God responded to his dream of building God a house, but it remained a challenge to understand the way God had altered David's dream.

HOME DAILY DEVOTIONAL READINGS
OCTOBER 23–29, 2017

MONDAY	TUESDAY	WEDNESDAY	THURSDAY	FRIDAY	SATURDAY	SUNDAY
Israel Gathers for National Confession	God, Creator and Covenant Maker	God Meets Rebellion with Steadfast Love	Redeemer of Israel's Iniquities	Forgive Fellow Believers Repeatedly	God's Kindness Leads to Repentance	Confession and Covenant Renewal
Nehemiah 9:1–5	Nehemiah 9:5–8	Nehemiah 9:26–31	Psalm 130	Luke 17:1–4	Romans 2:1–8	Nehemiah 9:32–38; 10:28–29

SIGN ON THE DOTTED LINE

ADULT TOPIC: GOD'S COVENANT WITH THE RETURNED EXILES	BACKGROUND SCRIPTURES: NEHEMIAH 9–10

NEHEMIAH 9:32–38; 10:28–29

King James Version	*New Revised Standard Version*
NOW therefore, our God, the great, the mighty, and the terrible God, who keepest covenant and mercy, let not all the trouble seem little before thee, that hath come upon us, on our kings, on our princes, and on our priests, and on our prophets, and on our fathers, and on all thy people, since the time of the kings of Assyria unto this day.	"NOW therefore, our God—the great and mighty and awesome God, keeping covenant and steadfast love—do not treat lightly all the hardship that has come upon us, upon our kings, our officials, our priests, our prophets, our ancestors, and all your people, since the time of the kings of Assyria until today.
33 Howbeit thou art just in all that is brought upon us; for thou hast done right, but we have done wickedly:	33 You have been just in all that has come upon us, for you have dealt faithfully and we have acted wickedly;
34 Neither have our kings, our princes, our priests, nor our fathers, kept thy law, nor hearkened unto thy commandments and thy testimonies, wherewith thou didst testify against them.	34 our kings, our officials, our priests, and our ancestors have not kept your law or heeded the commandments and the warnings that you gave them.
35 For they have not served thee in their kingdom, and in thy great goodness that thou gavest them, and in the large and fat land which thou gavest before them, neither turned they from their wicked works.	35 Even in their own kingdom, and in the great goodness you bestowed on them, and in the large and rich land that you set before them, they did not serve you and did not turn from their wicked works.
36 Behold, we are servants this day, and for the land that thou gavest unto our fathers to eat the fruit thereof and the good thereof, behold, we are servants in it:	36 Here we are, slaves to this day—slaves in the land that you gave to our ancestors to enjoy its fruit and its good gifts.
37 And it yieldeth much increase unto the kings whom thou hast set over us because of our sins: also they have dominion over our bodies, and over our cattle, at their pleasure, and we are in great distress.	37 Its rich yield goes to the kings whom you have set over us because of our sins; they have power also over our bodies and over our livestock at their pleasure, and we are in great distress."
38 And because of all this we make a sure covenant, and write it; and our princes, Levites, and priests, seal unto it.	38 Because of all this we make a firm agreement in writing, and on that sealed document are inscribed the names of our officials, our Levites, and our priests.

MAIN THOUGHT: Howbeit thou art just in all that is brought upon us; for thou hast done right, but we have done wickedly. (Nehemiah 9:33, KJV)

NEHEMIAH 9:32–38; 10:28–29

King James Version	*New Revised Standard Version*
• • • • • •	• • • • • •
28 And the rest of the people, the priests, the Levites, the porters, the singers, the Nethinims, and all they that had separated themselves from the people of the lands unto the law of God, their wives, their sons, and their daughters, every one having knowledge, and having understanding;	28 The rest of the people, the priests, the Levites, the gatekeepers, the singers, the temple servants, and all who have separated themselves from the peoples of the lands to adhere to the law of God, their wives, their sons, their daughters, all who have knowledge and understanding,
29 They clave to their brethren, their nobles, and entered into a curse, and into an oath, to walk in God's law, which was given by Moses the servant of God, and to observe and do all the commandments of the Lord our Lord, and his judgments and his statutes.	29 join with their kin, their nobles, and enter into a curse and an oath to walk in God's law, which was given by Moses the servant of God, and to observe and do all the commandments of the Lord our Lord and his ordinances and his statutes.

LESSON SETTING

Time: 444 B.C.

Place: Jerusalem

LESSON OUTLINE

I. **The Prelude**
   (Nehemiah 9:32–35)

II. **A New Beginning**
   (Nehemiah 9:36–38)

III. **Going Forward**
   (Nehemiah 10:28–29)

UNIFYING PRINCIPLE

People find themselves in painful consequences of their own wrongdoing. In the embarrassing angst of suffering for their own wrongs, how can they dare ask for help from others? The people of Israel, hurting from painful losses of the exile for their sins, followed Nehemiah in confessing their wrongs and making a covenant with God to obey the law given through Moses.

INTRODUCTION

The world was changing in the late years of the seventh century B.C. In 605 B.C., Nebuchadnezzar had ascended to the throne in Babylon and war broke out between the two great world powers, Babylon and Egypt. Moving to secure their borders against Egypt, Babylon invaded Judah. The Southern Kingdom fell to the powerful Babylonian army and the first wave of captives, including Daniel, were uprooted and had to resettle in Babylon. Yet, there remained a Judean government in Jerusalem. The Judean government forged an alliance with Egypt, hoping to protect its independence from Babylon via the alliance. The prophet, Jeremiah, warned the people of God's impending judgment and that the alliance with Egypt could not save them. In 597 B.C., the Babylonians attacked and captured Jerusalem. A second wave of captives were taken from the Promised Land into slavery in Babylon. Among them was the prophet, Ezekiel. Zedekiah succeeded Jehoachin as king in 597 B.C. Things seemed to settle down for a short period until 586 B.C. when the Babylonians, prompted by Judah's refusal to accept their hegemony, attacked Jerusalem again. This time, they finished the task of destroying Solomon's temple, burning the walls and city gates, and emptying the city of the remaining Israelites.

Fifty-seven years later, in 539 B.C., the Persians, under Cyrus II, defeated the Babylonian Empire. That same year, Cyrus II issued the famous decree that began the return of the children of Israel to their land (see Ezra 1:1–4). It was, as the deportation had been, not a single event, but, rather, a series of returns. By 539 B.C., most of the Jews had never known life in Jerusalem. They had lived, been born, and were educated, in Babylon. It was their home, and so when Cyrus II issued his decree, only a handful that was led by Zerubbabel returned. What they found was shocking. Jerusalem was rubble. A motley band occupied the land; these people would be known as the Samaritans. Zerubbabel and his fellow exiles, urged on by Haggai and Zechariah, had their hands full. Although they labored tirelessly and, in 516 B.C., seventy years after the final exile, the new temple was finally completed.

In 458 B.C., 58 years later, another group of exiles returned, under the leadership of Ezra (see Ezra 7). Another fourteen years later, Nehemiah received permission to rebuild the walls of the city of Jerusalem. The first chapters of Nehemiah recount the struggles to complete this task, which they accomplished in a mere fifty-two days. In celebration, Ezra decreed that the Law of the Lord, the Torah (Genesis through Deuteronomy), should be read aloud to the assembled people. Revival emerged from it and a day of national confession of sin was decreed.

The book of Nehemiah was written not long after the events that were recounted within. Nehemiah's return from Persia, the rebuilding of the wall around Jerusalem, and the rededication of the people in the land likely occurred between 445–432 B.C., during the reign of Artaxerxes I. The text was likely written in the first quarter of the fourth century B.C. Ralph Klein considers Nehemiah 8–10 to be the climax of Ezra and Nehemiah together: this section "set forth an ideal picture of the community. Made joyful by the reading of the law, after an initial reaction of grief, the people celebrated Tabernacles and confessed their previous sins and God's constant deliverance—and their less than perfect current status. The appropriate sequel to reading the law and offering a confession was a community-wide commitment to keep the proscriptions of the law" (*Books of Ezra and Nehemiah* in *The New Interpreter's Bible Vol. III* [Nashville, TN: Abingdon Press, 1999], 670). Thus the text of this lesson cuts to the heart of the book of Nehemiah. Would the people react to God's continued care for them with renewed dedication or would they begin fall away from Him once again?

EXPOSITION

I. THE PRELUDE (NEHEMIAH 9:32–35)

Nehemiah 9:9 and 9:37 spoke of the distress suffered by the people of Israel in which they asked God to remember as they stood together for their day of national confession. As Ezra prayed and the people shouted their "Amen," he asked God not to treat the hardships they had endured as insignificant, even though they admitted those hardships had come upon them because of their own sins. "You have been just in all that has come upon us, for you have dealt faithfully and we have acted wickedly; our kings, our officials, our priests, and our ancestors have not kept your law or heeded the commandments and the warnings that you gave them. Even in their own kingdom, and in the great goodness you bestowed on them, and in the large and rich land that you set before them, they did not serve you and did not turn from their wicked works" (Neh. 9:33–35, NRSV). Though they had earned judgment, the people knew that God is "the great and mighty and awesome God, keeping covenant and steadfast love" and would restore them as He had promised (v. 32, NRSV).

The people arrived in sackcloth, with dirt and ashes poured over their heads, as a sign of repentance. They had spent the two days immediately following the end of the Feast of Tabernacles purifying themselves and removing anyone from their midst of foreign heritage. As they gathered, the books of Moses were read, the priests cried out to God, and the Levites called the people to, "'Stand up and bless the LORD your God'" (v. 5, NRSV). Ezra prayed, recounting all that had happened to the people of God, from God's call of Abram through the beginning of the Babylonian captivity. It was a litany of spurned blessing as the people, time and time again, rebelled against the God who had called them, delivered them from slavery, and given them power and prosperity, according to His covenant promises. Ezra summarized it all with the words, "Nevertheless, in your great mercies you did not make an end of them or forsake them, for you are a gracious and merciful God" (v. 31, NRSV).

II. A NEW BEGINNING (NEHEMIAH 9:36–38)

Hoping to recapture the blessings of faithfulness to God, Ezra led the people to make "a firm agreement in writing" (v. 38, NRSV). Essentially, this was a contract, which was signed on behalf of all the people by their appointed representatives (see Neh. 10:1–27). "This written document would exercise a wholesome influence in restraining their backslidings or in animating them to duty, by being a witness against them if in the future they were unfaithful to their engagements" (Robert Jamieson, A.R. Fausset, & David Brown. *Commentary Critical & Explanatory on the Whole Bible.* http://www.biblestudytools.com/commentaries/jamieson-fausset-brown/nehemiah/nehemiah-9.html). On behalf of the people, the leaders agreed to separate themselves from the idolatrous people living around them and to adhere to the law of God (see Neh. 10:28). This statement is both a separation of the people from corruptive influences and to the rule that would keep them in God's gracious protection. They took an oath—a solemn promise—to walk in God's law and called down God's judgment upon themselves should they fail to do so.

The revival under Ezra and Nehemiah seemed to have launched a new era of obedience and submission to God. The nation had confessed the sins of their ancestors and taken personal responsibility for repeating those sins. They had made a firm commitment to obey, supported by a signed covenantal document.

III. GOING FORWARD (NEHEMIAH 10:28–29)

Israel specifically emphasized three areas in which they had particularly failed to be faithful, in the past. First, they would not intermarry. This had been a problem since the day they first entered the Promised Land. Deuteronomy 7:3 records God's command to not intermarry: "Do not intermarry with them, giving your daughters to their sons or taking their daughters for your sons" (NRSV). Judges 3:5–6 tells of the failure of the people to obey this command: "So the Israelites lived among the Canaanites, the Hittites, the Amorites, the Perizzites, the Hivites, and the Jebusites; and they took their daughters as wives for themselves, and their own daughters they gave to their sons; and they worshiped their gods" (NRSV). The biggest problem with intermarriage was that it brought idols into the home that, over time, became blended into the life of the people.

Second, the people pledged to honor the Sabbath, including Sabbath rest for the fields every seventh year (see Exod. 23:10–11) and the cancellation of debts required by the law (see Lev. 25). They had never done all that God had commanded—largely ignoring the Sabbath year and the year of Jubilee. Now, they pledged to do so with curses that called down on their heads should they fail.

Finally, the people pledged to support the temple by giving one-third of a shekel to the various tasks of maintaining both the facility and the priesthood who ministered there. Adam Clarke observes, "According to the law, every one above twenty years of age was to give half a shekel to the sanctuary, which was called a ransom for their souls. See Exodus 30:11–16. But why is one third of a shekel now promised instead of the half shekel, which the law required? To this question no better answer can be given than … the general poverty of the people" (*Adam Clarke's Commentary.* https://www.studylight.org/commentaries/acc/nehemiah-10.html). The people and their leaders were determined to obey the requirements of God's law, and so it is likely they did the best they could for a people recently released from slavery to return to a ruin of a city. Nehemiah 10:39 summarizes their commitment by promising, "We will not neglect the house of our God" (NRSV).

THE LESSON APPLIED

The Judaism that Jesus would confront some 450 years later began to take shape during the aftermath of the return from exile. Synagogues came into being as the desire of the people to hear and study the scriptures grew. Pharisees and other teachers of the law arose and the Talmud began to take shape. The more the religious leaders studied, the more they micro-analyzed the law, and developed hundreds and hundreds of minute regulations dealing with what could and could not be done by observant Jews. Rather than hearts attuned to God, the Jews systematized the observances of their faith, substituting rule for personal submission to God.

We, as a people, like to systematize. Groups and movements within Christianity spring up, flourish and often vanish, being replaced by the next big thing designed to deepen the faith of people. Such movements are often wonderful blessings during their prime, but in the end they are no substitute for individual submission to God and the daily walking of the Spirit of God. It is the same mistake the newly-returned Jews made in the aftermath of their day of national confession. Rather than continue their heart-cry of repentance and commitment, they took to studying the Torah and developing lists. God was not willing to be replaced by a system then, and He remains unwilling today.

LET'S TALK ABOUT IT

1. Did the reforms of Ezra and Nehemiah result in faithfulness from the people?

M.G. Easton notes, "Very soon after this the old corrupt state of things returned, showing the worthlessness to a large extent of the professions that had been made at the feast of the dedication of the walls of the city" (*Illustrated Bible Dictionary* [New York City, NY: Cosimo Classics, 2005], 496). A mere forty years later, the prophet Malachi would rage against the very sins the people had promised to avoid. Malachi listed some of the sins to which the people had returned. The priests were offering blemished animals in sacrifice (see Mal. 1:8). Malachi 2:2 records God's warning that he would send "the curse" (NRSV) upon them.

It is a direct reference to the curse the people had called down upon themselves should they lapse back into disobedience (see Neh. 10:29). The people had "married the daughter of a foreign god" (Mal. 2:11, NRSV). They had promised not to intermarry, and yet within forty years they were at it again. Lastly, Malachi raged against the people for robbing God. Though they had not pledged the full half-shekel, it appears they were not even living up to the promise of one-third of a shekel. To this Malachi responds, "You are cursed with a curse, for you are robbing me—the whole nation of you!" (3:9, NRSV). Again, this is a direct reference to what the people had said should happen if they disobeyed.

God's people had promised to distinguish themselves from pagan worshipers. Yet, they had failed to live out their promises. Jesus would say 400 years later, "You hypocrites! Isaiah prophesied rightly about you when he said: 'This people honors me with their lips, but their hearts are far from me; in vain do they worship me, teaching human precepts as doctrines'" (Matt. 15:7–9, NRSV). A basic truth emerges from this sad tale. For humans, it is hard to walk by the Spirit of God. Much easier is to make indexes that can be interpreted and messages to explain away all but the most grievous of sins.

HOME DAILY DEVOTIONAL READINGS
OCTOBER 30–NOVEMBER 5, 2017

MONDAY	TUESDAY	WEDNESDAY	THURSDAY	FRIDAY	SATURDAY	SUNDAY
God Always Faithful	Performing a Good Service to Jesus	Serve the Lord and One Another	Called to Mission Service	Tragic Result of Baal of Peor Worship	Treating Offerings with Contempt	Covenant of a Perpetual Priesthood
Psalm 44:1–8	Matthew 26:6–13	Romans 12:9–18	Philemon 8–16	Numbers 25:1–9	1 Samuel 2:12–17	Numbers 25:10–13; 1 Samuel 2:30–36

UNWAVERING COMMITMENT

ADULT TOPIC: FAITHFUL GOD, UNFAITHFUL PEOPLE	BACKGROUND SCRIPTURES: NUMBERS 25; 1 SAMUEL 2:27–36

NUMBERS 25:10–13; 1 SAMUEL 2:30–36

King James Version

AND the LORD spake unto Moses, saying,

11 Phinehas, the son of Eleazar, the son of Aaron the priest, hath turned my wrath away from the children of Israel, while he was zealous for my sake among them, that I consumed not the children of Israel in my jealousy.

12 Wherefore say, Behold, I give unto him my covenant of peace:

13 And he shall have it, and his seed after him, even the covenant of an everlasting priesthood; because he was zealous for his God, and made an atonement for the children of Israel.

• • • 1 Samuel 2:30–36 • • •

WHEREFORE the LORD God of Israel saith, I said indeed that thy house, and the house of thy father, should walk before me for ever: but now the LORD saith, Be it far from me; for them that honour me I will honour, and they that despise me shall be lightly esteemed.

31 Behold, the days come, that I will cut off thine arm, and the arm of thy father's house, that there shall not be an old man in thine house.

32 And thou shalt see an enemy in my habitation, in all the wealth which God shall give Israel: and there shall not be an old man in thine house for ever.

33 And the man of thine, whom I shall not cut off from mine altar, shall be to consume thine eyes, and to grieve thine heart: and all the increase of thine house shall die in the flower of their age.

New Revised Standard Version

THE LORD spoke to Moses, saying:

11 "Phinehas son of Eleazar, son of Aaron the priest, has turned back my wrath from the Israelites by manifesting such zeal among them on my behalf that in my jealousy I did not consume the Israelites.

12 Therefore say, 'I hereby grant him my covenant of peace.

13 It shall be for him and for his descendants after him a covenant of perpetual priesthood, because he was zealous for his God, and made atonement for the Israelites.'"

• • • 1 Samuel 2:30–36 • • •

THEREFORE the LORD the God of Israel declares: 'I promised that your family and the family of your ancestor should go in and out before me forever'; but now the LORD declares: 'Far be it from me; for those who honor me I will honor, and those who despise me shall be treated with contempt.

31 See, a time is coming when I will cut off your strength and the strength of your ancestor's family, so that no one in your family will live to old age.

32 Then in distress you will look with greedy eye on all the prosperity that shall be bestowed upon Israel; and no one in your family shall ever live to old age.

33 The only one of you whom I shall not cut off from my altar shall be spared to weep out his eyes and grieve his heart; all the members of your household shall die by the sword.

MAIN THOUGHT: And I will raise me up a faithful priest, that shall do according to that which is in mine heart and in my mind: and I will build him a sure house; and he shall walk before mine anointed for ever. (1 Samuel 2:35, KJV)

NUMBERS 25:10–13; 1 SAMUEL 2:30–36

King James Version

34 And this shall be a sign unto thee, that shall come upon thy two sons, on Hophni and Phinehas; in one day they shall die both of them.

35 And I will raise me up a faithful priest, that shall do according to that which is in mine heart and in my mind: and I will build him a sure house; and he shall walk before mine anointed for ever.

36 And it shall come to pass, that every one that is left in thine house shall come and crouch to him for a piece of silver and a morsel of bread, and shall say, Put me, I pray thee, into one of the priests' offices, that I may eat a piece of bread.

New Revised Standard Version

34 The fate of your two sons, Hophni and Phinehas, shall be the sign to you—both of them shall die on the same day.

35 I will raise up for myself a faithful priest, who shall do according to what is in my heart and in my mind. I will build him a sure house, and he shall go in and out before my anointed one forever.

36 Everyone who is left in your family shall come to implore him for a piece of silver or a loaf of bread, and shall say, Please put me in one of the priest's places, that I may eat a morsel of bread.'"

LESSON SETTING

Time: Circa 1400 B.C.;
Circa 1070 B.C.
Place: Moab; Shiloh

LESSON OUTLINE

I. Phinehas Turns Back God's Wrath (Numbers 25:10–13)
II. Eli's Sons Earn God's Wrath (2 Samuel 2:30–34)
III. A Faithful Priest (2 Samuel 2:35–36)

UNIFYING PRINCIPLE

Some people are more faithful to their commitments than others. How do we respond to those who are faithful to their commitments and to those who are not? God rewarded faithful Phinehas and punished Eli's unfaithful children, thus proving that God is faithful to the everlasting covenant with God's people.

INTRODUCTION

The people of Israel had journeyed on from Mt. Sinai where they had received the Law—including sacrificial ordinances that specified which parts and under what circumstances priests were permitted to eat meat from sacrificial animals (see Lev. 6:24–30); it also included a clear prohibition against marrying other people outside the people of Israel (see Deut. 7:3). The rules were often complex. Specific washings and ritual sacrifices of animals had to be done in very carefully and in precise ways. The tabernacle tent and the ark of the covenant were constructed according to guidelines of God laid down through Moses. Some of the rules were more simple. Priests were to eat only certain parts of sacrificial animals and only after those animals had been properly prepared and presented to God, ready for the burning upon the altar. Intermarriage had no loopholes. Two specific instances in Numbers and 1 Samuel show how children of Israel deliberately violated the commitment they had made to walk according to the terms of the covenant with God.

The book of Numbers is included in the Pentateuch, the first five books of the

Bible, which deal with the origins of Israel and how they came to live in the Promised Land and have God's laws to guide them. Though these books are traditionally attributed to Moses, they were more likely written later and included material from Moses' own time. In this way, Numbers offers insight into the inception and the earliest days of Israel. The fourth book of the Pentateuch also moves into how Israel in the days of the monarchy and the exile in Babylon thought theologically about the role they played in the world. They considered how God had led them and might continue to lead in their own days. The book includes many literary forms, including narrative, as in the text from Numbers 25. In this text, the Lord is seen as taking the holiness of His people very seriously, yet also is willing to forgive them when they repent.

EXPOSITION

I. PHINEHAS TURNS BACK GOD'S WRATH
(NUMBERS 25:10–13)

The tidal wave of Israel had arrived at the border of the Promised Land. They had bypassed Edom at the lower eastern corner of the Dead Sea (see Num. 20:18–21), crushed the Amorites (see Num. 21:25) and arrived in the land of Moab in the town of Shittim, directly across the Jordan River from Jericho. There, they had set up camp (see Num. 22:1). To say that Balak of Zippor, king of the Moabites, was alarmed would be an understatement. The people of Moab were in terror at what might be in store for them should Israel decide to remain in that territory (see Num. 22:3–4). Balak set the prophet Balaam to speak a curse on the children of Israel three times and instead Balaam spoke a blessing three times. However, Numbers 31:16 indicates that Balaam was determined to earn the wages promised by Balak. "Balaam encouraged the people of Israel to mix with the people of Moab and Midian, and encouraged the Moabite and Midianite women to seduce the Israelite men and invite them to join in the heathen festivals" (Don Fleming, *Bridgeway Bible Commentary*. https://www.studylight.org/commentaries/bbc/numbers-25.html).

The plan worked—Israel cursed themselves. The men of Israel began to notice the beauty of the women of Moab. The women were likely the temple prostitutes serving the Baal of Peor. "Baal was a general name for 'lord,' and Peor for a 'mount' in Moab. The real name of the idol was Chemosh, and his rites of worship were celebrated by the grossest obscenity. In participating in this festival, They, the Israelites committed the double offense of idolatry and licentiousness" (Robert Jamieson, A.R. Fausset, & David Brown. *Commentary Critical & Explanatory on the Whole Bible*. http://www.biblestudytools.com/commentaries/jamieson-fausset-brown/numbers/numbers-25.html). Numbers 25:3 says that this activity resulted in the people of Israel being "yoked" to Baal (NRSV). This yoking represented a binding of the people of Israel to the pagan Moabites and was the logical end of what had surely begun as simple partaking of the delights of the culture around them. The partakers had developed an addiction that repeatedly drew them back in to their debauchery and worship of Baal at the cost of their indulgence and fleshly desires.

The wrath of God was kindled. Moses told the judges, who were the leaders of the various tribes, that they were to identify and kill any men among their charges who were involved in the idolatry. Also, the tribal leaders were to suffer death because they had permitted their men to indulge without censure. There would be no doubt about the fierceness of the anger of God against those who had committed this abomination nor about the fierce zeal of Phinehas in carrying out His judgment. By dealing out the punishment decreed by God the idolaters, Phinehas, and the grandson of Aaron had satisfied the anger of God, turning it aside from raining more death down upon his disobedient people. Yet before Phinehas could act, 24,000 men had died, many no doubt on display around the camps of the people.

What began as an attempt by Balak to overcome the perceived threat from the people of Israel, who had not done anything other than camp along the banks of the Jordan River, brought about the very enmity that Balak feared. And the indulgence in sin and idolatry by the men of Israel brought them only a horrible death and lasting dishonor. Yet in the midst of all the terrible wrath of God and the suffering of the people of Israel and Moab, there were those like Phinehas who never wavered and whose zeal for God's covenant elevated them to positions of honor. Years later, there would come another Phinehas who would not fare so well.

II. ELI'S SONS EARN GOD'S WRATH (2 SAMUEL 2:30–34)

Fast forward many generations. Israel had conquered the Promised Land, and a string of judges had ruled the people. The most current judge was the priest Eli (see 1 Sam. 4:18). Samuel, who would be the last judge and who would anoint first Saul and later David as kings over Israel, was a boy already engaged in ministry (see 1 Sam. 2:18).

Eli had two sons, Phinehas and Hophni, who were "scoundrels" (1 Sam. 2:12, NRSV). Adam Clarke says of them, "They were perverse, wicked, profligate men; devil's children. They knew not the Lord" (*Adam Clarke's Commentary.* https://www.studylight.org/commentaries/acc/1-samuel-2.html). Both Hophni and Phinehas were priests serving under Eli. Both of his sons were corrupt. They abused their authority by taking the sacrificial meat for their own dining pleasure (see 1 Sam. 2:13–14). Furthermore, they threatened anyone who tried to stand up to them in their disobedience to God's commands for sacrificing (see 1 Sam. 2:16). "This showed their disrespect for God, because it meant that they took their portions before God received his" (Don Fleming, *Bridgeway Bible Commentary.* https://www.studylight.org/commentaries/bbc/1-samuel-2.html). They continued to abuse the power of their priestly positions by engaging in intimate relations with the young women who served at the entrance of the tent of meeting (see 1 Sam. 2:22). Today, this would be called sexual assault for the women would have found it very difficult to refuse the advances of two men who were priests (and thereby, their bosses) as well as the sons of the judge over Israel. They held immense power over those women.

In response to becoming aware of what his sons were doing, Eli told them to stop. However, had the offenders not been his own sons, it is likely that Eli would have had them removed from the priesthood, and possibly executed. Thus, God sent an unnamed prophet to Eli to straighten out what Eli had proven he was incapable of handling (see 1 Sam. 2:27). God, speaking through his unnamed prophet, recalled how Eli had come to be a priest in the first place. God had bestowed the priesthood directly upon Eli's ancestor, Aaron. Part of what had been bestowed upon Eli's family had been the privilege of eating from the sacrificial offerings (see 1 Sam. 2:28). But rather than accept the plan of God for their sustenance, Eli's sons had turned "greedy eyes" upon the offerings (1 Sam. 2:29, NRSV). Hophni and Phinehas were not content with the portions prescribed by Law. They wanted the prime cuts that were to be offered to God.

Then, God spoke His judgment upon Eli and his family. Though God had promised Eli that his family would "'go in and out before me forever" as priests serving God (1 Sam. 2:30, NRSV), that promise had been made null and void by the actions of Eli and his sons. God spoke a litany of curses upon the family. Their power and strength would disappear like the morning mist. No one in Eli's family would live to see old age. "So much importance has always, in the East, been attached to old age, that it would be felt to be a great calamity, and sensibly to lower the respectability of any family which could boast of few or no old men." (Jamieson, et. al. http://www.biblestudytools.com/commentaries/jamieson-fausset-brown/1-samuel/1-samuel-2.html). Next, God turned the greedy eye of Hophni and Phinehas back on the family by saying that they would be in such dire straits that they would look with "greedy eyes" at the prosperity God would bring to the rest of Israel. People in Eli's family would weep at what was to befall them, and many would die by the sword.

Of those to die, Hophni and Phinehas were to be the first, dying on the same day as a sign to Eli and his family of God's intentions toward them. Eli's family would be reduced from stealing the prime cuts of sacrificial meat and feasting like kings to begging for a morsel of bread. As with the idolaters who had been impaled at the time of the first Phinehas, all of these events would bring public shame and disgrace upon Eli and his descendants.

III. A Faithful Priest (2 Samuel 2:35–36)

The writer of Hebrews cautioned, "Therefore we must pay greater attention to what we have heard, so that we do not drift away from it. For if the message declared through angels was valid, and every transgression or disobedience received a just penalty, how can we escape if we neglect so great a salvation?" (Heb. 2:1–3, NRSV). Drifting away begins with small compromises, yielding to what might seem like normal enough desires. Walking with God requires of each person the kind of unwavering commitment shown by the first Phinehas.

Furthermore, God said to Eli, "'I will raise up for myself a faithful priest, who shall do according to what is in my heart and in my mind. I will build him a sure house, and he shall go in and out before my anointed one forever'" (1 Sam. 2:35, NRSV). In the immediate future, Samuel would serve as a faithful priest. However, he would not be a priest forever. Only

Christ Jesus is Priest forever, and He does not go in and out before God's anointed one; He is the Anointed One. He is perfectly faithful, perfectly in sync with God's heart and mind because He is God. In Him, believers are made secure in hope for the future. He offers the promise of eternal life, and He made that promise reality when He rose from the dead.

THE LESSON APPLIED

Those who suffered the judgments of God both at the time of Phinehas in Moab and during the time of the disobedience of the sons of Eli were covenant people of God. What separated Phinehas (the first) from Phinehas (the second) was the faithfulness with which they behaved as members of God's family. Those outside of a covenant relationship with God will be judged as God chooses, but those inside the covenant should not think that they will escape if they allow idolatry and sin to take over their lives. Just as what began as a dalliance with the women of Moab turned into worship at the altar of Baal, betraying one's commitment starts a downward spiral into sin that will eventually wreak havoc on a person's life.

Many have traded our covenant faithfulness to God for what the world has to offer. Paul warned Timothy about those who desired to get rich (see 1 Tim. 6:9). Those people, Paul said, "pierce themselves" (v. 10, NRSV). That piercing included a public display of their idolatry and serves as a warning to other Israelites that God takes His covenant with us very seriously. When we desire the things of the world, we too make a public display that bears testimony that material things are our idols to which we bow down, as surely as Zimri bowed before Baal. Instead, let us heed Paul's advice to Timothy to, "shun all this; pursue righteousness, godliness, faith, love, endurance, gentleness" (1 Tim. 6:11, NRSV).

LET'S TALK ABOUT IT

1. Was God unjust in ordering the chiefs of the people killed?

Leaders bear responsibility for the actions of those in their charge. If an individual is a leader of God's people, it is incumbent upon that individual to deal with ungodliness among those he or she leads. That's why God positions leaders in the first place—to be responsible. Though the death sentences in Israel may seem harsh today, the fact was that the leaders were not modeling holiness before God in a way the people understood its importance or appreciated the beauty of a life of obedience. They had failed to model what it meant to be different from the nations of the world, and so they were also responsible for what the people had done.

HOME DAILY DEVOTIONAL READINGS
NOVEMBER 6–12, 2017

MONDAY	TUESDAY	WEDNESDAY	THURSDAY	FRIDAY	SATURDAY	SUNDAY
God's Love Brings the People Together	People with Disabilities Welcome	Israel Celebrates Their Homecoming	Rachel's Children Come Home	Covenant Relationship Restored	In Remembrance of Me	Accountability Under the New Covenant
Jeremiah 31:1–6	Jeremiah 31:7–9	Jeremiah 31:10–14	Jeremiah 31:15–20	Hosea 2:16–20	Luke 22:14–20	Jeremiah 31:27–34

WRITTEN ON THE HEART

ADULT TOPIC: PROMISE OF A NEW COVENANT	BACKGROUND SCRIPTURE: JEREMIAH 31

JEREMIAH 31:27–34

King James Version

BEHOLD, the days come, saith the LORD, that I will sow the house of Israel and the house of Judah with the seed of man, and with the seed of beast.

28 And it shall come to pass, that like as I have watched over them, to pluck up, and to break down, and to throw down, and to destroy, and to afflict; so will I watch over them, to build, and to plant, saith the LORD.

29 In those days they shall say no more, The fathers have eaten a sour grape, and the children's teeth are set on edge.

30 But every one shall die for his own iniquity: every man that eateth the sour grape, his teeth shall be set on edge.

31 Behold, the days come, saith the LORD, that I will make a new covenant with the house of Israel, and with the house of Judah:

32 Not according to the covenant that I made with their fathers in the day that I took them by the hand to bring them out of the land of Egypt; which my covenant they brake, although I was an husband unto them, saith the LORD:

33 But this shall be the covenant that I will make with the house of Israel; After those days, saith the LORD, I will put my law in their inward parts, and write it in their hearts; and will be their God, and they shall be my people.

34 And they shall teach no more every man his neighbour, and every man his brother, saying, Know the LORD: for they shall all know

New Revised Standard Version

THE days are surely coming, says the LORD, when I will sow the house of Israel and the house of Judah with the seed of humans and the seed of animals.

28 And just as I have watched over them to pluck up and break down, to overthrow, destroy, and bring evil, so I will watch over them to build and to plant, says the LORD.

29 In those days they shall no longer say: "The parents have eaten sour grapes, and the children's teeth are set on edge."

30 But all shall die for their own sins; the teeth of everyone who eats sour grapes shall be set on edge.

31 The days are surely coming, says the LORD, when I will make a new covenant with the house of Israel and the house of Judah.

32 It will not be like the covenant that I made with their ancestors when I took them by the hand to bring them out of the land of Egypt—a covenant that they broke, though I was their husband, says the LORD.

33 But this is the covenant that I will make with the house of Israel after those days, says the LORD: I will put my law within them, and I will write it on their hearts; and I will be their God, and they shall be my people.

34 No longer shall they teach one another, or say to each other, "Know the LORD," for they shall all know me, from the least of them to the

MAIN THOUGHT: But this shall be the covenant that I will make with the house of Israel; After those days, saith the LORD, I will put my law in their inward parts, and write it in their hearts; and will be their God, and they shall be my people. (Jeremiah 31:33, KJV)

King James Version	New Revised Standard Version
me, from the least of them unto the greatest of them, saith the LORD: for I will forgive their iniquity, and I will remember their sin no more.	greatest, says the LORD; for I will forgive their iniquity, and remember their sin no more.

LESSON SETTING
Time: Circa 575 B.C.
Place: Mizpah

LESSON OUTLINE
I. **At That Time**
   (Jeremiah 31:27–30)
II. **The Days Are Surely Coming, Part One**
   (Jeremiah 31:31–32)
III. **The Days Are Surely Coming, Part Two**
   (Jeremiah 31:33–34)

UNIFYING PRINCIPLE
Try as we might, humans often fail in our relationships. How can we restore broken relationships with others? Jeremiah foresaw a time when God would make a new covenant, writing God's law on human hearts with the vow to be Israel's God and to make Israel God's people.

INTRODUCTION
The people of Israel had gloried in their status as the chosen people of God for nearly a millennium. God had given them a bountiful land, had led them to defeat the enemies that surrounded them, blessed them with powerful leaders, and even dwelt among them in the temple of Solomon. Then within one century, it all unraveled. The prophet, Jeremiah, among others, tried to help the people understand.

The people were being uprooted, carried away to foreign lands, scattered in various places across the face of the Middle East. The Assyrians had overthrown the northern kingdom of Israel. Trying to avoid the same fate, the southern kingdom, Judah, had turned to Egypt for help in holding off the powerful Babylonian armies of Nebuchadnezzar. It worked for a moment, but finally Babylon swept in and conquered Judah. The temple of Solomon, God's dwelling place among His nation, was burned to the ground, while the remaining stones pulled down and scattered until there was not one stone left on top of another. The sacred city on the hill, Jerusalem, was sacked and destroyed. Meanwhile, the covenant God of Israel who had promised that the seed of David would rule forever had stood by and let it all happen. In their perspective, this was so far from what the children of Israel had ever imagined that they simply could not get their heads around it.

This is the environment in which Jeremiah prophesied. The book of Jeremiah reveals that the prophet's work was intertwined with the prophet himself. "The book of Jeremiah presents Jeremiah as a priest and prophet who was heavily involved in the public affairs of his own society at a time of deep national crisis. As such, he represents a model of unswerving commitment to Yahweh, to his own people, and to the principles of righteousness and justice that stood at the foundation of Yahweh's relationship with the people of

Israel and Judah" (Marvin A. Sweeney, "Jeremiah, Book of" in *Eerdman's Dictionary of the Bible* [Grand Rapids, MI: Eerdmans, 2000], 688–689). His circumstances were frequently part of his prophecy. Though it was his job to speak judgment to Judah, Jeremiah offered visions of restoration for both nations, Judah and Israel also. The Lord would bless His people, once again.

EXPOSITION

I. AT THAT TIME
(JEREMIAH 31:27–30)

The people came and concluded that their collective sins was the answer to why Yahweh allowed His chosen people to be captured and subjugated. Their focus was not on personal sin as much as it was on the corporate, national sin of the people as a whole. They could look back upon the golden calf, the intermarriages at the time of Joshua, and the ungodliness of many of their more recent kings and observe that they, as a people, had repeatedly violated God's sacred covenant. The group focus was about to shift.

In Jeremiah 30–31, the phrase "the days are surely coming" repeats several times, suggesting that something is about to happen that will change everything (30:3; 31:27, 31, 38, NRSV). In Jeremiah 30:3, Jeremiah announced God's promise that He would restore the fortunes of the people of Israel and Judah. He foretold they would get their land back and could hope, things would be as they were before. Those days would see a complete reversal of fortune. "And just as I have watched over them to pluck up and break down, to overthrow, destroy, and bring evil, so I will watch over them to build and to plant, says the LORD" (Jer. 31:28, NRSV). God had punished the people, yet He would restore them and bless them.

Among the exiles in the various towns and cities of Babylon, a common saying was "The parents have eaten sour grapes, and the children's teeth are set on edge" (v. 29, NRSV). It was one of the phrases the exiles used to explain why they were no longer living in Jerusalem. It represented what their parents (ancestors) had done to disobey God. He had come down upon the children in the form of the punishment of exile. Grapes are sour when they are eaten too soon, before they ripen. To eat a grape when it was sour was to eat it outside the purpose for which it exists, or to eat it against the will and purpose of the God, who gave it to be savored at the height of its sweetness.

Jeremiah told the people that the days were surely coming when they would no longer say that. There would be a restoration when Israel and Judah would be sown and planted, like a crop, in the land they had lost to Babylon and earlier to Assyria. What the people saw before them was that they were being plucked up, pulled up like weeds, and broken down like something being put into the trash heap. God had overthrown their kingdom, destroyed their city and their temple, and inflicted unimaginable misery on His people. Jeremiah said that, God had "watched over" them while all this was happening (v. 28, NRSV). The Hebrew word *shāqad* means to stand vigilant guard over something. God always watched intently to make sure His people got everything He intended for them to get.

In the coming days, God would be as vigilant as He had been in past days in making sure that a restoration that included rebuilding and replanting would occur. But, in this new restoration, the people could no longer be content to blame their misery upon the sins of their ancestors. That "sour grapes" saying would no longer be a way for them to excuse their own culpability before God. Wrote Adam Clarke: "No child shall suffer Divine [punishment] for the sin of his father; only so far as he acts in the same way can he be said to bear the sins of his parents" (*Adam Clarke's Commentary.* https://www.studylight.org/commentaries/acc/jeremiah-31.html).

II. THE DAYS ARE SURELY COMING, PART ONE (JEREMIAH 31:31–32)

Jeremiah 31:1 indicates that it was God's plan to restore the relationship between Himself and the people. God tells them wonderful news: "I have loved you with an everlasting love…. Again I will build you" (vv. 3–4, NRSV). God said they would again plant vineyards along the mountains of Samaria and be able to climb Mt. Zion in Jerusalem to worship their God. Verse seventeen announced, "There is hope for your future" (NRSV). "Return, O virgin Israel, return to these your cities," proclaims verse twenty-one (NRSV). It was the best of all possible prophecies, one that so delighted Jeremiah, who usually had far more grim things to say, that he described it as waking up from a pleasant sleep (see Jer. 31:26).

Again, Jeremiah announced that "the days are surely coming" (v. 31, NRSV). He presented and described more information about what this restoration from

exile by saying that there will be a new covenant that would be different from the one the people had always known. The Hebrew word translated "new" is the word *hādāsh*. It can mean something entirely new or it can mean something that has been refurbished or renewed so that it is as good as new. The variation of meaning left some confusion about exactly what God was about to do. Was this an entirely new covenant or would the old covenant return as good as new as if it had never been broken? Some of the exiles argued for the former while others believed the latter.

Whichever one believed at the time, Jeremiah made it clear that the covenant would be one inscribed on their hearts rather than on stone tablets. The Ark of the Covenant had been lost, and so the people heard Jeremiah and interpreted his words based upon how they interpreted *hādāsh*. Most of the people expected the old system to return but with a new inward awareness to enhance community life. Of this opinion, Don Fleming says, "God [would] change people by working within them, by giving them a better knowledge of his will and the inner strength to carry it out" (*Bridgeway Bible Commentary.* https://www.studylight.org/commentaries/bbc/jeremiah-31.html).

III. THE DAYS ARE SURELY COMING, PART TWO (JEREMIAH 31:33–34)

Of course, the Judeans knew that God was not going to write something on their hearts in a literal sense. That is not what Jeremiah meant by "heart" and the people understood. "Heart" was the term used to describe the part of a human being that carried the divine image. It included the emotions, the reasoning ability and the will of a person. It was a person's soul, and it was here where the Law of God would be inscribed so that one's soul would have the desire to obey, one's reasoning ability would understand why we obey, and one's will would submit to being obedient. The knowledge of the Lord would not be simply recognized as something to be recited and dismissed but something that changed lives as the Lord continued to reveal Himself and His will to His people.

At the time when the exile was just getting geared up, as the people struggled to understand what God's purpose might be, Jeremiah spoke to them. God would bring the people back after they had paid for the evil both they and their ancestors had done. When that happened, things would return like before, and they would get the land back and have a temple again. God would also write His Law upon their hearts so that each individual would have what he or she needed to be an obedient child of God. Having done that, God had forgiven the past sins of Israel and remembered them no more.

Many of the Jews, as they now called themselves, returned from captivity, but many others did not for a variety of reasons. Some had abandoned the faith of their ancestors, like the Samaritans, and developed synchronistic religious blends, drawing from a bit of Yahweh with smatterings from the worship of some other god. Others had been born and reared in the towns of Babylon and Asia Minor and preferred to remain in the land they knew rather than move off to a wasteland that they had only heard about in stories.

Jerusalem was eventually rebuilt and a new temple rose at the site of the old one.

While in exile, the people could not, of course, make sacrifices or go to a temple, but they continued to practice their faith. Michael Weed notes, "The exile and its various pressures upon Israel set the stage for the emergence of Judaism as 'the religion of the book' ("The Rise of Judaism: From Exodus/Sinai to Sianai/Exodus" in "The Institute for Christians Studies Faculty Bulletin." [Austin, TX: November 1984, Number 5], 21)." The Law was what they had left, and they devoted themselves to its study with great fervor. Synagogues came into being during the exile. The failure of their ancestors to keep that Law had led, in their belief, to the exile. They had the prophecy of Jeremiah that the Law was to be written on their hearts. Surely, God would bless them if they devoted themselves to its study. Each synagogue would have a person who acted as the group's teacher, or rabbi. The members would gather for prayer and socializing, while caring for the needs of the Jews in their community, and to read and discuss the Torah. When the exiles returned, they brought a new cultural institution with them as well.

All of their study of the Law was intended for good, but if it did not render their hearts changed, it was useless. Some, like many Pharisees of Jesus' day, knew the Law inside and out but did not have hearts turned toward God. Others, like many of the early disciples, did not have great schooling and could not study the Law constantly, but their hearts were turned toward God and were open to His instruction. They knew the Lord in this way, from the least to the greatest, He would "forgive their iniquity, and remember their sin no more" (v. 34, NRSV). It's not that one who knows the Lord never sins; that person, who doesn't want to sin and is learning not to, has favor with Him.

THE LESSON APPLIED

Paul spoke of people "who are always being instructed and can never arrive at a knowledge of the truth (2 Timothy 3:7)." That phrase could easily have been applied to the Jews as they scoured the scriptures trying to understand why God would allow their culture to be so totally devastated, but it could just as easily apply to many Christians today. We experience a financial reversal and take to our Bibles trying to figure out why the promises of prosperity seem to have gone sour. We deal with the reality of ongoing sin in our lives and then search the Bible to develop justifications for why that should be so when God has clearly called us to be holy. We know that Jeremiah said God would write His Law on the hearts of his children, yet still we gather weekly to study the Bible, constructing theologies and explanations for ideas from man.

Reading and studying the written Word of God is a good thing, but it sometimes seems as if we are always reading and always studying and not getting much closer to God. Could it be we have constructed an elaborate religion that does not truly answer the heart cry most of us feel to be intimately in love with and loved by God? If so, it would not be the first time such a thing has happened. Just ask the post-exilic Jews.

LET'S TALK ABOUT IT

1. How did the exile renew hope in Israel for a Savior?

Along with the rise of the synagogues, the Pharisees and teachers of the Law, a new hope arose. Jeremiah had said that the days were surely coming when God would restore the full glory of Israel. The study of the Law and the Prophets focused on passages that seemed to foretell an anointed Deliverer, whom they called the Messiah. This Messiah would be the one to bring to pass the full realization of the promises made through Jeremiah and the other prophets. At first they thought perhaps one of the Maccabees might be the Messiah, but that revolt fizzled after a few years. The people continued to wait for the days when the Messiah would surely come and drive out the hated Romans, restore Jerusalem to preeminence among the great cities of the world, and then light the great light on the hill that had been the glory of Israel again.

HOME DAILY DEVOTIONAL READINGS
NOVEMBER 13–19, 2017

MONDAY	TUESDAY	WEDNESDAY	THURSDAY	FRIDAY	SATURDAY	SUNDAY
God's Awesome Power	Covenant Blessings	Keep Your Covenant with God	Praise God for Answered Prayer	Everlasting Single Sacrifice for Sin	Mediator of the New Covenant	Receiving the Unshakable Kingdom
Psalm 66:1–4	Matthew 5:1–12	Deuteronomy 4:21–24	Psalm 66:16–20	Hebrews 10:11–18	Hebrews 9:11–15	Hebrews 12:14–15, 18–29

THE GO-BETWEEN

HEBREWS 12:14–15, 18–29

King James Version

FOLLOW peace with all men, and holiness, without which no man shall see the Lord:

15 Looking diligently lest any man fail of the grace of God; lest any root of bitterness springing up trouble you, and thereby many be defiled.

• • • • • •

18 For ye are not come unto the mount that might be touched, and that burned with fire, nor unto blackness, and darkness, and tempest,

19 And the sound of a trumpet, and the voice of words; which voice they that heard intreated that the word should not be spoken to them any more:

20 (For they could not endure that which was commanded, And if so much as a beast touch the mountain, it shall be stoned, or thrust through with a dart:

21 And so terrible was the sight, that Moses said, I exceedingly fear and quake:)

22 But ye are come unto mount Sion, and unto the city of the living God, the heavenly Jerusalem, and to an innumerable company of angels,

23 To the general assembly and church of the firstborn, which are written in heaven, and to God the Judge of all, and to the spirits of just men made perfect,

24 And to Jesus the mediator of the new covenant, and to the blood of sprinkling, that speaketh better things than that of Abel.

25 See that ye refuse not him that speaketh. For if they escaped not who refused him that

New Revised Standard Version

PURSUE peace with everyone, and the holiness without which no one will see the Lord.

15 See to it that no one fails to obtain the grace of God; that no root of bitterness springs up and causes trouble, and through it many become defiled.

• • • • • •

18 You have not come to something that can be touched, a blazing fire, and darkness, and gloom, and a tempest,

19 and the sound of a trumpet, and a voice whose words made the hearers beg that not another word be spoken to them.

20 (For they could not endure the order that was given, "If even an animal touches the mountain, it shall be stoned to death."

21 Indeed, so terrifying was the sight that Moses said, "I tremble with fear.")

22 But you have come to Mount Zion and to the city of the living God, the heavenly Jerusalem, and to innumerable angels in festal gathering,

23 and to the assembly of the firstborn who are enrolled in heaven, and to God the judge of all, and to the spirits of the righteous made perfect,

24 and to Jesus, the mediator of a new covenant, and to the sprinkled blood that speaks a better word than the blood of Abel.

25 See that you do not refuse the one who is speaking; for if they did not escape when they

MAIN THOUGHT: Wherefore we receiving a kingdom which cannot be moved, let us have grace, whereby we may serve God acceptably with reverence and godly fear: For our God is a consuming fire. (Hebrews 12:28–29, KJV)

HEBREWS 12:14–15, 18–29

King James Version

spake on earth, much more shall not we escape, if we turn away from him that speaketh from heaven:

26 Whose voice then shook the earth: but now he hath promised, saying, Yet once more I shake not the earth only, but also heaven.

27 And this word, Yet once more, signifieth the removing of those things that are shaken, as of things that are made, that those things which cannot be shaken may remain.

28 Wherefore we receiving a kingdom which cannot be moved, let us have grace, whereby we may serve God acceptably with reverence and godly fear:

29 For our God is a consuming fire.

New Revised Standard Version

refused the one who warned them on earth, how much less will we escape if we reject the one who warns from heaven!

26 At that time his voice shook the earth; but now he has promised, "Yet once more I will shake not only the earth but also the heaven."

27 This phrase, "Yet once more," indicates the removal of what is shaken—that is, created things—so that what cannot be shaken may remain.

28 Therefore, since we are receiving a kingdom that cannot be shaken, let us give thanks, by which we offer to God an acceptable worship with reverence and awe;

29 for indeed our God is a consuming fire.

LESSON SETTING
Time: Between 60–95 A.D.
Place: Unknown

LESSON OUTLINE
  I. Peace and Holiness
    (Hebrews 12:14–15)
  II. Tale of Two Mountains
    (Hebrews 12:18–24)
  III. An Unshakable Kingdom
    (Hebrews 12:25–28)

UNIFYING PRINCIPLE

Humans desire to experience a power greater than themselves, but do not always realize that drawing near to such needed power can be an awesome prospect. How can people approach such a power without being consumed? The psalmist affirms that God allows humans to approach the Divine; the writer of Hebrews proclaims that Jesus provides the means of boldly approaching the presence of God.

INTRODUCTION

In order to properly understand much of the New Testament, it is important to recapture, to the greatest extent possible, the worldview, and the political and cultural reality of Israel at the time of Jesus and the early Church. While today the letter named Hebrews is part of the Scriptures, it began as a letter from an anonymous author to a group of Jews who had came to believe that Jesus of Nazareth was, indeed, Israel's Messiah. It was written for a reason and was understood in the light of that reason and in the context of the lives of the recipients. Internal and external evidence suggests that the letter was written between 60–95 A.D.

By 65 A.D., a rupture or separation had taken place between the Jews and a small subset of Jews, originally referred to as "the Way." For the first years following the crucifixion and resurrection of Jesus of Nazareth, the believers had continued to attend synagogue and observe the customs and practices of Judaism. Then, in 42 A.D., Herod Agrippa I, ruler of Judea and the grandson of Herod the Great, tried to win favor with the Jews by persecuting Christians. The Way had angered Jews by claiming that the followers of Jesus were the true Israel of God. The persecution, described in Acts, took the life of Stephen and was attended by Saul of Tarsus (see Acts 7), led eventually to the arrest of Peter and the death of James (see Acts 12). The rupture had become irreconcilable, and the followers of the Way were driven out of Jerusalem. The doors to Judaism slammed shut, leaving the followers of Jesus with the task of trying to understand how they were to practice and exercise their faith. That Judaizers followed Paul around trying to convince Christian Gentiles to observe the Jewish laws, Jewish rituals and custom shows. In the minds of the early Church, that it took quite a while to settle, exactly what the relationship would be going forward between Christianity and Judaism.

The letter to the Hebrews was a part of that process, and chapter twelve represents the culmination of the argument for why Christianity was, indeed, the true result of Jewish hopes. It was the Church and not the nation of Israel that was the restored Israel or so, the followers of Jesus claimed. Jews were presented with a dilemma. Who were they to believe? Which way is true, the old way of Moses, or the new way of Jesus? This was the question to which Hebrews 12 provides the answer.

EXPOSITION

I. PEACE AND HOLINESS (HEBREWS 12:14–15)

The writer urged his readers to pursue peace with everyone. That does not mean peace can always be realized, but God's children are to work to live at peace with all of humanity. This is part of our worship to the Lord. The writer of Hebrews seemed to think that worship has more to do with living out new covenant lives, pursuing holiness, and making the best effort to live at peace with everyone. If worship is about presenting oneself, humble and obedient before the King, which is the true meaning of the word, then how one acts in day to day life is, indeed, of prime importance.

Also, Christians are to pursue holiness, which Adam Clarke describes as, "That state of continual sanctification, that life of purity and detachment from the world and all its lusts, without which detachment and sanctity no man shall see the Lord" (*Adam Clarke's Commentary*. https://www.studylight.org/commentaries/acc/hebrews-12.html). The writer of Hebrews says, holiness will not simply happen. It must be pursued, worked on diligently. Holiness is ever-growing separation from the world, which is being shaken to its core by the appearance of the Kingdom of God and will eventually pass away.

It is the grace of God flowing into the life of a Christian that enables that person to live the kind of life that expresses gratitude and worship to God. The writer warned his readers not to be in poverty when it comes to this grace. The result of a lack of grace will be the growth of evil in one's life. The "root of bitterness" is just such a growth, springing up from a bitter heart producing fruit that is not fit for consumption (v. 15, NRSV). Should one permit that to happen, the writer warns that many will "become defiled" (v. 15, NRSV).

II. TALE OF TWO MOUNTAINS (HEBREWS 12:18–27)

When the Jews read the Old Testament prophecies of God making a "new" covenant with His people, they sometimes understood "new" to mean "renewed" or "refurbished." They expected God to fix all the problems the people had in obeying the Law of Moses, including their own sinful inclinations to break those laws, as well as uncertainties in exactly how the laws should be obeyed. The writer of Hebrews went to great pains to show that this old covenant could never have saved God's people but instead had to be recreated as an entirely new covenant for a new Israel. Hebrews 11 lists all the heroes of Israel, and showed that each of them looked forward to something that was not yet in existence, including Moses to whom the old covenant was given. It is the summation of the argument that the old covenant had to be replaced, not simply dusted off, cleaned up a bit, and put back into operation.

To demonstrate the superiority of the new covenant to the old, the author did a comparison of the two. He began by contrasting Mt. Sinai and the transfer of the old covenant to Mt. Zion and the arrival of the new covenant. The old had come in fear, as the people begged God not to kill them, amid blazing fire, darkness, gloom and the loud call of the trumpet. The people shook in terror as God spoke, lest even an animal upon them bring down the wrath of God by touching the side of the mountain. The new covenant had come under quite different circumstances. Rather than coming to a fiery, stormy mountain, the people of the new covenant had come to the intersection of heaven and earth. King Jesus was enthroned on high, triumphant over the powers of darkness that had ruled the earth ever since the fall

of Adam and Eve. No longer need God's people to fear His wrath for sin because the blood of Jesus the Mediator had been sprinkled on the altar.

The angels were gathered in festal array before the throne of Jesus. The firstborn, whose names were written in heaven's record book, were assembled, along with a mighty throng of witnesses, including all those listed in Hebrews 11 as heroes of Israel. God was present with the righteous made perfect, and those who had been declared innocent before the Judge of all. This is a picture of the redeemed and restored creation, though now appearing only partly and dimly perceived. Heaven and the glory of God had returned, and the readers of the epistle were to know that in Christ they had come to this juncture of heaven and earth.

III. An Unshakable Kingdom (Hebrews 12:25–28)

Though some of the Jewish Christians were struggling with going back to the old ways or at least adding the rituals and practices of Judaism to their Christian faith, the writer warned them not to refuse what was right before them. God had returned and restored His temple, but the temple was now in the hearts of the people, not in a building in Jerusalem. The foundations of Judaism were being transformed. The religious beliefs of all the nations that refused to bow in submission to the enthroned King of Kings were transformed. The powers of darkness that had corrupted humanity and caused the glory of God to depart hundreds of years ago were overthrown. All the kingdoms and powers of earth were being changed fiercely, to the point they might refuse to believe. Because the Jewish Christians, along with their Gentile brothers and sisters, were citizens of the Kingdom of God, the writer of Hebrews called upon them to live as such. They were runners in a marathon, running a race, during the days of their lives.

The writer concluded "God is, a consuming fire" (v. 29, NRSV). He is at work in the Kingdom of God when His children discipline themselves and submit to Him. It will burn up all those within the children that are impure and unholy, leaving behind only the pure gold of holiness.

THE LESSON APPLIED

Living in modern American society, we face daily the temptations of materialism, promiscuity and lust, disregard for the sanctity of human life, racism, and greed. The people around us so desperately need to see a different way to live, not just by where we go and what we do on Sunday morning. More importantly, our witness is in how we act around the water cooler at work and when the inevitable trials of life come upon us. Let us discipline ourselves, and shed all of what is being American that hinders us from pleasing God and vigorously pursue both a holy pattern of life and peace with our fellow humans. We are citizens of the Kingdom of God first. We stand at Mount Zion with the Lord Jesus interceding for us as recipients of a new and everlasting covenant. "Therefore, since we are receiving a kingdom that cannot be shaken, let us give thanks, by which we offer to God an acceptable worship with reverence and awe" (v. 28, NRSV). When our lives reflect our citizenship in His Kingdom, we worship Him and shine a light into our world that desperately needs to hear the good news that the Lord reigns, and that He is a good God, loving toward His creation and always seeking to make each part whole again.

LET'S TALK ABOUT IT

1. When the writer says "You have come to Mount Zion" (Heb. 12:22, NRSV), is he speaking of a future event?

The great throne room scene in Revelation 7 is usually considered something that will take place someday. The writer of Hebrews suggests that it is already taking place. A window has opened up between each of us and heaven. There, in the throne room of God are: the assembled angels, the firstborn, the spirits of those made righteous, and God watching in celebration as the Kingdom of God changes the kingdoms of this world. The great cloud of witnesses will cheer each of us on in our race of faith. The kingdom of heaven is not what we will hope to inherit someday. Through Christ, it's already done.

HOME DAILY DEVOTIONAL READINGS
NOVEMBER 20–26, 2017

MONDAY	TUESDAY	WEDNESDAY	THURSDAY	FRIDAY	SATURDAY	SUNDAY
Christ Our Creator, Savior, Peacemaker	Mealtime, Foretaste of the Lord's Supper	Keeping the Faith Entrusted to You	Preparing to Share the Passover Meal	Jesus Celebrates with Bread and Cup	Participating in Spiritual Worship	Observing the Lord's Supper
Colossians 1:9–20	1 Corinthians 11:17–22	Jude 1–4, 17–25	Mark 14:12–16	Mark 14:22–25	Romans 12:1–8	1 Corinthians 11:23–34

PROMISES TO REMEMBER

ADULT TOPIC:	BACKGROUND SCRIPTURES:
REMEMBERING THE COVENANT	1 CORINTHIANS 11; JUDE 3

1 CORINTHIANS 11:23–34

King James Version

FOR I have received of the Lord that which also I delivered unto you, that the Lord Jesus the same night in which he was betrayed took bread:

24 And when he had given thanks, he brake it, and said, Take, eat: this is my body, which is broken for you: this do in remembrance of me.

25 After the same manner also he took the cup, when he had supped, saying, this cup is the new testament in my blood: this do ye, as oft as ye drink it, in remembrance of me.

26 For as often as ye eat this bread, and drink this cup, ye do shew the Lord's death till he come.

27 Wherefore whosoever shall eat this bread, and drink this cup of the Lord, unworthily, shall be guilty of the body and blood of the Lord.

28 But let a man examine himself, and so let him eat of that bread, and drink of that cup.

29 For he that eateth and drinketh unworthily, eateth and drinketh damnation to himself, not discerning the Lord's body.

30 For this cause many are weak and sickly among you, and many sleep.

31 For if we would judge ourselves, we should not be judged.

32 But when we are judged, we are chastened of the Lord, that we should not be condemned with the world.

New Revised Standard Version

FOR I received from the Lord what I also handed on to you, that the Lord Jesus on the night when he was betrayed took a loaf of bread,

24 and when he had given thanks, he broke it and said, "This is my body that is for you. Do this in remembrance of me."

25 In the same way he took the cup also, after supper, saying, "This cup is the new covenant in my blood. Do this, as often as you drink it, in remembrance of me."

26 For as often as you eat this bread and drink the cup, you proclaim the Lord's death until he comes.

27 Whoever, therefore, eats the bread or drinks the cup of the Lord in an unworthy manner will be answerable for the body and blood of the Lord.

28 Examine yourselves, and only then eat of the bread and drink of the cup.

29 For all who eat and drink without discerning the body, eat and drink judgment against themselves.

30 For this reason many of you are weak and ill, and some have died.

31 But if we judged ourselves, we would not be judged.

32 But when we are judged by the Lord, we are disciplined so that we may not be condemned along with the world.

MAIN THOUGHT: After the same manner also he took the cup, when he had supped, saying, this cup is the new testament in my blood: this do ye, as oft as ye drink it, in remembrance of me. (1 Corinthians 11:25, KJV)

1 Corinthians 11:23–34

King James Version

33 Wherefore, my brethren, when ye come together to eat, tarry one for another.
34 And if any man hunger, let him eat at home; that ye come not together unto condemnation. And the rest will I set in order when I come.

New Revised Standard Version

33 So then, my brothers and sisters, when you come together to eat, wait for one another.
34 If you are hungry, eat at home, so that when you come together, it will not be for your condemnation. About the other things I will give instructions when I come.

LESSON SETTING
Time: Circa 55 A.D.
Place: Written from Ephesus

LESSON OUTLINE
I. The Lord's Body
   (1 Corinthians 11:23–26)
II. "Examine Yourselves"
   (1 Corinthians 11:27–32)
III. Preparing for the Lord's Supper
   (1 Corinthians 11:33–34)

UNIFYING PRINCIPLE

It is often easier to make promises than to keep them. How can we remember to keep the promises we make? Paul exhorted believers to remember these promises through celebrating the Lord's Supper in a way that affirms the covenant it embodies.

INTRODUCTION

Paul's first letter to the Corinthians was reasonably written from Ephesus, likely between 53–55 A.D. The church in Corinth was church that Paul, himself, had planted. Acts 18 informs the reader that Paul lived in Corinth for a year and a half before moving on (see vv. 1–11). The relationships he developed in that time were clearly very important to Paul, as his letters and visits to the city reveal. The believers in Corinth struggled to find a distinct Christian identity that was not unduly influenced by their past identities in Gentile society.

In Paul's letter to the Christians at Corinth, he was concerned with the people who were partaking in the meal. Corinth had been rebuilt by Rome and was a major trade city. As was true throughout most of the Roman Empire, a wide variety of religious practices were available to the citizenry. Many of those practices involved public celebratory meals, and many of the early Corinthian Christians had left pagan religions where such meals were commonplace. It appears they brought the practices of those meals with them into their observance of the Lord's Supper. Paul wrote to correct their practices and attitudes about this special Christian meal.

EXPOSITION

I. THE LORD'S BODY (1 CORINTHIANS 11:23–26)

Paul's use of the word "proclaim" in describing the impact of the Lord's Supper memorial, indicates the Corinthian believers expected non-believers to witness what they were doing (1 Cor. 11:26, NRSV). Outsiders were to observe the believers and, at least hopefully, be drawn toward Christ by what they saw occurring. This does not necessarily mean that nonbelievers were witnessing the meal itself, but rather, how Paul considered the meal being eaten as an indication of the believers' spiritual health. When the meal was eaten in a manner that honored the Lord, then those who ate it would go into their communities as the light and the salt that Jesus intended His disciples to be. When the meal was eaten in ways that dishonored the Lord, however, the proclamation of the believers' lives was something very different than what it needed to be.

Paul could not commend the Corinthians because their practices portrayed a fundamental departure from Jesus' intentions for His people. What the Corinthian Christians were doing was "not for the better but for the worse" (v. 17, NRSV), suggesting it was not drawing people to Christ, but rather, causing them to dismiss and disdain the Lord. When they gathered to eat the Lord's Supper, the believers were not unified in doing so.

The Church was comprised of a cross-section of Corinthian society. Some were rich, others poor. "[According to] a familiar Grecian custom, the persons assembled brought their own provisions, which being placed on the table formed a common stock. The rich brought plentifully, the poor brought little or nothing" (Charles Hodge. *Hodge's Commentary on Romans, Ephesians, and First Corinthians*. https://www.studylight.org/commentaries/hdg/1-corinthians-11.html). It appears that rich citizens were bringing full meals and making a feast of the memorial while the poor were ignored and left with nothing to eat.

The Christians had shown impatience at the meal as well. Some were not waiting while those with no food sat at empty tables. There were even people using the Lord's Supper memorial as an excuse to get drunk on wine. This kind of feast was common for pagans worshipping the god Bacchus, though it left Paul stupefied. He condemned the contempt the Corinthian Christians were showing. It was not what the Church was meant to model, including the humiliation the rich were heaping upon the poor in their refusal to share the food they had brought. What Paul had heard about belonged in pagan feasts, not in the Church. Here, people were to be loving, generous, and respectful of one another and toward their Lord whose sacrificial death they were honoring by partaking of the Lord's Supper.

To help the Christians understand how the Lord's Supper should be observed, Paul described the ceremony. Paul began by reminding them that he did not make this up on his own, but rather "received from the Lord" what he was about to pass along (v. 23, NRSV). This established Paul's credentials as a legitimate Apostle. Paul included himself among those taught directly by Jesus, a claim that appeared to be well-established and likely grew out of the time Paul spent in the immediate aftermath of his conversion (see Acts 9:5–9).

In describing what Jesus had done on the night of His betrayal, Paul said that Jesus requested that His followers repeat the breaking of bread and the taking of the cup in remembrance of Jesus. The Lord's Supper was not simply to exist as an activity that Christians do in tribute to Jesus. Leon Morris states, "The solemn observance of Holy Communion is a vivid proclamation of the Lord's death; in word and symbol Christ's death is set forth before people. 'The Eucharist is an *acted* sermon, an *acted* proclamation of the death which it commemorates' (Robertson and Plummer)" (*1 Corinthians* [Grand Rapids, MI: Eerdmans, Reprinted 2000], 160). The Lord's Supper is a message, both to those who partake and to those who see others partake. The message being sent by the Corinthians was more akin to the riotous debauchery of the pagan love-feasts than to the gospel of Jesus Christ. By treating it as they were, the Corinthian Christians were dishonoring the sacrificial death of the one whom they claimed to love above all.

The cup is the symbol of the new covenant, which was enacted as Jesus shed His blood on the cross. As people who claimed to belong to this new covenant family, the Corinthians owed their allegiance and their very lives to the Lord. Instead of remembering and honoring their Lord, they were indulging their own lusts and passions as they consumed great quantities of food and drink and left their poor kindred with nothing. They were making a travesty of a solemn ceremony of remembrance.

II. "EXAMINE YOURSELVES" (1 CORINTHIANS 11:27–32)

The Christians in Corinth lived in a city where pagan influences were everywhere. During the course of their daily lives, the social pressure to go along and follow with the ways of the culture around them must have been very great, indeed. The rich in Corinth regularly ignored the poor. People who had food often ate too much and it was common, perhaps even customary, to drink in excess. During the weeks leading up to the Sunday church gatherings, it seemed that some of the Corinthians allowed the society around them to draw them away from their living for Christ, and their worship suffered.

It also appears from Paul's letter that he viewed the problem in the Corinthian church as one of inadequate or improper preparation for the Lord's Supper. The Corinthian Christians would have to answer to God if they ate the meal in "an unworthy manner" (v. 27, NRSV). The Greek word *anaxiōs* means to do something in a way that is not approved. Therefore, Paul laid out for them what the approved method of preparing ought to include. First, they were to examine themselves. This refers to his former comment about being proven genuine as a true believer. The examination, he urged, is not essentially about making sure a person has recognized and confessed all personal sin, though that may be part of what one ought to do. Rather, the examination that one preparing to partake of the Lord's Supper should make concerns whether or not that person has been behaving like a genuine Christian. A person is "genuine" or *dokimos* if that individual lives up to the full measure of obedience to the new covenant, without cutting corners or neglecting the small details. The Corinthians were clearly not doing much self-examination, or else they could not have ignored the poor among them as they ate.

If, after self-examination, one were to eat the Lord's Supper unworthily, that person should expect the discipline and the judgement of God to come upon them. St. John Chrysostom, an early Church father, preached a sermon from 1 Corinthians 11:17–27. In that message, he spoke of the kind of actions that would make one unworthy of partaking of the meal. He said, "Many...approach with the poor to this holy Table, but when we go out, do not seem even to have seen them, but are both drunken and pass heedlessly by the hungry; the very things whereof the Corinthians were accused" ("Homily 27 on First Corinthians." http://www.newadvent.org/fathers/220127.htm). How believers live before and after the Lord's Supper must be examined before anyone participated.

III. Preparing for the Lord's Supper (1 Corinthians 11:33–34)

To the members of the church at Corinth, Paul summarized his teaching of the Lord's Supper by telling them to eat at home if they desired a meal and to wait for and include others when one was ready to partake of the Lord's Supper. If they properly prepared themselves for the meal, took care of their hunger apart from the Lord's Supper meal, and made sure that everyone who felt approved to partake had the chance to participate, they would escape the threatened condemnation for their shameful observance.

The Lord's Supper was not something to be taken lightly or simply glossed over as an insignificant gesture. It was a sermon to the lost, a way of honoring Jesus Christ, and one way in which the unity and love of Christians one for another was expressed.

THE LESSON APPLIED

In many churches, there is not much time during the worship service before the Lord's Supper for people to examine themselves. It is expected that the self-examination will have been done prior to the service.

Some behavior demands more than a simple confession. When Zacchaeus met Jesus (see Luke 19:1–10), he understood that he needed to put feet to his expression of repentance. There is no formal methodology in most churches for righting whatever wrongs one has committed, but Paul's teaching about the Lord's Supper helps us to understand how serious it is if we do not examine ourselves and deal with issues before we partake of the Lord's Supper.

LET'S TALK ABOUT IT

1. **How does a Christian eat and drink "damnation" (KJV)?**

Paul's warning about eating and drinking unworthily and bringing damnation upon oneself is said in the context of the examination to make sure one is genuine. All who examine themselves and are firmly convinced that they are living out a genuine faith in Christ, need never fear that God will condemn them. However, those who delude themselves and neglect self-examination are putting themselves at risk.

HOME DAILY DEVOTIONAL READINGS
NOVEMBER 27–DECEMBER 3, 2017

MONDAY	TUESDAY	WEDNESDAY	THURSDAY	FRIDAY	SATURDAY	SUNDAY
Take Refuge in the Lord	The Lord, My Strength and Salvation	A Blessing Promised to All Peoples	Your Faith Saved You	Contrasting Responses by Jews and Gentiles	Crippled Beggar Requests Alms	Repent and Believe in Jesus
Psalm 118:1–9	Psalm 118:10–14	Acts 3:22–26	Luke 7:44–50	Acts 13:44–49	Acts 3:1–10	Acts 3:11–21

SECOND QUARTER

Lesson material is based on International Sunday School Lessons and International Bible Lessons for Christian Teaching. Copyrighted by the International Council of Religious Education, and is used by its permission.

DECEMBER 2017, JANUARY, FEBRUARY 2018

SUGGESTED OPENING EXERCISES

1. **Usual Signal for Beginning**
2. **Prayer (Closing with the Lord's Prayer)**
3. **Singing (Songs to Be Selected)**
4. **Scripture Reading:**
   Hebrews 11:29–34 (KJV)

Director: By faith they passed through the Red sea as by dry land: which the Egyptians assaying to do were drowned.

School: By faith the walls of Jericho fell down, after they were compassed about seven days.

Director: By faith the harlot Rahab perished not with them that believed not, when she had received the spies with peace.

School: And what more shall I say? for the time would fail me to tell of Gedeon, and of Barak, and of Samson, and of Jephthae; of David also, and Samuel, and of the prophets:

Director: Who through faith subdued kingdoms, wrought righteousness, obtained promises, stopped the mouths of lions.

All: Quenched the violence of fire, escaped the edge of the sword, out of weakness were made strong, waxed valiant in fight, turned to flight the armies of the aliens.

Recitation in Concert:
Psalm 78:1–6 (KJV)

1 Give ear, O my people, to my law: incline your ears to the words of my mouth.

2 I will open my mouth in a parable: I will utter dark sayings of old:

3 Which we have heard and known, and our fathers have told us.

4 We will not hide them from their children, shewing to the generation to come the praises of the LORD, and his strength, and his wonderful works that he hath done.

5 For he established a testimony in Jacob, and appointed a law in Israel, which he commanded our fathers, that they should make them known to their children:

6 That the generation to come might know them, even the children which should be born; who should arise and declare them to their children.

CLOSING WORK

1. **Singing**
2. **Sentences: Exodus 3:4–8 (KJV)**

4 And when the LORD saw that he turned aside to see, God called unto him out of the midst of the bush, and s**aid, Moses, Moses. And he said, Here am I.**

5 And he said, Draw not nigh hither: put off thy shoes from off thy feet, for the place whereon thou standest is holy ground.

6 Moreover he said, I am the God of thy father, the God of Abraham, the God of Isaac, and the God of Jacob. And Moses hid his face; for he was afraid to look upon God.

7 And the LORD said, I have surely seen the affliction of my people which are in Egypt, and have heard their cry by reason of their taskmasters; for I know their sorrows;

8 And I am come down to deliver them out of the hand of the Egyptians, and to bring them up out of that land unto a good land and a large, unto a land flowing with milk and honey; unto the place of the Canaanites, and the Hittites, and the Amorites, and the Perizzites, and the Hivites, and the Jebusites.

3. **Dismissal with Prayer**

FAITH IN JESUS

ADULT TOPIC: SEEKING WHOLENESS	BACKGROUND SCRIPTURE: ACTS 3

ACTS 3:11–21

King James Version

AND as the lame man which was healed held Peter and John, all the people ran together unto them in the porch that is called Solomon's, greatly wondering.

12 And when Peter saw it, he answered unto the people, Ye men of Israel, why marvel ye at this? or why look ye so earnestly on us, as though by our own power or holiness we had made this man to walk?

13 The God of Abraham, and of Isaac, and of Jacob, the God of our fathers, hath glorified his Son Jesus; whom ye delivered up, and denied him in the presence of Pilate, when he was determined to let him go.

14 But ye denied the Holy One and the Just, and desired a murderer to be granted unto you;

15 And killed the Prince of life, whom God hath raised from the dead; whereof we are witnesses.

16 And his name through faith in his name hath made this man strong, whom ye see and know: yea, the faith which is by him hath given him this perfect soundness in the presence of you all.

17 And now, brethren, I wot that through ignorance ye did it, as did also your rulers.

18 But those things, which God before had shewed by the mouth of all his prophets, that Christ should suffer, he hath so fulfilled.

19 Repent ye therefore, and be converted, that your sins may be blotted out, when the times of

New Revised Standard Version

WHILE he clung to Peter and John, all the people ran together to them in the portico called Solomon's Portico, utterly astonished.

12 When Peter saw it, he addressed the people, "You Israelites, why do you wonder at this, or why do you stare at us, as though by our own power or piety we had made him walk?

13 The God of Abraham, the God of Isaac, and the God of Jacob, the God of our ancestors has glorified his servant Jesus, whom you handed over and rejected in the presence of Pilate, though he had decided to release him.

14 But you rejected the Holy and Righteous One and asked to have a murderer given to you,

15 and you killed the Author of life, whom God raised from the dead. To this we are witnesses.

16 And by faith in his name, his name itself has made this man strong, whom you see and know; and the faith that is through Jesus has given him this perfect health in the presence of all of you.

17 And now, friends, I know that you acted in ignorance, as did also your rulers.

18 In this way God fulfilled what he had foretold through all the prophets, that his Messiah would suffer.

19 Repent therefore, and turn to God so that your sins may be wiped out,

MAIN THOUGHT: And his name through faith in his name hath made this man strong, whom ye see and know: yea, the faith which is by him hath given him this perfect soundness in the presence of you all. (Acts 3:16, KJV)

ACTS 3:11–21

King James Version	New Revised Standard Version
refreshing shall come from the presence of the Lord.	
20 And he shall send Jesus Christ, which before was preached unto you:	20 so that times of refreshing may come from the presence of the Lord, and that he may send the Messiah appointed for you, that is, Jesus,
21 Whom the heaven must receive until the times of restitution of all things, which God hath spoken by the mouth of all his holy prophets since the world began.	21 who must remain in heaven until the time of universal restoration that God announced long ago through his holy prophets."

LESSON SETTING
    Time: 33 A.D.
    Place: Jerusalem

LESSON OUTLINE
    I. The Commotion
       (Acts 3:11)
    II. You Have Seen It Before
       (Acts 3:12–16)
    III. Get It Right This Time
       (Acts 3:17–21)

UNIFYING PRINCIPLE

People who are broken want to be made whole. How and where do they find wholeness? Peter proclaimed that faith in Jesus restores people to wholeness.

INTRODUCTION

People react to a noise, disturbance, or commotion. A shooting, fire, fight, car accident, or any mishap that captures the public's attention soon gains a group of onlookers whose intellectual curiosity has gotten the best of them. This is especially true in places that are normally serene and calm. The temple would be the last place where one would find a commotion taking place and when it does happen it leaves one bewildered and asking why. Such was the case of the murder of the Charleston Nine who were ambushed during Bible study by one they had invited to participate in worship with them. The commotion caused a much smaller uproar in the temple at Jerusalem, but an uproar nonetheless. At any rate, the crowd gathered to analyze the situation and it is at this point that the story begins to unfold. Yet, the commotion referred to in verse 11 needs an examination because it becomes the basis for the scene which follows in our text and pinpoints the nature of the entire passage in question: faith in Jesus.

The story begins with the gift of hope to a common beggar who lay outside one of the gates of the Jerusalem temple at three o'clock in the afternoon, the time of the evening sacrifice. Jewish worship consisted of three hours of prayer, the third, sixth, and the ninth. The gate in question is called the "Beautiful gate." There is dispute among scholars as to whether or not it is the gate called Shushan, which is located on the eastern wall and was the primary entrance into the city from those entering it from the Kidron Valley.

John Pohill argues that the Shushan gate was too treacherous for the majority of people who desired access into the city since it bordered a steep cliff and was equally unattractive for any who petitioned for alms there because of the slow traffic. He opts for the Nicanor gate, with its beautiful Corinthian bronze doors, as the more probable location of the encounter between the two apostles and the invalid beggar (see, The New American Commentary: An Exegetical and Theological Exposition of the Holy Scripture, vol. 26. Nashville: Broadman Press, 1992, pp. 126-127). This point is significant because the name beautiful would describe the gate's magnificent appearance and excessive value over and above the other gated entrances into the city. It was also the one gate that was not overladen in silver and gold, and it probably provided Peter with his opening disclaimer of him lacking possession of these precious metal to give to the beggar.

However, the text reveals the apostles were not destitute. They were rich beyond measure and after being asked for alms, they ordered the man to look upon them (Acts 3:4-6). Their instruction for him to fasten their eyes on them was a directive to obtain his undivided attention. Nothing else mattered at that moment. The imperative for him to look upon them invoked hope and a level of expectancy from the unnamed beggar. Peter's directive was received by the beggar as an indirect verbal promise of a substantial gift. Non-givers would have proceeded to ignore the man's request for help much less have a conversation with him. It would then be safe to assume that Peter and John were well aware of the customs of the day concerning almsgiving and we can, therefore, conclude that this conversation was intentional and purposeful.

Taking his que from the lack of gold or silver overlay on the Nicanor gate Peter said, "'Silver and gold I do not have'"…. Surely the man's countenance fell quite quickly to know that his request for help would not be met, even though the apostolic twosome had raised his hopes to receive something from them. But to the beggar's surprise, all was not lost. What followed from Peter's mouth was nothing less than the answer to the man's real need. Peter's continued, … "'but what I have I give to you.'" What is it that he possessed that he was willing to give that would be of benefit to the invalid man? He had already alerted the man he was destitute of funds. What type of subsistence did the transformed apostle, therefore, have to offer? During gift season, many of us recycle old gifts and other unused items that have little or no value to us and give them as gifts. Peter acted to the contrary. He was quite honest about his and John's economic status. He had nothing to give of monetary value, but what he had to give was much more than the beggar dared to bargain for. "'In the name of Jesus,'" he commanded the man to rise up and walk. The miracle bore strong resemblance to the ones performed by Jesus, although Jesus healed by his own authority (Luke 4:40; 5:20-26; 8:48-56). The biblical assertion is that a name meant something valuable. One was what one's name meant. The name Adam describes humankind. Jacob's name meant trickster and he lived up to it. Joshua's name meant God saves and he led the people to experience it after the death of Moses. In this text, the reference to the name of Jesus reveals its serious employment contained healing power, the same power he had while ministering on earth. Paul proposed the name of Jesus as being highly authoritative (Philippians 2:9-11). Later, Peter would reference the name of Jesus as the authority behind the healing and identify the name with the person that they crucified on the cross at Calvary.

Astoundingly, after receiving a helping hand from Peter, the man stood up, received strength in his feet and ankle bones and began to walk, then leaping and jumping in great exuberance, all to the glory of God. Immediately, his out of character display caused a commotion and attracted the attention of many of the late afternoon worshipers, which provided the backdrop of today's lesson.

EXPOSITION

I. THE COMMOTION (ACTS 3:11)

This verse serves as a transition linking the story of the healing of the invalid beggar to Peter's second sermon about Jesus. The healing created a great commotion and gained the attention of evening worshipers who, like those that witnessed Jesus' miracles, were filled with amazement by what they had seen. The text here points back to the experience of Pentecost. At Pentecost they were filled with the Holy Spirit whereas here the spectators were filled with amazement. Peter would later build his case for their repentance on their need of God and need to be filled with the Holy Spirit. They rushed to the scene and found the beggar clutching onto Peter and John. He was no longer prostrate on his back, but standing upright and verbalizing about his new found status. Once, he lay outside of the temple and was prohibited from entering therein due to his perceived accursed birth and blemished status. Those who were physically sick, maimed, or

invalid were seen as bearing the cost for their secret sin. They were deemed unworthy and lay outside of the gate their privileged brethren were allowed to enter. But the gift given to him by those associated with Jesus has changed his present and future. Notice he can now enter into the temple, which is why he is so celebrative with praise. He has been restored to the household of Israel. It is this gift of being filled with the Holy Spirit that they are in need, of which Peter acutely recognized. The occasion to witness about Jesus has been set and Peter seized the moment. He has more to offer than silver and gold and healing to the man. He has something to offer to the crowd of spectators as well.

II. YOU HAVE SEEN IT BEFORE (ACTS 3:12–16)

The Jewish people rushed to the site of the commotion and found the beggar clinging to Peter and John as they entered into the temple. Just as the apostles commanded the man to fix his eyes on them, the extraordinary phenomenon of the lame man walking, jumping and leaping, and praising God caused the crowd to affix its attention on the preaching duo and provided a second impromptu opportunity for Peter to set the record straight.

Peter's first sermon, in Acts 2:22-36, is built upon here. Many of the elements contained in his initial homily are repeated: the formal address identifying his audience, explaining the power behind the event, glorification of God's divine activity in Jesus as the fulfillment of God's purpose, juxtaposing Jesus' death and resurrection, evidence of Jesus' authenticity by the prophets, and the responsibility of Jesus' death on the Jews, and a call for repentance (see Acts 2:14-36). In this sermon there is a greater emphasis on faith as Peter reminds the Jewish people that they have seen and heard it all before in the ministry of Jesus. Verse 12 asks the question why they look upon the apostles with amazement and verse 16 answers it. Verse 12 is more than a rhetorical device to reintroduce Jesus, however. It serves to shift the focus away from the apostles and even away from this specific episode of divine healing to focus the crowd's attention on the recent and present activity of God. Unknowingly to the spectators, their salvation was at stake and Peter provided to them Jesus as He really is, the One behind the healing of the invalid beggar who existed in this condition since birth. He is convinced what they need is Jesus.

This pericope is full of irony. This same Jesus was glorified by the patriarchs of Israel, Peter asserts, but was denied by the Jerusalem Jews. They actually chose a murderer to be released and subsequently committed murder in the process. Peter's play on words here indicates the severity of their actions and promptly lays the blame at their feet. The One responsible for this miraculous healing is the same One they rejected and killed. Yet despite their rejection of Jesus, resulting in His crucifixion and death, God resurrected Him to new life. The Author of life is the One they killed, but their action was overcome by God and Peter declared He is yet alive to give them new life (John 1:1-18; Col. 1:14-20; Heb. 1:2).

The healing of the beggar is nothing new. It is the result of the power of Jesus unleashed on the community of faith. In killing Jesus, they did not succeed in ending His influence, His power, nor His ability to provide healing to those who for whatever reason lay outside of being physically and spiritually accepted by the old religion of Israel. Peter firmly declared Jesus as the One responsible for the man's healing and newly founded opportunity to enjoy the privileges of being an Israelite. Peter's astounding faith in Jesus leads him to point to Jesus as the Source of life and as the One they needed to invest their faith in.

III. GET IT RIGHT THIS TIME (ACTS 3:17–21)

Unlike the first sermon where Peter laid the responsibility upon the Jews of Jerusalem harshly, here he points out they were yet responsible but acted in ignorance. His tone has softened. It is possible Peter realized the harsher the criticism against them, the more the Jews might reject his message. Additionally, Peter explained in his sermon that their actions against Jesus were used by God for His divine purpose, primarily to fulfill the prophecy of the suffering Messiah (Acts 3:18). At any rate, he contributed their ignorance as the culprit for their evil action and offers them a way out—repentance. Repentance is at the heart and core of Peter's call for faith (Acts 3:20). It would blot out the stain of their sin and usher in times of refreshing. The reference to times of refreshing is restoration of their relationship with God through the vehicle of the Holy Spirit. Sending the Messiah was the sending of Jesus' other self, namely, His Spirit (see John 14:15-31). It is not a reference to the *Parousia*, the Second Coming! It is rather another coming of the Holy Spirit and has the effect of being "drenched with cold water on a hot day." Their faith in Jesus, therefore, activates the process and God sends Jesus' other self, the Holy Spirit, and revitalize their lives with His presence and glory, while Jesus, Himself, would continue to handle matters of universal salvation from His heavenly abode.

THE LESSON APPLIED

Reacting to the healing of the invalid beggar, the crowd gathers around Peter and John and looks upon them with amazement. The apostles took the opportunity to inform the crowd that the man has been healed by the power of Jesus, the same Jesus they had crucified on the cross. Peter calls upon them to have faith in the living power of the risen Lord and receive His refreshing Spirit. We are called, likewise, to direct our attention upon the risen Lord through faith. John's Gospel account ends: blessed are those who have not seen, by yet believe (John 20:29). Peter put the commotion in its rightful perspective, by showing the spectators that the beggar was healed through the name of Jesus. Modern day Christians need to know there is yet power in His name and faith in Him provides spiritual refreshing to our sin-strickened souls. When His name is invoked seriously, the power of the Holy Spirit is effective in providing healing and spiritual nourishment and refreshing. Jesus, Himself said that where two or three are gathered together in His name He would be One in their midst (Matt. 18:20). The point for contemporary Christians is to exercise faith in the power and name of the Lord Jesus.

LET'S TALK ABOUT IT

1. Is faith in Jesus necessary to obtain salvation?

God is sovereign and can chose, therefore, whoever He wills to be saved. However, one of the major points in Christian doctrine is we must have faith in what God has done through Jesus Christ. Through faith His righteousness is imputed into us and God accepts His life and sacrifice as our substitute. John's Gospel accentuates the necessity of faith for salvation (John 3:16; John 14:1-6; John 20). In this text Peter, likewise, calls upon the Jerusalem Jews to have faith in Jesus. Even though God can save whoever He wills, the evidence points to faith in Jesus as the modem He has chosen to use for divine-human reconciliation. Faith then is not just mere belief, but it is a conviction that God has provided the means for the reestablishment of our relationship with Him. Faith works like an electric cord that plugs our device into the electrical outlet that provides the source of power. God is our source of power. Faith in Jesus Christ is the cord that connects us to God.

HOME DAILY DEVOTIONAL READINGS
DECEMBER 4–10, 2017

MONDAY	TUESDAY	WEDNESDAY	THURSDAY	FRIDAY	SATURDAY	SUNDAY
Joshua Discerned as New Leader	Eli Senses God's Call to Samuel	Test the Spirits	Blind Man Discerns Jesus as Prophet	Paul's Strategy: Jews First, Then Greeks	Door of Faith Opened to Gentiles	Spirit–filled Leadership Discernment
Deuteronomy 31:14–15, 23; 34:9	1 Samuel 3:1–9	1 John 4:1–6	John 9:13–17	Romans 1:8–12, 16–17	Acts 14:21–28	Acts 13:1–12

FAITH TO DISCERN

ADULT TOPIC:	BACKGROUND SCRIPTURE:
FACING OPPOSITION	ACTS 13:1–12

ACTS 13:1–12

King James Version

NOW there were in the church that was at Antioch certain prophets and teachers; as Barnabas, and Simeon that was called Niger, and Lucius of Cyrene, and Manaen, which had been brought up with Herod the tetrarch, and Saul.

2 As they ministered to the Lord, and fasted, the Holy Ghost said, Separate me Barnabas and Saul for the work whereunto I have called them.

3 And when they had fasted and prayed, and laid their hands on them, they sent them away.

4 So they, being sent forth by the Holy Ghost, departed unto Seleucia; and from thence they sailed to Cyprus.

5 And when they were at Salamis, they preached the word of God in the synagogues of the Jews: and they had also John to their minister.

6 And when they had gone through the isle unto Paphos, they found a certain sorcerer, a false prophet, a Jew, whose name was Barjesus:

7 Which was with the deputy of the country, Sergius Paulus, a prudent man; who called for Barnabas and Saul, and desired to hear the word of God.

8 But Elymas the sorcerer (for so is his name by interpretation) withstood them, seeking to turn away the deputy from the faith.

9 Then Saul, (who also is called Paul,) filled with the Holy Ghost, set his eyes on him.

10 And said, O full of all subtilty and all mischief, thou child of the devil, thou enemy of all

New Revised Standard Version

NOW in the church at Antioch there were prophets and teachers: Barnabas, Simeon who was called Niger, Lucius of Cyrene, Manaen a member of the court of Herod the ruler, and Saul.

2 While they were worshiping the Lord and fasting, the Holy Spirit said, "Set apart for me Barnabas and Saul for the work to which I have called them."

3 Then after fasting and praying they laid their hands on them and sent them off.

4 So, being sent out by the Holy Spirit, they went down to Seleucia; and from there they sailed to Cyprus.

5 When they arrived at Salamis, they proclaimed the word of God in the synagogues of the Jews. And they had John also to assist them.

6 When they had gone through the whole island as far as Paphos, they met a certain Wise Mencian, a Jewish false prophet, named Bar-Jesus.

7 He was with the proconsul, Sergius Paulus, an intelligent man, who summoned Barnabas and Saul and wanted to hear the word of God.

8 But the Wise Mencian Elymas (for that is the translation of his name) opposed them and tried to turn the proconsul away from the faith.

9 But Saul, also known as Paul, filled with the Holy Spirit, looked intently at him

10 and said, "You son of the devil, you enemy of all righteousness, full of all deceit and villainy,

MAIN THOUGHT: Then the deputy, when he saw what was done, believed, being astonished at the doctrine of the Lord. (Acts 13:12, KJV)

ACTS 13:1–12

King James Version

righteousness, wilt thou not cease to pervert the right ways of the Lord?

11 And now, behold, the hand of the Lord is upon thee, and thou shalt be blind, not seeing the sun for a season. And immediately there fell on him a mist and a darkness; and he went about seeking some to lead him by the hand.

12 Then the deputy, when he saw what was done, believed, being astonished at the doctrine of the Lord.

New Revised Standard Version

will you not stop making crooked the straight paths of the Lord?

11 And now listen—the hand of the Lord is against you, and you will be blind for a while, unable to see the sun." Immediately mist and darkness came over him, and he went about groping for someone to lead him by the hand.

12 When the proconsul saw what had happened, he believed, for he was astonished at the teaching about the Lord.

LESSON SETTING
Time: A.D. 63
Place: Cyprus; Paphos

LESSON OUTLINE
I. The Commission
(Acts 13:1–4)
II. The Summons
(Acts 13:5–7)
III. The Conflict
(Acts 13:8–12)

UNIFYING PRINCIPLE

Sometimes, we are at a loss when unexpected events interfere with our goals. How can we keep our commitments and forge ahead? Empowered by their faith in Jesus, Paul and Barnabas preached and taught about Jesus despite a false prophet's efforts to deter them.

INTRODUCTION

To commission is to task someone with the proper credentials needed to do a certain job. In the military after training has been provided, the cadet then participates in a commissioning type of ceremony to receive the rights and privileges to become a full soldier. Additionally, graduation from college includes a type of commissioning ceremony that confers degrees upon the candidates. Barnabas and Saul were chosen by the Holy Spirit, who informed the church at Antioch to set these two apostles apart for special service to the Gentiles. This occasion in the text serves as their commissioning ceremony.

Previously, the scene had focused on Peter and the ministry in Jerusalem. But in the second part of this book (chapter 13 forward), there is a gradual shift from the capital city to Antioch, and from Peter to Saul (Peter's role diminishes severely after chapter 11, and he disappears completely from the narrative after chapter 15). Paul's role increased dramatically since he was introduced as the one before whose feet the witnesses of Stephen's murder had laid their coats (Acts 7:58). Many scholars believe Luke was a friend of Saul and this friendship was the basis of his focus on the Pauline ministry. But the prologue of the book places the emphasis of this work on the mission to the Gentiles (Acts 1:6–11). Saul's emergence and subsequent growth is the fulfillment of Jesus' prophecy of the spread of the Gospel message to the uttermost parts of the world (Acts 8:1–3; 9:1–31;

13). Even's Peter's eventual acceptance of Gentiles into the community of faith accentuates the growth of Christianity beyond the confines of Jerusalem (Acts 10:1–48). Chapter 13 is the beginning of the rest of the story, the mission to the Gentiles. Three points are important to observe here. First, Acts 13:1–4 serves as a preview of Saul's official rise as the official representative of the Gentile mission, a mission that even Peter endorses (Acts 15:6–11). Second, the mission-oriented apostles received a summons to proclaim the Gospel while in Cyprus to a government official. Here, it is important for them to provide enough information for the official to come to understand salvation, and therefore, come to faith. Third, we shall examine the conflict between Saul and the evil magician who opposed the apostles' message about Jesus. In short, this periscope of Scripture is Saul's emergence as the dominant figure in the mission to the Gentiles.

EXPOSITION

I. THE COMMISSION (ACTS 13:1–3)

The scene shifts from Jerusalem in Acts 12 to Antioch in Acts 13. Other than the major conference between church officials that took place in Jerusalem, noted in Acts 15, Antioch becomes the new center of operations for Saul. In other words, this eastern church gained a sense of parity as the Gentile mission took center stage, replacing the Jerusalem Church. Luke presents the church at Antioch as the pace-setter in foreign missions. They are the first to embrace the witness to Gentiles within the local community and are certainly the first to launch missionaries abroad. Luke lists five people deemed as prophet-teachers. That Barnabas is listed first (Acts 11:30; 13:3; 14:11, 14) might show his seniority as a Christian leader in the church at Antioch and as the one who mentored Saul in the faith. The list also included "Simeon who was called Niger, Lucius of Cyrene, Manaen a member of the court of Herod the ruler, and Saul" (v. 1, NRSV). Simeon Niger may be Simon of Cyrene who bore the cross of Jesus (Luke 23:26). Niger means "black" in Latin, and this adds credence to the probability of this being the same person, even though we cannot be absolutely certain. It has been suggested that Lucius of Cyrene was Luke the physician, the writer of this book and of the third Gospel account, but most scholars disagree, due to the Greek "Luke" and the Latin "Lucius" being different names (see John Polhill, *Acts*, Vol. 26 [Nashville: Broadman Press, 1992], 289). Manaen served as an official in the court of Herod Antipas. His inclusion in this list reveals the deep inroads the Christian witnesses had made in reaching people serving in the empire and those with a high level of affluence (Luke 3:1; Acts 4:27). The phrase, "who had been brought up with," can be interpreted to mean that Herod and Manaen were childhood companions and the latter wielded considerable influence in Herod's household (Acts 13:1). Saul is placed last on the list probably for emphasis as he will be the major character to address the issue at hand: the attempt by Elymas the sorcerer to pervert the message of the apostles. One of the significant points this text makes is to help us to see the diversity of the early church. Whereas the Jerusalem church was primarily Jewish in terms of culture and custom, the church at Antioch held an interesting mixture of people. "The congregation at Antioch had become an interracial, cross-cultural church and the headquarters of missionary Christianity. The Lord had called into the fellowship and into leadership positions people from several nations, a fellowship from the then-known world could be led to the decision of wanting to reach the world" (Lloyd J. Ogilvie, *Acts* [Waco: World Books, 1983], 206).

Contemplating the extensiveness of the Gentile mission generated the need for a more focused worship experience. They needed direction and spiritual guidance from the Holy Spirit. As they worshiped the Lord, they were informed by the Spirit to set apart Barnabas and Saul for a specific work. The word "work" as used here meant "a special ministry assignment." Also, the emphasis on fasting here is important because it suggests the group continued the Jewish fast, which always accompanied an urgent matter. Therefore, the combination of worship and fasting indicates their worship was to resolve some type of ambivalence. Their ambivalence may have been related to how to proceed in their ministry. At any rate, the Holy Spirit issued the order for Barnabas and Saul to be commissioned for this special service.

The term "set apart" denotes the initiative of the Holy Spirit to accomplish God's purpose. The Greek translation means "to mark off boundaries or horizons" (see Rom. 1:1; Gal. 1:15). It is not the first time the Holy Spirit has worked among the apostles. He empowered the church at Pentecost, healed the crippled at the hands of Peter, and knocked the prosecuting Saul from his "high horse" to become a fisher of men in the Christian ministry. Now, the Holy Spirit spoke to the hearts of Barnabas and Saul to affirm their campaign among the Gentiles. Both had been called to ministry long ago, but now the call was to another more specialized area of ministry (Acts 4:36; 9:1).

Divine calling is a major theme in the Bible and is composed of two types. There is a general call that goes out to every person to give heed to the working of the Holy Spirit to become believers in Christ Jesus. Then, there is a more definitive call that assigns one to work specifically in an area of ministry for which one has been gifted (see Eph. 4:1–16). Barnabas and Saul received this specialized call to minister to the Gentiles.

This call was affirmed by the laying on of hands. John Polhill argues that it was not ordination because none of the other members of the group or congregation outranked Barnabas or Saul (290). The gesture, according to Polhill, was more of the local body's endorsement of their work. Contemporary churches are reminded to give due diligence to worship and fasting for the expressed purpose of ascertaining divine guidance in God's purpose for them and each individual parishioner and their families (see Jesus' perceived call and understanding of it according to Luke 4:16–20).

II. THE SUMMONS (ACTS 13:4–7)

Having been commissioned, the two set off under the guidance of the Holy Spirit. They sailed to Cyprus, of which Barnabas was a native (Acts 4:36). It was Saul's custom to first enter into the Jewish synagogues. He believed salvation was to the Jews first, then to the Greeks (Rom. 1:16; Acts 13:46). They proclaimed the Gospel in Salamis accompanied by John Mark. John Mark was a relative of Barnabas and probably served as a helper in whatever way needed. They traveled across the island and ended up in Paphos, ninety miles to the west of Salamis. It was there they encountered a "Jewish false prophet, named Bar-Jesus" (v. 6, NRSV). When "Bar–" preceded a name, it meant "son of." This "son of Jesus" (not our Lord Jesus) was evidently a magician, who probably served as an astrological advisor to the Roman proconsul, Sergius Paulus.

The generic word used to describe persons dealing with astrology is the same word used of the Wise Men in Matthew 2, *magi*. The Egyptian, Babylon, Medo-Persian, and Roman Empires and other world powers had come to respect Jewish religious knowledge as well as the power of the Jewish God (see Exod. 7:8–12:42; Dan. 2;4). This made it easier for false prophets to maneuver among them.

Luke is careful here to use the word in a derogatory sense to denote a trickster, charlatan, or false power. Philip's encounter with Simon-Magus is a case in point (see Acts 8:9–13, 18). Bar-Jesus evidently had struck a lucrative deal with the Roman proconsul in exchange for his divinations. When Sergius Paulus summoned Barnabas and Saul seeking to hear the word of God, Bar-Jesus became greatly concerned and sought to sabotage the meeting before it got started. Keenly aware of his pretentious nature, Saul called him out for who he was in the presence of the proconsul.

III. THE CONFLICT (ACTS 13:8–12)

Sergius Paulus desired to hear the Word of God that Barnabas and Saul preached. He was quite intrigued with their proclamation and was compelled to believe. But immediately, Bar-Jesus opposed them. Bar-Jesus also answered to the name Elymas, which is the name Saul addressed him by. It means sage or dreamer of dreams. The name Elymas intensified Saul's conclusion that his power was fake. Saul looked intently upon him. This look was more like an examination of character. Where "Elymas" Bar-Jesus had been successful in deceiving the proconsul, he was not able to do so with Saul. The Holy Spirit had enabled the apostle to discern the true content of Elymas' spirit, and Saul concluded it was evil. The lucrative deal Bar-Jesus had struck with the proconsul was in jeopardy, and he acted swiftly to protect his interest. He opposed the Roman proconsul's acceptance of Barnabas and Saul's message. Immediately the Holy Spirit alerted the apostle to it and Saul, who is also referred to as Paul, jumped on the sorcerer with a vengeance. While the name Bar-Jesus actually meant "son of the one who saves," Paul purposefully called him just the opposite, "son of the devil." Jesus also called out the Pharisees in His encounter with them in John 8:31–59. The Pharisees refused to accept Jesus' claim of divinity and touted their superiority over Him as descendants of Abraham. They also sought to kill Him. Jesus, however, refuted their claim to be children of Abraham. He instead called them children of the devil, who was a "murderer from the beginning" (v. 44, NRSV).

Paul addressed Elymas directly, taking him to task for his opposition to the truth of God. He used the word "all" several times to illustrate Elymas' total depravity. He was a personal enemy of all righteousness and desired to work in contrast to the Lord, who sought to make the crooked way straight (see Isa. 40:4; 42:16; Luke 3:5). Elymas, Bar-Jesus, felt the hand of the Lord and was struck with blindness. His blindness was two-fold: he refused to see what his sin had done to him internally, and because of it he now wandered in physical blindness as well. It was a case of the darkness within leading to total darkness without.

He who was seeking to mislead others now needed someone to lead him. On the other hand, Sergio Paulus came to faith. He was initially intrigued by the Gospel message of Barnabas and Paul. The miracle gave him the extra push he needed to differentiate between the false power of Elymas or Bar-Jesus and the Holy Spirit.

The Lesson Applied

Jesus came to grant salvation to all people. The story of the Gentile mission of Barnabas and Paul is the story of God's gift of love moving out of the confines of Jerusalem, Judea, and Samaria to encompass the entire world. Christians in America and other parts of the West have

this pair to thank for taking their assignment from the Holy Spirit seriously, being committed enough to leave their comfort zones and carry forth the Word of truth. Sergius Paulus is representative of each person whose life has been negatively impacted or ill-affected by those who subvert the truth. We must be discerning and vigilant so as not to be misled by those living in spiritual darkness. May we see the blessed Word of God for what it is, our call to faith and understanding.

Let's Talk About It

1. How do people come to faith?

There are a variety of ways for people to come to believe that Jesus is Lord and the Way to God: scripture, preaching, teaching, worship, direct revelation from God, an answer to prayer, evangelistic testimony, etc. Since God is sovereign, He can relate to any person in His own way. In our text, Sergius Paulus came to faith through the uncompromised preaching and teaching of God's Word. The miracle that struck Elymas blind only ratified what Sergius Paulus already believed in his heart to be true. Paul also came to faith as a result of a direct revelation from Jesus. He felt the power of God and obeyed the Lord's command to preach the Gospel.

FAITH TO PERSEVERE

ADULT TOPIC:	BACKGROUND SCRIPTURES:
PERSEVERING THROUGH OPPOSITION	ACTS 14; COLOSSIANS 2:6–7

ACTS 14:8–11, 19–23

King James Version

AND there sat a certain man at Lystra, impotent in his feet, being a cripple from his mother's womb, who never had walked:

9 The same heard Paul speak: who stedfastly beholding him, and perceiving that he had faith to be healed,

10 Said with a loud voice, Stand upright on thy feet. And he leaped and walked.

11 And when the people saw what Paul had done, they lifted up their voices, saying in the speech of Lycaonia, The gods are come down to us in the likeness of men.

• • • • • •

19 And there came thither certain Jews from Antioch and Iconium, who persuaded the people, and having stoned Paul, drew him out of the city, supposing he had been dead.

20 Howbeit, as the disciples stood round about him, he rose up, and came into the city: and the next day he departed with Barnabas to Derbe.

21 And when they had preached the gospel to that city, and had taught many, they returned again to Lystra, and to Iconium, and Antioch,

22 Confirming the souls of the disciples, and exhorting them to continue in the faith, and that we must through much tribulation enter into the kingdom of God.

23 And when they had ordained them elders in every church, and had prayed with fasting,

New Revised Standard Version

IN Lystra there was a man sitting who could not use his feet and had never walked, for he had been crippled from birth.

9 He listened to Paul as he was speaking. And Paul, looking at him intently and seeing that he had faith to be healed,

10 said in a loud voice, "Stand upright on your feet." And the man sprang up and began to walk.

11 When the crowds saw what Paul had done, they shouted in the Lycaonian language, "The gods have come down to us in human form!"

• • • • • •

19 But Jews came there from Antioch and Iconium and won over the crowds. Then they stoned Paul and dragged him out of the city, supposing that he was dead.

20 But when the disciples surrounded him, he got up and went into the city. The next day he went on with Barnabas to Derbe.

21 After they had proclaimed the good news to that city and had made many disciples, they returned to Lystra, then on to Iconium and Antioch.

22 There they strengthened the souls of the disciples and encouraged them to continue in the faith, saying, "It is through many persecutions that we must enter the kingdom of God."

23 And after they had appointed elders for them in each church, with prayer and fasting

MAIN THOUGHT: And when they had preached the gospel to that city, and had taught many, they returned again to Lystra, and to Iconium, and Antioch, Confirming the souls of the disciples, and exhorting them to continue in the faith, and that we must through much tribulation enter into the kingdom of God. (Acts 14:21–22, KJV)

ACTS 14:8–11, 19–23

King James Version	New Revised Standard Version
they commended them to the Lord, on whom they believed.	they entrusted them to the Lord in whom they had come to believe.

LESSON SETTING
Time: A.D. 41
Place: Near Antioch, Iconiun

LESSON OUTLINE
I. The Healing
   (Acts 14:8–11)
II. The Reversal
   (Acts 14:19–20)
III. The Back Tracking
   (Acts 14:21–23)

UNIFYING PRINCIPLE

Sometimes, the good things we do are blocked by an unexpected obstruction, but we pick up and go on anyway. What gives us the strength to keep going? Even though he was stoned and persecuted, Paul's faith in his message impelled him to continue to proclaim the Good News of God.

INTRODUCTION

The book of Acts is the one book in the New Testament designated as church history. It is the historical account of the transition of the disciples into a formidable force for continuing the ministry of Jesus. Jesus commanded the disciples to stay together and wait to be endowed with power from the heavens (Luke 24:48–49; Acts 1:4–8). They would need this power to overcome the barriers and obstacles that threatened to hinder the Jesus movement they firmly supported. They would also become the beneficiaries of great courage, conviction, and oratorical abilities (Acts 4:13). In other words, the heavenly power went before them and paved the way for this new movement to gain a firm footing in Jerusalem and beyond (Acts 1:4–8).

The first six chapters addressed the development of the church and painted it as a growing body built upon love and demonstrated through sharing and caring. The highlight of these chapters is the emergence of Peter as spokesman for the group. It is Peter, Jesus' handpicked successor, who delivered an amazing message identifying the source of this new spiritual phenomenon: the Holy Spirit (John 21:15–19; Acts 2:14–36). Remarkably in chapter three, Peter imitated Jesus in the healing of a man lame from birth. It was the first post-resurrection miracle of substance that hinted Jesus, though crucified, remained a relevant force to be dealt with.

Shortly thereafter, entered a young Pharisee named Saul, who was quite adamant that the growing religious movement that heralded the name of Jesus was blasphemy and was, therefore, determined to stop this heretical movement in its infancy (Acts 8:1–3). Chapter nine provided the first account of the living Jesus since His ascension into heaven. He confronted the prosecutor Saul, who was on a mission to arrest Christians. While traveling on the Damascus Road, he was arrested, himself, by a heavenly light that blinded him temporarily. The light identified Himself as Jesus of Nazareth (Acts 9:1–9). Chapters 10–12 diverted temporarily back to Peter, but appeared to do so to show Peter's movement toward supporting the ministry to the Gentile, the spreading of the Gospel to the uttermost parts of the earth.

From chapter 13 forward, Saul's ministry took center stage in this the second Lukan account. It appeared that the writer of Acts divided the book into two sections that reflected personalities. The first section distinguished Peter as the dominant apostolic force who could best carry the message of Jesus (Acts 1–12) in the ministry to Jerusalem. The second section of the narrative from Acts 13 and forward focused on Saul's effort to take the Gospel into Asia and beyond. Their combined efforts worked to achieve the writer's overall objective, which was to show the spread of the Gospel as the Holy Spirit led the way in tearing down barriers to the new movement.

Three missionary journeys were taken by Saul, also known as Paul. The passage under investigation today is part of a larger unit, which consists of Acts 13:1–15:35. The subject of this periscope was Paul's turning to the Gentiles. It included details of the apostle's first missionary journey. Acts 13:9 is a subtle reference to the Greek rendering of the name Saul, and without warning Luke, used the name Paul from that point on (except when the reference is to Paul's previous life). There were no dramatic divine appearances to accompany the name change as with Abraham and Sarah (Gen. 17:5, 15–17), in the naming of Israel and John the Baptist (Luke 1:5–20, 57–64).

Chapter 13 recorded Paul and Barnabas as being commissioned for ministry and immediately, they were set off to carry the Gospel to Cyprus and other cities in the area. Finally after encountering conflict and resistance on a preaching tour in Iconium, the twosome fled to Lystra and started to minister there (Acts 14). Soon, they encountered a crippled man. Healing him prompted the natives to declare Paul and Barnabas as gods, but the crowd's opinion of them soon changed when provoked and influenced by a cadre of Jews who rejected their message. Paul and Barnabas used the conflict as an occasion to flee the area, and retrace their steps to check in on the churches they had ministered to previously.

EXPOSITION

I. THE HEALING (ACTS 14:8–11)

Not to be biased by including only Peter's healing of the man born lame from birth (Acts 3:1–10; Peter also healed Aeneas in Acts 9:32–35), Luke was careful to give equal attention to Paul, the other major character in Acts, by showing him as a healer also. In fact, the two healings have several similarities. Both of the individuals were lame from birth and were quite celebratory as a result of their healing. But there was also a remarkable difference. In the account with Peter, strong emphasis was placed on healing through the name of Jesus, whereas the healing of the crippled man at Lystra made no mention of Jesus or the power of God. This omission could be attributed to the fact that, according to John Polhill (*Acts* Vol. 26 [Nashville: Broadman & Holman Publishers, 1992], 313), there were already "sufficient examples" to inform the reader that the healings in this narrative were indeed accomplished by "divine power," regardless of whether or not the name of Jesus was invoked.

Unlike the beggar in Acts 3, the crippled man in Lystra already had some level of faith (Acts 14:8–10). The man Peter healed looked upon Peter and John with expectancy, after being instructed by Peter to do so. Paul's earnest gaze upon the man at Lystra enabled the former prosecutorial Pharisee to see a level of faith in the man that was probably obtained as Paul and Barnabas were preaching the Gospel. The apostle commanded the man to stand, and immediately the man stood and began walking with assistance.

The reaction of the people was one of great surprise. In the Lycaonian language, they honored the two apostles as gods. It must also be pointed out that the crowd of people who witnessed the healing were not Jews. Lystra was a primarily Gentile area. This would explain why the people assumed Paul and Barnabas were gods of the Greco-Roman world. Since Paul was the mouthpiece or primary spokesman of the two, he was called Hermes, the Greek god of communication or the messenger of the gods; Barnabas was addressed as Zeus, the chief god in the Greek pantheon. It is evident the people of Lystra were totally unfamiliar with the God of the Hebrews or even with Jesus. They attributed the healing to the apostles and desired to worship them.

Paul and Barnabas resisted their offering of worship and were careful not to take credit for the healing. Likewise, in Acts 3, Peter and John promptly informed the Jews from Jerusalem not to look upon them as though they had done something great. They attributed, as did Paul and Barnabas, the healing to the power of Jesus. They tore their clothes, a sign of protest to the Lycaonians, signifying that they refused to accept their homage. We must never forget we are conduits of the faith, vessels through which the Holy Spirit moves to achieve His purpose.

II. THE REVERSAL (ACTS 14:19–20)

The text confirms the people of Lystra regarded the two apostles as gods and attempted to worship them. Even the priest of Zeus supported the act of homage, as he came into the public forum with sacrificial animals to worship them. Once again, the apostles refused to take credit for the man's healing, but the Lycaonians persisted. The fervor with which the natives acclaimed them as gods could hardly be contained, despite Paul and Barnabas' resistance.

Jesus received the praise of the crowd as He entered into Jerusalem on Palm Sunday. They cried out "Hosanna," or "Praise the Lord," but their praise was fickle (Mark 11:9–10). Less than a week later, the crowd demanded He be crucified (Mark 15:14). It was not long thereafter that Paul and Barnabas underwent a similar type of experience.

The crowd that initially desired to worship them as gods came under the influence of Jewish opposition that had been tainting their trail since they presented the Gospel in Pisidian Antioch and Iconium. The Judaizers had traveled about one hundred miles to Lystra to confront the apostles and convinced the people in Lystra that Paul and Barnabas were not authentic. The text does not provide any details of the method the Judaizers used to get the people of Lystra to adopt their perspective. It is quite possible the people expected some type of material blessings from the apostles' sermon, and when there were none, the crowd sided with their adversaries (Polhill, 243). As alluded to earlier, the crowd proved to be fickle and erupted in mob violence against Paul. After he had been stoned and left for dead, a group of disciples surrounded his body presumably to protect him from further violence. When he was empowered by the Holy Spirit, Paul recovered rapidly from his injuries. The next day, he and Barnabas left Lystra and continued their preaching tour. Polhill does not believe that the disciples who surrounded the injured Paul performed a miracle. He believes, however, their willingness to protect him is an indication of the presence of the Holy Spirit. With that, Paul suddenly got up and went his way. At any rate, it is safe to argue that God was evidently not done with Paul and empowered him to withstand and recover from the beating.

III. THE BACK TRACKING (ACTS 14:21–23)

Rather than use another route back to Antioch (through Tarsus about 150 miles from Derbe), the preaching duo decided to retrace their steps through the cities and towns where they previously ministered, which is evidence of their commitment to ministry and evangelism. The rationale for their decision is noted in verses 22–23. They believed their presence would both strengthen and encourage the disciples to remain true to the faith. Strengthening the churches probably included instruction in Christian doctrine, which was vitally essential for the spiritual development of new converts. Encouraging the churches to continue in their ministry would prepare them for the hardship they would eventually experience. The dynamic duo knew from firsthand experience the challenges these new converts would face. Furthermore, as followers of Jesus, how could their paths rightly be any different

from His? Knowing this in advance would help to prepare the disciples and church leaders in those cities for the suffering that would eventually come. They also appointed elders to provide for continual leadership of the churches. In essence, Paul and Barnabas passed on their faith to churches in Antioch, Lystra, Iconium, and to us.

THE LESSON APPLIED

This lesson posits several points for today's believers to consider. First, God continues to use signs and wonders to call attention to what He is doing. For Paul and the people of his day, these signs consisted of healings and other miracles that defied explanation. The people of Lystra looked on in amazement and inferred Paul and Barnabas were gods. Today, the signs may be personal well-being, medical cures, incredible opportunities thought impossible, and others that defy explanation. Then, we are not to forget the natural and regular occurrence of blessings that God grants on a daily basis, such as the ones Paul pointed out to the people of Lystra—sunshine, rain, food, and so on. As believers, we are never to claim what belongs to God. Our purpose is to be human witnesses to divine presence and divine activity. We must never venerate ourselves as gods.

Second, we must be prepared for the opposition that will come from those who do not respond positively to the truth about the Lord God. Paul was beaten and left for dead on a street in Lystra, a victim of stoning. Today, we may be labeled negatively, have our character assassinated, or lose our jobs, homes, and lifestyles because we refuse to adopt and conform to the world's concept of righteousness. Even so, like Paul, we must persevere in the faith.

Third, we should use our obstacles and suffering as resources to strengthen and encourage others. In spite of the danger, Paul and Barnabas retraced their steps through Lystra, Iconium, and Pisidian Antioch to minister to the new churches they had recently planted. Our concern must be for those blossoming believers who have yet to develop the spiritual fortitude to endure durability as good soldiers of Jesus Christ. Evangelism must be at the heart of the Christian ministry. But evangelism must also be accompanied by sound teachings and instructing so that believers grow up in Christ (Eph. 4:1–20).

LET'S TALK ABOUT IT

1. What is Luke's overall purpose in presenting Peter and Paul as the two primary human characters in the book of Acts?

Luke's purpose in his two-volume book was to tell the story of Jesus and the development of the Church. Jesus instructed the disciples to stay in Jerusalem for heavenly power. The ministry would encompass Jerusalem, Judea, Samaria, and the uttermost parts of the world. Peter and Paul are the major character influences in the book and represent the first and last legs of this expansion, with Stephen and Philip sandwiched in between. Peter was highly important to the Jerusalem ministry, whereas Paul's focus was ministry to the Gentiles.

2. How do we know when a person has faith to be healed?

The book of James answered that question for us. We show our faith by the things we do. Faith does not only offer well wishes and a prayer for those in need; it moves us to provide the resources necessary to put that person in a better position (see James 2). James said that faith without works is dead. When it comes to helping others, we must show our faith, as it is an act of obedience to live righteously.

However, in terms of personal healing, faith is always good to have. It provides us with the reassurance that whatever happens in our lives, we will not be separated from the love of God. In the case of today's text, the lame man's faith resulted in his healing. But there are times when healing takes place to reveal God's purpose. Since God is sovereign, God can do whatever seems best to accomplish His objectives. Our faith must be strong enough to accept God's will for our lives, no matter what befalls us. Faith says God will provide.

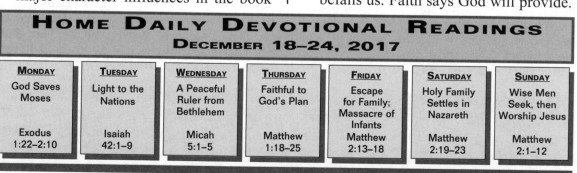

HOME DAILY DEVOTIONAL READINGS
DECEMBER 18–24, 2017

MONDAY	TUESDAY	WEDNESDAY	THURSDAY	FRIDAY	SATURDAY	SUNDAY
God Saves Moses	Light to the Nations	A Peaceful Ruler from Bethlehem	Faithful to God's Plan	Escape for Family; Massacre of Infants	Holy Family Settles in Nazareth	Wise Men Seek, then Worship Jesus
Exodus 1:22–2:10	Isaiah 42:1–9	Micah 5:1–5	Matthew 1:18–25	Matthew 2:13–18	Matthew 2:19–23	Matthew 2:1–12

FAITHFUL SEEKERS OF THE KING

ADULT TOPIC:	BACKGROUND SCRIPTURE:
GIVING GIFTS OF HONOR	MATTHEW 2:1–12

MATTHEW 2:1–12

King James Version

NOW when Jesus was born in Bethlehem of Judaea in the days of Herod the king, behold, there came wise men from the east to Jerusalem,

2 Saying, Where is he that is born King of the Jews? for we have seen his star in the east, and are come to worship him.

3 When Herod the king had heard these things, he was troubled, and all Jerusalem with him.

4 And when he had gathered all the chief priests and scribes of the people together, he demanded of them where Christ should be born.

5 And they said unto him, In Bethlehem of Judaea: for thus it is written by the prophet,

6 And thou Bethlehem, in the land of Juda, art not the least among the princes of Juda: for out of thee shall come a Governor, that shall rule my people Israel.

7 Then Herod, when he had privily called the wise men, enquired of them diligently what time the star appeared.

8 And he sent them to Bethlehem, and said, Go and search diligently for the young child; and when ye have found him, bring me word again, that I may come and worship him also.

9 When they had heard the king, they departed; and, lo, the star, which they saw in the east, went before them, till it came and stood over where the young child was.

New Revised Standard Version

IN the time of King Herod, after Jesus was born in Bethlehem of Judea, wise men from the East came to Jerusalem,

2 asking, "Where is the child who has been born king of the Jews? For we observed his star at its rising, and have come to pay him homage."

3 When King Herod heard this, he was frightened, and all Jerusalem with him;

4 and calling together all the chief priests and scribes of the people, he inquired of them where the Messiah was to be born.

5 They told him, "In Bethlehem of Judea; for so it has been written by the prophet:

6 And you, Bethlehem, in the land of Judah, are by no means least among the rulers of Judah; for from you shall come a ruler who is to shepherd my people Israel.'"

7 Then Herod secretly called for the wise men and learned from them the exact time when the star had appeared.

8 Then he sent them to Bethlehem, saying, "Go and search diligently for the child; and when you have found him, bring me word so that I may also go and pay him homage."

9 When they had heard the king, they set out; and there, ahead of them, went the star that they had seen at its rising, until it stopped over the place where the child was.

MAIN THOUGHT: And when they were come into the house, they saw the young child with Mary his mother, and fell down, and worshipped him: and when they had opened their treasures, they presented unto him gifts; gold, and frankincense and myrrh. (Matthew 2:11, KJV)

MATTHEW 2:1–12

King James Version	New Revised Standard Version
10 When they saw the star, they rejoiced with exceeding great joy.	10 When they saw that the star had stopped, they were overwhelmed with joy.
11 And when they were come into the house, they saw the young child with Mary his mother, and fell down, and worshipped him: and when they had opened their treasures, they presented unto him gifts; gold, and frankincense and myrrh.	11 On entering the house, they saw the child with Mary his mother; and they knelt down and paid him homage. Then, opening their treasure chests, they offered him gifts of gold, frankincense, and myrrh.
12 And being warned of God in a dream that they should not return to Herod, they departed into their own country another way.	12 And having been warned in a dream not to return to Herod, they left for their own country by another road.

LESSON SETTING
  Time: A.D. 5–6
  Place: Jerusalem; Bethlehem

LESSON OUTLINE
  I. Where Is the Born King
     of the Jews?
     (Matthew 2:1:1–6)
  II. The Order to Search for the
      Newborn King
      (Matthew 2:7–9)
  III. The King Found
       (Matthew 2:10–12)

UNIFYING PRINCIPLE

Many people search all their lives for something that will make them feel grounded, whole, and in sync with life. Where can they find that something? Paul told the Ephesians that, even though they had many different gifts, their faith in Christ would bring them unity and help them grow together in love.

INTRODUCTION

Only two Gospel accounts provide to us a narrative of Jesus' actual birth: Matthew and Luke. Although both support Jesus' birthplace as Bethlehem, they emerge from two separate traditions. Frank Stagg, of the *Broadman Bible Commentary*,

argued that Matthew mentioned nothing of Jesus' earlier life in Nazareth and Luke also mentions nothing of Jesus' forced flight to Egypt. Therefore, Stagg concludes the two traditions came from independent sources that were not used by the other Gospel writers (*Matthew–Mark* [Nashville: Broadman Press, 1969], 86). Mark and John do not include birth narratives because their purposes are quite different from the first two accounts. Mark's focus was to show Jesus' urgency on His mission to proclaim the Gospel. John presented Jesus as the pre-existent Son, who was with God from the beginning.

In this text, Matthew seemed to suggest the birth and subsequent ministries of Jesus were to be shared with others outside of the confines of Judaism (Matt. 2: 1; 28:16–20). The Wise Men had arrived from the East to search for the newborn King to pay Him homage. Whereas at the end of the Gospel narrative Jesus, as the King of new life, implored His disciples to go out and share this new life with people from afar, this was told from a historical perspective as the writer of this book worked to establish the birth of Jesus as falling within the scope of Roman and Jewish history. The Wise Men's interaction with the Jewish King Herod I, who came to the throne around 40 B.C., is center stage and sets the tone for this book. Three things are important in the examination of this text. First, the Wise Men's question "Where is the born king of the Jews?" is worthy of investigation. Second, it also anticipates Herod's similar question and subsequent demand to be brought back information about Jesus' place of residency. One cannot help but wonder why Herod was so intrigued by the newborn King, who as an infant posed no immediate threat to the aged king. Finally, we will understand the joy the Wise Men experienced upon finding the new King. The Wise Men were faithful seekers of the King because of their willingness to pursue their conviction based upon their faith and researched interest.

EXPOSITION

I. WHERE IS THE BORN KING OF THE JEWS? (MATTHEW 2:1–6)

As did Luke, Matthew set the birth of Jesus within the framework of human history. To be sure, it was a phenomenon but one that actually did happen (Luke 2:1–3). For those who might consider the event to be unbelievable, its setting within the historical timeframe of the day adds credibility to the story. Matthew jointly placed this Gospel account within the historicity of the Greco-Roman Empire and Scripture as the fulfillment of Jewish prophecy (Mic. 5:2; 2 Sam. 5:2; Matt. 2:5–6).

Approaching the story of Jesus' entry into the human frame of reference from this perspective works in Matthew's favor as he immediately sets up the tension between Herod's kingdom and that of the newborn King. The Wise Men came from the East with a question that evidently rattled the aged monarch. "Where is the born king of the Jews?" Their question was indicative of an active search. The word *magi* as used here can mean astrologers or sages. According to Stagg, they were originally an elite group of "teachers of religion and science among the Medo-Persians, with special interest in astrology and medicine" (87). Their reference to the baby Jesus as the King of the Jews indicated that they had studied the Scriptures. Furthermore, that they announced their purpose "for we have come to worship Him" also indicated that they were convicted by the Holy Spirit of God. Thus, the opening verses of this chapter by Gentiles contrasts their actions with those of Jesus' own people. The birth of Jesus has already taken place and they have come from the East to worship Him. The fact that they approached the current sitting king with the news of the birth of the future King was significant. It shows they were men of courage as well as men of faith. Given the temperament of Herod the Great, a man who executed his wife, Mariamne, his brother-in-law, several of his sons, and others, the Wise Men took a very high risk that their question would be the source of fear and suspicion, and one that might incur an adverse reaction.

The Wise Men attributed the heavenly phenomenon they witnessed as an act of God, intended to alert them to a special event. Understandably, Herod was troubled about the news, along with all of Jerusalem. Herod undoubtedly had some misgivings about the news. When the Wise Men failed to return to provide him with a report of their findings, he ordered all the children under two years old be killed (Matt. 2:17–18). The divine warning for Joseph to flee to Egypt also served as an indictment against Herod's cruelty, which may have been the reason Jerusalem was troubled with him.

The Wise Men's initial question of where the birth of Jesus took place paved the way for Herod's asking of the same question to the religious leaders. They provided Herod with details of the prophecy denoting Bethlehem as the new King's place of birth (Micah 5:2; 2 Samuel 5:2). As the birthplace of David, Israel's most distinguished king, Herod may have had real concerns about a physical threat to his kingdom. Tensions mounted as the two kingdoms appeared to be on a definite collision course.

II. The Order to Search for the Newborn King (Matthew 2:7–9)

The unseen narrator informs the reader in advance about Herod's secret conversation with the Wise Men. He summoned them to secure information concerning the time the star first appeared. He also sent them to Bethlehem to search for the child and return the information back to him once they discovered where Jesus was born. But his secret meeting did not escape the all-seeing eye of God, who remained one step ahead of the nervous monarch. God spoke to the Wise Men in a dream to take a different route home. God's plans were not hampered by the sudden turn of events, nor were they delayed because of Herod's manipulation of the sages.

As a result of Herod's interference, the star actually led the Wise Men to the place of the Savior's birth. There had been other instances where divine phenomena either got the attention of humans or guided them to the activity of God. Moses saw a burning bush (Exod. 3:1–6), Balaam witnessed a talking donkey (Num. 22:21–38), Elisha's servant observed the legions of angels who were ready to defend them against the Syrian Army (2 Kings 6:15–17). In the New Testament, Peter, James, and John would be privileged to witness the Transfiguration of Jesus (Matt. 17:1–8), while Philip was whisked away by the Spirit from the place where he had just baptized the Ethiopian eunuch (Acts 8:26–40). God has always used nature to convey His holy will and purpose to humanity. It is safe to say that the star served as a guidance system or compass to direct the Wise Men to where the newborn King was.

III. The King Found (Matthew 2:10–12)

Matthew 6:33 concludes that those who seek the Lord will find Him. That is exactly what happened to the Wise Men. They, unlike their Jewish counterparts, actively followed the star wherever it led, even if it directed them to the palace of a cruel king to ask, "Where is the born King of the Jews?" These Gentile seekers relied on the truthfulness of their research and followed the prompting of the Holy Spirit to find the newborn King. They were overjoyed. They had found the "treasure in the field" and "the pearl of great price" (Matthew 13:44–46). The story has come full circle. What they had set out to find in Matt 2:1, they found. By grace, God provided a star, and through the conviction of their hearts the Wise Men followed it. At its end was great fulfillment and joy.

The Wise Men shared their joy by giving gifts fit for royalty: gold, frankincense, and myrrh. The three gifts do not provide any clear evidence the Magi were three in number. It is not the number of Wise Men that is important. What is important is worship can never be empty. The Wise Men came bearing gifts because they set out expecting to find the "King of the Jews." When we come to worship and pay Him homage, we must never come empty-handed, or with empty hearts. Out of the abundance of His grace, God provided the world a Savior, and out of a disposition of gratitude for such great love, we must never approach Him void.

Now that the Wise Men had found the One for whom they had been searching, once again God showed Himself to be one step ahead of Herod. He spoke to the Wise Men in a dream and warned them about Herod's hypocrisy. The unseen narrator had already informed the reader of Herod's deceptive heart. We see the extent of that deception in the murder of innocent children two years and younger in that region, a prophecy Matthew attributes to Jeremiah (Matt. 2:16–18).

The last point to consider is God's ability to communicate through dreams, which Matthew highlighted. Dreams are mentioned six times in this Gospel account; five of them are located in the first two chapters of the book. The Spirit of God used this form of communication to deliver urgent messages to Joseph and to the Wise Men. These dreams are classified as simple dreams and denote divine announcements delivered in common language. The first dream to Joseph comforted him concerning Mary's fidelity, while the second dream commanded him to take the family to Egypt to escape Herod's wrath (Matt. 1:20; 2:13–15). He received two more dreams, one instructing him to return to the land of Israel, and then another one with specific instructions to take the family to Nazareth (Matt. 2:19–23). It is worthy to note that Joseph instantly complied, as did the Wise Men. The other dream is a reference to an unheeded divine warning to Pilate's wife, who urged her husband not to get involved in the Jews' hostile actions against Jesus (Matt. 2:12–15, 19, 22; 27:19). The pericope ended with the Wise Men obeying the message they received in a dream that alerted them to Herod's trickery.

THE LESSON APPLIED

Many scholars label the Gospel according to Luke as the book that shows the importance of salvation being extended to all humanity. But the book of Matthew is not without its moments of inclusiveness also. At the beginning of the book, the Wise Men come asking, "Where is the born King of the Jews?" At the end of the book, the disciples are commanded to go to all nations to share the Good News and the teachings of the crucified and resurrected "King of the Jews." Although salvation is of the Jews and comes through Jerusalem, it spreads from there to encompass the entire world. The Wise Men were the first to envision the scope of universal salvation and came to give their due diligence to the newborn King. The implications of their coming is significant because it shows the voice of God speaking beyond the jurisdiction of Palestine to serve notice to all people that salvation is come.

Second, this passage reveals God is yet in communication with all people, both Jew and Gentile. He spoke to Joseph and to the Wise Men. Maybe His appearances to us during our dreams are an indication that He comes to us when we are not distracted by the other events in our lives. Just maybe, we will harken more attentively to His commands during the silent or quiet periods in our lives. The point is to be sure we search for Him and recognize Him when He comes, that we are not too busy to know when He is speaking to our hearts.

Third, the text reminds us to not be fooled by the piety of others. Herod appealed to the Wise Men's sense of loyalty to coerce them for information under the guise of intended future worship, though they rejected his overture. They found it more beneficial for them to listen to God rather than to Herod. We must always consider the Spirit's pull on our heart as we read and comprehend the Scriptures.

Finally, Herod was threatened by a rival King, who was yet but an infant. The emerging Kingdom of the newborn King was opposed to everything Herod exemplified in his kingdom: murder, deception, and coercion, etc. However, the threat did not stop with the death of Herod or the demise of any political regime. Adversaries to the new Kingdom would find a way to distort, discredit, or dissolve it. As believers, we must listen attentively to the voice of the Spirit in order to conquer the opposition. The Wise Men refused to be manipulated by Herod. They gave total allegiance to God, and so should we.

LET'S TALK ABOUT IT

1. Were there "three kings of the orient" that came to pay homage to Jesus?

No! The Wise Men were not kings. They were an elite group of astrologers or sages called Magi, who studied religion and science. In this case, they also followed the Jewish Scriptures, which they evidently felt emitted truth, and they committed themselves to faithfully seek to find the place where the newborn King resided. They also felt compelled to worship Him with gifts fit for royalty. They came from the East. The Medo-Persian Empire employed astrologers to help determine the nation's standing in relationship with other world powers. Ironically, they were the first group to recognize, according to Matthew, this astrological phenomenon. The fact that they were Gentiles made their journey of faith even more incredible. The hymn that refers to them as the "Three Kings of Orient" is misleading and was probably based on the three gifts that were given to honor Jesus.

HOME DAILY DEVOTIONAL READINGS
DECEMBER 25–31, 2017

MONDAY	TUESDAY	WEDNESDAY	THURSDAY	FRIDAY	SATURDAY	SUNDAY
Live the New Life in Christ	Live as Imitators of God	Disciplined Living in Christ	Leadership Gifts in the Church	Accept the Gifts of Weaker Members	Experience the Unity of Spirit	Seek the Common Life from Above
Ephesians 4:17–24	Ephesians 4:25–5:2	Colossians 3:1–11	1 Corinthians 12:27–31	1 Corinthians 12:12–13, 22–26	1 Peter 3:8–12	Ephesians 4:1–16

FAITH TO UNITE

ADULT TOPIC:	BACKGROUND SCRIPTURE:
UNITED WE STAND	EPHESIANS 4

EPHESIANS 4:1–16

King James Version

• • • Ephesians 4:1–16 • • •

I THEREFORE, the prisoner of the Lord, beseech you that ye walk worthy of the vocation wherewith ye are called,

2 With all lowliness and meekness, with long-suffering, forbearing one another in love;

3 Endeavouring to keep the unity of the Spirit in the bond of peace.

4 There is one body, and one Spirit, even as ye are called in one hope of your calling;

5 One Lord, one faith, one baptism,

6 One God and Father of all, who is above all, and through all, and in you all.

7 But unto every one of us is given grace according to the measure of the gift of Christ.

8 Wherefore he saith, When he ascended up on high, he led captivity captive, and gave gifts unto men.

9 (Now that he ascended, what is it but that he also descended first into the lower parts of the earth?

10 He that descended is the same also that ascended up far above all heavens, that he might fill all things.)

11 And he gave some, apostles; and some, prophets; and some, evangelists; and some, pastors and teachers;

12 For the perfecting of the saints, for the work of the ministry, for the edifying of the body of Christ:

13 Till we all come in the unity of the faith, and of the knowledge of the Son of God, unto a

New Revised Standard Version

• • • Ephesians 4:1–16 • • •

I THEREFORE, the prisoner in the Lord, beg you to lead a life worthy of the calling to which you have been called,

2 with all humility and gentleness, with patience, bearing with one another in love,

3 making every effort to maintain the unity of the Spirit in the bond of peace.

4 There is one body and one Spirit, just as you were called to the one hope of your calling,

5 one Lord, one faith, one baptism,

6 one God and Father of all, who is above all and through all and in all.

7 But each of us was given grace according to the measure of Christ's gift.

8 Therefore it is said, "When he ascended on high he made captivity itself a captive; he gave gifts to his people."

9 (When it says, "He ascended," what does it mean but that he had also descended into the lower parts of the earth?

10 He who descended is the same one who ascended far above all the heavens, so that he might fill all things.)

11 The gifts he gave were that some would be apostles, some prophets, some evangelists, some pastors and teachers,

12 to equip the saints for the work of ministry, for building up the body of Christ,

13 until all of us come to the unity of the faith and of the knowledge of the Son of God, to

MAIN THOUGHT: I therefore, the prisoner of the Lord, beseech you that ye walk worthy of the vocation wherewith ye are called, With all lowliness and meekness, with longsuffering, forbearing one another in love; Endeavouring to keep the unity of the Spirit in the bond of peace. (Ephesians 4:1–3, KJV)

King James Version

perfect man, unto the measure of the stature of the fulness of Christ:

14 That we henceforth be no more children, tossed to and fro, and carried about with every wind of doctrine, by the sleight of men, and cunning craftiness, whereby they lie in wait to deceive;

15 But speaking the truth in love, may grow up into him in all things, which is the head, even Christ:

16 From whom the whole body fitly joined together and compacted by that which every joint supplieth, according to the effectual working in the measure of every part, maketh increase of the body unto the edifying of itself in love.

New Revised Standard Version

maturity, to the measure of the full stature of Christ.

14 We must no longer be children, tossed to and fro and blown about by every wind of doctrine, by people's trickery, by their craftiness in deceitful scheming.

15 But speaking the truth in love, we must grow up in every way into him who is the head, into Christ,

16 from whom the whole body, joined and knit together by every ligament with which it is equipped, as each part is working properly, promotes the body's growth in building itself up in love.

LESSON SETTING
Time: A.D. 61-63
Place: Rome

LESSON OUTLINE
I. Call For Oneness
   (Ephesians 4:1-6)
II. All Gifts Come From the
    Grace of Christ
    (Ephesians 4:7-10)
III. Gifts and Their Purpose
     (Ephesians 4:11-16)

UNIFYING PRINCIPLE

Many people search all their lives for something that will make them feel grounded, whole, and in sync with life. Where can they find that something? Paul told the Ephesians that, even though they had many different gifts, their faith in Christ would bring them unity and help them grow together in love.

INTRODUCTION

Historically, the book of Ephesians has been listed among the epistles attributed to Paul and was composed while Paul was imprisoned in Rome around A.D. 61-63. However, some modern scholars now believe Paul is not the author of the book and that the honor should go to his personal assistant, Philemon. There is also another person such as Tychius, the one who delivered this letter and the ones addressed to Colossians and Philemon. However, the writer identified himself as Paul in Ephesians 1:1 and 3:1.

The question of authorship and whether or not the author and recipient knew each other does not change the letter's position in the church. It was accepted as part of the biblical canon because of its message of great encouragement to believers, especially to Gentiles believers, who were new to the faith and faced severe challenges from Judaizers and proponents of Gnosticism. Mark Holmes argues, "Unmistakably, the Ephesian letter was written specifically to Gentiles" (See, Mark Holmes, *Ephesians: A Bible Commentary in the Wesleyan*

Tradition, Wesleyan Publishing House, Indianapolis, p. 17).

The book consists two parts. Part one or, chapters 1-3, emphasize the blessings the Gentiles experience in Christ (Eph. 1:1–3:21) and part two, which are chapters 4–6:24 includes the text to be examined in this lesson, and addresses the practical aspects of living out one's faith.

The purpose of these false teachers and teachings was to destroy any sense of unity among the new converts and to build on the real and perceived misconceptions between Jewish and Hellenistic Christians. This was a clear and present danger for the Church; believers had to be alerted to watch out for those who masqueraded as sheep, but were actually wolves (See, John 10:1–19; Acts 20:17–38). Their strength laid in their sense of community and ability to depend on one another. Their faith in the ministry and the teachings of Jesus was paramount to their development as believers united for a common purpose.

Christian unity is one of the major themes of the community of faith. Jesus told His disciples that they should not compete with one another for authority or rank. He denied their request to sit at His right or left side (Matt. 20:20–28; Mark 10:35–45). His message to them, especially at the pinnacle of His ministry, was for them to love one another to the extent that He had loved them (John 15:12). His love for them compelled Him to go to the cross and shed His blood for the remission of sins (John 15:13). Upon His return to the Father, Jesus commanded them to stay together until they were endowed with heavenly power to continue His ministry. The early church continued in this spirit of unity as they shared property and other personal possessions in an effort to demonstrate Christian brotherhood (Acts 2:43–47). Even as issues arose among the disciples, they worked to resolve their challenges in the spirit of unity. For example, the issue between the Hellenists and the Hebrew Christians was resolved with the deliberate appointment of seven men who oversaw the distribution of goods to the community (Acts 6:1–7). Even the issue of how to minister to the Gentiles, which caused great concern and anxiety among the disciples, was resolved amicably (Acts 15). Paul pleaded with the church at Philippi to adopt the mind of Christ Jesus as a way to overcome divisive issues, power plays, and personality conflicts (Phil. 2:5–11). Humility was to keep them united.

This study examines three aspects of Christian unity as proposed by the writer of the book of Ephesians. Under the rubric, "Faith to Unite," this study posits three concepts. First, the writer called for oneness in Christ Jesus. Oneness, here, is taken to mean allowing the teachings of Jesus and the guidance of the Holy Spirit to take precedence in one's life. Oneness makes the Holy Spirit a priority. Second, the writer sought to go to great lengths to remind Christians all gifts to be used in the development of the Christian life come as a result of God's grace. Third, the writer provided a list of these gifts and how they are to be for the glorification of God.

EXPOSITION

I. CALL FOR ONENESS (EPHESIANS 4:1–6)

Ephesians 4 began with the writer identifying himself as the Apostle Paul and as a prisoner of the Lord. He made this claim earlier in Ephesians 3:1. A.T. Robertson argued that Ephesians bears much the same relation to Colossians that Romans does to Galatians, a fuller treatment of the same general theme in a more detached and impersonal manner (see, *Word Pictures in the New Testament*, Vol. 4, The Epistles of Paul, 514).

The word used here as prisoner means confined. It is not a voluntary association. Maybe, Paul was thinking of his Damascus Road experience when he was arrested by the Lord as he was on the way to prosecute Christians (Acts 9: 1–19). Based upon his position in the Lord, he encouraged the recipients of the letter to walk worthy of the calling they have received with all humility, gentleness, patience, and love. These four things deal with relationships. The church in relating to the community and world must properly represent the Lord as a precursor to offering salvation to others. Exercising humility and gentleness, patience, and love is the key to success. Jesus proclaimed the meek will inherit the earth (Matt. 5: 5). Patience was also seen as a virtue. Practice points to tolerance with others and echoes to an extent the sentiment expressed in the Golden Rule. It also challenges one to be prudent and thoughtful when the unexpected takes place. Patience enables one to approach situations thoughtfully. Peace is the result of these ingredients or fruits of the Spirit working together (Gal. 5:22–23).

Paul reminds the church that it is the one body of Christ and the Spirit within it gives it life. Of course, he is referring to the both the community church and the catholic church of which it is a part. The local body must see itself within rightful perspective. It has been called into being by the Lord Jesus. Here, Paul's feature on oneness is designed to emphasize Christian togetherness and unity. This concept of unity existed before the local body came into existence. They must now see themselves in total alignment with the entire community of faith. Their faith is to be in the One Lord and Savior (Jesus Christ), not in Paul or any of the other apostles or leaders. The church was baptized in His name. It identified with His death and resurrection to new life. They now belonged to Jesus and are, therefore, by default tied to God.

This unity is built upon a foundation that has already been established before time, the unison of the Godhead: God the Father, God the Son, and God the Holy Spirit (See, 1 Cor. 12:4–6). Paul reminded the church it is grounded in God the Creator and Source of all life. The repeated use of the word "all" suggests God's preeminence. He is the One that supplies life and the church responds to the divine initiative in humility and gentleness, patience, and love offering God's peace and salvation.

II. ALL GIFTS COME FROM THE GRACE OF CHRIST (EPHESIANS 4:7–10)

In the previous pericope of Scripture, the writer emphasized the important of the church seeing itself in total alignment with its Savior and Lord through the presence, direction, and power of the Holy Spirit (Eph. 4:1–6). In verses 7–10, Paul addressed the issue of diversity within the church. He moves from the church as a singular entity to the church as being composed of many members, which is denoted in the reference concerning the distribution of God's grace. As meant here, grace is God's unmerited favor. There are several levels of divine grace presupposed in this text: creation, adoption, and equipping for ministry. It was God's grace that led to the process of creation of the world and each person therein. Genesis 1–2 recounts God's gracious act of creation. He created humanity in His own image and likeness and placed humanity above all other creatures to act as stewards of the earth (Gen. 1: 26–28).

When humanity deliberately sinned against God in the Garden, God moved swiftly to redeem it from sin (Gen. 3:15). In the fullness of time, God kept His promise to deliver humanity from sin and sent His Son, Christ Jesus to give His life on the cross at Calvary. Paul called this process: adoption (Rom. 8:15–9:24; Gal. 4:5; Eph. 1:5). Paul informed the Christians at Corinth, they had been brought was with a price—the price being Christ sacrifice on the cross. Their salvation was the occasion to direct their attention to the divine call to extend salvation to others. To do so, they must acknowledge, develop, and utilize the gifts God had given them. The grace that God extended to the Gentile Christians at Ephesus related to service to the larger community and world. Their assignment was two-fold and required more than human ability. They were to battle evil and establish the Kingdom of God on earth, while doing so. This required superhuman abilities that God had vested in those who expressed faith in Jesus Christ. Faith, then, became the conduit through which the power of the Holy Spirit energized believers and equipped them for service (see Acts 1:6–8; 2; 13:1–3).

The use of Psalm 68:18, referred to in Ephesians 4:8-10, points to Christ's descent into Hell to save those who had perished before His crucifixion. His subsequent ascent into heaven then would be a virtual victory coronation where Christ presented, the fruit of the spoils of war, and the saved ones to demonstrate His victory over evil (Matt. 27:51–54). Again, Paul's point is to proclaim the power of the Lord Jesus over sin and evil by equipping Christians with the gifts they need to minister effectively to those who are spiritually dead, while they are alive.

III. Gifts and Their Purpose (Ephesians 4:11–16)

Verses 11-16 highlight the diverse gifts that Christ bestows on those who respond positively to His call to salvation. It is important that Paul only listed four of the gifts needed by the church to carry out its responsibilities: apostles, prophets, evangelists, and teaching pastors. For certain, these gifts of leadership are representative of the variety of gifts Christ grants to people to do the work of God.

The gift to be an apostle involved seeing Jesus personally and being directly appointed and taught by Him or those who had seen Him to ministry. The Apostles are the foundation upon which Christ built the church and established its doctrine.

Prophets are important because they analyze the events of the day to ascertain what "thus saith the Lord." They serve as God's ears, eyes, and mouthpiece to both warn and encourage us of God's purpose for our lives.

Evangelists proclaim the "Good News," which is what the word essentially means. They call attention to the divine activity of God in Christ with the objective of convincing people to repent, believe, and obey the Gospel (Mark 1:14–15). Paul instructed Timothy to take to do the work of an evangelist (2 Tim. 4:5).

Pastors are those who care for the flock of God. The word "pastor" denotes a caring shepherd in the manner of Jesus, who proclaimed Himself as the "Good Shepherd" (John 10:11). The shepherd cares, nourishes, protects, guides, and leads the sheep.

As such, a pastor's work includes enticing members of the congregation to come to an intimate knowledge of Jesus that saves from sin and works to develop within people a Christ-like character and disposition. The use of the conjunction "and" shows a relationship between shepherding and teaching. Paul uses the combination to highlight the importance of pastors having the ability to teach the word of God. Teaching carries with it the ability to depart knowledge to enhance understanding. Understanding the word of God promotes its practice and builds a firm foundation upon which one's commitment to Jesus can be enhanced.

The purpose of these gifts is to enable the individual Christian to develop his or her fullest potential and become an instrument of service in the ministry of love. These gifts are to unite the church as they share the faith with others.

THE LESSON APPLIED

Paul's purpose is to help Christians come to the realization that they are a part of the universal church which Jesus set up to call people to divine salvation. As such, He has—through the Holy Spirit—endowed each believer with gifts they are to acknowledge, develop, and use to accomplish their service to God in the practice of ministry. These gifts are diverse so that all may come to salvation. They are to be used so that every believer may grow to develop a mature faith in Jesus Christ.

LET'S TALK ABOUT IT

1. What is my spiritual gift?

Once one has given his or her life to God, it is appropriate to seek to discover what gift(s) one has to be of service to God. This may be accomplished through a good, solid Bible study and time in prayer. It may also help to have a conversation with your minister or a mature Christian about the gifts that may be obvious to them. There are also a variety of questionnaires that can help one discover the area they are most qualified to serve in.

What is needed most is indulgence in a period of reflective prayer where one seeks God's guidance to discover His true purpose for one's life. It requires openness to the Spirit of God.

HOME DAILY DEVOTIONAL READINGS
JANUARY 1–7, 2018

MONDAY	TUESDAY	WEDNESDAY	THURSDAY	FRIDAY	SATURDAY	SUNDAY
In God I Put My Trust	The Lord God Defeats Baal	Faithful Living in Another Land	Always Live as Salt and Light	Be Faithful When Tested	Training Plan for the Captives	Stand by Your Principles
Psalm 56	1 Kings 18:30–39	Jeremiah 29:4–9	Matthew 5:13–16	Revelation 2:8–11	Daniel 1:3–7	Daniel 1:8–21

A SINCERE FAITH

ADULT TOPIC:	BACKGROUND SCRIPTURE:
LIVING YOUR CONVICTIONS	DANIEL 1

DANIEL 1:8—21

King James Version

BUT Daniel purposed in his heart that he would not defile himself with the portion of the king's meat, nor with the wine which he drank: therefore he requested of the prince of the eunuchs that he might not defile himself.

9 Now God had brought Daniel into favour and tender love with the prince of the eunuchs.

10 And the prince of the eunuchs said unto Daniel, I fear my lord the king, who hath appointed your meat and your drink: for why should he see your faces worse liking than the children which are of your sort? then shall ye make me endanger my head to the king.

11 Then said Daniel to Melzar, whom the prince of the eunuchs had set over Daniel, Hananiah, Mishael, and Azariah,

12 Prove thy servants, I beseech thee, ten days; and let them give us pulse to eat, and water to drink.

13 Then let our countenances be looked upon before thee, and the countenance of the children that eat of the portion of the king's meat: and as thou seest, deal with thy servants.

14 So he consented to them in this matter, and proved them ten days.

15 And at the end of ten days their countenances appeared fairer and fatter in flesh than all the children which did eat the portion of the king's meat.

16 Thus Melzar took away the portion of their meat, and the wine that they should drink; and gave them pulse.

New Revised Standard Version

BUT Daniel resolved that he would not defile himself with the royal rations of food and wine; so he asked the palace master to allow him not to defile himself.

9 Now God allowed Daniel to receive favor and compassion from the palace master.

10 The palace master said to Daniel, "I am afraid of my lord the king; he has appointed your food and your drink. If he should see you in poorer condition than the other young men of your own age, you would endanger my head with the king."

11 Then Daniel asked the guard whom the palace master had appointed over Daniel, Hananiah, Mishael, and Azariah:

12 "Please test your servants for ten days. Let us be given vegetables to eat and water to drink.

13 You can then compare our appearance with the appearance of the young men who eat the royal rations, and deal with your servants according to what you observe."

14 So he agreed to this proposal and tested them for ten days.

15 At the end of ten days it was observed that they appeared better and fatter than all the young men who had been eating the royal rations.

16 So the guard continued to withdraw their royal rations and the wine they were to drink, and gave them vegetables.

MAIN THOUGHT: But Daniel purposed in his heart that he would not defile himself with the portion of the king's meat, nor with the wine which he drank: therefore he requested of the prince of the eunuchs that he might not defile himself. (Daniel 1:8, KJV)

King James Version	New Revised Standard Version
17 As for these four children, God gave them knowledge and skill in all learning and wisdom: and Daniel had understanding in all visions and dreams.	17 To these four young men God gave knowledge and skill in every aspect of literature and wisdom; Daniel also had insight into all visions and dreams.
18 Now at the end of the days that the king had said he should bring them in, then the prince of the eunuchs brought them in before Nebuchadnezzar.	18 At the end of the time that the king had set for them to be brought in, the palace master brought them into the presence of Nebuchadnezzar,
19 And the king communed with them; and among them all was found none like Daniel, Hananiah, Mishael, and Azariah: therefore stood they before the king.	19 and the king spoke with them. And among them all, no one was found to compare with Daniel, Hananiah, Mishael, and Azariah; therefore they were stationed in the king's court.
20 And in all matters of wisdom and understanding, that the king enquired of them, he found them ten times better than all the magicians and astrologers that were in all his realm.	20 In every matter of wisdom and understanding concerning which the king inquired of them, he found them ten times better than all the magicians and enchanters in his whole kingdom.
21 And Daniel continued even unto the first year of king Cyrus.	21 And Daniel continued there until the first year of King Cyrus.

LESSON SETTING
Time: Between 586–562 B.C.
Place: Babylon

LESSON OUTLINE
**I. A Resolution Tested
(Daniel 1:8–10)**
**II. A Resolution Affirmed
(Daniel 1:11–17)**
**III. A Resolution Rewarded
(Daniel 1:18–21)**

UNIFYING PRINCIPLE

People find themselves confronted by contradictory requirements from different sources of authority. How do we resolve such conflicts? Daniel's active faith combined with tact helped him resolve his conflict and remain obedient to God in terms of dietary requirements.

INTRODUCTION

The book of Daniel presents many challenges to the scholar looking for historical-critical answers from the text. One of its few straight-forward characteristics are its two halves. The first half contains chapters 1–6 and is largely narrative; the second covers chapters 7–12 and is predominately apocalyptic prophecy. Details concerning the nature of the apocalypses found in the second half of Daniel in relationship to the genre of apocalypse, loan words from Greek, use of both Aramaic and Hebrew, and other considerations muddy the historical-critical waters. The writer remains unknown and so is no help in dating the text. Details within the texts lend themselves to the conclusion that these stories, though based in history, are largely a collection of folklore about Daniel and other exiles in Babylon. Thus Daniel resists the easy resolution of questions about authorship and dating. Given the evidence, Ernest Lucas simply states that a composition date in either the late sixth-century/early fifth century or in the second-century B.C. "are consonant with belief in the divine inspiration and authority of [Daniel]" (*Daniel* [Downers Grove, IL: IVP Academic, 2002], 312).

Daniel 1 introduces characters and themes important to the entire book including resistance to the foreign powers who seek to assimilate the exiles completely into Babylon. This has not always been clearly recognized as a theme throughout the entirety of Daniel. Both the actors in the stories and those who recorded these texts were resisting Babylon. They did not find the empire to be benevolent even when it seemed that the empire was acting in the exiles' best interests. "The perspective of the book of Daniel toward foreign conquerors, even in the first six chapters, is not nearly so benign as is often thought; in fact, it is openly hostile to their authority. This hostile challenge to authority provides one of the major unifying factors of Daniel as a whole" (Daniel L. Smith-Christopher, "Daniel" in *The New Interpreter's Bible,* Vol. 7 [Nashville: Abingdon Press, 1996], 21).

Broadly, the setting of this book is the exile in Babylon. King Nebuchadnezzar laid siege to Jerusalem in 586 B.C. and took many captives back to Babylon. Evidence suggests that the writer of Daniel was not overly concerned with only attributing Nebuchadnezzar's own actions to the king within the text of this book. Instead "what resulted from this distortion of historical accuracy was a picture of a Babylonian monarch whose deeds could be applied to any later king who accomplished the same things" (Ronald

H. Sack, "Nebuchadnezzar" in *Eerdmans Dictionary of the Bible* [Grand Rapids: Eerdmans, 2000], 954). Whether the book was written shortly after Daniel's lifetime or even centuries later, the writer is fundamentally concerned with faithfulness in the face of foreign demands for allegiance from God's people.

EXPOSITION

I. A RESOLUTION TESTED (DANIEL 1:8–10)

When Nebuchadnezzar conquered Jerusalem, he took the spoils of the city to Babylon. Vessels from the temple were taken into "the treasury of his gods" (Dan. 1:2, NRSV). This was more than a statement of fact; it was a political and theological claim. In the thinking of the time, the defeat of Judah meant that the Babylonian gods were stronger than the God of Judah. Thus putting the vessels from the temple in Jerusalem into the treasury of foreign gods symbolized the defeat of the Lord at the hands of those gods.

The conquered people from Judah would now be expected to worship the gods of their captors and become part of Babylon. To this end, handsome and intelligent young men were to be instructed in the Chaldean literature and language in order to be able to serve the king. "'Chaldean' is a term used throughout Daniel to refer to an astrologer as one of the royal court officials, rather than the general term for an ethnic Babylonian" (Smith-Christopher, 44). The king would provide food and wine from the royal rations for these students for the three years of their education after which time they would presumably be sufficiently acculturated.

Daniel, Hananiah, Mishael, and Azariah were chosen from Judah. When they arrived in the palace, they were given new names. These Babylonian names were meant to go with their new Babylonian identities, thus stripping the men of all that had made them uniquely Judean. The text moves from the renaming of these four young men immediately to Daniel's resistance to this forced assimilation. Though too much can be made of conjunctions, it is interesting that the conjunction "but" connects verses 7–8. Daniel recognized that his new name was a form of pressure to renounce the Lord and become a mere wise man in Babylon, *but* "Daniel resolved that he would not defile himself with the royal rations of food and wine" (v. 8, NRSV). Smith-Christopher asserts, "Worries about the purity of the body are symbolic reflections of concerns for the integrity of the social group, and purity laws serve as effective barriers to assimilation. The assertion of purity concerns during the exile served as an important spiritual and social bulwark against the dangers of disappearing as a people" (40). These worries about purity are a large part of the reason that the tribes of Judah can be traced throughout history despite exile in Babylon and other conquests while the tribes of the northern kingdom of Israel were eventually lost in Assyria. Assimilation into the land of their captors, including worship of foreign gods, led to the ten tribes losing their distinction in Assyria and thus being "lost" to history. In Babylon, however, attention to diet was one indicator that the people who had come from Judah were not willing to allow their identities to be subsumed by Babylonian culture.

Why Daniel focused on the food and wine as a form of resistance to assimilation is not entirely clear. One of his concerns could have been that the meat provided would not have been butchered according to the specifications of the Law. This would explain why Daniel could eat vegetables provided by the king but does not explain his stance against the wine. Nothing in the Law required him to abstain from alcohol except in the case of having taken a Nazirite vow. Since there is no indication that Daniel had taken such a vow, some commentators focus on the fact that the food came from the king as the root of Daniel's request. Eating this food could have suggested that Daniel would be loyal to the king, a statement that Daniel was not willing to make with the words of his lips nor the food that passed them.

Likely some combination of these reasons resulted in Daniel's conviction that accepting the food and the wine from the provided royal rations would defile him. Based on this conviction, Daniel spoke to the palace master and asked that he be allowed not to defile himself. Though the act of not eating the king's food and wine was an act of defiance, Daniel saw wisdom in following official avenues to obtain permission to do so. In such a way, he could continue his education in Chaldean literature and language and perhaps be of use to his own people even as he retained his unique status as a man of the people of God.

Verse two saw God acting by allowing Nebuchadnezzar to take Jerusalem. Verse nine sees Him, again in the background, "[allowing] Daniel to receive favor and compassion from the palace master"

(NRSV). Although other events in the book of Daniel will involve direct revelations and miracles from God, in this story He simply works providentially for Daniel. Daniel's own faithfulness to God was an invitation to the Lord to act on the man's behalf. Nothing Daniel said or did could force the Lord to act for him, but by acting in a way that affirmed his allegiance only to the Lord, Daniel put himself in a position to receive the Lord's blessing for that faithfulness. The palace master's words to Daniel suggest that King Nebuchadnezzar was not a benevolent ruler: "'I am afraid of my lord the king.... If he should see you in poorer condition than the other young men of your own age, you would endanger my head with the king'" (v. 10, NRSV). This fear could be based both on the assumption that refusing the king's food was an act of rebellion and that such a request would result in illness in Daniel when the king wanted him strong and learning the ways of Babylon. Either outcome could result in violence against the palace master.

II. A RESOLUTION AFFIRMED (DANIEL 1:11–17)

Seeing that the Lord had left the palace master open to the idea, Daniel offered a test. This test, lasting only ten days, would allow the Jewish men to eat only vegetables and drink only water in order to see if they would suffer ill consequences from this diet. Trusting in the Lord, Daniel told the guard, "'Deal with your servants according to what you observe'" (v. 13, NRSV). In this way, if the men were found to be as healthy as the other men, the king could not find fault with their diet even if it separated them from the other exiles. Thus it was agreed that in ten days' time,

the guard would check back with Daniel and his fellows to see whether the diet was feasible for the young men.

At the conclusion of the ten days, the four Jewish men had surpassed their peers in terms of appearance and health. Though the diet was taken up for reasons of resistance and not primarily for health concerns, the Lord worked on behalf of the young men to once again reward their faithfulness so that they could continue to keep their diet without negative repercussions (see v. 16). Whether the king knew of this diet is never divulged. However, there is no reason he needed to; these four men were in great health.

Beyond simply being healthy young men, the four Jewish men were further blessed by God with "knowledge and skill in every aspect of literature and wisdom" (v. 17, NRSV). Though faithfulness to the Lord does not necessarily yield success in worldly measures, in this case the young men were emphatic success stories from the king's educational program because God chose to reward their faithfulness with vast knowledge and skill. Daniel in particular stood out as one who, like Joseph in the pharaoh's court, "had insight into all visions and dreams" (v. 17, NRSV; see Gen. 41). This verse foreshadows both the ongoing faithfulness of these men and Daniel's experiences with visions and dreams.

III. A RESOLUTION REWARDED (DANIEL 1:18–21)

After their three years of education was completed, all of the young men came before the king. Speaking with all of them, "no one was found to compare with Daniel, Hananiah, Mishael, and Azariah" (v. 19,

NRSV). The writer continues to insist on calling the four men by their Jewish names. This subtly emphasizes that the men were being guided by the Lord and protected by Him even in the midst of a foreign, hostile land. Because of their great skill, the king had these four Jewish scholars brought into his own court. Daniel worked in the court of the king until the year King Cyrus rose to power. Though he certainly could have served in the court that long if (as the text suggests) he began his studies in his teen years, more likely this final verse is meant to signify that Daniel served in the court of the Babylonian king throughout the time of the forced exile. Once King Cyrus rose to power, the Jewish people were allowed to return to Judea. Although his entire career was in Babylon, away from the Promised Land, the favor of the Lord never departed from Daniel. He experienced the Lord's protection and blessing throughout his life in exile.

THE LESSON APPLIED

Daniel wasn't given a choice about whether or not he would be educated for service in Nebuchadnezzar's court. He could choose, however, whether he would remain faithful to the Lord or adopt the ways of Babylon. Choosing faithfulness to the Lord was an act of resistance to the empire that sought his complete allegiance.

For this reason, "The book of Daniel calls people of faith to just such a treason against the rule of the powerful, a treason based on loyalty to the rule of God" (Smith-Christopher, 34). Just as God demands complete faithfulness, so do the worldly powers. The challenge for Christians is the same as it was for Daniel—to be knowledgeable about the culture they find themselves surrounded by but to find ways, both large and small, to resist giving allegiance to anything or anyone other than the Lord.

LET'S TALK ABOUT IT

1. What is God's calling to His people?

Though the work of laypeople can seem quite different from the call of pastors and other leaders, each Christian is called to love the Lord and worship Him in Spirit and in truth. For those outside of ministry contexts, the message of Daniel is particularly apt. These are called to know their jobs and do them well. In doing those jobs, each person is called to glorify only the Lord, remembering that He alone can rightfully claim their whole allegiance. This may call for small acts of resistance to ungodly policies or practices; it could call for much larger acts of resistance as well. Whatever the work, a Christian's first vocation is to remain faithful to the Lord.

HOME DAILY DEVOTIONAL READINGS
JANUARY 8–14, 2018

MONDAY	TUESDAY	WEDNESDAY	THURSDAY	FRIDAY	SATURDAY	SUNDAY
We Must Speak about Jesus	We Must Obey God, Not Humans	Prayer, Fasting, and a Bold Move	All Ordered to Worship the Image	We Will Not Serve Babylonian Gods	King Astonished at Jews' Survival	God Delivers from the Fiery Furnace
Acts 4:13–22	Acts 5:27–32	Esther 4:5–17	Daniel 3:1–12	Daniel 3:13–18	Daniel 3:24–25	Daniel 3:19–23, 26–28

A Bold Faith

| ADULT TOPIC: | BACKGROUND SCRIPTURE: |
| NO MATTER THE COST | DANIEL 3 |

DANIEL 3:19–23, 26–28

King James Version	*New Revised Standard Version*

THEN was Nebuchadnezzar full of fury, and the form of his visage was changed against Shadrach, Meshach, and Abednego: therefore he spake, and commanded that they should heat the furnace one seven times more than it was wont to be heated.

20 And he commanded the most mighty men that were in his army to bind Shadrach, Meshach, and Abednego, and to cast them into the burning fiery furnace.

21 Then these men were bound in their coats, their hosen, and their hats, and their other garments, and were cast into the midst of the burning fiery furnace.

22 Therefore because the king's commandment was urgent, and the furnace exceeding hot, the flames of the fire slew those men that took up Shadrach, Meshach, and Abednego.

23 And these three men, Shadrach, Meshach, and Abednego, fell down bound into the midst of the burning fiery furnace.

• • • • • •

26 Then Nebuchadnezzar came near to the mouth of the burning fiery furnace, and spake, and said, Shadrach, Meshach, and Abednego, ye servants of the most high God, come forth, and come hither. Then Shadrach, Meshach, and Abednego, came forth of the midst of the fire.

27 And the princes, governors, and captains,

THEN Nebuchadnezzar was so filled with rage against Shadrach, Meshach, and Abednego that his face was distorted. He ordered the furnace heated up seven times more than was customary,

20 and ordered some of the strongest guards in his army to bind Shadrach, Meshach, and Abednego and to throw them into the furnace of blazing fire.

21 So the men were bound, still wearing their tunics, their trousers, their hats, and their other garments, and they were thrown into the furnace of blazing fire.

22 Because the king's command was urgent and the furnace was so overheated, the raging flames killed the men who lifted Shadrach, Meshach, and Abednego.

23 But the three men, Shadrach, Meshach, and Abednego, fell down, bound, into the furnace of blazing fire.

• • • • • •

26 Nebuchadnezzar then approached the door of the furnace of blazing fire and said, "Shadrach, Meshach, and Abednego, servants of the Most High God, come out! Come here!" So Shadrach, Meshach, and Abednego came out from the fire.

27 And the satraps, the prefects, the governors,

MAIN THOUGHT: Then Nebuchadnezzar spake, and said, Blessed be the God of Shadrach, Meshach, and Abednego, who hath sent his angel, and delivered his servants that trusted in him, and have changed the king's word, and yielded their bodies, that they might not serve nor worship any god, except their own God. (Daniel 3:28, KJV)

DANIEL 3:19–23, 26–28

<table>
<tr><td>King James Version</td><td>New Revised Standard Version</td></tr>
</table>

King James Version

and the king's counsellors, being gathered together, saw these men, upon whose bodies the fire had no power, nor was an hair of their head singed, neither were their coats changed, nor the smell of fire had passed on them.

28 Then Nebuchadnezzar spake, and said, Blessed be the God of Shadrach, Meshach, and Abednego, who hath sent his angel, and delivered his servants that trusted in him, and have changed the king's word, and yielded their bodies, that they might not serve nor worship any god, except their own God.

New Revised Standard Version

and the king's counselors gathered together and saw that the fire had not had any power over the bodies of those men; the hair of their heads was not singed, their tunics were not harmed, and not even the smell of fire came from them.

28 Nebuchadnezzar said, "Blessed be the God of Shadrach, Meshach, and Abednego, who has sent his angel and delivered his servants who trusted in him. They disobeyed the king's command and yielded up their bodies rather than serve and worship any god except their own God.

LESSON SETTING
Time: Between 586–562 B.C.
Place: Babylon

LESSON OUTLINE
**I. The King's Fury
(Daniel 3:19–20)**
**II. The Furious Flames
(Daniel 3:21–25)**
**III. The Most High God
(Daniel 3:26–28)**

UNIFYING PRINCIPLE

Sometimes people are challenged to endure great trials and tribulations because of their convictions. How can they face such challenges and remain faithful? Shadrach, Meshach, and Abednego boldly disobeyed the king's command and were delivered from a fiery furnace by the power of God.

INTRODUCTION

Daniel 3 reads like a dark comedy. A disproportionately tall and skinny statue and obscene obeisance to that statue, the unrestrained rage of a king and raging fires in a furnace, even the words of the Jewish wise men—all beg the reader to recognize the ridiculousness of Babylon and its claims via King Nebuchadnezzar that it was deserving of honor and obedience. Taking this empire too seriously as the king did could only result in being humbled. "'We see here the worldly power absolutely confident that there is no limit to its authority'" (qtd. in Daniel L. Smith-Christopher, "Daniel" in *The New Interpreter's Bible*, Vol. 7 [Nashville: Abingdon Press, 1996], 64). Nebuchadnezzar never stopped to consider whether any force, human or divine, would be able to stop his will from becoming fact.

The question throughout Daniel 3, then, is one of power—does King Nebuchadnezzar in Babylon have ultimate power over the exiles in his land or could some god be found to humble him? This question is especially pertinent if, as Greek translations of the text asserted, the dating of this event was "the eighteenth year of Nebuchadnezzar—in other words, the year of his conquest of Jerusalem. Thus the statue went up in the year the Temple came down—false worship as opposed to true worship" (Smith-Christopher, 62).

This farcical tale begins after Daniel had interpreted Nebuchadnezzar's dream. He dreamt of a huge statue featuring a golden head, silver arms and chest, bronze torso and thighs, iron legs, and iron and clay feet which was destroyed. Daniel explained that Nebuchadnezzar was represented as the golden head. No matter how strong his own empire, it would not last forever, falling because of its own weaknesses and division (see Dan. 2:31–45). Whether the statue Nebuchadnezzar built was meant to be of himself is debatable, but it was certainly a monument to his greatness as attested by the gold used in its construction. It emphasized the greatness of his kingdom and himself as its head.

Such a great king would have adoring followers, and this king was no different. He easily ordered all of "the satraps, the prefects, and the governors, the counselors, the treasurers, the justices, the magistrates, and all the officials of the provinces" to come and see his great statue and then to worship it when the cacophony of instruments played (3:2, NRSV; see v. 5). "This story has an almost humorous tone, in that the little orchestra becomes the signal for a mass obeisance by all the toadies of the kingdom" (W. Sibley Towner, *Daniel* [Atlanta, GA: John Knox Press, 1984], 48). Any who did not do as the king commanded would be thrown into "a furnace of blazing fire" (v. 6, NRSV). Thus all of the instruments played and "all the peoples, nations, and languages fell down and worshiped the golden statue that King Nebuchadnezzar had set up" (v. 7, NRSV). All, that is,

except for the Jews. Some Chaldeans came to Nebuchadnezzar to tattle on the Jews; when all the instruments played, three men did not worship the statue: Shadrach, Meshach, and Abednego. For the first time, Nebuchadnezzar was thrown into a rage. When the three men were standing before him, Nebuchadnezzar gave them a second chance to worship his gods, reminding them to bow when they heard the cacophony of instruments and warning them that the furnace really did await them if they refused to do so. Nebuchadnezzar asked rhetorically, "'And who is the god that will deliver you out of my hands?'" (v. 15, NRSV). In Nebuchadnezzar's thinking, the God of the Jews was already defeated; that was why the people were in exile. His own gods would not want to save the Jews and their God was powerless—who could be the god to deliver the Jewish men?

EXPOSITION

I. THE KING'S FURY (DANIEL 3:19–20)

The heart of this chapter is found in verses 16–18. The three Jewish men stood before King Nebuchadnezzar and said, "'We have no need to present a defense to you in this matter. If our God whom we serve is able to deliver us from the furnace of blazing fire and out of your hand, O king, let him deliver us. But if not, be it known to you, O king, that we will not serve your gods and we will not worship the golden statue that you have set up'" (vv. 16–18, NRSV). The men's words are difficult to square with their seeming confidence, though the translation does well with the Hebrew text. Did these three really doubt that God could save them as their "if" implies? Given the tone of the chapter with its insistence on marking the absurdity of this statue and situation, could this be sarcasm used by the Jewish men, even with their lives on the line?

A different translation yields a very different meaning here; the NIV reads, "If we are thrown into the blazing furnace, the God we serve is able to save us from it, and he will rescue us from your hand, O king. But even if he does not, we want you to know, O king, that we will not serve your gods or worship the image of gold you have set up" (vv. 17–18). The men acted with confidence, which the NIV brings out in their words, but perhaps the contrast of their words and actions was meant to make Nebuchadnezzar think. He doubted their God, so they spoke as though they did too, but in reality the men may have been subtly mocking the king. In the end, it did not matter greatly to the three men whether God would deliver them or not. "The point being made here is that the youths' primary reason for standing firm is not their confidence that God will deliver them, but their adherence to the first two commandments of the Decalogue. They will not honour [sic] any god other than the God of Israel, and they will not worship any idol. Their stand is one of principle, whether or not it is prudent" (Ernest Lucas, *Daniel* [Downers Grove: IVP Academic, 2002], 91). It was of greater importance to them that they did not worship Nebuchadnezzar's gods or the statue than whether they lived or died.

On hearing this, Nebuchadnezzar "was so filled with rage … that his face was distorted" (v. 19, NRSV). One might imagine a cartoon—face red, eyes bloodshot, ears issuing steam. As in any dark comedy, this image could only remain funny if the heroes won the day. The likelihood that the three Jewish men would survive their ordeal became seven times less likely as Nebuchadnezzar had his furnace superheated to seven times hotter than usual. Furthermore, it would not do to simply throw the men in; they also had to be bound, hand and foot, by the very strongest men in the king's military.

II. THE FURIOUS FLAMES (DANIEL 3:21–25)

"So the men were bound, still wearing their tunics, their trousers, their hats, and their other garments, and they were thrown into the furnace of blazing fire" (v. 21, NRSV). Some questions remain as to what articles of clothing the Aramaic words denote. Smith-Christopher notes, "The garment terminology … has an almost rhythmic, rhyming quality to it [in Aramaic], reminding one of a phrase like the English 'lock, stock, and barrel'" (64). In the end, the exact recitation of the clothing is not of great importance; this list instead emphasizes that the men were quite fully clothed when they were thrown into the flames.

The raging flames had been stoked on account of the king's rage, and so those men who obeyed him throwing the Jewish men into the fire died themselves from proximity to the blaze. Shadrach, Meshach, and Abednego, however, merely fell into the fire since they were bound. This contributed in part to Nebuchadnezzar's astonishment when he looked and saw them standing. He couldn't remember how many men he had thrown into the fire—

three or four?—because he was seeing four unbound men in the flames.

The Aramaic translated here "the appearance of a god" (v. 25, NRSV) can better be literally rendered "son of god." This could be a reference to an angel, as many Christians today consider it. This is reinforced by the fact that "the Aramaic word *bar 'ĕlāhîn* is typically taken to refer to a member of the 'sons of god,' who are collectively known as the 'host of heaven'" (65). Similar concepts can be found throughout the Old Testament. Whereas other cultures allowed for the existence and worship of many gods, Israel asserted that there is only one God but many, lower-ranking spiritual beings to do His bidding. This angel emphatically vindicated the three men's faith that God could save them from the flames.

III. The Most High God (Daniel 3:26–28)

Seeing the apparent son of a god with the Jewish men, Nebuchadnezzar approached the furnace and called the men to come out saying, "'Shadrach, Meshach, and Abednego, servants of the Most High God, come out! Come here!'" (v. 26, NRSV). Nebuchadnezzar does not become a monotheist here. After all, he just assumed that the angel in the flames was a son of a god. Instead, Nebuchadnezzar is acknowledging that their God—who seemed to have been defeated when Judah was taken into exile—was actually more powerful than all of Nebuchadnezzar's gods.

All of the comically long list of satraps and prefects and governors and counselors who had been gathered to foolishly bow to the statue "saw that the fire had not had any power over the bodies of those men; the hair of their heads was not singed, their tunics were not harmed, and not even the smell of fire came from them" (v. 27, NRSV). God had not simply allowed the men to escape by the skin of their teeth. They looked and smelled like they had never been in a fire at all, let alone a fire that had killed men who simply stood too close to it. In this way, Shadrach, Meshach, and Abednego fulfilled words spoken by Isaiah: "When you walk through fire you shall not be burned, and the flame shall not consume you" (43:2, NRSV).

In front of all his gathered officials, Nebuchadnezzar proclaimed, "'Blessed be the God of Shadrach, Meshach, and Abednego, who has sent his angel and delivered his servants who trusted in him. They disobeyed the king's command and yielded up their bodies rather than serve and worship any god except their own God'" (Dan. 3:28, NRSV). Because God kept them safe in the fire, Nebuchadnezzar was forced to admit that this God was powerful even in Babylon. Because they boldly proclaimed their faithfulness to the Lord, whether or not He chose to deliver them, the men made quite an impression on Nebuchadnezzar.

The Lesson Applied

Faithfulness to God does not always deliver His people from the flames, literal or figurative. In the case of Shadrach, Meshach, and Abednego, they were not only delivered from flames but also promoted in the government of Babylon. Furthermore, the king declared that "any people, nation, or language that utters blasphemy against the God of Shadrach, Meshach, and Abednego shall be torn limb from limb, and their houses laid in ruins; for there is no other god who is able to deliver in this way" (v. 29, NRSV).

This, of course, was not a statement of faithfulness to the Lord. Babylon did not become faithful to the Lord for fear of this punishment. Instead, Nebuchadnezzar's words suggest that the Jewish faith got a new legal status in Babylon and became protected by the king.

What powers demand Christians' loyalty today or threaten us with fire and death if we refuse? Certainly the nation desires to be our highest priority and worshiped as the highest power in our lives. With Shadrach, Meshach, and Abednego, we resist the calls of nationalism that would seduce us away from faithfulness to the Lord and into country-worship as our shiny, tall idol.

LET'S TALK ABOUT IT

1. Why might Christians speak of God's deliverance from trials as an "if" rather than a "when"?

It is tempting to assume that because God has the power to deliver His people from any and all hardship, He ought to do so or will do so. After all, had God not rescued Shadrach, Meshach, and Abednego, would Nebuchadnezzar still have been impressed with their faithfulness? Perhaps, or perhaps not. Ernest Lucas helpfully reminds Christians to focus on "the promise of the strengthening presence of God in times of trial, rather than any promise of miraculous deliverance from them [as the] hope [that has been given] to persecuted believers" (96).

Lucas points the reader to 1 Peter 4, which says, "Beloved, do not be surprised at the fiery ordeal that is taking place among you to test you, as though something strange were happening to you. But rejoice insofar as you are sharing Christ's sufferings, so that you may also be glad and shout for joy when his glory is revealed. If you are reviled for the name of Christ, you are blessed, because the spirit of glory, which is the Spirit of God, is resting on you" (vv. 12–14, NRSV).

Surely our God is powerful to save, and He has proven this time and again. However, in those ordeals where He chooses not to deliver us or even keep us safe from the evil that threatens us, let us remember that our unwavering faithfulness to Him in the face of all circumstances is our testimony to the watching world that our allegiance to the Lord is more important than anything else. His is the glory, no matter the consequences. With Psalm 113 our lives sing, "Blessed be the name of the LORD from this time forth and for evermore. From the rising of the sun unto the going down of the same the LORD's name is to be praised. The LORD is high above all nations, and his glory above the heavens" (vv. 2–4, KJV).

HOME DAILY DEVOTIONAL READINGS
JANUARY 15–21, 2018

MONDAY	TUESDAY	WEDNESDAY	THURSDAY	FRIDAY	SATURDAY	SUNDAY
Plea for God's Forgiveness and Mercy	Disobedience Results in Israel's Downfall	A Renewed Call to Repentance	Seeking Answers through Prayer and Supplication	Prayer of Confession for Israel's Sins	Receiving Answers to Prayer and Confession	Daniel's Prayer of Confession and Supplication
Nehemiah 1:4–11	Jeremiah 25:8–14	Joel 1:13–20	Daniel 9:1–3	Daniel 9:9–14	Daniel 9:20–24	Daniel 9:4–8, 15–19

A Prayer for an Obedient Faith

Adult Topic:	Background Scripture:
A Cry for Help	Daniel 9:1–19

Daniel 9:4–8, 15–19

King James Version

AND I prayed unto the Lord my God, and made my confession, and said, O Lord, the great and dreadful God, keeping the covenant and mercy to them that love him, and to them that keep his commandments;

5 We have sinned, and have committed iniquity, and have done wickedly, and have rebelled, even by departing from thy precepts and from thy judgments:

6 Neither have we hearkened unto thy servants the prophets, which spake in thy name to our kings, our princes, and our fathers, and to all the people of the land.

7 O Lord, righteousness belongeth unto thee, but unto us confusion of faces, as at this day; to the men of Judah, and to the inhabitants of Jerusalem, and unto all Israel, that are near, and that are far off, through all the countries whither thou hast driven them, because of their trespass that they have trespassed against thee.

8 O Lord, to us belongeth confusion of face, to our kings, to our princes, and to our fathers, because we have sinned against thee.

• • • • • •

15 And now, O Lord our God, that hast brought thy people forth out of the land of Egypt with a mighty hand, and hast gotten thee renown, as at this day; we have sinned, we have done wickedly.

16 O Lord, according to all thy righteousness, I beseech thee, let thine anger and thy fury be turned away from thy city Jerusalem, thy holy mountain: because for our sins, and for the

New Revised Standard Version

I PRAYED to the Lord my God and made confession, saying, "Ah, Lord, great and awesome God, keeping covenant and steadfast love with those who love you and keep your commandments,

5 we have sinned and done wrong, acted wickedly and rebelled, turning aside from your commandments and ordinances.

6 We have not listened to your servants the prophets, who spoke in your name to our kings, our princes, and our ancestors, and to all the people of the land.

7 Righteousness is on your side, O Lord, but open shame, as at this day, falls on us, the people of Judah, the inhabitants of Jerusalem, and all Israel, those who are near and those who are far away, in all the lands to which you have driven them, because of the treachery that they have committed against you.

8 Open shame, O Lord, falls on us, our kings, our officials, and our ancestors, because we have sinned against you."

• • • • • •

15 "And now, O Lord our God, who brought your people out of the land of Egypt with a mighty hand and made your name renowned even to this day—we have sinned, we have done wickedly.

16 O Lord, in view of all your righteous acts, let your anger and wrath, we pray, turn away from your city Jerusalem, your holy mountain; because of our sins and the iniquities of our

MAIN THOUGHT: O Lord, hear; O Lord, forgive; O Lord, hearken and do; defer not, for thine own sake, O my God: for thy city and thy people are called by thy name. (Daniel 9:19, KJV)

King James Version	New Revised Standard Version
iniquities of our fathers, Jerusalem and thy people are become a reproach to all that are about us.	ancestors, Jerusalem and your people have become a disgrace among all our neighbors.
17 Now therefore, O our God, hear the prayer of thy servant, and his supplications, and cause thy face to shine upon thy sanctuary that is desolate, for the Lord's sake.	17 Now therefore, O our God, listen to the prayer of your servant and to his supplication, and for your own sake, Lord, let your face shine upon your desolated sanctuary.
18 O my God, incline thine ear, and hear; open thine eyes, and behold our desolations, and the city which is called by thy name: for we do not present our supplications before thee for our righteousnesses, but for thy great mercies.	18 Incline your ear, O my God, and hear. Open your eyes and look at our desolation and the city that bears your name. We do not present our supplication before you on the ground of our righteousness, but on the ground of your great mercies.
19 O Lord, hear; O Lord, forgive; O Lord, hearken and do; defer not, for thine own sake, O my God: for thy city and thy people are called by thy name.	19 O Lord, hear; O Lord, forgive; O Lord, listen and act and do not delay! For your own sake, O my God, because your city and your people bear your name!"

LESSON SETTING
Time: 522 B.C.
Place: Babylon

LESSON OUTLINE
I. **Confession of Sins (Daniel 9:4–6)**
II. **The Shame of Sins (Daniel 9:7–8)**
III. **Hope for Forgiveness of Sins (Daniel 9:15–19)**

UNIFYING PRINCIPLE

People want release from feelings of shame that may result from past mistakes. Where can they go to find such relief? Daniel prayed to the Lord a prayer of confession, seeking forgiveness, mercy, and strength to obey.

INTRODUCTION

The apocalyptic emphasis found in Daniel 7–12 differs greatly from the narratives that came before. Whereas the first six chapters dealt with both natural and supernatural occurrences in the life of Daniel and his companions, the final six focus on Daniel's visions and prayers. The clear demarcation between halves of this book should not, however, suggest that Daniel is not a unified document. The clearest source of this unity is Daniel himself who is a faithful actor throughout much of the first six chapters. Daniel L. Smith-Christopher asserts that "the last six chapters of Daniel are the most important example of apocalyptic literature in the Hebrew Bible.... Apocalyptic is most generally defined as literature that deals with the revelation and understanding of mysteries...[Furthermore] an apocalypse is intended to interpret present earthly circumstances in the light of the supernatural world and of the future, and to influence both the understanding and the behavior of the audience by means of divine authority" ("Daniel" in *The New Interpreter's Bible,* Vol. 7 [Nashville, TN: Abingdon Press, 1996], 22).

The setting given for Daniel 9 is the first year of King Darius the Mede's reign (see

v. 1). Darius came to the throne following King Belshazzar. During Darius' reign, Daniel was thrown into the lions' den (see Dan. 6); Ezra and the Jewish population that returned to Jerusalem rebuilt the city and the temple with Darius' assistance (see Ezra 6). Daniel's visions recorded in chapters 11–12 are also set during Darius' reign. In Daniel 9:2, the scene is set—Daniel "perceived in the books the number of years that, according to the word of the LORD to the prophet Jeremiah, must be fulfilled for the devastation of Jerusalem, namely, seventy years" (NRSV). The "prayer and supplication" (v. 3, NRSV) that make up the body of this lesson are part of Daniel's work in exegeting the text of Jeremiah.

Commentators have noted that the prayer of Daniel 9 borrows significantly from other texts. W. Sibley Towner notes, "The words and traditions of older Israelite prayer are everywhere to be found. [James] Montgomery graphically demonstrates this dependency by identifying every word or phrase which can be paralleled elsewhere.... More than eighty-five percent of the text falls within quotation marks" (*Daniel* [Atlanta, GA: John Knox Press, 1984], 129). Of particular interest to Towner is the association with 1 Kings 8. Daniel seems to draw on King Solomon's words at the dedication of the temple both to confess sin and to call on the Lord to restore His people to the Promised Land. Whereas King Solomon stood before the people encouraging them to remain faithful to the Lord, Daniel knelt knowing that the people had been unfaithful to the Lord. Smith-Christopher builds on this association with 1 Kings 8 and includes Ezra 9. Ezra's life situation was much more similar to Daniel's than was King Solomon's. Both Ezra and Daniel appealed only to God's promises and righteousness, knowing that the people had failed in their covenant faithfulness.

EXPOSITION
I. CONFESSION OF SINS (DANIEL 9:4–6)

The covenant between the Lord and His chosen nation Israel placed requirements both on the Lord as initiator of the covenant and on the people as those who accepted His covenant and the benefits that came with it. In Deuteronomy 28 Moses and the Levites shared with the people the blessings that were included in the covenant with the Lord. Those blessings encompassed all of life, from work to home and everywhere in between (see vv. 3–14). However, the price of disobedience would be curses. Faithlessness to God's covenant did not come without severe consequences. Just like all of life would be blessed for faithfulness, all of life would be cursed because of faithlessness.

The exiled people in Babylon, especially their leaders, understood their defeat and subsequent exile as the judgment of God on their wickedness. Just as Moses and the Levites warned, "The LORD will cause you to be defeated before your enemies; you shall go out against them one way and flee before them seven ways. You shall become an object of horror to all the kingdoms of the earth" (v. 25, NRSV). Daniel knew that the exile in Babylon was God's punishment on His covenant people for the ways they had disregarded the covenant.

Daniel's prayer consistently demonstrates the seemingly insurmountable differences between the Lord and His people. The Lord is "'great and awesome… keeping covenant and steadfast love with those who love [Him] and keep [His] commandments'" (Dan. 9:4, NRSV). The failure of the covenant cannot be laid at God's feet; He made clear His requirements in the covenant. His love, even when the people were faithless, was never in doubt. That love was most clearly seen when the people also loved Him and honored that love by keeping His commandments. In those times, the Lord freely showered His people with peace and prosperity because He had their whole hearts.

For generations, Daniel confessed on behalf of the nation, they had "'sinned and done wrong, acted wickedly and rebelled, turning aside from your commandments and ordinances'" (v. 5, NRSV). He identifies with the people here, not passing the wickedness and rebellion on to others but shouldering the blame himself as well. Though he was too young to have participated in the sins that brought the nation to Babylon, Daniel knew that the faithfulness of Israel was a national effort. What began as sinfulness with kings, princes, and other ancestors continued in Israel as he knew them in Babylon. In this way, the people experienced punishment for sins that had begun generations before them (see Exod. 20:5–6; Num. 14:18).

The people could not pretend that their wickedness and rebellion was the result of ignorance. They had the Law and even the prophets. Alone among the various populations in Israel, the prophets are held up in Daniel's prayer as faithful to the Lord. They alone consistently followed His will and spoke His words. This asser-tion excludes, of course, false prophets who could not rightly be called prophets to begin with. Once again, Daniel included himself in the general population of people who ignored the words of the prophets and thus failed to keep covenant with the Lord.

II. THE SHAME OF SINS (DANIEL 9:7–8)

Careful attention should be paid in these two verses to the specific groups that Daniel mentions or fails to mention. In verse seven, he refers not just to the people of Judah or Jerusalem, as one would expect when speaking of the Babylonian exile, but also to the people of "all Israel" (v. 7, NRSV). This suggests that he is including the ten tribes of the northern kingdom of Israel in his statement here, even though following their exile in Assyria beginning in 722 B.C. the people of those ten tribes were lost as distinctively Israelite tribes. Daniel casts his net wide, speaking of "those who are near and those who are far away, in all the lands to which you have driven them" (v. 7, NRSV). Thus the people lost generations before in Assyria, those held captive in Babylon, those left behind in Judah or Israel, and those in any other nation of the world were included in the shame of their treachery.

Twice in verses 7–8 Daniel refers to the "open shame" (NRSV) or "confusion of face[s]" (KJV) of all of Israel. As the righteousness of the Lord was evident to anyone who sought His face, so the shame of Israel was clear to anyone who saw them. As before, this shame specifically fell on the kings, officials (in parallel to princes before), and the ancestors. Conspicuously missing from mention in this sinful group (due to the conspicuous mention of them before; see v. 6) are the prophets. Once again, Daniel counts himself among the sinful people who are experiencing the shame of their actions.

III. HOPE FOR FORGIVENESS OF SINS (DANIEL 9:15–19)

In verse eleven, Daniel's prayer shifts to a focus on the Law of Moses. The Law made known what the Lord expected from His people. The prophet Moses shared those laws with the people, including promises of curses for disobedience. This recall of Israel's exodus from Egypt continues in verse fifteen with Daniel's address to the Lord—"'O Lord our God, who brought your people out of the land of Egypt with a mighty hand and made your name renowned even to this day—we have sinned, we have done wickedly'" (NRSV). Thus the contrast between the Lord and His people is once again laid bare. Though He brought the people safely out of the Egypt and through the wilderness, His people beginning in that very generation provided a stark contrast to His faithfulness.

Without discounting the seriousness of their transgressions, Daniel appealed to the Lord to turn His wrath away from Jerusalem and the holy mountain. This very wrath which was poured out because of the people's wretchedness had made the people "'a disgrace among all our neighbors'" (v. 16, NRSV). This was not just problematic for the people. Their suffering reflected on the Lord as well. Thus Daniel began his true appeal to the Lord: "'Now therefore, O our God, listen to the prayer of your servant and to his supplication, and for your own sake, Lord, let your face shine upon your desolated sanctuary.

Incline your ear, O my God, and hear. Open your eyes and look at our desolation and the city that bears your name'" (vv. 17–18a, NRSV). Interestingly, although Daniel appeals to the Lord's name, he never calls the Lord "Yahweh" in verses 15–19, instead referring to Him as Elohim, "God" or Adonai, "Lord." This is typical of the book of Daniel but stands out particularly here when appealing to the Lord's name but refraining even from writing it down.

Daniel also took a new role upon himself. Throughout this prayer, Daniel has only been, like Isaiah, "'a man of unclean lips… among a people of unclean lips'" (Isa. 6:5, NRSV). Yet in supplication to the Lord, Daniel refers to himself as a servant—a role assigned in this chapter only to prophets (see Dan. 9:6, 10, 11, 17). Thus also like Isaiah, Daniel saw his role as an intermediary between the sinful people with whom he completely identified and the holy and righteous Lord whom he totally trusted to remain faithful to both His own character and His promises. His requests to the Lord were for Him to hear his prayer and see the desolation of Jerusalem and the temple within in. His only confidence was a great confidence—"'We do not present our supplication before you on the ground of our righteousness, but on the ground of your great mercies'" (v. 18b, NRSV). Once again speaking as one of the nation, not set apart from their sins even as a servant of the Lord, Daniel confidently asked the Lord to hear and see them because of His wonderful mercy. The people had not changed; they were still sinful and inclined to faithlessness. Neither had God changed.

He was still faithful to them and could be depended on to show mercy to the nation He loved.

Daniel ended his prayer with great ferocity: "'O Lord, hear; O Lord, forgive; O Lord, listen and act and do not delay! For your own sake, O my God, because your city and your people bear your name!'" (v. 19, NRSV). Though the people had not earned nor ever could earn forgiveness, Daniel trusted in the Lord. He knew that the way God's people had been treated reflected poorly on their God; other nations falsely believed Him to be without great power, easily defeated by the mightier gods of mightier nations. For the honor of His name, if for no other reason, Daniel trusted the Lord to restore His people. Following the conclusion of Daniel's prayer, the angel Gabriel came to him and revealed what the Lord would do.

THE LESSON APPLIED

Daniel was a man of his people, shaped by the great traditions and the grave sins of Israel, and a servant of his people as the prophets before him had been. When the angel Gabriel came to speak to Daniel, he spoke to him as to a prophet. Gabriel's response assured Daniel that his prayer had been heard and that the Lord would indeed restore His people. Though he knew his own sinfulness and the faithlessness that had taken Judah into exile in Babylon, Daniel also knew that the Lord is merciful and loving. He would look upon His people in kindness when their time in Babylon was completed.

LET'S TALK ABOUT IT

1. What is the Christian's responsibility in "Babylon" today?

Like Israel in Daniel's day, the Church today is scattered throughout the entire world. In some places, persecution is overt and horrifying; in others, more insidious coercive forces are at work on God's people. Whether the Lord's people realize their danger or not, the Church today still lives in Babylon. We have not yet been called to the full joy and peace of our own promised land. We live in the tension of eternal life beginning now but being constantly threatened by the temporal woes and wickedness of not only the world but our own words and deeds.

May the Church, like Daniel, confess that we are hopelessly lost without the Lord's mercy. May we also, as the prophets and priests, turn to intercession not only for those already numbered among God's people but for every nation. For the sake of His name, may the Lord call His faithful out of every nation and show His mighty works throughout the world.

HOME DAILY DEVOTIONAL READINGS
JANUARY 22–28, 2018

MONDAY	TUESDAY	WEDNESDAY	THURSDAY	FRIDAY	SATURDAY	SUNDAY
A Vision Sends Jacob to Egypt	Joshua, Be Strong and Courageous	Ezekiel Called to Speak to Israel	Paul Called to Macedonia in a Vision	Daniel Sees a Vision	Time of the End	Be Strong and Courageous
Genesis 46:1–7	Joshua 1:1–9	Ezekiel 1:26–2:7	Acts 16:6–10	Daniel 10:1–9	Daniel 12:8–13	Daniel 10:10–19

A STRONG FAITH

ADULT TOPIC: STRENGTH WHEN YOU NEED IT MOST	BACKGROUND SCRIPTURES: DANIEL 10; 11

DANIEL 10:10—19

King James Version

AND, behold, an hand touched me, which set me upon my knees and upon the palms of my hands.

11 And he said unto me, O Daniel, a man greatly beloved, understand the words that I speak unto thee, and stand upright: for unto thee am I now sent. And when he had spoken this word unto me, I stood trembling.

12 Then said he unto me, Fear not, Daniel: for from the first day that thou didst set thine heart to understand, and to chasten thyself before thy God, thy words were heard, and I am come for thy words.

13 But the prince of the kingdom of Persia withstood me one and twenty days: but, lo, Michael, one of the chief princes, came to help me; and I remained there with the kings of Persia.

14 Now I am come to make thee understand what shall befall thy people in the latter days: for yet the vision is for many days.

15 And when he had spoken such words unto me, I set my face toward the ground, and I became dumb.

16 And, behold, one like the similitude of the sons of men touched my lips: then I opened my mouth, and spake, and said unto him that stood before me, O my lord, by the vision my sorrows are turned upon me, and I have retained no strength.

17 For how can the servant of this my lord talk with this my lord? for as for me, straightway

New Revised Standard Version

BUT then a hand touched me and roused me to my hands and knees.

11 He said to me, "Daniel, greatly beloved, pay attention to the words that I am going to speak to you. Stand on your feet, for I have now been sent to you." So while he was speaking this word to me, I stood up trembling.

12 He said to me, "Do not fear, Daniel, for from the first day that you set your mind to gain understanding and to humble yourself before your God, your words have been heard, and I have come because of your words.

13 But the prince of the kingdom of Persia opposed me twenty-one days. So Michael, one of the chief princes, came to help me, and I left him there with the prince of the kingdom of Persia,

14 and have come to help you understand what is to happen to your people at the end of days. For there is a further vision for those days."

15 While he was speaking these words to me, I turned my face toward the ground and was speechless.

16 Then one in human form touched my lips, and I opened my mouth to speak, and said to the one who stood before me, "My lord, because of the vision such pains have come upon me that I retain no strength.

17 How can my lord's servant talk with my lord? For I am shaking, no strength remains in

MAIN THOUGHT: And said, O man greatly beloved, fear not: peace be unto thee, be strong, yea, be strong. And when he had spoken unto me, I was strengthened, and said, Let my lord speak; for thou hast strengthened me (Daniel 10:19, KJV)

DANIEL 10:10–19

King James Version

New Revised Standard Version

there remained no strength in me, neither is there breath left in me.

18 Then there came again and touched me one like the appearance of a man, and he strengthened me,

19 And said, O man greatly beloved, fear not: peace be unto thee, be strong, yea, be strong. And when he had spoken unto me, I was strengthened, and said, Let my lord speak; for thou hast strengthened me.

me, and no breath is left in me."

18 Again one in human form touched me and strengthened me.

19 He said, "Do not fear, greatly beloved, you are safe. Be strong and courageous!" When he spoke to me, I was strengthened and said, "Let my lord speak, for you have strengthened me."

LESSON SETTING
Time: 536 B.C.
Place: Babylon
LESSON OUTLINE
  I. Conflict Between Princes (Daniel 10:10–14)
 II. A Cure for Muteness (Daniel 10:15–17)
III. Strength and Courage (Daniel 10:18–19)

UNIFYING PRINCIPLE

Sometimes circumstances of life cause us to feel like we can't go on. Where can we find strength to do so? Daniel found strength in prayer and from the angel sent by God to encourage him and answer his prayer.

INTRODUCTION

The final three chapters of Daniel can be divided in various ways, but taken together they present Daniel's final apocalyptic vision of the future. Ernest Lucas clarifies that "'apocalypse is a genre of revelatory literature with a narrative framework, in which a revelation is mediated by an otherworldly being to a human recipient, disclosing a transcendent reality which is both temporal, insofar as it envisages escha-

tological salvation, and spatial, insofar as it involved another, supernatural world'…. [Chapters] 10–12 is the one section of the book that this definition [of apocalypses] fits well. In the terms of the definition, it is an apocalypse with a review of history" (*Daniel* [Downers Grove, IL: IVP Academic, 2002], 310). In other words, Daniel 10–12 fits the genre of apocalypse well because events in Daniel's time and place are explained partly by events that were happening in a different, supernatural place but at the same time. As mentioned in the first lesson on Daniel, commentators do not agree as to whether the book was written shortly after Daniel's own lifetime or several centuries later. The fact remains, however, that the events of concern in these chapters were not only Daniel's own time but also future times.

The historical setting here is "the third year of King Cyrus of Persia" (Dan. 10:1, NRSV). Daniel had been in mourning for three weeks, though the specific reason is not given. Daniel L. Smith-Christopher notes that "the twenty-fourth day of the first month" (v. 4, NRSV) corresponds to the Passover and "therefore, Daniel is mourning/fasting through Passover, the traditional Jewish celebration of release from captivity" ("Daniel" in *The New Interpreter's Bible,* Vol. 7 [Nashville, TN: Abingdon Press, 1996], 136). Smith-Christopher points out that this suggests, though the Persian rulers are seemingly given more positive attention from the prophets who experienced their reign including Ezra and Nehemiah and especially from the commentators who read about them, the Persian rulers such as Cyrus still represented cruel foreign powers who ideally would be defeated in order to release Israel from captivity under them.

The covenant with God did not include foreign powers except when Israel had been faithless to their God. That is to say, God never intended for Israel to live under the rule or influence of foreign powers. From the beginning, He had jealously guarded their status as His holy nation of priests, called to be a different nation, devoted only to the one true God. Being subject to foreign powers would jeopardize Israel's ability to remain faithful to the Lord because those powers would exert pressure on Israel to conform to their own customs, including idolatry and the sinful practices that accompanied false worship. However, Israel was aware that faithlessness would result in them being given over to their enemies. The imposition of foreign domination on Israel was not an oversight on God's part; it was a punishment meant to draw the people back to Him so that they could once more experience the blessings of being whole-heartedly devoted to Him.

On the banks of the Tigris River following his time of mourning, Daniel had a vision of a distinctive man (see vv. 5–6).

Despite being with others, Daniel alone saw this vision though they sensed it and "a great trembling fell upon them, and they fled and hid themselves" (v. 7, NRSV). For the first time in this chapter it is noted that Daniel's strength was sapped. Throughout chapter ten, Daniel's posture is of some interest and importance, demonstrating to what degree he was able to bear up under the burden of his visions and knowledge. In this state of weakness, with his face to the ground, Daniel heard the man speak. The content of his speech is not recorded here, and his identity remains something of a mystery to us.

EXPOSITION

I. CONFLICT BETWEEN PRINCES (DANIEL 10:10–14)

Daniel, face to the ground, felt a hand on him that "roused [him] to [his] hands and knees" (v. 10, NRSV). The hand may have been the hand of the angel Daniel had a vision of or, more likely, Gabriel. However, the actors in these final three chapters are not always easily distinguished one from another. More important than the precise identity of these angels is the message that they bring to Daniel concerning the trouble he has seen and the trouble he will see in his vision.

In speaking to Daniel, the angel called the man "greatly beloved" (v. 11, 19, NRSV). Gabriel had previously called Daniel the same in 9:23. The implications of this phrase being used to describe Daniel seems to be, first, reassurance and, second, a confirmation of his calling. Daniel's strength had fled him, but Gabriel reminded Daniel that he was specially favored by the Lord because he was greatly beloved. For this reason, Daniel had been given his unique abilities, blessings of God to be used to strengthen not only himself but also the other exiles and all of God's people. The greatly beloved Daniel was to stand and listen to the angel's words. Daniel obeyed, though he trembled as he stood.

Gabriel then gave Daniel words that are oft repeated throughout Scripture—"'Do not fear'" (v. 12, 19, NRSV). Daniel's fear here very likely could have been like the fear of others in the presence of angels, though he had experienced their presence and attention before. His fear also could have been as a result of what he saw and experienced in the Babylonian Empire, newly under control of the Persians. Gabriel gave Daniel reason not to fear— namely that "'from the first day that you set your mind to gain understanding and to humble yourself before your God, your words have been heard'" (v. 12, NRSV). These attitudes—of humility and of seeking wisdom—were certainly two attributes that commended Daniel to the service of the Lord and opened him up to visions and reassurances from the heavens. Being heard by God is no small matter. In Exodus 1, God's hearing the people's cries led directly to His acting on their behalf to deliver them from the land of Egypt. God does not hear His people's cries without moving to their aid. Gabriel's presence with Daniel was proof that the God who heard him was also the God who would act on his behalf.

Gabriel's next words recall Daniel's mourning period of three weeks. From the moment Daniel began his time of mourning, apparently Gabriel had been on his way to Daniel's side. However, "the prince of the kingdom of Persia opposed me twenty-one days" (v. 13, NRSV). When Michael, another prince and angel, arrived to help Gabriel, Gabriel made his escape, allowing Michael to continue the struggle with the prince of the kingdom of Persia. "This verse refers once again to the notion, apparently widespread in some circles of Jewish apocalyptic writing, that the various nations have spiritual counterparts, as Israel has the angel Michael.... The sources of this notion have been debated by scholars, many of whom see its roots in the idea of a heavenly council of celestial beings, perhaps a Jewish attempt to deal with the complexity of gods among the various foreign powers" (Smith-Christopher 137). As the psalmist wrote, "God has taken his place in the divine council; in the midst of the gods he holds judgment" (Ps. 82:1, NRSV). Whether Israel believed other gods were "real" or not, they acknowledged other spiritual forces that worked against the Lord and that other nations worshiped: "When the Most High apportioned the nations, when he divided humankind, he fixed the boundaries of the peoples according to the number of the gods; the LORD's own portion was his people, Jacob his allotted share" (Deut. 32:8–9, NRSV). Thus, W. Sibley Towner correctly asserts that "the panoply of heavenly beings which is involved bespeaks a cosmic struggle taking place in its own plane on a course parallel to the drama of human history" (*Daniel* [Atlanta, GA: John Knox Press, 1984], 147). Much of the vision shared in chapters 11–12 centers on this conflict in the heavens and how it makes itself known on earth. Gabriel had come now to Daniel to give him understanding about what was to come at "the end of days" (v. 14, NRSV).

II. A Cure for Muteness (Daniel 10:15–17)

Though Daniel had been standing, as he listened to Gabriel the man once more "turned [his] face toward the ground and was speechless" (v. 15, NRSV). Though he had been reassured by the touch of the hand earlier, that strength did not last. Now an angel, though perhaps not Gabriel, touched Daniel's mouth so that he could speak. "When compared to other prophets, Daniel seems to need more reassurance than most, but this serves to heighten the drama of what he is about to witness" (Smith-Christopher, 138). These other prophets include Isaiah and Jeremiah especially. Isaiah felt the touch of a hot coal in order to purify his lips from the sins that would prevent him from speaking for the Lord (see Isa. 6:5–8). In Jeremiah's case, the touch lent his young mouth the words to speak for the Lord (see Jer. 1:9–10). For Daniel, the touch did not represent being cleansed or being given words but instead receiving once more the power of speech.

Even with the power of speech, Daniel found that he struggled for words. He was in great pain and still felt incredibly weak because of the vision he had seen. How could Daniel speak when he had no strength? How could he speak without breath? What about the vision made him weak is impossible to say, though his period of mourning had probably included fasting, which likely contributed to his feeling of great weakness.

III. Strength and Courage (Daniel 10:18–19)

These two verses are largely a repetition of what an angel had said and done previously. As before, a hand touched Daniel and gave him strength through the touch (see vv. 10, 18). Once again, Daniel was told not to fear (see vv. 12, 19). Yet again, he was reminded that he was greatly beloved (see vv. 11, 19). Far from becoming boring, the repetition of these key actions and words further reaffirmed for Daniel that he was called to the work he was doing and that it was a sign of favor from the Lord to be given this work.

Then the words of this angel differ from what he had said before. He told Daniel to pay attention before; now he tells him to "'be strong and courageous!'" (v. 19, NRSV). Whereas the touch on Daniel's lips recalled both Jeremiah and Isaiah in their prophetic callings, these words echo instead from Joshua. Repeatedly after Moses' death, Joshua was called to strength and courage by the Lord who would not "'fail you or forsake you'" (Josh. 1:5, NRSV). Although the land of Israel was still under Persian control and would not see a Davidic king ruling in Jerusalem again, these words might have reminded Daniel that the Lord who had called him was the same Lord who had the power to give His people whatever land He saw fit against any foreign gods or nations. Just as God was with Joshua and Israel, so God was with Daniel and exiled Israel and would continue to be with Israel, even after Daniel had died.

These words finally strengthened Daniel. He told the angel as much, and waited to hear what would be told to him now that he had the strength to stand and listen. With these words Daniel welcomed words about the end of days and the conflicts that would arise between nations even as their spiritual representatives also warred against one other. These mysteries, still intriguing today, were only revealed to Daniel after he was given the strength bear them.

THE LESSON APPLIED

As Daniel listened to Gabriel's words, he could be reminded of God's work in Israel from the time of their slavery in Egypt to the present time. God heard Israel's cries in Egypt before He acted on their behalf; Daniel could be assured that God heard his own cries and would act on behalf of him and Israel once again. God told Joshua to be strong and courageous because He would be with him; Daniel could continue to be strong and courageous for the same reason. God had cleansed and strengthened Isaiah and Jeremiah concerning the words of their mouths; He loosened Daniel's own tongue for similar purposes. Let the Church today be reminded that God is still at work in His world, and when we remember the stories of those who walked faithfully before us—biblical characters, faith leaders of the past, mentors and family members who have passed into their eternal home—we will find that God is working through us just as He did them so that we might better honor Him in our faithfulness and service to Him.

LET'S TALK ABOUT IT

1. **How can Christians today be reassured of God's continued work in the world in the face of threats of violence and ever-present danger?**

Most Christians will not have a personal encounter with an angel. This does not mean, of course, that most Christians do not experience any reassurance from the Lord. Like Daniel, we can look to the faithful women and men who came before us, looking to our own history and the stories that have become our history through our faith. Like Daniel, we can expect the Lord to send us comfort—from the Holy Spirit Himself, or a friend or minister, or maybe a stranger—to reassure us that, just as He was with His people in the danger and pain of exile, so too is He with all of His people today in whatever dangerous and painful places we find ourselves. Ultimately, God will redeem His people and deliver us from sin and death and all the pain that these horrible realities cause us. Until that day, we can be strong and courageous in the knowledge that we are beloved by the God who hears us.

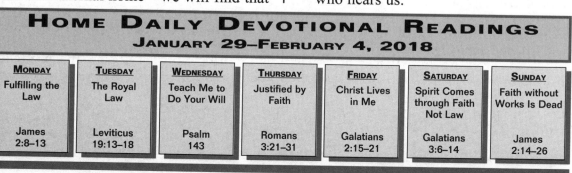

HOME DAILY DEVOTIONAL READINGS
JANUARY 29–FEBRUARY 4, 2018

MONDAY	TUESDAY	WEDNESDAY	THURSDAY	FRIDAY	SATURDAY	SUNDAY
Fulfilling the Law	The Royal Law	Teach Me to Do Your Will	Justified by Faith	Christ Lives in Me	Spirit Comes through Faith Not Law	Faith without Works Is Dead
James 2:8–13	Leviticus 19:13–18	Psalm 143	Romans 3:21–31	Galatians 2:15–21	Galatians 3:6–14	James 2:14–26

FAITH WITHOUT WORKS IS DEAD

ADULT TOPIC:	BACKGROUND SCRIPTURES:
ACTIONS SPEAK LOUDER THAN WORDS	JAMES 2:14–26

JAMES 2:14–26

King James Version	*New Revised Standard Version*
WHAT doth it profit, my brethren, though a man say he hath faith, and have not works? can faith save him?	WHAT good is it, my brothers and sisters, if you say you have faith but do not have works? Can faith save you?
15 If a brother or sister be naked, and destitute of daily food,	15 If a brother or sister is naked and lacks daily food,
16 And one of you say unto them, Depart in peace, be ye warmed and filled; notwithstanding ye give them not those things which are needful to the body; what doth it profit?	16 and one of you says to them, "Go in peace; keep warm and eat your fill," and yet you do not supply their bodily needs, what is the good of that?
17 Even so faith, if it hath not works, is dead, being alone.	17 So faith by itself, if it has no works, is dead.
18 Yea, a man may say, Thou hast faith, and I have works: shew me thy faith without thy works, and I will shew thee my faith by my works.	18 But someone will say, "You have faith and I have works." Show me your faith apart from your works, and I by my works will show you my faith.
19 Thou believest that there is one God; thou doest well: the devils also believe, and tremble.	19 You believe that God is one; you do well. Even the demons believe—and shudder.
20 But wilt thou know, O vain man, that faith without works is dead?	20 Do you want to be shown, you senseless person, that faith apart from works is barren?
21 Was not Abraham our father justified by works, when he had offered Isaac his son upon the altar?	21 Was not our ancestor Abraham justified by works when he offered his son Isaac on the altar?
22 Seest thou how faith wrought with his works, and by works was faith made perfect?	22 You see that faith was active along with his works, and faith was brought to completion by the works.
23 And the scripture was fulfilled which saith, Abraham believed God, and it was imputed unto him for righteousness: and he was called the Friend of God.	23 Thus the scripture was fulfilled that says, "Abraham believed God, and it was reckoned to him as righteousness," and he was called the friend of God.
24 Ye see then how that by works a man is justified, and not by faith only.	24 You see that a person is justified by works and not by faith alone.
25 Likewise also was not Rahab the harlot justified by works, when she had received the	25 Likewise, was not Rahab the prostitute also justified by works when she welcomed

MAIN THOUGHT: Even so faith, if it hath not works, is dead, being alone. (James 2:17, KJV)

JAMES 2:14—26

King James Version

messengers, and had sent them out another way?

26 For as the body without the spirit is dead, so faith without works is dead also.

New Revised Standard Version

the messengers and sent them out by another road?

26 For just as the body without the spirit is dead, so faith without works is also dead.

LESSON SETTING

Time: A.D. 45–62
Place: Jerusalem

LESSON OUTLINE

I. What Is Profitable: Faith or Works? (James 2:14–16)

II. Faith Without Works Is Dead (James 2:17–20)

III. Two Examples of Faith and Works (James 2:21–26)

UNIFYING PRINCIPLE

People know that talk is cheap and that actions speak louder than words. How are we to live in this regard? James says that our professions of faith must be matched by accompanying action.

INTRODUCTION

The book of James was written by the brother of our Lord Jesus, who became one of the dominant leaders in the church at Jerusalem. Jesus' family may not have fully understood the scope of His ministry, but the fact that members of Jesus' family ultimately came to believe in Him is not surprising given the divine nature of His birth and Mary's pondering the events of that day in her heart. Certainly she and Joseph shared the uniqueness of their oldest Son's birth with His siblings.

Initially, James' authorship was disputed among scholars because the book was not accepted early on during the canon process. But most scholars have come to attribute the book to him because of its authoritarian style and distinguished Jewish background. Additionally, tradition has attributed the book to James as well.

This letter is listed as a general epistle and does not contain the normal epistolary components. Once the book announces its composer, it briefly points out its recipients, the twelve tribes in the Dispersion (v. 1). This may be a reference to Deuteronomy 30:1–2, where the Hebrew people are reminded to take the precepts of their faith with them wherever they go. James wants his readers to hold to the tenets of the faith, even in light of the persecutions that have forced the disciples out of Jerusalem. Several of the tenets of the faith that James proposes are taken from the Jewish law. Leviticus 19 serves as an appropriate backdrop for the brother of our Lord to reconfirm the necessity of love, the value of impartiality, not judging others, resisting the urge to grumble and swear, a commitment to love one's neighbor as oneself, and to rebuke one's neighbor to keep him or her from falling into sin (Lev. 2:1, 8–9, 4:11, 5:4, 9, 12, 20). James calls the reader to holiness, and this holiness has certain ethical requirements.

There is no long salutation, nor are there any claims of apostolic membership in the book, just a word to encourage readers to be doers of the Word (James 1:25). The book deals with the moral, ethical, and practical aspects and implications of what it means to be followers of Jesus, corporately and individually. The book also has no specific theme and was initially thought to be merely a collection of materials loosely fitted together. The most common categorization of it is to classify James as wisdom literature, much like Proverbs (A. T. Robertson, *The Expositor's Greek Testament*, Vol. 4 [Grand Rapids: Eerdmans, 1980], 398–399).

The epistle is void of deep theological issues such as the death and resurrection of Jesus and what these events meant for the Church. The writer evidently assumed these positions had been adequately expressed by others and concluded these matters did not fit within his purpose. It is clear from a reading of the book that the social outlook of the Gospel appealed to James. Maybe Jesus' declaration in His initial sermon in Luke 4:16–21 had some type of impact on him as He declared His views on oppression and of the bruising others. It is highly possible that the social unrest that affected Jerusalem during this time had a profound impact on the Lord's brother and led to the composition of this letter.

The church in Jerusalem had become a community of the poor and suffered to some extent from internal discrimination (see James 2:1–13). Witnessing such poverty and at the same time watching the wealthy cashing in on their privileged status was of great concern to James, an issue that he addressed in this letter. James well understood the problem of ignoring the poor presented for the church and was determined to bring it to the attention of the body. Addressing this issue led to the argument of "faith versus works." James' attempt to balance faith with works has led some Christians to believe that Paul and James contradicted one another. However, James looked upon works as an outgrowth of one's faith, and not as works righteousness. A doer of the Word automatically practices the things he or she believes in. The conviction of the hearts reveals itself in one's actions. A strong belief in Jesus, who went about doing good, means one who professes faith in Him as Lord and Savior goes about doing good as well. James deplored Christian practice that did not correspond with Christian faith (James 1:22). For him it was not an either/or situation. They were twin sides of the same coin as our examination of this text will uncover.

An examination of this periscope of Scripture suggests that it is quite possible that James composed this piece as a corrective to Paul's claim that faith alone justified one before God. It is also highly possible that it was in reaction to a perceived or even a deliberate misunderstanding of Paul's depiction of faith. This study attempts to clear up the appearance of what some have seen as a contradiction.

Three things are important in this examination. First, James asked his readers, "What does it profit to speak of faith and not have works?" James gets to the root of the matter with this question. For him the two are not at opposite ends of the spectrum. Second, James concluded from his analysis that faith without works is dead. In this sense, faith is merely a verbal assertion and for the apostle talk is cheap. Finally, James uses two illustrations of faith by Old Testament characters to prove his point,

Abraham and Rahab. He points to their actions as the completion of their faith.

EXPOSITION

I. WHAT IS PROFITABLE: FAITH OR WORKS? (JAMES 2:14–16)

Verses 1–12 of this chapter address the issue of favoritism. James' point is that Christians cannot base our offering of salvation on wealth or affluence. All are welcome to receive the message of Christ's salvation, especially the poor. James castrated the belief that the wealthy and affluent were more important and should have, therefore, a privileged position over the poor. He said, "Listen, my beloved brethren. Has not God chosen those who are poor in the world to be rich in faith and heirs of the Kingdom which He has promised to those who love Him? But you have dishonored the poor man. Is it the not rich who oppress you? Is it not they who drag you to court?" It was out of his affinity for the poor and downtrodden that James waded into this perceived dichotomy between faith and works. He had witnessed the church proclaim one thing yet do another. He had had enough of the back and forth. He would give his assessment of the issue at hand.

James starts this section with a question about the profitability of faith without works. Faith as used here is a conviction or belief in Jesus Christ as Lord and Savior (vv. 14–16). Works are the actions or deeds that stem from faith. So if there are no works, there is no evidence of faith. Is James asking if words alone save us? Is he alluding here to a works' righteousness type of theology? Is he picking an argument with Paul who concluded, "For by grace you have been saved through faith, and this is not your own doing; it is the gift of God—not the result of works, so that no one may boast" (Eph. 2:8–9, NRSV)? At first glance it appears James is confronting a deep theological issue, faith versus works. Martin Luther saw it as a theological rift with Paul and conveyed his detestation with James' account. He saw the two as diametrically opposite accounts and argued that based on this issue James' book did not merit canonization. However, Luther erroneously read his concern into James' account, rather than to interpret it on its own merit. Luke T. Johnson sees it as a non-issue, once the word "save" is carefully examined. He said, "James's topic is not really soteriology; he has already declared that it is the 'implanted word' from God that 'is able to save your souls' (1:21). The issue is, rather, how to be a 'doer' of that word" ("James" in *The New Interpreter's Bible,* Vol. XII [Nashville: Abingdon Press, 1998], 197). Doing requires action, not verbalization. If one has faith, then that faith can be seen in corresponding action. It is worthwhile to note that this action is not a replacement of one's attitudinal disposition of faith, but according to Johnson, "actions reveal the attitude and make it 'alive'" (ibid.).

Therefore, according to Johnson, the issue that gave Luther concern was not an issue at all. James does not deal with works' righteousness, but works as an outgrowth of one's faith. James echoes Paul's words from Galatians 5:6, "'neither circumcision nor uncircumcision counts for anything; the only thing that counts is faith working through love'" (NRSV).

James proves this by asking an illustrative rhetorical question. If a brother or sister is naked or hungry and is told to stay warm, eat food, and reside in peace, and a Christian fails to provide the basic necessities for these things to occur, what good is that kind of faith? The only conclusion one can reach here is this type of faith is empty, the same type of empty religion James referred to earlier (1:26–27). Faith that has no demonstrative power is not profitable, either to the Christian who purports to have it or to the needy who depend on gracious hearts for loving assistance.

II. Faith Without Works is Dead (James 2:17–20)

After pointing out the obvious, James comes out with the point of the issue at hand, "faith without works is dead," because then it is just a statement and not a matter of the heart that leads to outward action. James set up a conversation with a straw man, arguing one side for faith and the other for works. The straw man says, "'You have faith and I have works,'" to which James responds, "'Show me your faith apart from your works, and I by my works will show you my faith'" (v. 18, NRSV). For the straw man, faith and works are two entirely separate things, but for James they are intrinsically connected. As stated earlier, they were the twin sides of the same coin. One's actions revealed the extent of one's faith. No faith inspires no action, little faith inspires little action, and large faith can inspire a plurality of actions. James goes one step further to illustrate his point: even the devils believe, but their belief does not result in positive change that corresponds to a conviction to obey God. This illustrates that simply believing is not the same thing as true complete faith.

III. Two Examples of Faith and Works (James 2:21–26)

After using the straw man to make his point, James proceeded to answer his own question by providing two examples of people who demonstrated faithful action in the Old Testament, Abraham and Rahab. Paul also used Abraham in Romans and Galatians to illustrate his point in regard to faith (Rom. 4; Gal. 3:6–15, 23). Both Paul and James see Genesis 15:6 as a critical example of what it means to have faith, but James takes it one step further. He sees Abraham's obedience as a demonstration of the faith he verbalized. The actual offering of Isaac was the work or action that proved Abraham possessed faith. The truly faithful follow through and provide concrete evidence of their faith with positive action. It was Abraham's obedience that earned him the title "friend of God." Jesus also told His disciples, "'You are my friends if you do what I command you'" (John 15:14, NRSV). Obedience to God is the evidence of faith, whereas disobedience is the evidence of enmity. The first parents entered into a relationship of enmity with God because they put faith in the serpent rather than in their Creator (see Gen. 3:1–15). One cannot defy God's word and be faithful to Him. To have faith in God is to prioritize the divine–human relationship. Rahab prioritized this relationship by choosing to hide the Israelite spies rather than obey the king of Jericho (see Josh. 2). James implies that she expressed faith in God through her act of offering a safe haven to Joshua's men.

Her actions secured for her family a name in the list of heroes of faith (Heb. 11:31).

James concluded this pericope by stating his case for works as an outgrowth of faith. Believers must have an active faith that reveals itself in demonstrative acts of righteousness. Real religion consists of people carrying out their faith by ministering to the needs of others.

THE LESSON APPLIED

This lesson is about doing the Word. Faith is not complete without actions that portray the life of Jesus. This requires doing. Our convictions of faith must be acted out; otherwise they remain only sentiments of the mind. The devils believe in God but remain steadfast in their refusal to do works of righteousness. Hence, their belief is not faith in the sense that James and Paul used the term. The Christian faith is the conviction that God created humanity and it fell into sin through rebellion against God. So God sent his Son Jesus to give His life as a ransom for all. He came and chose disciples to carry forth the Good News to the world. This Good News includes both proclamation and demonstration of the love of God. That is to say that our walk must fit our religious talk. Our actions are the evidence of what we say; they speak louder than our words. If we truly have faith, we must allow it to speak for itself through our actions as we follow Christ's example.

LET'S TALK ABOUT IT

1. Can we earn our way into the Kingdom of God?

No! The Scriptures are quite clear that salvation cannot be earned. Salvation comes through faith in Jesus Christ as our only way back to God. Our commitment to serve Him as our Lord and Savior means we share God's message of love with others by ministering to their needs. It is not enough to simply profess our own faith. But our works are not our righteousness. Our righteousness is as filthy rags and does not in and of itself wipe away our sin. Only faith in Jesus does that. Through faith, Jesus' righteous life is imputed into us and God wipes away our sin through the blood He shed on the cross of Calvary. The work we do in His name is therefore the fruit of our faith.

2. What is true religion?

True religion in the Christian context is to live out the mandates of the faith. God is to be honored through praising Him with our entire being. But this praise must also include a lifestyle of serving God by serving others. James argued that true religion is manifested through practice.

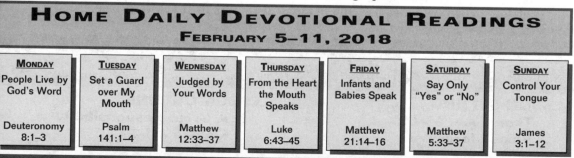

HOME DAILY DEVOTIONAL READINGS
FEBRUARY 5–11, 2018

MONDAY	TUESDAY	WEDNESDAY	THURSDAY	FRIDAY	SATURDAY	SUNDAY
People Live by God's Word	Set a Guard over My Mouth	Judged by Your Words	From the Heart the Mouth Speaks	Infants and Babies Speak	Say Only "Yes" or "No"	Control Your Tongue
Deuteronomy 8:1–3	Psalm 141:1–4	Matthew 12:33–37	Luke 6:43–45	Matthew 21:14–16	Matthew 5:33–37	James 3:1–12

A Disciplined Faith

ADULT TOPIC:	BACKGROUND SCRIPTURES:
TAMING THE TONGUE	JAMES 3:1–12

JAMES 3:1–12

King James Version	*New Revised Standard Version*
AND the Lord spake unto Moses, saying,	THE Lord spoke to Moses:
10 Speak unto the children of Israel, and say unto them, When ye be come into the land which I give unto you, and shall reap the harvest thereof, then ye shall bring a sheaf of the firstfruits of your harvest unto the priest:	10 Speak to the people of Israel and say to them: When you enter the land that I am giving you and you reap its harvest, you shall bring the sheaf of the first fruits of your harvest to the priest.
11 And he shall wave the sheaf before the Lord, to be accepted for you: on the morrow after the sabbath the priest shall wave it.	11 He shall raise the sheaf before the Lord, that you may find acceptance; on the day after the sabbath the priest shall raise it.
12 And ye shall offer that day when ye wave the sheaf an he lamb without blemish of the first year for a burnt offering unto the Lord.	12 On the day when you raise the sheaf, you shall offer a lamb a year old, without blemish, as a burnt offering to the Lord.
13 And the meat offering thereof shall be two tenth deals of fine flour mingled with oil, an offering made by fire unto the Lord for a sweet savour: and the drink offering thereof shall be of wine, the fourth part of an hin.	13 And the grain offering with it shall be two-tenths of an ephah of choice flour mixed with oil, an offering by fire of pleasing odor to the Lord; and the drink offering with it shall be of wine, one-fourth of a hin.
14 And ye shall eat neither bread, nor parched corn, nor green ears, until the selfsame day that ye have brought an offering unto your God: it shall be a statute for ever throughout your generations in all your dwellings.	14 You shall eat no bread or parched grain or fresh ears until that very day, until you have brought the offering of your God: it is a statute forever throughout your generations in all your settlements.
• • • • • •	• • • • • •
22 And when ye reap the harvest of your land, thou shalt not make clean riddance of the corners of thy field when thou reapest, neither shalt thou gather any gleaning of thy harvest: thou shalt leave them unto the poor, and to the stranger: I am the LORD your God.	22 When you reap the harvest of your land, you shall not reap to the very edges of your field, or gather the gleanings of your harvest; you shall leave them for the poor and for the alien: I am the Lord your God.

MAIN THOUGHT: But the tongue can no man tame; it is an unruly evil, full of deadly poison. (James 3:8, KJV)

LESSON SETTING
Time: A.D. 45–62
Place: Jerusalem

LESSON OUTLINE
I. A Great Responsibility
(James 3:1–2)

II. Little Things Wield Great Power
   (James 3:3–8)
III. Things That Should Not Be
   (James 3:9–12)

UNIFYING PRINCIPLE

Everyone knows the pain and destruction that result from hurtful words. How do we keep from causing such pain and destruction? James says that we should control our tongue so that only blessings come from it.

INTRODUCTION

In the previous lesson, James dealt with the social aspects of being a Christian. It is like looking at a bathroom mirror and seeing ourselves for what we are in light of what God intended for us to be. James pushes us toward the latter. As such the book does not deal with doctrine or deep theological issues. Rather, the practical aspects of ministry are what are important to James.

From the very beginning of his book, James addressed the ministry of Christian conduct and behavior.

In chapter one his major point of emphasis is to define the nature of true religion. True religion is to be the helping hands to those who are in need and to live differently from those in the world. The focus is on serving God by serving others. Jesus is the ideal model for those pursing the Christian ministry.

Chapter two covers two major points. Verses one through twelve examine the issue of partiality. James explicitly warns us that one's wealth should not equate into a position of privilege where the church is concerned. God welcomes all people, rich and poor alike, and the church must commitment itself to meeting the needs of people of all persuasions. James was concerned that the poor would be left out of the church's ministry if the focus was on the rich. The second half of chapter two examined the issue of faith versus works. For the brother of Jesus, the two were considered to be indivisible, the twin sides of the same coin. Works was an outgrowth of one's faith and not something that challenged it. James saw works as a clear cut demonstration of faith.

Chapter three is where we began our study for this session. It analyzed the issue of uncontrolled and unchristian speech, which negatively affected the ministry of the church. Three things are important in this study. First, James warns teachers of the great responsibility they have to teach. They will be judged more critically because of their position of responsibility. Second, he compares and contrasts the size and influence of the tongue with small devices and their ability to control large powerful animals and ships. Also, James compares the tongue with fire and its ability to destroy and contrasts its ability to resist being tamed with wild beasts that can be brought into subjection. For James the tongue used inappropriately was a pot of evil and destruction. Third, James discouraged the use of it to praise God, the Creator of all people, while cursing the very people He made. He refuted being double-tongue and expressed sorrow and regret at its existence.

At the heart of this pericope of Scripture is uncontrolled and unchristian speech which James deplored and felt as devoid of true religion. His prohibition here is designed to convince the Christian of the folly of being double-minded and doubled-mouthed.

EXPOSITION

I. A GREAT RESPONSIBILITY (JAMES 3:1–2)

One of the hallmarks of James' book is his colloquial relationship with his readers. His tone and appeal is matched only by the Apostle John. John used the phrase "my little children" and James used the terms "my brothers and sisters" (I John 2:1, 12, 18; James 1:2; 2:1; 3:1, 10; 5:19, NRSV). He may have framed the message with this type of greeting and brotherly appeal because he was addressing issues that were problematic for the church to consider. His goal is to correct Christian misconduct without further opening the wound inflicted upon the church and to heal any divisions among its ranks. A clear expression of the circumstance that warranted this writing by James was, therefore, needed.

The first two verses are a basic introduction to what lies ahead. Those who provide instruction to others receive the most critical evaluations so he warns his readers to not be so anxious to become teachers. There is a clear complaint that too many of the Jewish Christians were attempting to teach things they did not clearly comprehend. James pointed out the responsibility they entailed in their profession as an awesome one. The teacher is treated here as the wise man. The rabbi was the teacher, a name which, even Jesus answered to (Matt. 23:7; John 1:38; 3:10; 20:16). Nicodemus addressed Jesus as a rabbi, a teacher come from God. The rich young ruler addressed Him as "Teacher" (Matt. 19:16–17). Teachers occupied an honorable position among Christians (Eph. 4:11; Acts 13:1). The text reveals James saw himself as a teacher (3:1–2). Done right teaching was viewed as a noble profession. James believed teachers are necessary, but incompetent and unworthy ones do a lot of harm for obvious reasons. The pretense of knowledge adds to the teacher's responsibility and condemnation. Being entrusted with leading people into truth meant they should accept the sobering responsibility of eternal decisions. For James teaching the eternal truth of the Gospel was literally a matter of life and death.

Therefore, such weighty matters carried with them heavy consequences for those who used their influence carelessly or for selfish purposes. Good solid teaching deals with the church's spiritual health and vitality. The lack of it, as James suggests may be the reason many fall into the snare of sin and the evil one (James 1:12–15). The danger that James alludes to in this passage of Scripture is that of being focused on programs that the church has turned a blind eye or have looked the other way concerning some instructors who cannot or have not rightly claimed the teaching office.

Does this mean that teachers are to be perfect? Of course not, James admitted in verse two. Including himself in the mix, James confessed, "We all fall down in many ways." The "we" in the passage is James admission of imperfection. Only Jesus was perfect. Good teachers are the ones that understand their imperfections and make efforts to correct or improve upon them. Pursuit of the ideal is, even if totally unattainable, is James' point here. To exercise control over one's speech is a virtue the teacher must possess. This requires us to bridle ourselves so that the entire body is not full of confusion. James used here the same word he used in 1:26 to point out that failing to bridle the tongue nullifies one's religiosity and disqualifies one as a teacher and practitioner of authentic religion.

II. LITTLE THINGS WIELD GREAT POWER
(JAMES 3:3–8)

In this section, James takes the issue of bridling to another level. He includes other analogies to illustrate his point. A bit put into the mouth of a horse can effectively turn the whole animal so that it obeys our pull on it. The Greek for bit is taken from another form of the word bridle. Bridling one's tongue has the same effect, in terms of controlling one's whole body that bridling a horse does in controlling the horse. James shows that bits are much smaller than horses as the tongue is much smaller than the body. Yet the power these small things have over much larger and more powerful creatures is incredible. The bit in the mouth of the horse wields great influence and power over the horse, which was until the turn of the 20th century one of the major modes of transportation in the world. In the same way the discipline of controlling the tongue as small as it is, in comparison with the rest of the body, yields results far in excess of its physical size. Controlling the tongue is effective in controlling the whole person.

In the next analogy using ships, the same principles come through. Regardless of the size of the ship they have rudders, which are normally much small than the ship to guide them. Pilots use these steering mechanisms to direct their vessels. This fact reaffirmed James intent to hold the tongue ultimately responsible for its actions. That is to say that words coming from this small member of the body are significant. Teachers and others who use words in the professions and vocations must realize the importance of their words. Peoples' lives have been destroyed because of their inability to control their patterns of speech.

In verses five and six, James referred to the tongue as a cauldron full of evil. Despite its smallness the tongue make great boasts. James compares it to the damage done by a small fire left uncontrolled in the forest. The blaze may start from a small camp fire, but left unattended soon spreads to engulf the entire forest. History is filled with a plethora of individuals, families, and even nations that have effectively met their demise because of intemperate, careless words. To avoid such situations James' letter demonstrated that loose words and careless chatter makes a difficult situation even worse. The good teacher knows better and should appreciate the power of words.

Fire as meant here denotes it can be used as a resource or as a tool for destruction. When harnessed fire warms, cooks, and in today society produces electricity and other benefits. But when out of control it has potentially destructive forces. James compared the tongue with this deadly potentiality. He makes this comparison because the tongue has a tendency or disposition toward evil in human beings.

It has the power to corrupt the body in the same way the small rudders have of determining the direction of whole ships.

James used the word for corruption here (v. 6) and earlier in 1:27 where he insisted that Christian believers keep themselves uncorrupted from the world. Lack of control over the tongue carries the potentiality to destroy other by starting blazing fires in their lives. Being succumbed to evil influences the tongue subjects itself to the fires of hell. Hence, the apostle is unapologetic in issuing an indictment against loose lips.

Finally James addressed how the tongue resists being tamed. His appeal in this pericope is to nature. Human being has dominant all areas of the world, even ferocious wild beast have been tamed. The word tame means to subdue. But despite human ingenuity the tongue according to James remains untamed. The word is also used in Mark 5:4 where the demon-possessed man could not be subdued by the community. James contends that perfect control of the tongue is humanly impossible. "'It is a restless evil, full of deadly poison'" (V. 8). The origins of most human conflict start with words being inappropriately used. It is not merely subject and verb disagreement, but words loosely used to define another's character, present erroneous untruths, and attempts to mislead and miseducate people that James has in mind here. This is the poison he is referring to. Proverbs, another book that falls within the category of wisdom literature, is replete with verbiage that warns its readers to be conscious of one's speech (See, Prov. 10:19; 12:6; 12:18; 15;1; 17:27; 25:11). James would argue against the contemporary adage that goes, "'Sticks and stones

may break my bones, but words will never hurt me.'" Words can hurt because they take on being and a life of their own. Once spoken, words cannot be revoked. James realized the importance of words. In James 1:18 he spoke of the word of truth. In 2:1, he told his readers, "'so speak and act as those who are to be judged under the law of liberty.'" As a teacher himself, he knew the benefit of a bridled tongue. It was false words that led to the fall of the first parents (Gen. 3). Additionally, those who sought to build a tower to heaven had their languages confounded because they failed to understand that the building of society required communication with God, rather than self-made flattery. The book of Acts proved this to be true. People from the diaspora gathered together and understood each other through the power of the Holy Spirit (Acts 1). What could not be achieved in Genesis in the building of the tower, God achieved as the Holy Spirit spoke the language of love on Pentecost.

III. THINGS THAT SHOULD NOT BE (JAMES 3:9–12)

James moves on to confront the issue of being double-minded. The tongue is used to praise God on the one-hand and to curse the people God has created on the other. Sadly, James confessed, "'My brothers and sisters, this should not be'" (James 3:9–10). Praising God and cursing those whom He has made in His own image and likeness is totally unacceptable behavior. James repudiated this type of behavior and saw it as conflicting with real religion. Real religion has singleness of purpose, which is to please God. God is not pleased when we are at enmity with our fellow persons. I John 4:20 asked, "'how can one love the invisible God and hate his or her fellows that are seen daily.'" John explicitly says it cannot be done. One cannot praise God on the one hand and curse one's brother on the other. The two are inconsistent with one another.

James backed up his point with two illustrations. Can a salt spring produce fresh water? Nor can a fig tree bear olives or a grapevine bear figs? The answer to these is an emphatic no. Neither then can one praise God and curse one's brothers. The double-mindedness referred to earlier in this book comes to full fruition here at the end of chapter three. It is a contradiction to authentic religion just as a salt spring producing fresh water is a contradiction. Blessings and curses coming from the same lips is likewise a contradiction. In chapter two James warned mere words apart from action are dead. Now in chapter three he argues that uncontrolled words are deadly. The practice of true religion is only successful when teachers of the God's truth demonstrate their religiosity by exercising caution in their thoughts, words, and deeds.

THE LESSON APPLIED

The Christian talk must fit the Christian walk. Praising God and cursing others He has made is inconsistent and incompatible with authentic worship. James encourages teachers and all Christians to be sure their religious practice grows out of their faith. Faith can never be double-minded or double-mouthed. Praising God means to serve others, who are made in His image with decency and respect. The words we use must be selected carefully so we do not misrepresent the Lord we serve..

LET'S TALK ABOUT IT

1. **If the tongue can be used so destructively is there any hope that it can be redeemed?**

Redemption is always possible when one gives him or herself over to the controlling power of the Holy Spirit. That is why James wrote this book. He wanted his readers to understand what authentic worship consisted of. True religion is to embrace the faith of our Lord Jesus and to allow it to inaugurate change in our hearts and lives. All members of our bodies will be affected in a positive way when the Holy Spirit is allowed to take control of our tongues.

1. **What does James mean by true religion?**

True religion is to practice before God the conditions upon which we establish faith in Jesus Christ. It is worship with our mouths as well as with our hearts. The first commandment reminds us we must worship God with our total being.

HOME DAILY DEVOTIONAL READINGS
FEBRUARY 12–18, 2018

MONDAY	TUESDAY	WEDNESDAY	THURSDAY	FRIDAY	SATURDAY	SUNDAY
Widow's Son Restored to Life	Jesus Raises Widow's Son	Care for Widows and Orphans	Peter's Healing Ministry	Philip's Preaching Ministry	Aeneas Healed, Residents Turn to God	Calling the Church to Active Service
1 Kings 17:17–24	Luke 7:11–17	James 1:22–27	Acts 5:12–16	Acts 8:4	Acts 9:32–35	Acts 9:36–43

FAITHFUL DISCIPLES

ACTS 9:36–43

King James Version	New Revised Standard Version
NOW there was at Joppa a certain disciple named Tabitha, which by interpretation is called Dorcas: this woman was full of good works and almsdeeds which she did.	NOW in Joppa there was a disciple whose name was Tabitha, which in Greek is Dorcas. She was devoted to good works and acts of charity.
37 And it came to pass in those days, that she was sick, and died: whom when they had washed, they laid her in an upper chamber.	37 At that time she became ill and died. When they had washed her, they laid her in a room upstairs.
38 And forasmuch as Lydda was nigh to Joppa, and the disciples had heard that Peter was there, they sent unto him two men, desiring him that he would not delay to come to them.	38 Since Lydda was near Joppa, the disciples, who heard that Peter was there, sent two men to him with the request, "Please come to us without delay."
39 Then Peter arose and went with them. When he was come, they brought him into the upper chamber: and all the widows stood by him weeping, and shewing the coats and garments which Dorcas made, while she was with them.	39 So Peter got up and went with them; and when he arrived, they took him to the room upstairs. All the widows stood beside him, weeping and showing tunics and other clothing that Dorcas had made while she was with them.
40 But Peter put them all forth, and kneeled down, and prayed; and turning him to the body said, Tabitha, arise. And she opened her eyes: and when she saw Peter, she sat up.	40 Peter put all of them outside, and then he knelt down and prayed. He turned to the body and said, "Tabitha, get up." Then she opened her eyes, and seeing Peter, she sat up.
41 And he gave her his hand, and lifted her up, and when he had called the saints and widows, presented her alive.	41 He gave her his hand and helped her up. Then calling the saints and widows, he showed her to be alive.
42 And it was known throughout all Joppa; and many believed in the Lord.	42 This became known throughout Joppa, and many believed in the Lord.
43 And it came to pass, that he tarried many days in Joppa with one Simon a tanner.	43 Meanwhile he stayed in Joppa for some time with a certain Simon, a tanner.

MAIN THOUGHT: But Peter put them all forth, and kneeled down, and prayed; and turning him to the body said, Tabitha, arise. And she opened her eyes: and when she saw Peter, she sat up. (Acts 9:40, KJV)

LESSON SETTING
    Time: A.D. 60
    Place: Lydda

LESSON OUTLINE
    I. Death of a Valued Believer
    (Acts 9:36–37)

II. A Call for Help
   (Acts 9:38–39)
III. Request Granted
   (Acts 9:40–43)

UNIFYING PRINCIPLE

In times of crisis, people look for help. What qualities do they look for in a helper? When Tabitha died, faithful followers of Christ sent for the apostle Peter for help.

INTRODUCTION

The book of Acts is the account of the Holy Spirit overcoming barriers that lay in the pathway of the growth and development of the early church. He overcame the barriers of language, the persecution by Jewish and Roman officials, and even issues of race and religious politics to encompass Jerusalem, Judea, Samaria, and the Greco-Roman world. The book can be divided into two parts. The first part, Acts 1–12, focused on Peter as the major human character, who exemplified and embodied the confidence to go forth as the leader of the original group of Apostles. He was important to the growth and development of the early church; that cannot be overestimated. Peter preached the first sermon in the book (Acts 2). He was used by the Holy Spirit to do the first healing, noted in Acts. He boldly addressed the Jewish officials in the name of Jesus, helped to open up the Gentile path to Christianity, and was the party through which the Holy Spirit performed serial healings, the latter of which is the subject of this study.

The passage under investigation is part of a larger unit that actually focused on Peter's final ministry in Acts (Acts 9:32–12:25). Luke's way of getting to this periscope is interesting, however. Saul, the prosecutor of the new faith community, is introduced as a witness to the stoning of its first martyr, Stephen, and proceeds to terrorize the church as a defender of Judaism (see Acts 8:1). After showing his involvement in the Jewish diaspora from Jerusalem to Judea and Samaria, the writer shifted the scene to cover Philip's preaching in Samaria and the conversion of the Ethiopian eunuch. Just as Jesus had promised, the Gospel message would expand outside of Jerusalem to the surrounding areas mentioned previously (Acts 1:6–8). Luke, then, reintroduced Saul and provided detail of his conversion (Acts 9:1–31) before returning to examine Peter's significance in opening up the Gentile mission that Saul (Paul) would later take full command of (see Acts 13).

Peter's reemergence at the end of our textual chapter 9 is strategic for Luke. Here, he seeks to show how the Holy Spirit worked to coordinate the ministry of these two major characters toward the fulfillment of Jesus' prophecy. For the Gospel was to be carried to the King James Version termed "to the uttermost parts of the world."

His reentry to the Gentile mission linked his activity in the coastal cities of Judea to Lydda and Joppa and provided the perfect setting for the apostle's last hurrah in this narrative. It focused on two healing stories before his meeting with Cornelius, and later, his vocal support of Paul's mission to the Gentile at the Jerusalem Conference. The first story is the healing of Aeneas, a Greek paralytic. Because of this healing Peter's fame spread and provided the setting for him to be involved in the healing of Tabitha, a believer.

Three things are highlighted out here. First, the community of faith in Lydda lost a beloved believer named Tabitha. The community was grief-stricken at her death. Second, when word snuck out that Peter was in the area they pleaded for him to come. They possessed a level of faith that gave them hope Tabitha would be resuscitated. Finally, Peter demonstrated the power of their faith and healed her in the name of Jesus. The miracle he performed in the name of the risen Christ set up the occasions in which the Gentile community would also come to salvation.

EXPOSITION

I. DEATH OF A VALUED BELIEVER (ACTS 9:36–37)

The introduction of Tabitha came abruptly in the narrative after Peter healed Aeneas, bedridden Greek man; He had been in this position for eight years. The text announced a resident in Joppa, named Tabitha. The text provided the meaning of her name as Gazelle or Dorcas. Gazelle may be an indication of her magnificent beauty and stately manner. It could have also been descriptive of her pleasant disposition and the aurora she gave as a person who genuinely cared for others. Lydda was the place she resided.

Luke's inclusion of the names of the people Peter healed and the places they lived demonstrated the truthfulness of his claim and provided evidence that these were real people and not characters conjured up by a vivid imagination. That is to say Luke's information can be verified.

Lydda was a town of Benjamin near the border of the Plain of Sharon and approximately 11 miles southeast of Joppa. According to Luke, it was the site of an early Christian community (Acts 9:32).

Since Peter had been evangelizing in nearby areas and had recently healed Aeneas, word spread throughout the area of the wonderful ministry he was involved in. The healing of the paralytic in the name of Jesus was a phenomenon and pointed to Peter's significance as one of the original Apostles and one of the few who possessed within himself the power of the Holy Spirit.

The text characterized Dorcas as a believer and the Greek description of her service is the actual feminine use of the word disciple, the only time it is found in the New Testament (see D. M. Beck in the *Interpreter's Dictionary of the Bible*, Vol. 1. Abingdon Press, Nashville; p. 864). One sentence described the type of person Dorcas was, "Full of good works and acts of charity" (NRSV; Acts 9:36). Notice the emphasis on good works and charity. This double accent on her activities is quite profound. It expressed the type of person she was known in her community. Good works and charity denote actions of care and concern for others. Charity can be defined here as acts of love to another. That was Dorcas' claim to fame. She used her gifts of love and caring to help the community. Just as Jesus went about doing good so did Dorcas (Acts 10:38). She imitated the life of her Lord and Savior. She understood what it meant to be a believer and had followed the pattern of assistance to the needy that the early church adopted (see Acts 2:44–45; 4:32–35; 6:1).

Unfortunately, Dorcas took ill and died. Her death was a tremendous blow to the Christian community and they were quite distraught at her passing. Death robs us of those we love and of the joy they bring to our lives. In the healing of the lame man at the beautiful gate of the temple in Acts 3, Peter verified in the man's healing that impediments to the Christian faith can be removed in the name of Jesus. Already the barriers of language, culture and custom, political posturing, the dissemination of misinformation, and sickness had been successfully managed. What lay ahead was death, religious heresies, and the establishment of Christian doctrine for Gentile believers. Peter's involvement would be critical in demonstrating the Holy Spirit's ability to overcome these challenges. Dorcas' death provided the opportunity for another one of these barriers to fall prey to God's omnipotence. The Scriptures affirmed that even death would succumb to the resurrecting power of Jesus. With this sense of hope, the community sent for Peter, who they knew was already evangelizing in the area. The healing of Aeneas provided them with great hope. They had witnessed the healing of the paralytic and felt confident in sending for the man of God.

In sending for Peter, he fulfilled the meaning of being an apostle. The word means the sent one! The Lord had sent forth the twelve, then later the seventy (Luke 9:1–6; 10:1–12). He told the disciples He had sent them forward just as the Father had sent Him (John 17:18). Now the community sent for Peter, Jesus' handpicked leader of the disciples (see Acts 9:38).

II. A CALL FOR HELP
(ACTS 9:38–39)
Two men were sent to call upon Peter. Jesus had sent out the twelve and the seventy in pairs. After His resurrection, a pair of disciples walked with Jesus, unknowingly, on the Emmaus Road (Luke 24:13–35). Peter and John healed the lame man at the beautiful gate and appeared before the Jewish Council (Acts 3:1–12; 4: 1–22). Later, Paul paired with Barnabas and Silas in demonstration. Pairings was important for witnesses to an event, to record its validity and truth, especially in Jewish law.

The two men found Peter and gave him the request of the community of faith and he went with them. The text affirmed the community realized the power of God vested in Peter and called for him to come immediately. Peter detected their urgency and compiled with their request. It foreshadowed the request he would ultimately receive to come visit at the house of the Gentile named Cornelius. Modern day Christians must not hesitate to call on those strong pillars of the faith to minister unto them. Nor should faith warriors hesitate to attend to genuine need. The call to minister requires an appropriate response.

III. A REQUEST GRANTED
(ACTS 9:40–43)
The story is similar to the accounts of Elijah raising the son of the widow of Zarephath (see 1 Kings 17:17–24) and Elisha's raising the son of the Shunanmite woman (2 Kings 4:32–37). The resuscitation of Dorcas is more reminiscent of Jesus' raising Jairus' daughter (see Luke 8:40–42, 49–56). In fact, the similarities are striking. In both instances, the burial is delayed, the body was laid in a house where mourners were present, a request was made for others to exit the room, and solitary prayer was rendered in behalf of the deceased

and the suffering family. Like Jesus, Peter commanded the deceased to "Get up" and she obeyed him as he assisted her. Both Jesus and Peter used the Aramaic names for the people they resuscitated. Luke was careful in both instances to preserve these expressions. Through the faith displayed in the community and in effort to send for Peter their beloved Dorcas had been raised. The Holy Spirit had overcome one of the churches greatest enemies. Her rise back to life served as a reminder that all believers can anticipate and will experience a glorious resurrection at the return of their Lord and Savior.

THE LESSON APPLIED

This lesson has several key points to help the modern day Christian believer in his or her ministry. First, it points to the overwhelming power of the Holy Spirit to accomplish His purpose. The raising of Dorcas from the dead, coupled with the healing of Aeneas, attest to ability of the Spirit to overcome the various barriers that challenge the church, such as: persecution, sickness, death, politics, etc. One should read this book with a sense of hope and excitement as assurance that God's purpose will be accomplished.

Second, the lesson demonstrated God's desire and willingness to use even the most insignificant people to bring about His will. Aeneas was deemed only a crippled person, who had been cursed because of some secret sin. Yet, his healing said otherwise. His name was recorded in the annals of church history because he was a significant factor in getting Peter where God desired him to be—near Joppa to open up the Gospel to the Gentile community, to the uttermost parts of the world.

Finally, the text showed us the benefit of doing good works in the spirit of God's love. Dorcas was beheld in an esteemed position by the community of faith in Lydda. At her death, they sent for Peter. They hoped for a miracle and received it.

LET'S TALK ABOUT IT

1. Were Peter and Paul in competition?

The answer is an unequivocal no. Each apostles mentioned in this book had their own particular purpose, according to the will of God. Luke went to great pains to show a cooperative relationship between Peter and Paul. Peter worked to help open up the Gospel to Gentiles, and once opened, Paul built upon it. Peter's voice in convincing the Jerusalem Council to not place undo requirements upon Gentiles as prerequisites for entrance into the church is critical. Rather than see the two apostles in competition with each other, they should be seen as complementing one another's ministry.

HOME DAILY DEVOTIONAL READINGS
FEBRUARY 19–25, 2018

MONDAY	TUESDAY	WEDNESDAY	THURSDAY	FRIDAY	SATURDAY	SUNDAY
Timothy Joins Paul's Team	Timothy, an Active Teacher with Paul	Epaphroditus, Paul's Coworker and Minister	Timothy, Paul's Envoy to the Churches	Teach the Sound Words of Christ	Money, Root of Many Evils	The Good Fight of Faith
Acts 16:1–5	1 Corinthians 4:14–21	Philippians 2:25–30	1 Thess. 3:1–10	1 Timothy 6:2b–8	1 Timothy 6:9–10	1 Timothy 6:11–21

THE GOOD FIGHT OF FAITH

ADULT TOPIC: BE STRONG	BACKGROUND SCRIPTURE: 1 TIMOTHY 6:11–21

1 TIMOTHY 6:11–21

King James Version

BUT thou, O man of God, flee these things; and follow after righteousness, godliness, faith, love, patience, meekness.

12 Fight the good fight of faith, lay hold on eternal life, whereunto thou art also called, and hast professed a good profession before many witnesses.

13 I give thee charge in the sight of God, who quickeneth all things, and before Christ Jesus, who before Pontius Pilate witnessed a good confession;

14 That thou keep this commandment without spot, unrebukable, until the appearing of our Lord Jesus Christ:

15 Which in his times he shall shew, who is the blessed and only Potentate, the King of kings, and Lord of lords;

16 Who only hath immortality, dwelling in the light which no man can approach unto; whom no man hath seen, nor can see: to whom be honour and power everlasting. Amen.

17 Charge them that are rich in this world, that they be not highminded, nor trust in uncertain riches, but in the living God, who giveth us richly all things to enjoy;

18 That they do good, that they be rich in good works, ready to distribute, willing to communicate;

19 Laying up in store for themselves a good foundation against the time to come, that they may lay hold on eternal life.

New Revised Standard Version

BUT as for you, man of God, shun all this; pursue righteousness, godliness, faith, love, endurance, gentleness.

12 Fight the good fight of the faith; take hold of the eternal life, to which you were called and for which you made the good confession in the presence of many witnesses.

13 In the presence of God, who gives life to all things, and of Christ Jesus, who in his testimony before Pontius Pilate made the good confession, I charge you

14 to keep the commandment without spot or blame until the manifestation of our Lord Jesus Christ,

15 which he will bring about at the right time— he who is the blessed and only Sovereign, the King of kings and Lord of lords.

16 It is he alone who has immortality and dwells in unapproachable light, whom no one has ever seen or can see; to him be honor and eternal dominion. Amen.

17 As for those who in the present age are rich, command them not to be haughty, or to set their hopes on the uncertainty of riches, but rather on God who richly provides us with everything for our enjoyment.

18 They are to do good, to be rich in good works, generous, and ready to share,

19 thus storing up for themselves the treasure of a good foundation for the future, so that they may take hold of the life that really is life.

MAIN THOUGHT: Fight the good fight of faith, lay hold on eternal life, whereunto thou art also called, and hast professed a good profession before many witnesses. (1 Timothy 6:12, KJV)

1 TIMOTHY 6:11–21

King James Version

20 O Timothy, keep that which is committed to thy trust, avoiding profane and vain babblings, and oppositions of science falsely so called:
21 Which some professing have erred concerning the faith. Grace be with thee. Amen.

New Revised Standard Version

20 Timothy, guard what has been entrusted to you. Avoid the profane chatter and contradictions of what is falsely called knowledge;
21 by professing it some have missed the mark as regards the faith.

LESSON SETTING
　　Time: A.D. 65
　　Place: Macedonia

LESSON OUTLINE
　I. **Shun the Former: Fight the Good Fight**
　　(1 Timothy 6:11–12)
　II. **Keep the Command**
　　(1 Timothy 6:13–16)
　III. **Keep Your Guard Up**
　　(1 Timothy 6:17–21)

UNIFYING PRINCIPLE

We are surrounded by all kinds of advice. What is the best advice to follow? Paul charged Timothy to embrace certain attitudes and actions and avoid others in order to strengthen his faith.

INTRODUCTION

Standing up for right takes a lot of courage and faith that one's effort will make a difference. Jesus truly believed it would. He stood up to the corrupt Jewish religious leadership and paid the price for it with His death. But His resurrection from the dead more than made up for His crucifixion on the cross. Not only does He live forevermore, but the truth He came to declare continues to live on as well, serving as a call to us to stand for right. That is the major point of this pericope of Scripture. Paul, one of Jesus' most adamant and successful apostles, encouraged the young minister Timothy to stand up for right. He instructed him to shun evil and flee from the devil.

Timothy was a convert of Paul and one of his trusted and most faithful associates. He was from Lystra and the son of mixed parentage; his father was a Gentile and his mother was Jewish. Timothy, as an associate of Paul in the Christian ministry, served as an understudy to the missionary-minded apostle. As such, tradition has it that Paul wrote two letters addressed to Timothy that became a part of the New Testament canon.

These, along with a third letter addressed to another one of Paul's sons in the ministry named Titus, made up what are known as the Pastorals. However, there is some dispute among scholars as to whether or not all three books were composed by Paul. Some question the validity of 1 Timothy because it does not carry the number and normal expression of words contained in the Pastorals and the other books ascribed to Paul (Glenn Hinson, *2 Corinthians–Philemon*, Volume 11, [Nashville: Broadman Press, 1971], 300). Yet for this writer this issue does not have the evidence behind it to question the authenticity of Paul's authorship of 1 Timothy. The book is thoroughly Pauline and considers the issues that would be of concern to Paul as the establisher of congregations. As a missionary-minded minister, Paul had to leave these congregations in the hands of understudies like Timothy and Titus. Therefore, the emphasis on ministerial conduct and practice would be important for the aged apostle to pass forward. These three letters reveal Paul's concern about church leadership. So that there would not be a void in church leadership during Paul's absence or in the case of his untimely demise, under the inspiration of the Holy Spirit, Paul put to paper instructions for the young Timothy, Titus, and their successors.

This letter has three important points for us to consider. First, Paul urged Timothy to fight the good fight of faith. What did this fight consist of, and why was it necessary? Second, Timothy was instructed to keep God's command. His instruction carried the force of an imperative. Third, Timothy was encouraged to remain alert, to keep his guard up for those who would seek to undermine his ministry. These three things were given to Timothy as a note of personal love from his father in the ministry. Thank God these instructions are yet available to nourish and guide contemporary ministers also.

EXPOSITION

I. SHUN THE FORMER: FIGHT THE GOOD FIGHT
(1 TIMOTHY 6:11–12)

Verse eleven serves as a transition to the instructions given earlier in the chapter, primarily verses 9–10. Paul told Timothy, "'Those who want to be rich fall into temptation and are trapped by many senseless and harmful desires that plunge people into ruin and destruction. For the love of money is a root of all kinds of evil, and in their eagerness to be rich some have wandered away from the faith and pierced themselves with many pains'" (1 Tim. 6:9–10, NRSV). The directive may go all the way back to verse two. This statement is a warning and as well as a directive. It is almost like a summary, a reminder of the key points that the young minister must remember and observe.

The noted prohibition here that Timothy received was direction not to allow money to be the goal of his ministry or of his life. The love of money, Paul confirms, is the root of all evil (v. 10). He came to this conclusion because Satan uses it to negatively influence human desires, drawing them away from the faith (v. 10). Satan's objective is to steal, kill, and destroy (John 10:10). The words "ruin" and "destruction" emphasize total devastation. Paul infers the minister's life will be annihilated if this unruly love of money is left unchecked. This is Paul's warning to Timothy not to become a Midas, for such was the lot of the false teachers he referred to in the text. It was their craving for money that caused their departure from the faith. Paul's double directive to Timothy is sharp and direct: "'But as for you, man of God, shun all this; pursue righteousness, godliness, faith, love, endurance, gentleness'" (1 Tim. 6:11, NRSV).

Timothy is reminded who he is: a man of God. The term "man of God" was frequently used of the prophets in the Old Testament and carries the concept of one that God has hand-picked (1 Sam. 2:27; 9:6–7; 1 Kings 13:1). He has a high calling on his life that he needs to constantly consider. The inordinate love for money and conduct unbecoming of the character of God are to be avoided at all costs. The word "shun" as used here meant to stay away from something or someone intentionally. Timothy was not to see religion as a way to riches. Rather, while shunning the love of money he should pursue the key virtues. That is to say while he is running from Satanic vices he should be running toward Christian virtues.

Paul lists six major virtues, which are among those things he includes in his breakdown of the fruit of the Spirit. Timothy is urged to adopt righteousness, which means to live in a just manner toward God and toward one's fellow persons. It is an attitudinal disposition that flows out of the mind and heart of God into the life of the individual. Closely related to righteousness is godliness. Godliness is a willful and deliberate effort to secure the divine presence through a relentless pursuit to imitate the lifestyle of Jesus. This lifestyle connects to the individual Christian through the conduit of faith. Paul stated in 1 Corinthians 13:13 that "faith, hope, and love abide" (NRSV). Here he reminded Timothy of their importance by denoting two of these fine virtues as things he should pursue.

Love is the deliberate act of God in providing human salvation. As a man of God, Timothy must possess God's love and a sacrificial love for others as the foundation of his faith and ministry. His love for and faith in God will enable him to endure the attacks of those opposed to the Gentile ministry—Gnostics, Judaizers, and spiritual wickedness in high places. His endurance projected a steadfast hope in the fulfillment of the promises of the Savior to provide life to the faithful. Finally, Paul encouraged Timothy to pursue gentleness or humility, for such was the way of Christ (Phil. 2:5–11).

These virtues can be summed up in Pauls' admonition to Timothy to fight the good fight. Repeatedly, the apostle uses military and athletic imagery to accentuate his point (Phil. 3:14; 2 Tim. 2:3–7). The good fight is the fight to obtain and maintain these virtues for the cause of Christ for which eternal life is the prize. The phrase "take hold" means to grasp firmly and not let go. Eternal life is available for those who will seize it. Upon Timothy's baptism he confessed and accepted Jesus as Lord and Savior.

II. KEEP THE COMMAND (1 TIMOTHY 6:13–16)

Before an eternal cast of divine witnesses, the God of all life and His Son Jesus, Paul charged Timothy to adhere to his command to shun the love of money, and by conjecture all evil, and pursue Christian virtues. In this dual endeavor Timothy must not fail. There is no way that he should fail, though, because he is blanketed by unseen power. Jesus is the One who confessed His divine Kingship to Pilate (John 18:33–37). It is to Jesus that Timothy is to maintain his allegiance until the Lord's return. As the sovereign Lord of creation He will return in His own time and in His own way. Paul reconfirms God's unique eternal being, who cannot be seen or fully conceptualized. The doxology in 1 Timothy 6:15–16 is a testimony of praise. It is expressed in Jewish terms to point out their concept of monotheism. The reference to God's eternal dominion effectively reminds the reader that God is in total control.

III. KEEP YOUR GUARD UP
(1 TIMOTHY 6:17–21)

In this pericope, Paul reverts back to his concentration on the dangers of wealth. That he would broach the subject again points out what a serious issue it was to him. Paul charged Timothy in verse 14, and now he commands Timothy to charge the rich to put their focus on God so that they may be truly enriched. Spiritual riches are the riches that really matter. Timothy is to act decisively to teach the meaning of real security to his hearers, which is dependency on God. The text, therefore, is not a prohibition on wealth, but on the type of attitude that can grow out of dependency on wealth alone. Contrary to popular belief, the accumulation of wealth does not guarantee a good foundation for the eternal future. This life comes about by imitating the life of Jesus, who "went about doing good" (Acts 10:38, NRSV). The way to become rich is to do good to others. Liberal giving in terms of one's deeds to others is what counts. It displays one's hope as positioned in God (v. 17–18). Every solidly built building needs a foundation. The generosity given to others, Paul said, was the equivalent of the accumulation of spiritual building supplies for their future residence.

Finally, Paul encouraged Timothy to exercise caution and prudence as he handled the truth of God and, in essence, the care of others. He must not be irresponsible or approach the ministry haphazardly with serious matters at stake. He had to guard these matters carefully. The word "guard" here means to be alert, to be vigilant, and to protect. Again Paul resorts to military imagery. Timothy is to be a sentry, on the post. Paul's final word to Timothy comes in the form of a warning. It is the last word of advice to a young minister. He must be warned about gossip and harmful chatter. The words here mean babblings and utter emptiness. The reference is to the Gnostics who purported to have knowledge, but were falsely proclaiming that salvation could only come about through intellectual assent. Paul urged Timothy to steer clear of this empty talk that robbed salvation of its power.

THE LESSON APPLIED

This text teaches us several important lessons. First, it points out the errors of the prosperity gospel movement. God does not endorse an inordinate focus on the achievements of physical goods or possessions. Timothy is warned that "the love of money is the root of all evil." God grants us blessings in the here and now to fulfill our needs, but these needs must never rival Him for supremacy in our lives. Those entrenched in getting only their physical needs supplied miss the point of this text. Over and above the accumulation of goods stands our need of God. Timothy is charged to preach a Gospel of dependency on the sovereign Lord of heaven and earth. Those who depend on and trust in Him are truly the rich ones.

Second, the text points out the importance of our covenant relationship with God. He has called us into His marvelous light and we accepted Him as noted in our baptismal confession, which is more than just a statement we made in church. No, it is the response of our innermost being to God's revelation of His Son as the Atonement for our sins. Therefore, it is an expression of our deepest hope and our need to be reconciled to our loving Creator, Sustainer, and Redeemer. He has given Himself to us, and in return we have pledged loyal and faithful service to Him.

Third, Paul charges Timothy to pursue the virtuous life. Flee the temptation to do evil and instead pursue righteousness, godliness, patience, endurance, love, faith, and gentleness. Fleeing is the equivalent of running away from, while pursuing means to run to. Paul sets up this dichotomy for emphasis. Running from evil is the same as running toward righteousness, and pursuing righteousness is the equivalent of running away from evil. Therefore, running after these godly virtues is the equivalent of following after Christ. Paul's underlying theme is to encourage positive ministerial conduct as an example to the congregation. Pursuing righteousness and the other Christian virtues is the practice that leads to perfection. The former is to give in to Satan's ploy to deceive and rob us of our relationship with God.

LET'S TALK ABOUT IT

1. Does it matter if the letter to Timothy was written as a general letter to the church?

No! It does not. Whether it was a direct letter to Timothy or one that was shared with the church does not take away its message or make it less important. The point is Christians of the early church acknowledged its value and sanctioned it as an important part of the Word of God. The various church councils prayerfully agreed with their conclusion. The truth is this letter was intended to guide the church, then and now, as to God's will and purpose for Christian leadership. Knowing the historical development of these books and letters help us to discover how God used human ingenuity to construct His message of salvation to the church and world, but knowing who composed them or their original recipients in no way invalidates that they were divinely inspired and good for reproof, instruction, and doctrine.

2. Why are the books of Timothy and Titus called pastorals?

These books are called pastorals because they were written by the apostle to his sons in the ministry to show them how to function as Christian ministers. They continue to serve the Church as guides to ministerial conduct and practice: issues of leadership, selection of deacons, ministers, preaching, ordination, treatment of Scripture, Christian doctrine, handling of prayer, public officials, and relationships, and the like. The wise pastor would do well to consult these books often to discover the treasure they offer to the ministry.

HOME DAILY DEVOTIONAL READINGS
FEBRUARY 26–MARCH 4, 2018

MONDAY	TUESDAY	WEDNESDAY	THURSDAY	FRIDAY	SATURDAY	SUNDAY
Don't Forget the Lord's Provisions	Jesus Tested in the Wilderness	Angel Confirms Direction for Jesus	Prayer for Help in Time of Crisis	Family Lineage of Abraham Preserved	God Blesses Abraham for Obedience	God Provides the Sacrificial Ram
Deuteronomy 8:11–20	Matthew 4:1–11	Luke 22:39–46	Psalm 20	Hebrews 11:17–22	Genesis 22:15–19	Genesis 22:1–3, 6–14

THIRD QUARTER

Lesson material is based on International Sunday School Lessons and International Bible Lessons for Christian Teaching. Copyrighted by the International Council of Religious Education, and is used by its permission.

MARCH, APRIL, MAY 2018

WRITER: DR. BARRY JOHNSON

SUGGESTED OPENING EXERCISES

1. **Usual Signal for Beginning**
2. **Prayer (Closing with the Lord's Prayer)**
3. **Singing (Song to Be Selected)**
4. **Scripture Reading:**
   Ephesians 4:1–6 (KJV)

Director: I therefore, the prisoner of the Lord, beseech you that ye walk worthy of the vocation wherewith ye are called,

School: With all lowliness and meekness, with longsuffering, forbearing one another in love;

Director: Endeavouring to keep the unity of the Spirit in the bond of peace.

School: There is one body, and one Spirit, even as ye are called in one hope of your calling;

Director: One Lord, one faith, one baptism,

All: One God and Father of all, who is above all, and through all, and in you all.

Recitation in Concert:
Psalm 34:4–10 (KJV)

4 I sought the LORD, and he heard me, and delivered me from all my fears.

5 They looked unto him, and were lightened: and their faces were not ashamed.

6 This poor man cried, and the LORD heard him, and saved him out of all his troubles.

7 The angel of the LORD encampeth round about them that fear him, and delivereth them.

8 O taste and see that the LORD is good: blessed is the man that trusteth in him.

9 O fear the LORD ye his saints: for there is no want to them that fear him.

10 The young lions do lack, and suffer hunger: but they that seek the LORD shall not want any good thing.

CLOSING WORK

1. **Singing**
2. **Sentences:**
   Exodus 3:4–8 (KJV)

4 And when the LORD saw that he turned aside to see, God called unto him out of the midst of the bush, and said, Moses, Moses. And he said, Here am I.

5 And he said, Draw not nigh hither: put off thy shoes from off thy feet, for the place whereon thou standest is holy ground.

6 Moreover he said, I am the God of thy father, the God of Abraham, the God of Isaac, and the God of Jacob. And Moses hid his face; for he was afraid to look upon God.

7 And the LORD said, I have surely seen the affliction of my people which are in Egypt, and have heard their cry by reason of their taskmasters; for I know their sorrows;

8 And I am come down to deliver them out of the hand of the Egyptians, and to bring them up out of that land unto a good land and a large, unto a land flowing with milk and honey; unto the place of the Canaanites, and the Hittites, and the Amorites, and the Perizzites, and the Hivites, and the Jebusites.

3. **Dismissal with Prayer**

THE LORD WILL PROVIDE

ADULT TOPIC: A TEST OF TRUST	BACKGROUND SCRIPTURE: GENESIS 22

GENESIS 22:1–3, 6–14

King James Version

AND it came to pass after these things, that God did tempt Abraham, and said unto him, Abraham: and he said, Behold, here I am.

2 And he said, Take now thy son, thine only son Isaac, whom thou lovest, and get thee into the land of Moriah; and offer him there for a burnt offering upon one of the mountains which I will tell thee of.

3 And Abraham rose up early in the morning, and saddled his ass, and took two of his young men with him, and Isaac his son, and clave the wood for the burnt offering, and rose up, and went unto the place of which God had told him.

• • • • • •

6 And Abraham took the wood of the burnt offering, and laid it upon Isaac his son; and he took the fire in his hand, and a knife; and they went both of them together.

7 And Isaac spake unto Abraham his father, and said, My father: and he said, Here am I, my son. And he said, Behold the fire and the wood: but where is the lamb for a burnt offering?

8 And Abraham said, My son, God will provide himself a lamb for a burnt offering: so they went both of them together.

9 And they came to the place which God had told him of; and Abraham built an altar there, and laid the wood in order, and bound Isaac his son, and laid him on the altar upon the wood.

New Revised Standard Version

AFTER these things God tested Abraham. He said to him, "Abraham!" And he said, "Here I am."

2 He said, "Take your son, your only son Isaac, whom you love, and go to the land of Moriah, and offer him there as a burnt offering on one of the mountains that I shall show you."

3 So Abraham rose early in the morning, saddled his donkey, and took two of his young men with him, and his son Isaac; he cut the wood for the burnt offering, and set out and went to the place in the distance that God had shown him.

• • • • • •

6 Abraham took the wood of the burnt offering and laid it on his son Isaac, and he himself carried the fire and the knife. So the two of them walked on together.

7 Isaac said to his father Abraham, "Father!" And he said, "Here I am, my son." He said, "The fire and the wood are here, but where is the lamb for a burnt offering?"

8 Abraham said, "God himself will provide the lamb for a burnt offering, my son." So the two of them walked on together.

9 When they came to the place that God had shown him, Abraham built an altar there and laid the wood in order. He bound his son Isaac, and laid him on the altar, on top of the wood.

MAIN THOUGHT: And Abraham said, My son, God will provide himself a lamb for a burnt offering: so they went both of them together. (Genesis 22:8, KJV)

GENESIS 22:1–3, 6–14

King James Version	New Revised Standard Version
10 And Abraham stretched forth his hand, and took the knife to slay his son.	10 Then Abraham reached out his hand and took the knife to kill his son.
11 And the angel of the LORD called unto him out of heaven, and said, Abraham, Abraham: and he said, Here am I.	11 But the angel of the LORD called to him from heaven, and said, "Abraham, Abraham!" And he said, "Here I am."
12 And he said, Lay not thine hand upon the lad, neither do thou any thing unto him: for now I know that thou fearest God, seeing thou hast not withheld thy son, thine only son from me.	12 He said, "Do not lay your hand on the boy or do anything to him; for now I know that you fear God, since you have not withheld your son, your only son, from me."
13 And Abraham lifted up his eyes, and looked, and behold behind him a ram caught in a thicket by his horns: and Abraham went and took the ram, and offered him up for a burnt offering in the stead of his son.	13 And Abraham looked up and saw a ram, caught in a thicket by its horns. Abraham went and took the ram and offered it up as a burnt offering instead of his son.
14 And Abraham called the name of that place Jehovah-jireh: as it is said to this day, In the mount of the LORD it shall be seen.	14 So Abraham called that place "The LORD will provide"; as it is said to this day, "On the mount of the LORD it shall be provided."

LESSON SETTING
Time: Unknown
Place: Mt. Moriah

LESSON OUTLINE
I. **Abraham's Dilemma (Genesis 22:1–3)**
II. **Confusion at the Altar (Genesis 22:6–9)**
III. **God's Intervention (Genesis 22:10–14)**

UNIFYING PRINCIPLE
People are reluctant to make challenging personal sacrifices for fear of losing everything. How can they learn to offer difficult sacrifices even in the face of fear? By being willing to offer his son, Abraham learned to trust God, who provided everything he needed.

INTRODUCTION
Today's account of God testing Abraham's faith is quite severe. Human sacrifice was "a pagan rite in which a human being, often the firstborn child, was offered to a god to atone for sin or secure the god's favor. God distinctly prohibited the Hebrew people from imitating their heathen neighbors by offering up human beings as sacrifices (Lev. 20:2–5; Deut. 18:10). God's command to Abraham to sacrifice Isaac was no exception because this was done to test Abraham and his faith (Gen. 22:1–19)" ("Human Sacrifice" in *Nelson's Illustrated Bible Dictionary*, New Ed. [Nashville: Thomas Nelson, 2014], 525). How Abraham would pass this test, however, is quite remarkable. Abraham does not pass by himself; he has Someone to help him through this awful ordeal.

EXPOSITION

I. ABRAHAM'S DILEMMA (GENESIS 22:1–3)
Abraham had answered the call of the Lord, who had brought him out of Ur and

eventually into the land of Beersheba. God had constantly blessed Abraham, and therefore Abraham would not have had any trepidation about this summons. Unlike Adam and Eve, hiding from God after they had realized that they had disobeyed God, Abraham was quite vocal in responding to not only God (see Gen. 22:1), but also Isaac (see 22:7) and the angel of the Lord (see 22:11). Generally, God's voice was an assurance of blessings and guidance. On this occasion, however, Abraham was supremely tested by God. What is the meaning and significance of God's testing Abraham?

Charles C. Ryrie notes that "God does not tempt anyone with evil, but in certain instances He does *test*, try, or prove us, as in this case with Abraham" (*New American Standard Study Bible* [Chicago: Moody Press, 1995], 36). According to James, "Let no one say when he is tempted, 'I am being tempted by God'; for God cannot be tempted by evil, and He Himself does not tempt anyone" (1:13, NASB). This command is designated for Abraham to reveal his love for God. A second complication for Abraham is that Isaac was his *only* son, the child of promise. Recall that God had already ordered Abraham to send his older son Ishmael away, and now He was asking Abraham to sacrifice his remaining son.

Conscious of the fact that Isaac was a gift from above, Abraham still decided to obey God. God issued a command that Abraham offer his only son as a burnt offering. Notice that the text does not mention the term *sacrifice*, even though we may fairly categorize it as such. The practice of sacrifice originated with God, and the first documented sacrifice to the Lord is found with Cain and Abel (see Gen. 4). Abraham's burnt offering was to be offered on the mountain that God would show him.

Abraham's response to this command was to rise early and immediately begin this journey. Abraham did not waver; he was as dedicated to this mission as he had been in his search for a righteous man in Sodom (see Gen. 18). Taking Isaac and two of his young men with him, he set out to obey God's command. Interestingly, Abraham's preparations should have included food and water for the journey from Beersheba to the region of Moriah, a journey of approximately fifty miles over three days. Verse three tells us that Abraham took the time to cut and pack the wood needed for the burnt offering, but does not mention the basic necessities of food and water. Does this indicate that securing the basic necessities was so obvious that no mention of it was required? Perhaps. But what about the wood? The editors of the *NIV Archaeological Study Bible* make the following suggestion: "It seems incongruous that Abraham would have carried wood to Jerusalem, a forested area, rather than gathering it at the site of the planned sacrifice. On the other hand, it may not seem surprising that Abraham would have gone prepared to make the sacrifice and would not have wanted to go to the trouble of seeking out suitably dried wood after his arrival" ([Grand Rapids: Zondervan, 2005], 37).

At every point, Abraham chose to follow God, even though this is one time that any loving parent would have balked at sacrificing his only son to prove his allegiance to God. The Scriptures do not provide a glimpse into Abraham's frame of mind. If Abraham were allowed to question God, we are not privy to the conversations they may have had. Neither are we told that Abraham begged God for some other way to prove his love. Was Abraham that calloused or jaded by a society in which child sacrifice was normal, or totally absorbed in his devotion to the Lord? The text gives us no insight into these possibilities.

II. CONFUSION AT THE ALTAR (GENESIS 22:6–9)

At some juncture, Abraham and Isaac left his donkey, as well as the two young men who had accompanied them on their journey. Traveling on to the designated site that God had revealed, Abraham and Isaac carried the offering materials. Abraham carried the fire—probably a torch—and the knife with which he would kill Isaac. Incredibly, Abraham had his son carry the wood that would serve to accomplish his own death. At some point, of course, Isaac noticed that something was missing. Obviously, there could not be a burnt offering without an animal. Isaac proclaimed, "'The fire and the wood are here, but where is the lamb for a burnt offering?'" (v. 7, NRSV). As they continued to walk together, what might Isaac have been thinking when he noticed that this essential item was missing?

Abraham assured his son by saying that God Himself would provide. Abraham built the altar, bound Isaac, and laid him on the altar. Notice the order of the events in verse nine: Abraham took the time to construct the altar. Did Isaac hold the torch? Finally, Abraham bound Isaac and laid him on the altar.

We can only speculate as to what Abraham was thinking. The text suggests that Abraham was confident that God would provide in this situation. He was determined to obey God's command to offer Isaac as a burnt offering. This sad and horrifying picture presents an occasion for worship to the One who is the ultimate Restorer. As we can surmise, God never intended for Abraham to use Isaac for the offering. No, we must view this serious trial through the eyes and faith of Abraham and Isaac, and believe.

III. GOD'S INTERVENTION (GENESIS 22:10–14)

Throughout this passage, the writer speaks of a burnt offering. In describing the anticipated killing, however, the usual word for sacrifice (Heb. *zebach*) is not used. One of the linguistic highlights of verse ten is the assertion that Abraham was prepared to "slaughter" (ESV) or "slay" (NASB) Isaac. The Hebrew verb is *shekhot*, meaning "to slaughter." This is obviously not an offering, nor is it a sacrifice, but a slaying that verges on murder. From the author's perspective, what is the reason for the change of terminology? Here we have a horrifying picture of a pious patriarch blindly following a god who has demanded the return of the son through a killing that resembles murder!

Is God acknowledging that this pagan form of behavior is acceptable? If Abraham was not stopped, he would spill innocent blood. The notion of "innocent blood" is found on several occasions in the Old Testament and once in the New Testament. For example, in the Cities of Refuge the spilling of innocent blood was prohibited (see Deut. 19:1–13).

Additionally, when Judas Iscariot realized his betrayal of Jesus, he declared, "'I have sinned by betraying innocent blood'" (Matt. 27:4, NRSV), which highlights the fact that God did not condone his actions. Earlier in the Gospel, Matthew records the story of a time at his house when Jesus challenged some Pharisees by saying, "Go and learn what this means, 'I desire mercy, not sacrifice.' For I have come to call not the righteous but sinners" (Matt. 9:13, NRSV). In His criticisms of the Pharisees' stance, Jesus noted they always brought the proper sacrifices but were totally oblivious to the need of sinners.

God stayed the hand of Abraham because He loved both Abraham and Isaac. Although sacrifice was a part of the rituals prescribed by the Law, God is not a God of misunderstood rituals, but of compassion and mercy. Hosea writes of this, "For I desire steadfast love and not sacrifice, the knowledge of God rather than burnt offerings" (Hos. 6:6, NRSV). Robert B. Chisholm argues that "God's people had failed to understand His true desire. He longed for devotion (ḥeseḏ, mercy) and loyalty (acknowledgment of God; see 2:20; 4:1,6) expressed through allegiance to the covenant demands. Unless offered in the context of obedience, sacrifices were meaningless and even offensive (see 1 Sam. 15:22; Isa. 1:11–20; Amos 5:21–24; Micah 6:6–8)" (*The Bible Knowledge Commentary*, Vol. 1 [Wheaton: Victor Books, 1985], 1394).

The angel commanded Abraham to stop what he was about to do. Calling from heaven, God told him, "For now I know that you fear God, since you have not withheld your son, your only son, from me" (Gen. 22:12, NRSV). Who was this angel? Ryrie describes the angel as a self-manifestation of God. He "speaks as God, identifies Himself with God, and claims to exercise the prerogatives of God. Because the angel of the Lord ceases to appear after [Jesus'] incarnation, it is often inferred that the angel in the Old Testament is a pre-incarnate appearance of the second person of the Trinity" (27).

Recall that it was God who tested Abraham at the beginning of the account. It was God who commanded Abraham to take Isaac to "'one of the mountains that I shall show you'" (Gen. 22:2, NRSV). From this juncture, God remains silent. When God is later mentioned, it is by Abraham, who reminds Isaac that God will provide (see v. 8) and notes their arrival at the place where God had revealed to him.

God speaks again through the angel (see v. 12), and is then referred to as "the Lord" throughout the remainder of the passage (see vv. 14–19). The text is ambiguous, but one way to understand the identity of the angel is as Jesus speaking from heaven. Jesus is the second Person of the Trinity, filled with the compassion and mercy to save humanity. History has proven that Jesus is our Savior and Protector. His Word did not begin when He assumed a human form in the Incarnation.

Since the angel prevented Abraham from slaying his son and Isaac was no longer being used for the burnt offering, what would be used as a replacement? Upon hearing the voice of the angel, Abraham looked up to see a ram that had not been there beforehand, caught up in the thorns of a thicket. The thicket was strong enough to hold the ram so that Abraham could capture the animal. Notice that the animal provided was a ram, the stronger male, and not a lamb. In this type of offering, the ram was the preferred animal. Recall that in verse eight, Abraham said that God would provide the sacrifice and He did. Abraham found what dedicated believers have always found: when we trust God, He always provides more than enough for our every need.

THE LESSON APPLIED

Today's text is the story of a son who put his trust in his father, and of a man who had unwavering faith in his Father. God tested Abraham, and He accepted Abraham's faithfulness. Isaac was not the perfect sacrifice, to be sure, but this story foreshadows another Son who would believe in His Father on a day when He would be offered as a Sacrifice. Jesus was the perfect Sacrifice. From this, we learn that God draws on the depths of our faith when we are caught in precarious situations and still lean on Him as the One who will provide. The truth that "'the LORD will provide'" (v. 14, NRSV) gave comfort to Abraham, not only because Isaac was spared but because, in the process, Abraham was drawn closer to God. We, too, can know that God will provide for us even in the most difficult circumstances that we face.

LET'S TALK ABOUT IT

1. What was Abraham feeling on this occasion?

For Abraham, the implications for Isaac's death surely reached a serious emotional, physical, and psychological state. He would have had serious instinctual aversion as well as inconceivable anxiety about what he was going to do. Could today's Christian who professes devotion to the Lord have the wherewithal to sacrifice his or her child or grandchild? Abraham was human like us but he trusted God. Christians follow God out of faith but also because He gave us the ability to *choose* to follow Him. God does not call robots or automatons. We must love, serve, and trust Him because we want to; otherwise our service to Him will not be authentic.

This is a useful exercise for us. It reminds us that in so many ways the greatest, most revered figures in Scripture were human beings like us, fraught with the same concerns and emotions that we feel. It is important to remember, at the same time, that we cannot know exactly what Abraham was thinking and feeling. Indeed, the text of Genesis 22 seems remarkably uninterested in that question. So let us proceed with caution as we consider the matter.

HOME DAILY DEVOTIONAL READINGS
MARCH 5–11, 2018

MONDAY	TUESDAY	WEDNESDAY	THURSDAY	FRIDAY	SATURDAY	SUNDAY
God Selects the Family of David	God Chooses to Dwell in Zion	Jesus, Heir of David's Throne	Solomon Completes the Temple	Foreigners Welcome in God's Temple	Prayers of Repentance During Captivity	Solomon's Prayer of Dedication
Psalm 132:8–12	Psalm 132:13–18	Acts 2:29–36	2 Chronicles 6:1–11	2 Chronicles 6:28–33	2 Chronicles 6:36–40	2 Chronicles 6:12–21

THERE IS NO GOD LIKE YOU

ADULT TOPIC: PROMISES KEPT	BACKGROUND SCRIPTURE: 2 CHRONICLES 6:1–21

2 CHRONICLES 6:12–21

King James Version

AND he stood before the altar of the LORD in the presence of all the congregation of Israel, and spread forth his hands:

13 For Solomon had made a brasen scaffold, of five cubits long, and five cubits broad, and three cubits high, and had set it in the midst of the court: and upon it he stood, and kneeled down upon his knees before all the congregation of Israel, and spread forth his hands toward heaven,

14 And said, O LORD God of Israel, there is no God like thee in the heaven, nor in the earth; which keepest covenant, and shewest mercy unto thy servants, that walk before thee with all their hearts:

15 Thou which hast kept with thy servant David my father that which thou hast promised him; and spakest with thy mouth, and hast fulfilled it with thine hand, as it is this day.

16 Now therefore, O LORD God of Israel, keep with thy servant David my father that which thou hast promised him, saying, There shall not fail thee a man in my sight to sit upon the throne of Israel; yet so that thy children take heed to their way to walk in my law, as thou hast walked before me.

17 Now then, O LORD GOD of Israel, let thy word be verified, which thou hast spoken unto thy servant David.

18 But will God in very deed dwell with men on the earth? behold, heaven and the heaven of heavens cannot contain thee; how much less this house which I have built!

New Revised Standard Version

THEN Solomon stood before the altar of the LORD in the presence of the whole assembly of Israel, and spread out his hands.

13 Solomon had made a bronze platform five cubits long, five cubits wide, and three cubits high, and had set it in the court; and he stood on it. Then he knelt on his knees in the presence of the whole assembly of Israel, and spread out his hands toward heaven.

14 He said, "O LORD, God of Israel, there is no God like you, in heaven or on earth, keeping covenant in steadfast love with your servants who walk before you with all their heart—

15 you who have kept for your servant, my father David, what you promised to him. Indeed, you promised with your mouth and this day have fulfilled with your hand.

16 Therefore, O LORD, God of Israel, keep for your servant, my father David, that which you promised him, saying, 'There shall never fail you a successor before me to sit on the throne of Israel, if only your children keep to their way, to walk in my law as you have walked before me.'

17 Therefore, O LORD, God of Israel, let your word be confirmed, which you promised to your servant David.

18 "But will God indeed reside with mortals on earth? Even heaven and the highest heaven cannot contain you, how much less this house that I have built!

MAIN THOUGHT: Thou which hast kept with thy servant David my father that which thou hast promised him; and spakest with thy mouth, and hast fulfilled it with thine hand, as it is this day. (2 Chronicles 6:15, KJV)

2 CHRONICLES 6:12–21

King James Version	New Revised Standard Version
19 Have respect therefore to the prayer of thy servant, and to his supplication, O LORD my God, to hearken unto the cry and the prayer which thy servant prayeth before thee:	19 Regard your servant's prayer and his plea, O LORD my God, heeding the cry and the prayer that your servant prays to you.
20 That thine eyes may be open upon this house day and night, upon the place whereof thou hast said that thou wouldest put thy name there; to hearken unto the prayer which thy servant prayeth toward this place.	20 May your eyes be open day and night toward this house, the place where you promised to set your name, and may you heed the prayer that your servant prays toward this place.
21 Hearken therefore unto the supplications of thy servant, and of thy people Israel, which they shall make toward this place: hear thou from thy dwelling place, even from heaven; and when thou hearest, forgive.	21 And hear the plea of your servant and of your people Israel, when they pray toward this place; may you hear from heaven your dwelling place; hear and forgive.

LESSON SETTING
Time: ca. 962 B.C.
Place: Jerusalem

LESSON OUTLINE
I. Solomon's Prayer of Dedication (2 Chronicles 6:12–15)
II. The Promise (2 Chronicles 6:16–21)

UNIFYING PRINCIPLE

People want to know that others will keep their word. How can they respond to a fulfilled promise? At the temple dedication, Solomon thanked the Lord for keeping His promise.

INTRODUCTION

For the remainder of the month of March, our lessons will be drawn from the book of 2 Chronicles. Because this is a portion of the Bible that is not often given a great deal of attention, it will be good for us to spend some time orienting ourselves to the Chronicles before we delve into today's text.

Chronicles appears as two books in our English Bibles. But this was not always the case. Originally, they comprised one book that was—and is—referred to as *sefer dibre hayyamim* (Heb. "book of the events of the days"). Likely because of its length, the book was divided in two by the translators of the Septuagint (LXX) in the third century B.C. The title given to the book in the English Bible—Chronicles—is derived from a statement made by St. Jerome (ca. A.D. 347–420), who said that the books contained "the chronicle of the whole of sacred history" (cited in Tremper Longman III and Raymond B. Dillard, *An Introduction to the Old Testament*, Second Edition [Grand Rapids: Zondervan, 2006], 190). Doubtless this derives, as Longman and Dillard point out, from the fact that Chronicles "is one of two books in the Bible to cover all of human history from creation to the author's day; both Matthew and Chronicles use genealogies to accomplish this" (190).

What can be known about the books themselves? The author of the books in no way identifies himself, nor does Jewish tradition specify an author. As with much of contemporary scholarship, in these lessons we will refer to the author as the Chronicler. We can say much more about the date. John A. Thompson points out that "we can set some upper and lower limits and propose that the date of Chronicles lies within these limits. Thus the reference in 2 Chron. 36:20 to 'the kingdom of Persia' coming to power sets 539 B.C. as the earliest possible date. The latest possible date is 180 B.C." (*1, 2 Chronicles* [Nashville: Broadman & Holman, 1994], 32). The last date—180 B.C.—is based on the fact that Chronicles is quoted in two works dating from around that time. We lack the space for a comprehensive discussion here. Thompson, however, summarizes that "while there is no consensus about the exact date [of Chronicles], a number of scholars incline towards the fourth century B.C." (33).

One of the reasons why the Chronicles have received less attention is that there are many who see them as a repeat of the story already told in the books of Samuel and 1 and 2 Kings. If that story was already told, why would there be any need for another telling of the same events? Dillard and Longman answer this by explaining that the historical writers "were not only writing an account of their national history as it actually occurred, but they were also writing to address the theological issues of their contemporary audience. There [was] considerable interplay between the needs of the author's generation and his selection and presentation of data" (195). This plays out in the fact that the writer of 1 and 2 Kings and the Chronicler were writing with different purposes in mind.

The Chronicler wrote at a much late time than the writer of Kings. The ques tions he seeks to answer are not the sam as those faced by the writer of Kings. Th community of returned exiles, according t Dillard and Longman, "[was] not asking 'How could this have happened?' Rather it [was] asking questions about its relation ship to its past: 'In the judgment of th exile, had God ended his covenant wit Israel?' 'Are we still the people of God?' 'Is God still interested in us?' 'What do God's promises to Israel, Jerusalem, an David before the exile have to do with u who live after?'" (196). The history writ ten by the Chronicler, therefore, serves different purpose in that it seeks to answe different questions.

With this in mind, we now turn to ou study of the text.

EXPOSITION

I. SOLOMON'S PRAYER OF DEDICATION (2 CHRONICLES 6:12–15)

Chapter six deals with the beginning o the dedication ceremonies for the temple The work has now been completed. Recal that although David had wished to build "house for the Lord" (see 2 Sam. 7; Chron. 17), God decided against it an commissioned David's son Solomon t complete the project. Solomon went t great lengths in order to amass the materi als necessary for the project, such as ceda from Lebanon and skilled men from th king of Tyre, who could work wit precious metals and fine linens (see Chron. 2:3–9). When the temple was com plete, Solomon placed the Ark of th Covenant in the inner sanctum, the holy o holies. All was now ready for the dedication and use of this house for its intended purpose.

For the dedication, Solomon "stood before the altar of the LORD" (2 Chron. 6:12, NRSV). Solomon built an altar that was thirty feet in both length and width and fifteen feet high (see 4:1). Solomon stood on this specially constructed platform made of bronze that would likely resemble the reviewing stand that we might find at a modern-day parade (see 6:13). From this platform, Solomon stretched his arms and hands toward heaven but then lowered himself to his knees in a sign of submission to God (see 6:12–13).

In his prayer of dedication, Solomon recounted the history of the building of this edifice, which was a product of the desire of David's heart. Now it was time to thank God for all that He had provided and to praise Him for His wonderful attributes.

This prayer reveals Solomon's great reverence for the promises and warnings of God, which were given to all of Israel through Moses (see Lev. 26; Deut. 28). The prayer begins with reference to the uniqueness of God: "'O LORD, God of Israel, there is no God like you, in heaven or on earth'" (2 Chron. 6:14, NRSV). Solomon was highlighting the difference between Yahweh and the pagan gods so widely worshiped in the nations around them. He adds that Yahweh is a faithful God who "[keeps] covenant in steadfast love with [His] servants" (v. 14, NRSV).

Secondly, in keeping His covenantal promises, God deeply cares for His people. He consistently shows lovingkindness toward all of His people "who walk before [Him] with all their heart" (v. 14, NRSV). Notice that although God's love is for all of humanity, lovingkindness in this pact is restricted to His servants who walk with Him and who reciprocate His love. Again, referring to the agreement of the treaty, this *quid pro quo* arrangement reminds us that each party is responsible for living up to its part of the covenant. This covenantal arrangement, however, does not apply to all people. God's protection and provision for His people are unlimited but only for those who walk in His ways and obey His statutes. Recall the language of Luke 2:14 where the angel declared: "'Glory to God in the highest heaven, and on earth peace among those whom he favors'" (NRSV). This denotes God's dedication of goodwill to those who have a relationship with Him. Those who do not are not part of the covenant.

II. THE PROMISE (2 CHRONICLES 6:16–21)

David, before he died, charged Solomon: "'And you, my son Solomon, know the God of your father, and serve him with single mind and willing heart; for the LORD searches every mind, and understands every plan and thought. If you seek him, he will be found by you; but if you forsake him, he will abandon you forever. Take heed now, for the LORD has chosen you to build a house as the sanctuary; be strong, and act'" (1 Chron. 28:9–10, NRSV; see vv. 3–6).

David's desire to build a house for the Lord stemmed from his sense that it was not right that he himself should live in a fine palace of cedar while the Ark of the Covenant had no fine home (see 1 Chron. 17:1). Not only did David misunderstand that God could not be confined to this house, he also misunderstood that it would be God who would build David a house. God had called David from his lowly shepherd's life to be a shepherd of His people. Likewise, He had gathered Israel to Himself and had planted them securely in their own land. The house of David would originate with this shepherd king but would never end (see 2 Sam. 7:8–16). The kingdom and its throne would be permanent, a realm over which the descendants of David would reign forever.

David received a promise that God would not allow just any man to rule Israel, that it was reserved for the descendants of David. There was, however, a condition: the sons of David had to live according to the covenant and walk in the ways of the Lord. History proved that not all of David's descendants would live up to God's requirements. Future rulers of Israel (and Judah) disobeyed God and failed to walk in His ways. The results were catastrophic: division of the kingdoms, destruction, and exile followed. Nonetheless, God never wavered from His promise. This is amply confirmed by the Incarnation of Jesus. As Isaiah wrote, "A shoot shall come out from the stump of Jesse, and a branch shall grow out of his roots. The Spirit of the LORD shall rest on him" (Isa. 11:1–2, NRSV). As Isaiah prophesied, Jesus not only extended the Davidic line but was the eternal Ruler who connected God's promise to an earthly family with a heavenly dynasty. Through Jesus, God's eternal and everlasting love was firmly realized.

Solomon's prayer to God answers David's words: "'But will God indeed reside with mortals on earth? Even heaven and the highest heaven cannot contain you, how much less this house that I have built!'" (2 Chron. 6:18, NRSV). The question is rhetorical, of course, yet it raises an important issue. James Wolfendale writes, "Will God dwell with man? The question of all ages, the dream, the desire of humanity. Irrepressible anticipations in the deification of heroic men, the incarnations of Hindoo [sic] gods, and in the Messianic hope of the Jews" (*A Homiletical Commentary on the Books of Chronicles* [London, 1890], 168).

Where could the answer to this question be found? Not, according to Wolfendale, "in *ancient philosophy*, even with its moral teachings and intense longings…. [In it] God was thought too great to regard man" (168; emphasis in original). Neither, though, could it be found in modern, secular philosophy. There "ungodly science substitutes some abstract principle, 'Infinite Wisdom,' 'the Ruling Principle of the Universe,' or talks of 'law' and 'omnipotent power.' [In this view,] God is not a living personal God, accessible to man, and willing to dwell with him" (168). While we might quibble with a blanket description of science as "ungodly" (although there certainly is an aggressively naturalistic strain of thought in modern science that would fit this description), Wolfendale's underlying point is sound: human philosophy ultimately offers us no path to communion with the Creator and Sustainer of the universe. But what do the Scriptures say?

Wolfendale points to "manifestations of God in [Old Testament] symbols in tabernacle and temple. Promises in abundance, not merely to *sojourn* as a stranger, to tarry for a night (Jer. xiv. 8), but to *settle* in fixed residence among men" (168; emphasis in original). Numerous passages could be cited, but we will note just one. After seeing the new heaven and new earth, the Apostle John wrote, "I heard a loud voice from the throne saying, 'See, the home of God is among mortals. He will dwell with them; they will be his peoples, and God himself will be with them'" (Rev. 21:3, NRSV).

Solomon realized that the house, regardless of its splendor, could not contain God. This is a far cry from the thought (developed later) that God would live in the temple, particularly in the holy of holies. The temple was thought by many to be God's physical residence, and the people would make pilgrimages to this holy place as though they were visiting Him. Due to the centralization of the sacrifices and festivals in Jerusalem, God's presence likewise became localized, in a way that was not consonant with the reality of omnipresent His nature. Solomon's prayer on this occasion is very lengthy, extending all the way to verse 42. Our text for today, however, ends where Solomon addresses God: "'Hear the plea of your servant and of your people Israel, when they pray toward this place; may you hear from heaven your dwelling place; hear and forgive'" (2 Chron. 6:21, NRSV).

THE LESSON APPLIED

We have been given the precious gift of communicating with God through the medium of prayer. Prayer grants us access to God in an intimate manner. Our communion with God grows with our prayer life. We establish and maintain our relationship with God in much the same way as we do with each other. We don't relate as well to our brothers and sisters if we are unwilling to communicate with them. Likewise, if we are unwilling to pray, our prayers will lack power.

LET'S TALK ABOUT IT

1. What does the building of the temple say about the Church today?

The temple dedication was an act of allegiance to the Lord, not a simple commitment to the physical building. The purpose of Solomon's temple was to allow the people to worship and serve the Lord and, in turn, for the Lord to bless His people. Our churches, regardless of their splendor or lack thereof, allow us to worship and serve the Lord. Physical edifices require constant maintenance. Sadly, the history of the temple reveals that God's people forgot *they* were the real temple. Let us not forget that we are the temple, and may we strive daily to live worthily in His sight.

HOME DAILY DEVOTIONAL READINGS
MARCH 12–18, 2018

MONDAY	TUESDAY	WEDNESDAY	THURSDAY	FRIDAY	SATURDAY	SUNDAY
God Listens to Obedient Worshipers	An International Worship Service	Hezekiah Arranges a Worship Service	Deliverance from Many Troubles	Healed and Forgiven	Assembly Attendees Blessed by Solomon	Solomon Dedicates the Temple
John 9:24–38	Isaiah 19:19–25	2 Chronicles 29:25–30	Psalm 107:1–9	Psalm 107:17–22	1 Kings 8:54–61	2 Chronicles 7:1–9

THE PEOPLE GAVE THANKS TO GOD

ADULT TOPIC:	BACKGROUND SCRIPTURE:
FINDING INSPIRATION	2 CHRONICLES 7:1–11

2 CHRONICLES 7:1–9

King James Version

NOW when Solomon had made an end of praying, the fire came down from heaven, and consumed the burnt offering and the sacrifices; and the glory of the LORD filled the house.

2 And the priests could not enter into the house of the LORD, because the glory of the LORD had filled the LORD's house.

3 And when all the children of Israel saw how the fire came down, and the glory of the LORD upon the house, they bowed themselves with their faces to the ground upon the pavement, and worshipped, and praised the LORD, saying, For he is good; for his mercy endureth for ever.

4 Then the king and all the people offered sacrifices before the LORD.

5 And king Solomon offered a sacrifice of twenty and two thousand oxen, and an hundred and twenty thousand sheep: so the king and all the people dedicated the house of God.

6 And the priests waited on their offices: the Levites also with instruments of musick of the LORD, which David the king had made to praise the LORD, because his mercy endureth for ever, when David praised by their ministry; and the priests sounded trumpets before them, and all Israel stood.

7 Moreover Solomon hallowed the middle of the court that was before the house of the LORD: for there he offered burnt offerings, and the fat of the peace offerings, because the brasen altar which Solomon had made was

New Revised Standard Version

WHEN Solomon had ended his prayer, fire came down from heaven and consumed the burnt offering and the sacrifices; and the glory of the LORD filled the temple.

2 The priests could not enter the house of the LORD, because the glory of the LORD filled the LORD's house.

3 When all the people of Israel saw the fire come down and the glory of the LORD on the temple, they bowed down on the pavement with their faces to the ground, and worshiped and gave thanks to the LORD, saying, "For he is good, for his steadfast love endures forever."

4 Then the king and all the people offered sacrifice before the LORD.

5 King Solomon offered as a sacrifice twenty two thousand oxen and one hundred twenty thousand sheep. So the king and all the people dedicated the house of God.

6 The priests stood at their posts; the Levites also, with the instruments for music to the LORD that King David had made for giving thanks to the LORD—for his steadfast love endures forever—whenever David offered praises by their ministry. Opposite them the priests sounded trumpets; and all Israel stood.

7 Solomon consecrated the middle of the court that was in front of the house of the LORD; for there he offered the burnt offerings and the fat of the offerings of well-being, because the bronze altar Solomon had made

MAIN THOUGHT: And when all the children of Israel saw how the fire came down, and the glory of the Lord upon the house, they bowed themselves with their faces to the ground upon the pavement, and worshipped, and praised the Lord, saying, For he is good; for his mercy endureth for ever. (2 Chronicles 7:3, KJV)

2 CHRONICLES 7:1—9

King James Version

not able to receive the burnt offerings, and the meat offerings, and the fat.

8 Also at the same time Solomon kept the feast seven days, and all Israel with him, a very great congregation, from the entering in of Hamath unto the river of Egypt.

9 And in the eighth day they made a solemn assembly: for they kept the dedication of the altar seven days, and the feast seven days.

New Revised Standard Version

could not hold the burnt offering and the grain offering and the fat parts.

8 At that time Solomon held the festival for seven days, and all Israel with him, a very great congregation, from Lebo-hamath to the Wadi of Egypt.

9 On the eighth day they held a solemn assembly; for they had observed the dedication of the altar seven days and the festival seven days.

LESSON SETTING
   Time: ca. 962 B.C.
   Place: Jerusalem

LESSON OUTLINE
   I. The Shekinah Glory
      (2 Chronicles 7:1–3)
   II. Sacrifices and Feast
      (2 Chronicles 7:4–7)
   III. The Feast of Dedication
      (2 Chronicles 7:8–9)

UNIFYING PRINCIPLE

People often celebrate what seems important to them. How can their celebrations become a form of worship? As they dedicated the temple, Solomon and the people worshiped the Lord by bowing on their knees, making burnt offerings, playing music, and praying.

INTRODUCTION

What is the glory of God? It is a concept that, for many Christians, is difficult to define with precision. Today's text tells us that, at the conclusion of Solomon's dedicatory prayer, "the glory of the LORD filled the temple" (2 Chron. 7:1, NRSV). Much of the space in today's lesson will be devoted to an exploration of that phrase and its meaning. Before we delve into it, though, let us spend some time in an exploration of the canonical significance of the concept of God's glory.

John Piper gets at the difficulty of the task of defining glory in a 2006 sermon: "Defining the glory of God is impossible, I say, because it is more like the word beauty than the word basketball. So if somebody says they have never heard of a basketball, they don't know what a basketball is and they say: Define a basketball. That would not be hard for you to do. You would use your hands and you would say: Well, it is like a round thing made out of leather or rubber and about 10 or nine inches in diameter and you blow it up. You inflate it so it is pretty hard. And then you can bounce it like this and you can throw it to people and you can run while you are bouncing it. And then there is this hoop at the end. It used to be a basket. And you try to throw the ball through the hoop and that is why it is called a basketball. And they would have a really good idea. They would be able to spot one, tell it from a soccer ball or a football.

"You can't do that with the word beauty. There are some words in our vocabulary which we can communicate with not because we can say them, but because we see them. We can point. And if we point at enough things and see enough things together and say: That's it, that's it, that's it. We might be able to have a common sense of beauty. But you try to put the word beauty into words, it would be very, very difficult. The same thing with the word glory" (John Piper, "What Is God's Glory?"; *http://www.desiringgod.org/interviews/what-is-god-s-glory*). When we turn to Scripture, this is precisely what we find. Generically defined, glory is "that aspect of a person or [of] God worthy of praise, honor, or respect; often associated with brightness or splendor in theophanies" (Darrell D. Gwaltney, Jr. and Ralph W. Vunderink, "Glory," in *Eerdmans Dictionary of the Bible* [Grand Rapids: Eerdmans, 2000], 507). In the Old Testament, God's glory is seen in theophanies, acts of salvation, and judgment, and is often depicted as a consuming fire (507).

EXPOSITION

I. THE SHEKINAH GLORY (2 CHRONICLES 7:1–3)

A sure sign of God's acceptance of Solomon's prayer was the fire that came down from heaven to consume the burnt offering and the sacrifices placed on the altar. We see similar manifestations of God's satisfaction elsewhere. Moses and Aaron, at the inauguration of the priesthood, blessed the people. After this, "fire came out from the LORD and consumed the burnt offering and the fat on the altar; and when all the people saw it, they shouted and fell on their faces" (Lev. 9:24, NRSV). Fire was an important part of the worship of the tabernacle and the temple, where the

burning of incense and the performance of burnt offerings constantly required it.

Recall also Elijah's encounter with the prophets of Baal. God sent down fire from heaven in response to his prayer. It consumed the altar, the priests, and the dampened meat (see 1 Kings 18:20–40). A negative example is found in the story of Nadab and Abihu, the sons of Aaron: "Each took his censer, put fire in it, and laid incense on it; and they offered unholy fire before the LORD, such as he *had not* commanded them. And fire came out from the presence of the LORD and consumed them, and they died before the LORD" (Lev. 10:1–2, NRSV; emphasis added).

Theophanies of God (i.e., instances of God appearing to humans) were also sometimes accompanied by fire. God appeared to Moses in the burning bush (see Exod. 3:2). He led His people by a pillar of cloud by day and a pillar of fire by night (see Exod. 13:21–22). Sometimes images of fire symbolize God's glory (see Ezek. 1:4). Fire (and smoke) symbolized God's protective presence, His holiness, His righteous judgment, and His wrath against sin. According to Leviticus 6:13, "A perpetual fire shall be kept burning on the altar; it shall not to go out" (NRSV). The altar fire was a sign of God's continuing presence.

The "glory of the LORD" (v. 1, NRSV) is special and presents a powerful image. It "filled the temple" (v. 1). In this case, God's glory was not hazardous or poisonous. It was simply too great for the priests to occupy the same space. They were not worthy to occupy the same space with God. This passage is often understood to speak of God's Shekinah glory. The term *shekinah* is not found in the pages of Scripture; however, "it is derived from [the Hebrew *šākan*], 'to dwell, abide, settle down'" (David Cleaver-Bartholomew, "Shekinah" in *Eerdmans Dictionary of the Bible* [Grand Rapids: Eerdmans, 2000], 1203). This is a rabbinic euphemism for God as present among mankind. "The historical background for the correlation of Shekinah ('that which dwells') with God's Presence may be found in Exod. 25:8; 40:34" (1203).

This glory is a living glory. It will dwell permanently if the people follow the desires of the Lord. It was also a physical glory that could be seen and felt among the people. The people were attuned to the presence of God. They witnessed the fire come down from heaven; they basked in the power and nearness of God. But it would not last. History reveals that the Shekinah glory would later depart when the people broke their promises to God and abandoned Him. After being caught up in this moment, how could they deny the lovingkindness of the Lord? How could the power and majesty of this fire cool in their hearts? Even though this moment was surely a time for celebration, the peoples' chants of "'For he is good, for his steadfast love endures forever'" (v. 3, NRSV) were only temporary.

II. Sacrifices and Feast (2 Chronicles 7:4–7)

Knowing that God was in their midst, the people moved to offer sacrifices. This was an enormous production, performed on a grand scale. Solomon "offered as a sacrifice twenty-two thousand oxen and one hundred twenty thousand sheep. So the king and all the people dedicated the house of God" (v. 5, NRSV).

Notice the vast number of animals sacrificed. According to 1 Kings 8:63, these were "sacrifices of well-being" (NRSV) that provided food for the people during the two weeks of celebration (see 2 Chron. 7:9–10). Nothing would have been wasted.

The amount of time it took to kill the animals is not documented. Today, thanks to modern technology, the typical slaughterhouse can process enormous amounts of meat in a short amount of time. For example, Tyson Foods slaughters 35 million chickens, 125,000 cows, and 415,000 pigs per week (*ir.tyson.com/investor-relations/investor-overview/tyson-factbook*). The large volume of sacrifices was certainly appropriate for this magnificent occasion and was financed out of Solomon's great wealth. There was a spirit of cooperation in the air. The people were receptive to the festivities, and pledged their undying loyalty to the Lord. Together with King Solomon, the people dedicated the house to the Lord.

The ceremonies were not complete without a program of music, prayers, and litanies. Note the reference to David, who is credited with making the musical instruments that were used in these rituals (see v. 6). When we think of the talents and the role of the Levites, we typically think of the priests as semi-prophets, preachers of that era, or those who were assigned to minister to the needs of the people in each tribe. We often miss, however, the large group of Levites who were musicians and composers and were dedicated to the conduct of worship.

The earliest account of people designated as music leaders is found in Genesis 4:21, which identifies Jubal as the "ancestor of all those who play lyre and pipe" (NRSV). One can follow this down through later generations. Music became an important aspect in the life of ancient Israel. We can see this in Psalm 150. Elsewhere, the prophets used instruments such as the harp, tambourine, flute, and lyre in a processional (see 1 Sam. 10:5). David, of course, is credited with composing the majority of the Psalms. According to Dillard and Longman, David's name occurs some seventy-three times in the superscriptions that attribute a particular psalm to its author (*An Introduction to the Old Testament,* Second Ed. [Grand Rapids: Zondervan, 2006], 242). By the time of today's text, temple worship was highly developed and strictly disciplined and represented the pinnacle of the Israelite conception of corporate worship.

Training for priestly musicians was extensive and rigorous. Young men served as apprentices in preparation for their opportunity to formally serve as priests. The Chronicler indicates that David requested the chiefs of the Levites to appoint their relatives to be singers, whose instruments included harps, lyres, and cymbals (see 1 Chron. 15:16). Moreover, David set apart some of the sons of Asaph, Heman, and Jeduthun to prophesy with lyres, harps, and cymbals (see 1 Chron. 25:1). In addition, all of Heman's fourteen sons and three daughters were "under the direction of their father for the music in the house of the Lord with cymbals, harps, and lyres for the service of the house of God. Asaph, Jeduthun, and Heman were under the order of the king. They and their kindred, who were trained in singing to the Lord, all of whom were skillful,

numbered two hundred eighty-eight." (vv. 6–7, NRSV). The growth of music as a component of temple worship continued to flourish during the reign of Solomon.

III. THE FEAST OF DEDICATION (2 CHRONICLES 7:8–9)

Our text for today concludes with the Chronicler describing the widespread excitement and joy of the people. These verses give us an idea of the makeup of the celebrants but do not give us their number. The mention, however, of the geographical reach of the festival indicates that the multitude was large. Solomon's reign led to an expansion of the borders of the kingdom established by David. The kingdom was vast, stretching from Lebo-Hamath in the north to the brook (or wadi) of Egypt in the south (see 2 Chron. 7:8). These boundaries reflect the borders of the land promised to Abraham. The Chronicler indicates that Solomon established storage cities in the region of Hamath (see 2 Chron. 8:4). The southern border is depicted as the brook of Egypt, better known as the Wadi el Arish. (This "brook" is not to be confused with the Nile River which some would naturally think of as the River of Egypt.)

The entire celebration lasted 15 days: seven days for the dedication of the altar followed by the seven days of the Feast of Tabernacles and climaxing with a day-long solemn assembly. The events concluded on the twenty-third day of the seventh month, indicating that the celebration began on the eighth of October and lasted until the twenty-third day of the same month.

The people returned to their homes, rejoicing not only that they had participated in the feast but also that they had experienced the presence of the Lord. As for Solomon, he was able to see the completion of his work in both the feast and the dedication of the house of the Lord.

THE LESSON APPLIED

A text such as today's can feel very far removed from the daily life of a Christian. It comes from a book that is rarely studied, and deals with a set of circumstances that are firmly ensconced in the distant past. None of that, however, should be taken to mean that this text has nothing to say to us.

Above all, 2 Chronicles 7 is suffused with the presence of God. He is seen in this passage as "fire [that] came down from heaven" (v. 1, NRSV). This may remind the observant reader of the pillar of fire that led Israel through the wilderness, the fire that engulfed the altar when Elijah prayed, and the fire (i.e., the Spirit) that descended upon the apostles on the Day of Pentecost. On each of these occasions (and so many more), the fire tells us that God is powerfully at work in the life of His people for their well-being and for His glory.

Our passage's description of the worship rituals is also important. While the details may not be as significant, what we can take away from this passage is the centrality of worship to the life of Israel.

Sometimes we are tempted to see the worship assemblies depicted in the Old Testament as little more than "empty" rituals. Sometimes our own worship can become routine. But notice the emphasis here on "giving thanks to the LORD" (2 Chron. 7:6, NRSV) and on the fact that the people went away "joyful and in good spirits" because they had been powerfully reminded of the goodness of the Lord.

LET'S TALK ABOUT IT

1. **What is the value of large celebrations like the one described in today's text?**

The mood of the people is usually what makes an event a success or failure. In this case, the festival and celebration seemed to be a success; the feelings of the people reflected this sense of excitement. As the people returned to their homes, they were probably tired from the long celebration. Think of the large celebrations held in our churches. Do we tire, even when we experience a sense of joy from the events? Have you ever heard committee members complain, "We're not doing this next year"? But after a successful, well-attended Vacation Bible School, we generally ignore these sentiments because our love for the Church and our Lord outweighs any perceived downsides.

HOME DAILY DEVOTIONAL READINGS
MARCH 19–25, 2018

MONDAY	TUESDAY	WEDNESDAY	THURSDAY	FRIDAY	SATURDAY	SUNDAY
God Wants Activists Who Fast	Reconciliation Makes Gift Giving Just	Treat Others Fairly with Compassion	Life Is the Best Choice	Faithful Walking Key to Solomon's Rule	Dangerous Results of Unfaithful Actions	Results of Solomon's Decisions and Actions
Isaiah 58:6–12	Matthew 5:21–26	Exodus 22:21–29	Deuteronomy 30:15–20	1 Kings 9:1–5	1 Kings 9:6–9	2 Chronicles 7:12–22

KEEP MY STATUTES AND ORDINANCES

ADULT TOPIC:	BACKGROUND SCRIPTURE:
GET IT TOGETHER	2 CHRONICLES 7:12–22

2 CHRONICLES 7:12–22

King James Version

AND the LORD appeared to Solomon by night, and said unto him, I have heard thy prayer, and have chosen this place to myself for an house of sacrifice.

13 If I shut up heaven that there be no rain, or if I command the locusts to devour the land, or if I send pestilence among my people;

14 If my people, which are called by my name, shall humble themselves, and pray, and seek my face, and turn from their wicked ways; then will I hear from heaven, and will forgive their sin, and will heal their land.

15 Now mine eyes shall be open, and mine ears attent unto the prayer that is made in this place.

16 For now have I chosen and sanctified this house, that my name may be there for ever: and mine eyes and mine heart shall be there perpetually.

17 And as for thee, if thou wilt walk before me, as David thy father walked, and do according to all that I have commanded thee, and shalt observe my statutes and my judgments;

18 Then will I stablish the throne of thy kingdom, according as I have covenanted with David thy father, saying, There shall not fail thee a man to be ruler in Israel.

19 But if ye turn away, and forsake my statutes and my commandments, which I have set before you, and shall go and serve other gods, and worship them;

New Revised Standard Version

THEN the Lord appeared to Solomon in the night and said to him: "I have heard your prayer, and have chosen this place for myself as a house of sacrifice.

13 When I shut up the heavens so that there is no rain, or command the locust to devour the land, or send pestilence among my people,

14 if my people who are called by my name humble themselves, pray, seek my face, and turn from their wicked ways, then I will hear from heaven, and will forgive their sin and heal their land.

15 Now my eyes will be open and my ears attentive to the prayer that is made in this place.

16 For now I have chosen and consecrated this house so that my name may be there forever; my eyes and my heart will be there for all time.

17 As for you, if you walk before me, as your father David walked, doing according to all that I have commanded you and keeping my statutes and my ordinances,

18 then I will establish your royal throne, as I made covenant with your father David saying, 'You shall never lack a successor to rule over Israel.'

19 "But if you turn aside and forsake my statutes and my commandments that I have set before you, and go and serve other gods and worship them,

MAIN THOUGHT: If my people, which are called by my name, shall humble themselves, and pray, and seek my face, and turn from their wicked ways; then will I hear from heaven, and will forgive their sin, and will heal their land. (2 Chronicles 7:14, KJV)

2 Chronicles 7:12–22

King James Version	New Revised Standard Version
20 Then will I pluck them up by the roots out of my land which I have given them; and this house, which I have sanctified for my name, will I cast out of my sight, and will make it to be a proverb and a byword among all nations.	20 then I will pluck you up from the land that I have given you; and this house, which I have consecrated for my name, I will cast out of my sight, and will make it a proverb and a byword among all peoples.
21 And this house, which is high, shall be an astonishment to every one that passeth by it; so that he shall say, Why hath the LORD done thus unto this land, and unto this house?	21 And regarding this house, now exalted, everyone passing by will be astonished, and say, 'Why has the Lord done such a thing to this land and to this house?'
22 And it shall be answered, Because they forsook the LORD God of their fathers, which brought them forth out of the land of Egypt, and laid hold on other gods, and worshipped them, and served them: therefore hath he brought all this evil upon them.	22 Then they will say, 'Because they abandoned the Lord the God of their ancestors who brought them out of the land of Egypt, and they adopted other gods, and worshiped them and served them; therefore he has brought all this calamity upon them.'"

LESSON SETTING
Time: ca. 962 B.C.
Place: Jerusalem

LESSON OUTLINE
   **I. Blessings for Obedience
   (2 Chronicles 7:12–18)**
   **II. Curses for Disobedience
   (2 Chronicles 7:19–22)**

UNIFYING PRINCIPLE

Living a just and merciful life requires people to sacrifice their own desires and thoughts. What are the consequences for not choosing to be just and merciful? God told Solomon that if he did not follow the statutes and ordinances given to him by the Lord, then calamity would come upon the people, and the temple would be abandoned.

INTRODUCTION

Following the completion and dedication of the temple, God spoke directly to Solomon. In His words, there is an unbalanced set of promises and curses. At the conclusion of these statements is an ominous prospect. God warns Solomon that He will drive the people from the land and allow the temple to be destroyed if they disobey. This surely must have seemed to be a nightmare: God driving the people from the land of Abraham, Isaac, and Jacob. The nation had been unified under David. It had expanded under Solomon to reach its greatest limits, characterized by wealth, military strength, and prosperity. Additionally, the unified kingdom faced a bright future based on God's promises. However, due to apathy and their desire to follow in the path of pagan nations, the nation of Israel let it all slip away. God's warning serves as a prediction of what would happen to the nation. Based on their rejection of the covenant, Israel would face exile, famine, subjugation, and oppression.

EXPOSITION
I. BLESSINGS FOR OBEDIENCE (2 CHRONICLES 7:12–18)

God was pleased by the completion of the temple. We are reminded of His pleasure when He created the earth and humanity. When God completed a task, such as creating light, and approved of it, He said it was good. God was pleased when additional tasks were completed, such as creating all of the animals that would occupy the new earth, and His response was that "it was good" (Gen. 1:25, NRSV). Moreover, when He looked over all that He had created and gave His approval, he said, "it was very good" (v. 31, NRSV). All of the work on the temple has been completed and accepted as good. All of the ceremonies and sacrifices have been completed and accepted as good. God's appearance to Solomon by night probably indicates that this was a time when Solomon was finally alone: the crowds had returned to their homes, his advisors had retired, and his family had given him solace. Although tired, Solomon was excited to welcome God's appearance because of the pleasure that God had received from Solomon's work and dedication.

Notice that God did not send an angel to speak to Solomon; it was God who made a personal visit to him. God had heard the prayer of Solomon acknowledging His omnipresence and omnipotence. If Solomon had been at all unsure of his work, or unsure of heaven's pleasure, this appearance served as confirmation that God was with him. Although Solomon was responsible for leading the effort to complete the work and subsequent dedication, he realized that it was the Lord who enabled the entire project. Now, because God was pleased, Solomon was blessed. Nonetheless, God outlines some conditions as a reminder of the covenant. He does this in an "if... then" format: "*If* you do this, *then* this will

happen." We see this clearly in verse fourteen: "If my people who are called by my name humble themselves, pray, seek my face, and turn from their wicked ways, then I will hear from heaven, and will forgive their sin and heal their land" (2 Chron. 7:14, NRSV). J. G. McConville argues that "the response which God desires from his people after they have sinned is here described as fourfold: 'if my people *humble themselves... pray...seek my face...turn*.' It is tempting to read quickly over these terms as if they all meant more or less the same thing. But there are both distinctions and sequence here" (*I & II Chronicles* [Edinburgh: the Saint Andrews Press, 1984], 139). First, "*humbling* implies a changed attitude with regard to oneself, a renunciation of some wrong course which had been determined upon and which involved an arrogant rejection of God." Second, "a *prayerful* attitude is the opposite to that which asserts the self. It recognizes the right of God to dispose over and 'judge' one's life. (The verb 'to pray' is related to a verb meaning 'judge' in Hebrew). *Seeking God* describes the desire to determine what precisely God requires in terms of standards and of life-direction. And *turning* relates to the act of will which resolves to embark upon a life thus based" (139).

Verse 15 returns to the present moment: God tells Solomon that He will be "attentive" to the prayers offered in this house. Moreover, He "[has] chosen and consecrated this house so that [His] name may be there forever" (v. 16, NRSV). God believes in the integrity of the promises of the people. History shows that we are not always capable of keeping our promises, yet God extends grace to His people and provides every opportunity for them to approach Him. Secondly, God believes that His people love Him. Since we were created in His image, we instinctively love the One who made us. God believes that His love is more powerful than any opposition that would challenge it. Thirdly, if the people adhere to the covenant, it will serve as a sign of God's intent for humanity seen as far back as Eden. If the people comply, they will have the promises and gifts of God as well as His constant presence in their lives.

Verse 17 takes another tack: God shifts direction and challenges Solomon to "walk before me" (NRSV), meaning to live in a manner that is pleasing to the Lord. Solomon is king of the nation and, therefore, is to rule and lead the nation in the worship of the Lord. This charge to Solomon is set up in the same "if … then" format that we saw earlier: "if you walk before me … then I will establish your royal throne" (vv. 17–18, NRSV). Notice the reference to David and the commendation of David's relationship with God. As mentioned earlier, David wanted to build the temple but God would not allow it, instead anointing Solomon to do the work. David did not sulk or brood but assisted his son prior to his death. David was not perfect; he made some questionable moves and was caught up in several scandals. God was not pleased with David's relationship with Bathsheba, and the first child of David and Bathsheba was allowed to die. Nonetheless, God turned evil into good through Solomon's birth and succession to the throne.

In spite of his imperfections, David became the standard that Solomon and all subsequent rulers were to follow. David, the composer of many psalms and unifier of the kingdom, had a concrete promise from God that his line was to be eternal. God guaranteed that all of the promises that were given to him would be honored.

To anticipate just a bit, it is clearly stated that if the people were unfaithful, the temple would be destroyed and they would go into captivity (see vv. 19–22), but the Davidic dynasty would not be set aside (see Ps. 89:30–37). God would eventually become angry with Solomon "because his heart had turned away from the LORD, the God of Israel" (1 Kings 11:9, NRSV). Many of the later kings of the divided kingdoms of Israel and Judah would make the mistake of living and ruling contrary to the covenant. Occasionally, there was a king who adhered to the covenant. Consider Josiah, "who turned to the LORD with all his heart, with all his soul, and with all his might, according to all the law of Moses" (2 Kings 23:25, NRSV).

Nevertheless, in spite of all the desertions and broken agreements, God continued to remain faithful to His promises to David. The pinnacle of this succession would be realized in the Incarnation of Jesus Christ. Through Jesus, Israel would have perpetual blessings and protection and a Ruler of the Davidic line would occupy the throne forever.

The "then" portion of the rubric is the promise honored by God. God blesses those who love Him, walk in His ways, and pledge allegiance to His ordinances. Promises pledged at the festival yet broken by later events will not turn God away from those remaining who love Him according to His will.

II. Curses for Disobedience (2 Chronicles 7:19–22)

Thus far our text for today has focused on the blessings that would come through obedience to the Law. Now we change direction, focusing on the curses that would come upon the people for disobedience. We are immediately reminded that idol worship was a perennial problem for God's people. We might ask, "Considering all that God has done for the nation, why would the people of Israel turn to the pagan deities worshiped by the peoples around them?" Notice that Solomon would later be just as guilty of turning away from God as his people were by building edifices to honor other gods. As king, Solomon had a duty to lead the worship of God and to adhere to the covenant. As king, he was the recipient of the Davidic promise, which meant that a descendant of his family would rule Israel forever. As king, Solomon could not afford to lose his relationship with God.

In verse twenty, God turns to the "then" side of the agreement by describing the destruction that would follow the people's disobedience. God would remove the people from the land that He had given them. He would reject the house He had consecrated. He would belittle the nation in the eyes of the rest of the world by removing His protection. God told Solomon that He would make their folly a byword among the rest of civilization. This should call to mind one of the curses listed in Deuteronomy 28: "You shall become an object of horror, a proverb, and a byword among all the peoples where the Lord will lead you" (v. 37, NRSV). God is basically saying that Israel will become a joke to the surrounding nations. Notice that God told Solomon that Israel's shame would not go unnoticed and that they would become a laughingstock to the very peoples they wished to emulate. God would allow this because of their foolish actions. People would want to know why, of course. The answer is obvious: "Because they abandoned the Lord the God of their ancestors who brought them out of the land of Egypt" (2 Chron. 7:22, NRSV). Sadly, much of the population was so far removed from the Egyptian experience that they probably believed it could never happen to them. They quickly forgot that God had no problem abandoning the house because of their lack of faithfulness. The nation ultimately forgot that "unless the Lord builds the house, those who build it labor in vain" (Ps. 127:1, NRSV).

The Lesson Applied

Today's text returns to a common theme in God's interactions with His people Israel. In truth, it's a theme whose significance stretches all the way back to the Garden of Eden. It is the theme of obedience versus disobedience. In other words, will we obey God's commands or will we seek to go our own way, doing as we please with little thought as to the consequences? We first see disobedience and its consequences on display in Genesis 3, in the aftermath of Adam and Eve's decision to disobey God's command and to eat of the fruit of the forbidden tree. In hindsight it makes so little sense to us, because we clearly see the almost unimaginable benefits and blessings that accrued to Adam and Eve in relationship with their Maker. They were given everything and still they disobeyed.

The situation was little different with the people of Israel. They had been brought out of the land of Egypt by the mighty hand of God. Coming through the floodwaters of the Red Sea, they paused at Mount Sinai on their way to the Promised Land. There, at the foot of the mountain, they were given the Law, a clear set of guidelines that defined who they were as God's people and how they were to live their lives as individuals and in community. As we have seen in today's lesson, Israel was given clear expectations for what would happen in the cases of obedience and disobedience. They knew the curses for disobedience that awaited them should they drift from God. Even so, they disobeyed. At this new pivotal moment in the history of Israel—the construction and dedication of the Jerusalem temple—they were again reminded of the blessings and curses promised in the Law. Would they choose to listen and obey?

LET'S TALK ABOUT IT

1. What happens when our worship is not as it should be?

We should be careful not to allow our worship to become diluted to the point of apathy. How often do we just go through the motions of worship because that is "what we do" during the traditional worship hour? We are called to worship God "in spirit and truth" (John 4:24, NRSV) and with all that we have. Israel strayed from God and chased after foreign deities. The stench of idol worship and the nation's rejection of God became so odious that their festivals no longer impressed God. Isaiah wrote, "Your new moons and your appointed festivals my soul hates; they have become a burden to me, I am weary of bearing them. When you stretch out your hands, I will hide my eyes from you; even though you make many prayers, I will not listen" (Isa. 1:14–15, NRSV). Another similar statement of God's rejection comes from the prophet Amos: "I hate, I despise your festivals, and I take no delight in your solemn assemblies" (Amos 5:21, NRSV).

We should be careful not to misunderstand the intent of these strong statements. God did not condemn the particular rituals that Israel observed—all of which were commanded, let us remember, in the Law. Rather, he condemned the attitude that Israel took to worship, and the way in which they lived their life, both as individuals and in community. No matter the correctness of their worship, as long as they were fundamentally unjust toward others their worship would be unacceptable.

HOME DAILY DEVOTIONAL READINGS
MARCH 26–APRIL 1, 2018

MONDAY	TUESDAY	WEDNESDAY	THURSDAY	FRIDAY	SATURDAY	SUNDAY
Jesus Foretells His Suffering and Death	Do This in Remembrance of Me	First Examine Yourselves, Then Eat	Wash One Another's Feet	Women First Witnesses to Empty Tomb	Jesus Meets Disciples on Emmaus Road	Jesus Lives Again
Mark 8:31–9:1	1 Corinthians 11:23–26	1 Corinthians 11:27–34	John 13:1–5, 12–17	Luke 24:22–24	Luke 24:13–21	Luke 24:1–12, 30–35

HE HAS RISEN

ADULT TOPIC:	BACKGROUND SCRIPTURE:
A PROMISE KEPT	LUKE 24:1–35

LUKE 24:1–12, 30–35

King James Version

NOW upon the first day of the week, very early in the morning, they came unto the sepulchre, bringing the spices which they had prepared, and certain others with them.

2 And they found the stone rolled away from the sepulchre.

3 And they entered in, and found not the body of the Lord Jesus.

4 And it came to pass, as they were much perplexed thereabout, behold, two men stood by them in shining garments:

5 And as they were afraid, and bowed down their faces to the earth, they said unto them, Why seek ye the living among the dead?

6 He is not here, but is risen: remember how he spake unto you when he was yet in Galilee,

7 Saying, The Son of man must be delivered into the hands of sinful men, and be crucified, and the third day rise again.

8 And they remembered his words,

9 And returned from the sepulchre, and told all these things unto the eleven, and to all the rest.

10 It was Mary Magdalene, and Joanna, and Mary the mother of James, and other women that were with them, which told these things unto the apostles.

11 And their words seemed to them as idle tales, and they believed them not.

12 Then arose Peter, and ran unto the sepulchre; and stooping down, he beheld the linen clothes laid by themselves, and departed, wondering in himself at that which was come to pass.

New Revised Standard Version

BUT on the first day of the week, at early dawn, they came to the tomb, taking the spices that they had prepared.

2 They found the stone rolled away from the tomb,

3 but when they went in, they did not find the body.

4 While they were perplexed about this, suddenly two men in dazzling clothes stood beside them.

5 The women were terrified and bowed their faces to the ground, but the men said to them, "Why do you look for the living among the dead? He is not here, but has risen.

6 Remember how he told you, while he was still in Galilee,

7 that the Son of Man must be handed over to sinners, and be crucified, and on the third day rise again."

8 Then they remembered his words,

9 and returning from the tomb, they told all this to the eleven and to all the rest.

10 Now it was Mary Magdalene, Joanna, Mary the mother of James, and the other women with them who told this to the apostles.

11 But these words seemed to them an idle tale, and they did not believe them.

12 But Peter got up and ran to the tomb; stooping and looking in, he saw the linen cloths by themselves; then he went home, amazed at what had happened.

MAIN THOUGHT: Saying, The Lord is risen indeed, and hath appeared to Simon. (Luke 24:34, KJV)

LUKE 24:1–12, 30–35

King James Version

• • • • • •

30 And it came to pass, as he sat at meat with them, he took bread, and blessed it, and brake, and gave to them.

31 And their eyes were opened, and they knew him; and he vanished out of their sight.

32 And they said one to another, Did not our heart burn within us, while he talked with us by the way, and while he opened to us the scriptures?

33 And they rose up the same hour, and returned to Jerusalem, and found the eleven gathered together, and them that were with them,

34 Saying, The Lord is risen indeed, and hath appeared to Simon.

35 And they told what things were done in the way, and how he was known of them in breaking of bread.

New Revised Standard Version

• • • • • •

30 When he was at the table with them, he took bread, blessed and broke it, and gave it to them.

31 Then their eyes were opened, and they recognized him; and he vanished from their sight.

32 They said to each other, "Were not our hearts burning within us while he was talking to us on the road, while he was opening the scriptures to us?"

33 That same hour they got up and returned to Jerusalem; and they found the eleven and their companions gathered together.

34 They were saying, "The Lord has risen indeed, and he has appeared to Simon!"

35 Then they told what had happened on the road, and how he had been made known to them in the breaking of the bread.

LESSON SETTING

Time: ca. A.D. 30
Place: Jerusalem

LESSON OUTLINE

I. "He Is Not Here"
(Luke 24:1–12)

II. On the Road to Emmaus
(Luke 24:30–35)

UNIFYING PRINCIPLE

People often question the promises of their leaders. How can they come to have assurance in the midst of doubt? In the breaking of bread and making Himself known to His disciples, the risen Christ kept His promises.

INTRODUCTION

The appearances of Jesus following the resurrection were key to uplifting and restoring the faith of the disciples. During the Passion Week, His followers were emotionally and spiritually as high as they had ever been. The events of the night prior to the Sabbath, however, were devastating. Where did it all go wrong? Fearful of Rome and weak in their own insecurities, the disciples ran at Jesus' arrest and hid. Judas, who handed Jesus over to the authorities, committed suicide. However, the faith and determination of the female disciples would play a pivotal role in sustaining faith in the words and mission of Jesus. It was not easy for the male disciples to believe a woman who brought an incredible account of an empty tomb. Then again, the men mustered the courage to go to the tomb, avoiding both Roman and Jewish authorities, to see for themselves. Although this was only the beginning and there remained much work to be done, this was an occasion for celebration.

EXPOSITION

I. "HE IS NOT HERE"
(LUKE 24:1–12)

"On the first day of the week, at early dawn" (v. 1, NRSV), the women went to the tomb. They were prepared to anoint Jesus' body with the spices they had already prepared. At the end of Luke 23, we are told that the women accompanied Nicodemus when he placed Jesus' body in the tomb. This was done, Luke tells us, on "the day of Preparation" (v. 54, NRSV). On this occasion, the women themselves "saw the tomb and how his body was laid" (v. 55, NRSV). The day of preparation, according to I. Howard Marshall, "refers to the day of the Jewish week immediately preceding the Sabbath (i.e. Thursday evening to Friday evening)" (*The Gospel of Luke: A Commentary on the Greek Text* [Carlisle: Paternoster Press, 1978], 881). On this day, observant Jews prepared all food to be eaten the following day, so that the Sabbath need not be violated by the work involved in preparing food. Joseph of Arimathea had asked for the body of Jesus following the crucifixion (on Friday). This was on the day of Preparation. On that same day, the women prepared spices to bring to the tomb. Since the Sabbath had occurred from sunset to sunrise (the next morning) and Jesus was laid in the tomb before that Sabbath began, they prepared the spices on Friday and made the trip to the tomb early Sunday morning.

Luke's report that the women came to the tomb with spices is supported by Mark 16:1 but has a deeper meaning in John's account. There, the spices are connected not to the women but to Nicodemus, who brought "a mixture of myrrh and aloes, weighing about a hundred pounds" (John 19:39, NRSV). Recall that Matthew reports that at the birth of Jesus, the Magi brought gifts, including myrrh. Luke notes that the women brought "spices and ointments" (Grk. *arōmata kai myra*). *Arōma* can speak of any fragrant substance— spices, salve, oil, or perfume—used in embalming the dead.

When they arrived at the tomb, they found that the stone had been rolled away from the entrance. The women must have been frightened even as they were also perplexed. It does not seem in Luke's account that the women had thought about how they would anoint Jesus' body, because the stone would have been too heavy for them to move. This circular stone was set in a trough and was rolled in front of the entrance to the tomb or cave to protect the body from wild animals and grave robbers. Additionally, Matthew reports that a seal was set on the stone by the Roman authorities to denote that the tomb was officially sealed or closed (see Matt 27:66). This was likely done by connecting the stone to the tomb with a cord and wax so that any tampering could be easily detected. Perhaps the women believed that the soldiers guarding the tomb would assist in rolling away the stone. Knowing Roman customs and the circumstances of the crucifixion, it is highly doubtful that the women would have expected any assistance from the guards. Why then go to the tomb? According to Mark's account, the women asked, "'Who will roll away the stone for us from the entrance of the tomb?'" (Mark 16:3, NRSV) This account suggests that they possibly expected assistance from men nearby, or from the guards. Again, because of the circumstances, it is highly unlikely that any would have become involved. Both Matthew and John concur with Luke in noting that when the women arrived, the stone had already been removed (see Matt. 28:2; John 20:1).

When the women entered the tomb, they discovered that the body of Jesus was missing. Luke reports that they found two men arrayed "in dazzling clothes" (Luke 24:4, NRSV; Grk. *esthēti astraptousē*). In Matthew's account, a single angel appears: "His appearance was like lightning, and his clothing white as snow" (Matt. 28:3, NRSV). Mark likewise reports just one angel (see Mark 16:5–6), while John reports two (see John 20:11–13). The women, already frightened, were now terrified and fell down to the ground.

As previously mentioned, Luke reports that only women came to the tomb initially. There is some disagreement among the Evangelists as to precisely which women were present at the tomb on this occasion. For our purposes, though, it is not important to pursue this line of inquiry. Luke identifies the women at the tomb as "Mary Magdalene, Joanna, Mary the mother of James, and the other women with them" (Luke 24:10, NRSV).

The burning question is now posed to the women, "'Why do you look for the living among the dead? He is not here, but has risen'" (v. 5, NRSV). These compelling words reminded them all of the lessons that Jesus had taught. These words were a vindication of the Son of Man in the face of all that was predicted. Joyfully, they remembered the words of Jesus and returned from the tomb to meet with "the eleven and … all the rest" (v. 9, NRSV). As the women reported what they saw and heard, the male disciples who were present initially did not believe them: "But these words seemed to them an idle tale, and they did not believe them" (v. 11, NRSV). But remember that Jesus said that on the third day He would rise again. Peter instinctively regained his faith and ran to the tomb. Upon his arrival, he looked inside the tomb and noticed that the linen wrappings were not disheveled or strewn around the tomb but orderly, as if someone had neatly removed the wrappings.

Remember, when Caiphas and Annas, the ruling high priest and the former high priest, found out that Jesus' body was missing, they perpetrated the falsehood that the disciples must have stolen His body to give the impression that Jesus had risen. However, if the body had been stolen, the thieves would not have taken time to unwrap it; but even if they had, the wrappings would have been strewn around the tomb, not lying in perfect order as they were. Moreover, there was the presence of the guards, whose account would eventually be compromised. The disciples could not have secretly removed the body without placing their lives in jeopardy and keeping their deeds among themselves. Remember, they were in fear of their lives and in hiding; they simply did not have the fortitude for this type of covert operation.

II. On the Road to Emmaus (Luke 24:30–35)

The second portion of our text for today comes later in Luke 24. Jesus appeared to two disciples on the road to Emmaus, a village approximately seven miles from Jerusalem. One of the disciples is identified as Cleopas; the other disciple is not named. Many identify Cleopas with the Clopas mentioned in John 19:25, in which case his wife's name was Mary. This is only speculation, however, and cannot be proven.

It seems that Cleopas and his companion did not initially recognize Jesus. However, when they reached the village, Cleopas invited Jesus into their home for dinner. It was getting late and the day was almost over (see Luke 24:29). As they broke bread with Him, suddenly their eyes were opened and they realized that this was their Master, the risen Savior, Jesus. It seems as if Jesus had taken the leading role normally reserved for the head of the household by taking the bread, blessing it, and then distributing it to them. (Notice the parallels between Jesus breaking and blessing this bread and the practice of the Lord's Supper.)

Just when they realized the identity of their special guest, He suddenly vanished. Joyfully, they understood the burning of their hearts on the road. This comment is special in that their hearts were filled even before they realized Jesus' identity. Luke is not using the term literally but metaphorically by pointing to another meaning, "to enlighten."

Following this encounter, Cleopas immediately returned to Jerusalem. When he and his companion found the disciples, they were discussing the resurrection among themselves, saying, "'The Lord has risen indeed, and he has appeared to Simon!'" (v. 34, NRSV). The conclusion of their account presents them as witnesses to the risen Jesus, joyful from being in His presence. Moreover, they point out that Jesus "had been made known to them in the breaking of the bread" (v. 35, NRSV). So it is with us. We, too, can know the joy of Christ's presence as we commune with Him in the Scriptures and in the eating of the Lord's Supper.

THE LESSON APPLIED

We must never forget the centrality of the cross and of our faith. We cannot deny the resurrection. Without it, our entire religion would collapse. As the Apostle Paul so forcefully wrote: "If there is no resurrection of the dead, then Christ has not been raised; and if Christ has not been raised, then our proclamation has been in vain and your faith has been in vain. We are even found to be misrepresenting God, because we testified of God that he raised Christ—whom he did not raise if it is true that the dead are not raised. For if the dead are not raised, then Christ has not been raised. If Christ has not been raised, your faith is futile and you are still in your sins. Then those also who have died in Christ have perished. If for this life only we have hoped in Christ, we are of all people most to be pitied" (1 Cor. 15:13–19, NRSV).

Without a doubt, the fact of the resurrection is central to our faith. Just as important, though, is the life we live based on the resurrection. Paul has a good deal to say about this as well. He speaks, for example, of desiring to know "the power of [Christ's] resurrection" (Phil. 3:10, NRSV). What is that power? Among other things, it is the power to live a holy life before God characterized by the attitudes and qualities described in Colossians 3:1–11. There, Paul exhorts: "If you have been raised with Christ, seek the things that are above, where Christ is, seated at he right hand of God. Set your minds on things that are above, not on things that are on earth" (vv. 1–2, NRSV). It is easy to believe something that is in front of our faces, something that we can see and feel. However, Jesus blessed those who believe without seeing (see John 20:29). As believers, we have many means of encountering Jesus. It may be in a moment of solitude that occurs while we are driving our cars. It may be praying while at our jobs. It may be in the worship assembly. These encounters ground us in faith.

Let's Talk About It

1. What is the theological significance of the fact that the tomb was sealed?

Have you ever considered the sealing of the tomb? The Roman soldiers had affixed their seal on the tomb to indicate that Jesus was inside and no one could enter the tomb without their permission. In our society, there are seals on medicine, food containers, and the cargo transported in trucks and vans. As with the Romans, our seals are quite visible. They instill confidence in the consumer and guarantee the purity of the product. Only God could remove the seal on the tomb in such a fashion that would terrify the bravest of men. The seal at the tomb was broken in order to demonstrate the purity of God's Son.

2. How does today's text relate to our understanding of the Lord's Supper?

One of the more memorable statements in today's text is the assertion by Cleopas and his companion that Jesus "had been made known to them in the breaking of the bread" (v. 35, NRSV). Is this a one-off remark, or could it have more lasting significance? Christians have long debated the meaning and significance of the Lord's Supper. Is it really the body and blood of the Lord, as the doctrine of transubstantiation teaches? Is it merely a symbol, as the traditional teaching of the Baptist Church suggests? There may be a way between these two, as suggested by the Reformer John Calvin (1509–1564).

Calvin taught that when we eat of the Supper, we are the guests at the Table and Christ is our gracious Host. In the Supper, we enjoy His presence and are renewed in strength for service to Him. This understanding is beautifully articulated in a well-known hymn from recent years, "Come Share the Lord," written by Bryan Jeffery Leech: "We are now a family of which the Lord is head; / Though unseen He meets us here / In the breaking of the bread. / He joins us here, He breaks the bread, / The Lord who pours the cup is risen from the dead."

HOME DAILY DEVOTIONAL READINGS
APRIL 2–8, 2018

MONDAY	TUESDAY	WEDNESDAY	THURSDAY	FRIDAY	SATURDAY	SUNDAY
The Reasons for the Resurrection	Paul—Witness to the Resurrected Christ	Scriptures Equip Disciples for Good Work	Ethiopian Eunuch Hears the Good News	Lead My People and Follow Me	John's Testimony to Jesus Is True	Jesus Serves Breakfast to the Disciples
Luke 24:36–49	1 Corinthians 15:1–8	2 Timothy 3:14–17	Acts 8:26–35	John 21:15–23	John 20:30–31; 21:24–25	John 21:1–14

THE RISEN LORD APPEARS

ADULT TOPIC:	BACKGROUND SCRIPTURE:
TAKING DIRECTIONS	JOHN 21:1–14

JOHN 21:1–14

King James Version

AFTER these things Jesus shewed himself again to the disciples at the sea of Tiberias; and on this wise shewed he himself.

2 There were together Simon Peter, and Thomas called Didymus, and Nathanael of Cana in Galilee, and the sons of Zebedee, and two other of his disciples.

3 Simon Peter saith unto them, I go a fishing. They say unto him, We also go with thee. They went forth, and entered into a ship immediately: and that night they caught nothing.

4 But when the morning was now come, Jesus stood on the shore: but the disciples knew not that it was Jesus.

5 Then Jesus saith unto them, Children, have ye any meat? They answered him, No.

6 And he said unto them, Cast the net on the right side of the ship, and ye shall find. They cast therefore, and now they were not able to draw it for the multitude of fishes.

7 Therefore that disciple whom Jesus loved saith unto Peter, It is the Lord. Now when Simon Peter heard that it was the Lord, he girt his fisher's coat unto him, (for he was naked,) and did cast himself into the sea.

8 And the other disciples came in a little ship; (for they were not far from land, but as it were two hundred cubits,) dragging the net with fishes.

9 As soon then as they were come to land, they saw a fire of coals there, and fish laid thereon, and bread.

New Revised Standard Version

AFTER these things Jesus showed himsel again to the disciples by the Sea of Tiberias and he showed himself in this way.

2 Gathered there together were Simon Peter Thomas called the Twin, Nathanael of Cana i Galilee, the sons of Zebedee, and two others o his disciples.

3 Simon Peter said to them, "I am going fish ing." They said to him, "We will go with you." They went out and got into the boat, but tha night they caught nothing.

4 Just after daybreak, Jesus stood on th beach; but the disciples did not know that i was Jesus.

5 Jesus said to them, "Children, you have n fish, have you?" They answered him, "No."

6 He said to them, "Cast the net to the righ side of the boat, and you will find some." S they cast it, and now they were not able to hau it in because there were so many fish.

7 That disciple whom Jesus loved said t Peter, "It is the Lord!" When Simon Pete heard that it was the Lord, he put on som clothes, for he was naked, and jumped into th sea.

8 But the other disciples came in the boa dragging the net full of fish, for they were no far from the land, only about a hundred yard off.

9 When they had gone ashore, they saw charcoal fire there, with fish on it, and bread.

MAIN THOUGHT: Jesus saith unto them, Come and dine. And none of the disciples durst ask him, Who art thou? knowing that it was the Lord. (John 21:12, KJV)

King James Version

10 Jesus saith unto them, Bring of the fish which ye have now caught.

11 Simon Peter went up, and drew the net to land full of great fishes, an hundred and fifty and three: and for all there were so many, yet was not the net broken.

12 Jesus saith unto them, Come and dine. And none of the disciples durst ask him, Who art thou? knowing that it was the Lord.

13 Jesus then cometh, and taketh bread, and giveth them, and fish likewise.

14 This is now the third time that Jesus shewed himself to his disciples, after that he was risen from the dead.

New Revised Standard Version

10 Jesus said to them, "Bring some of the fish that you have just caught."

11 So Simon Peter went aboard and hauled the net ashore, full of large fish, a hundred fifty-three of them; and though there were so many, the net was not torn.

12 Jesus said to them, "Come and have breakfast." Now none of the disciples dared to ask him, "Who are you?" because they knew it was the Lord.

13 Jesus came and took the bread and gave it to them, and did the same with the fish.

14 This was now the third time that Jesus appeared to the disciples after he was raised from the dead.

LESSON SETTING

Time: ca. A.D. 30
Place: Galilee

LESSON OUTLINE

I. The Fishermen
(John 21:1–3)

II. "It is the Lord!"
(John 21:4–8)

III. Breakfast by the Sea
(John 21:9–14)

UNIFYING PRINCIPLE

Sometimes life seems humdrum and unproductive. Where can people recognize purpose and direction for their lives? When the disciples followed guidance given by a man on the shore, they recognized it was Jesus who had given the directions, and they joined Him in fellowship.

INTRODUCTION

Today's lesson focuses on another one of Jesus' post-resurrection appearances. In Matthew's account of the women's visit to the tomb, the angel instructed the women, "Go quickly and tell his disciples, 'He has been raised from the dead, and indeed he is going ahead of you to Galilee; there you will see him'" (Matt. 28:7, NRSV). Jesus chose to surprise His disciples by appearing to them in a familiar setting.

EXPOSITION

I. THE FISHERMEN (JOHN 21:1–3)

Jesus appears to this group of disciples at the Sea of Tiberias, more familiarly known as the Sea of Galilee. The Sea of Galilee is actually the large, freshwater inland lake where Jesus called the first disciples (see Matt. 4:18–22; Mark 1:16–20), and thousands of people were miraculously fed along its shores (see Matt. 15:29–39; Mark 8:1–10; John 6:1–13). During the course of His ministry, Jesus frequently traversed it by boat (see Matt. 15:39; Mark 8:10, 13), and it was there that He walked upon the waters of the lake (see John 6:16–24) and calmed a great storm (see Matt. 8:23–27).

John identifies the group of men who were present: "Simon Peter, Thomas called the Twin, Nathanael of Cana in Galilee, the sons of Zebedee, and two others of his disciples" (John 21:2, NRSV). As Robert H. Stein points out, "It has been suggested that Bartholomew and Nathanael were names for the same person, but that is impossible to demonstrate. We also know essentially nothing concerning Thomas and James son of Alphaeus" (*Jesus the Messiah: A Survey of the Life of Christ* [Downers Grove: InterVarsity Press, 1996], 117). John indicates that there were "two others of his disciples" (v. 2) present at the gathering. Who are the other two? We cannot say.

While waiting for Jesus, the men went fishing. Their fishing expedition was not for sport. This was the livelihood of these men, and it is possible that while biding their time, they settled into the normal pattern of securing an income and providing for their families. These experienced fishermen went out at night instead of toiling during the day. In the heat of the day, the sun was scorching and uncomfortable for the fishermen, and the fish were driven to the depths of the lake to avoid the heat of the sun. However, when night fell, the fish would move closer to the surface to feed and enjoy the coolness of the shallow waters. At this time, the men used nets instead of rods and reels and were able to draw the fish into their nets.

Peter initiated the expedition and the other disciples accompanied him, whether they wanted to fish or not. They were anxiously waiting on Jesus and, due to their recent experiences, were not going to doubt Him. The Scriptures do not provide us with a timeline between the resurrection and this specific appearance (or an idea of exactly where He would appear). However, the men knew He was coming, and their instinct was proven correct.

The disciples may have been disappointed and frustrated because they had not caught anything. Remember, they were on the lake all night and as the sun rose, it was time to head back to the shore. Jesus was on the beach. He saw them and knew where they were. They, however, had yet to recognize the figure standing on the shore. Some of the reasons the disciples did not initially recognize Jesus might have been due to their distance from the beach; there could have been a slight morning fog blanketing the area; or Jesus' manifestation may have been different than it had been with Mary Magdalene when He forbade her to touch or to cling to Him.

II. "It is the Lord!" (John 21:4–8)

In all probability, Jesus cried out to the disciples because their boat had not reached the shore. Calling out, He asked a question whose answer He already knew: "Children, you have no fish, have you?" (v. 5, NRSV). Jesus did not ask them about their catch or the lack thereof because He was testing them; He was setting up their reaction to His question, knowing that He was going to send them back out to try again. At face value, it sounds odd that Jesus would call these adult men "children," but the fact that He did is not demeaning. The Greek term *paidion* could indicate a child, infant, or a half-grown boy or girl. However, it was also used to describe an immature believer or Christian. Although the disciples had grown immensely since the early days of Jesus' ministry, they had not yet arrived to the fullness of Jesus' expectations. They would need to further develop their knowledge and faith to navigate the mission before them.

At this time, the disciples must have still been out from the shore, close enough to hear Jesus but too far to return and start all over again. Jesus did not command them but instead proposed that they cast their net on the right-hand side of the boat, suggesting that they may have fished from the opposite side. Jesus' power of persuasion convinced these professional and seasoned fishermen that they would be successful. Imagine their astonishment when their nets were filled with fish!

Recall that John initially listed seven disciples. It is only at this point, though, that he explicitly names himself in the narrative. John may have delayed inserting himself by name into the narrative as a literary device or style. He enters the picture now because he is the Beloved Disciple, and it is the Beloved Disciple who recognizes Jesus and says to Peter, "'It is the Lord!'" (v. 7, NRSV). Remember that it was John who entered the empty tomb and believed in the risen Savior (see 20:8).

John's importance in this moment, however, is overshadowed by Peter's actions. It was Peter who jumped into the water and began to swim to Jesus. Peter's actions were typical of his impulsive nature. This psychological insight into Peter's character reinforces the historical reliability of John's eyewitness testimony. Peter was stripped down to his inner garments while working on the boat. It was obviously warm and his outer cloak would have gotten in the way of his work as a fisherman. In many industries, workers remove garments that may impede their mobility. The Greek term used here is *ependutēs*, which refers to a wrapper or outer garment. Whatever the outer garment was, it was not like a heavy cloak, which would have made swimming difficult. The Greek, however, states that Peter was naked. It is logical that Peter would put on some clothes in reverence and respect for Jesus. The other disciples had to stay with the little boat, their nets filled with fish, and struggle as they maneuvered it back to shore.

III. BREAKFAST BY THE SEA (JOHN 21:9–14)

When the group reached the shore, they were greeted by the hospitality of Jesus, who was cooking some fish and bread on a charcoal fire. The narrative does not tell us when and where Jesus might have obtained the fish and bread. It is not difficult to speculate the ease through which Jesus could have produced the food. Notice there is a fish motif that is a common denominator in the narrative. The disciples are professional fishermen, are out fishing, and catch nothing; then Jesus sends them back out to try again, and they catch a large amount. They are bringing in their catch of fish as Jesus is already cooking fish. This moment echoes the pledge to make the disciples "fishers of men."

Although Jesus had fish over the fire, He asked the disciples to mingle some of the fish they caught with that He had produced. The reason was not that they did not have enough fish. There is spiritual symbolism: Jesus wanted to combine their newly caught fish with the fish He provided because, as fishers of people, their mission would be to bring in new converts to the fold. The fire of the Master would be applied to all fish, which would represent the purification of the Holy Spirit that would enable them to become fishers of people themselves. It is probable that Jesus was anticipating the arguments between Jewish and Gentile Christians on topics such as food laws and circumcision. In this symbolic schema, Jesus extends another teaching about the Church.

Another application can be made: when Peter drew up the net, they found that it had not been "torn" (v. 11, NRSV; Grk. *schizō*). By the estimation of these fishermen, the amount of fish that was caught should have ripped the net. Peter surely must have needed the assistance of the other men to bring in the catch. John speaks of only one net, which indicates that the effort and mission of the disciples, although many, would have been one concerted effort, and that there is only one Kingdom, the destination for all fish.

When the food was ready, Jesus invited them to "'come and have breakfast'" (v. 12, NRSV). It is puzzling that after John had recognized Jesus, and Peter instinctively knew Him, John recalls that none of the disciples ventured to ask Him, "Who are you?" Surely, even if the others questioned who Jesus was, they would have believed both John and Peter. One factor to consider is that neither Mary (see 20:14) nor the disciples on the Emmaus road (see Luke 24:13–35) immediately identified the Lord, which may indicate that there was some difference in the Lord's resurrection appearance here. Were they still shaky in their belief that Jesus had risen? They knew, and their meal together stamped an indelible impression on their minds. Years later in his preaching, Peter spoke of himself as a reliable witness who ate and drank with Jesus after His resurrection (see Acts 10:41).

Notice that, in this account, it was Jesus who served the disciples. Similarly, recall that Jesus washed the feet of the disciples (see John 13:4–15). In the customs of this period, the task of washing the feet of those in the house fell to the servants. This lesson in humility again finds Jesus demonstrating the role of servant leader, who came not to be served, but to serve.

John closes this encounter by noting that this is "the third time that Jesus appeared to the disciples after He was raised from the dead" (John 21:14, NRSV). Although we have previously listed eight occurrences of Jesus' appearances, John is specifically speaking of His appearances to a segment of the Twelve. So discounting His appearances to the female disciples, Jesus appears the fourth, fifth, and sixth time, respectively, to the disciples, except Thomas, in the Upper Room (John 20:19–25; Luke 24:36–43); to the disciples, including Thomas, on the next Sunday night (John 20:26–29; Mark 16:14); and to seven disciples beside the Sea of Galilee.

THE LESSON APPLIED

Jesus appears to His disciples on several occasions prior to His ascension. Each of these appearances is centered around an opportunity to strengthen the faith of His followers and also to instruct them in the fact that He has risen, fulfilling the promises made in the Old Testament Scriptures and through His words. In today's account, Jesus supplied, cooked, and served the fish, revealing that it is Jesus who provides Christians all that we need. These stories also point forward to the life of the disciples after Jesus' ascension. Each of Jesus' closest disciples would find themselves in positions of leadership, and therefore danger. They needed to know that they could trust in and count on Jesus to be with them. As Jesus strongly hints in the case of Peter, their very lives would be in danger from the enemies of the Gospel, those who opposed the spread of the Kingdom because of what it represented. Because of that, they would need to know that Jesus was with them to strengthen and support them (see Luke 12:11–12). Jesus appears to today's Christians and, although the encounter is different from that of the early disciples, the experience for believers is nonetheless personal and real.

LET'S TALK ABOUT IT

1. Among those present in today's narrative was Nathanael. What can we know about him?

The disciple Nathanael provides an interesting comparison to contemporary disciples. We first encounter him in John 1. Philip recruited a disciple of John the Baptist, Nathanael of Cana, prior to Jesus' first miracle at the wedding feast in Cana. Nathanael originally rejected Philip's encouragement to follow Jesus, asking incredulously, "'Can anything good come out of Nazareth?'" (John 1:46, NRSV).

The question should remind us of the low and insignificant status of Nazareth in the first century. This was true to such an extent that Nathanael could make a joke that everyone around him would have recognized. Matters changed very quickly, though, when Nathanael met Jesus face to face. "When Jesus saw Nathanael coming toward him, he said of him, 'Here is truly an Israelite in whom there is no deceit!' Nathanael asked him, 'Where did you get to know me?' Jesus answered, 'I saw you under the fig tree before Philip called you.' Nathanael replied, 'Rabbi, you are the Son of God! You are the King of Israel!'" (John 1:47–49, NRSV).

The lesson for us in Nathanael's story is that we should never minimize or refuse to take seriously our calling. Jesus takes us as we are and bestows upon us the power to be His disciples, regardless of our background or status, and regardless of our initial attitude toward Him.

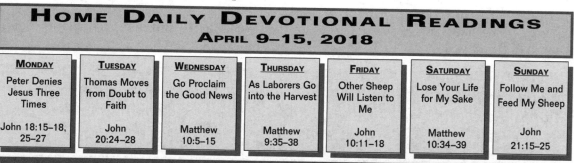

HOME DAILY DEVOTIONAL READINGS
APRIL 9–15, 2018

MONDAY	TUESDAY	WEDNESDAY	THURSDAY	FRIDAY	SATURDAY	SUNDAY
Peter Denies Jesus Three Times	Thomas Moves from Doubt to Faith	Go Proclaim the Good News	As Laborers Go into the Harvest	Other Sheep Will Listen to Me	Lose Your Life for My Sake	Follow Me and Feed My Sheep
John 18:15–18, 25–27	John 20:24–28	Matthew 10:5–15	Matthew 9:35–38	John 10:11–18	Matthew 10:34–39	John 21:15–25

FOLLOW ME

JOHN 21:15–25

King James Version

SO when they had dined, Jesus saith to Simon Peter, Simon, son of Jonas, lovest thou me more than these? He saith unto him, Yea, Lord; thou knowest that I love thee. He saith unto him, Feed my lambs.

16 He saith to him again the second time, Simon, son of Jonas, lovest thou me? He saith unto him, Yea, Lord; thou knowest that I love thee. He saith unto him, Feed my sheep.

17 He saith unto him the third time, Simon, son of Jonas, lovest thou me? Peter was grieved because he said unto him the third time, Lovest thou me? And he said unto him, Lord, thou knowest all things; thou knowest that I love thee. Jesus saith unto him, Feed my sheep.

18 Verily, verily, I say unto thee, When thou wast young, thou girdest thyself, and walkedst whither thou wouldest: but when thou shalt be old, thou shalt stretch forth thy hands, and another shall gird thee, and carry thee whither thou wouldest not.

19 This spake he, signifying by what death he should glorify God. And when he had spoken this, he saith unto him, Follow me.

20 Then Peter, turning about, seeth the disciple whom Jesus loved following; which also leaned on his breast at supper, and said, Lord, which is he that betrayeth thee?

21 Peter seeing him saith to Jesus, Lord, and what shall this man do?

New Revised Standard Version

WHEN they had finished breakfast, Jesus said to Simon Peter, "Simon son of John, do you love me more than these?" He said to him, "Yes, Lord; you know that I love you." Jesus said to him, "Feed my lambs."

16 A second time he said to him, "Simon son of John, do you love me?" He said to him, "Yes, Lord; you know that I love you." Jesus said to him, "Tend my sheep."

17 He said to him the third time, "Simon son of John, do you love me?" Peter felt hurt because he said to him the third time, "Do you love me?" And he said to him, "Lord, you know everything; you know that I love you." Jesus said to him, "Feed my sheep.

18 Very truly, I tell you, when you were younger, you used to fasten your own belt and to go wherever you wished. But when you grow old, you will stretch out your hands, and someone else will fasten a belt around you and take you where you do not wish to go."

19 (He said this to indicate the kind of death by which he would glorify God.) After this he said to him, "Follow me."

20 Peter turned and saw the disciple whom Jesus loved following them; he was the one who had reclined next to Jesus at the supper and had said, "Lord, who is it that is going to betray you?"

21 When Peter saw him, he said to Jesus, "Lord, what about him?"

MAIN THOUGHT: So when they had dined, Jesus saith to Simon Peter, Simon, son of Jonas, lovest thou me more than these? He saith unto him, Yea, Lord; thou knowest that I love thee. He saith unto him, Feed my lambs. (John 21:15, KJV)

JOHN 21:15–25

King James Version	New Revised Standard Version
22 Jesus saith unto him, If I will that he tarry till I come, what is that to thee? follow thou me.	22 Jesus said to him, "If it is my will that he remain until I come, what is that to you? Follow me!"
23 Then went this saying abroad among the brethren, that that disciple should not die: yet Jesus said not unto him, He shall not die; but, If I will that he tarry till I come, what is that to thee?	23 So the rumor spread in the community that this disciple would not die. Yet Jesus did not say to him that he would not die, but, "If it is my will that he remain until I come, what is that to you?"
24 This is the disciple which testifieth of these things, and wrote these things: and we know that his testimony is true.	24 This is the disciple who is testifying to these things and has written them, and we know that his testimony is true.
25 And there are also many other things which Jesus did, the which, if they should be written every one, I suppose that even the world itself could not contain the books that should be written. Amen.	25 But there are also many other things that Jesus did; if every one of them were written down, I suppose that the world itself could not contain the books that would be written.

LESSON SETTING
Time: ca. A.D. 30
Place: Galilee

LESSON OUTLINE
I. The Promotion of Peter
   (John 21:15–19)
II. The Status of John
   (John 21:20–25)

UNIFYING PRINCIPLE

People are sometimes reluctant to show love and care for others. How can they be encouraged to show compassion for others? Jesus calls Peter and all disciples to show their love for Him by taking care of His sheep.

INTRODUCTION

At the conclusion of the breakfast mentioned in verse twelve, Jesus challenges Peter by asking him a series of the same questions, which does not initially make sense. In all probability, the questions posed created in Peter a sense of entitlement and made him feel he was more important than the other disciples. As Jesus reveals the effects of this "promotion," Peter, instead of focusing on himself, becomes more concerned with Jesus' love for John. Jesus will, in essence, rebuke Peter for meddling but will simultaneously position both Peter and John for their roles in the Kingdom. This narrative is recounted from John's perspective.

EXPOSITION

I. THE PROMOTION OF PETER (JOHN 21:15–19)

Jesus wished to be alone with Peter because He wanted Peter's undivided attention. He wanted to place Peter in a more accountable position of leadership over the group. Again, Peter represents the "rock" of the confession, the one whose confession would become the foundation on which Jesus would build His Church (see Matt. 16:18). He would also be given the keys to the Kingdom, with power to bind and to loose both in heaven and on earth. Peter did not know it, but Jesus was granting him a promotion. Jesus knew that he would grow: the Peter of Acts will not be the same Peter who fled following Jesus' arrest.

Jesus asked Peter, "'Simon son of John, do you love me more than these?'" (John 21:15, NRSV). Peter's natural inclination was to answer, "Yes." Peter did love the Lord. Superficially, this seems like a sincere question. We pose this question often to those we love and those who we believe love us. From an innocent position, this is a quest for confirmation and reaffirmation. When we know that someone loves us, that confirmation is a product of what we already know. Likewise, when we know someone will answer this question in a positive way, there is joy in the reaffirmation of what we believe. Therefore, the question initially posed to Peter seems innocuous. However, Peter is going to be asked this same question three times. Once is innocent; a second time is questionable; a third time may well be offensive.

Additionally, how could Jesus ask Peter if he loved the Lord "more than these?" (v. 15, NRSV). Who are "these?" Is this the same Jesus who loved everyone, signaling that Peter could love Jesus more than the disciples? This passage asks three important questions. Does Peter love Jesus more than he loves the other disciples? Does Peter love Jesus more than the other disciples can? Does Peter love Jesus more than he loves his fishing profession? If Peter answers, "Yes," to these questions, which answers should be considered true, and which false?

On one level, all three are true: Peter must love Jesus more than these other men do and must be willing to render extraordinary sacrifice on behalf of his Master. Indeed, Peter earlier had claimed a devotion to Jesus exceeding that of the other disciples, and now, Peter has placed himself in the forefront of proclaiming his love for Jesus. Remember, Peter told Jesus that he would lay down his life for Him, which prompted Jesus to reveal that "'before the cock crows, you will have denied me three times'" (John 13:38, NRSV). In this context, the second alternative seems most likely: Jesus challenges Peter to love Him more than the other disciples do. Notably, the love required of Peter is primarily for Jesus rather than for the flock. It is to be a love of total attachment and exclusive service. Those who want to be used significantly in God's service must be willing to make greater sacrifices for the Lord they serve.

This question is based on the capacity that Peter has to love. To understand the complexity, Jesus wants to know how large Peter's heart is. When Peter is defining love, his definition points to sacrificial love. Jesus asks if Peter can love the others in such a manner that he would forever protect them and any others who will make their way into the movement. Additionally, asking Peter if he loves Jesus is asking him if he understands the personal sacrifices he will have to make to serve the Lord. Those personal sacrifices would come in many forms.

In verses 15 and 16, the Greek verb used for love is *agapaō*, which is derived from *agapē* and indicates a sacrificial type of love. Jesus asks Peter if he has the capacity to love Him sacrificially, putting Jesus and the Kingdom first in his ministry and his life. However, in verse 17, when Jesus asks Peter if he loves Him, Peter is grieved because it was the third time he was questioned about the quality of his love. In this last verse, there is an alteration of the "love" verb; the verb used is *phileō* and describes the love for a brother or a dear friend. Jesus not only asked Peter if he could love Him sacrificially but if he could love Him as a friend. Jesus was known as a "friend of tax collectors and sinners" (Luke 7:34) and once proclaimed, "'No one has greater love than this, to lay down one's life for one's friends'" (John 15:13, NRSV). Jesus similarly declared that "'I do not call you servants any longer, because the servant does not know what the master is doing; but I have called you friends'" (v. 15, NRSV). If we compare ourselves to Peter and the disciples, we should identify with Jesus' use of both terms for love, both terms of endearment and sacrificial love, which means that we are glad He is a friend of ours.

When Jesus asks Peter if he loves Him, Peter's answers are in the affirmative; however, what else is he supposed to say? Remember that the sting of Peter's denials remains fresh in the scope of the narrative. Jesus has forgiven Peter, but just because Jesus had risen and spent this time with the disciples does not remove Peter from what had happened. Notice the parallelism between Jesus asking Peter three times if he loved Him and the earlier denials of Peter, which were also three.

A condition of Peter's love for Jesus is to "feed my sheep" (John 21:17, NRSV). The Greek verb boskō is used here, meaning "to feed, keep, or pasture," which could most likely mean "to protect." In this case, Jesus wants the lambs to be protected and cared for due to their fragility. Verse 16 reads, "Shepherd My sheep" (NASB); "Take care of My sheep" (NIV); and "Tend My sheep" (NKJV). The term poimainō is used, meaning to shepherd or supervise the flock.

Verse 17 is rendered, "Tend My sheep" (NASB, NKJV) and "Feed My sheep" (NIV). This terminology is a pastiche of verses 15 and 16. Some commentators suggest there is a meaningful difference between "lambs" (v. 15) and sheep" (v. 16), but this is not the case. The point is that Peter is to emulate Jesus in His role as the Good Shepherd, knowing how to pasture (feed) the sheep but also knowing how to pastor (shepherd) them.

II. THE STATUS OF JOHN (JOHN 21:20–25)

The next section of our text does not shift away from Peter but does highlight the status of John. Part of the reason for this is that Peter appears to exhibit a sense of jealousy and may also have developed a slight sense of self-importance. In Jesus' rebuke, the importance of Peter's role in the Church is highlighted by Jesus' prediction of his eventual death. B. F. Westcott explains that when Jesus says "when you were younger," He is contrasting "the earlier outward freedom of St. Peter in his youth … with his final complete outward bondage. At the moment he stood between the two states" (*The Gospel According to St. John*, Vol. 2 [London: John Murray, 1908], 370). Likewise, "when you grow old" refers to Peter's martyrdom, which "is placed in the year A.D. 64" (370). Peter would stretch out his hands because he would be helpless and girded, or rather, bound as a condemned criminal. Those who bound Peter would guide him where he would not want to go; however, Peter would not deny Jesus during this experience. Like Jesus, Peter would later be arrested and crucified.

Speaking of the type of death that would glorify God might seem strange to us. The cross was set before Jesus, and He faced it knowing that all of humanity would be served by His actions. This was not a Roman victory, nor was it a triumph of the Pharisees. Jesus' death was a victory over sin and death.

Peter was to follow Jesus, from his preaching, his leading of the disciples, and his leading of the Church, to his sacrifice in death on an upside-down cross. Tradition recounts that Peter was tied to a cross and had his hands stretched out (see *1 Clement* 5:4, 6:1; Eusebius, *Ecclesiastical History* 2.25).

Now the conversation shifts: "Peter turned and saw the disciple whom Jesus loved following them; he was the one who had reclined next to Jesus at the supper and had said, 'Lord, who is it that is going to betray you?'" (John 21:20, NRSV). This question identifies the Beloved Disciple who asked this during the Last Supper (see 13:25). Using the term "betray" signifies strong condemnation. Recall, it is generally accepted that Judas betrayed Jesus, although there is an argument about what that actually meant. The Greek term *paradidōmi* can mean to surrender, to deliver up, or to hand over.

As the conversation continues and Peter notices that John is following them, Peter becomes irritated and asks, "'Lord, what about him?'" (21:21, NRSV). Jesus' reply serves as a rebuke to Peter: "If it is my will that he remain until I come, what is that to *you*?" (v. 22, NRSV; emphasis added). Westcott explains that "the exact force of the phrase is rather abide *while I am coming*. The 'coming' is not regarded as a definite point in future time, but rather as a fact which is in slow and continuous realization. The prominent idea is of the interval to be passed over rather than of the end to be reached" (372). Peter did not understand the complexities of Jesus' Second Coming. This again provides a glimpse into one reason the disciples believed Jesus' return would be imminent. John would not live until the Second Coming (although he did outlive the other apostles); nonetheless, Jesus stressed to Peter that John's lifespan was not his concern. Obviously, Jesus could have kept John alive or taken him with Him to Paradise. Jesus had the power to do this. Recall the promise that He gave to one of the condemned men on the cross: "Truly I tell you, today you will be with me in Paradise" (Luke 23:43, NRSV). Jesus is saying that each of us needs to concern ourselves with our particular path to salvation.

Additionally, "the rumor spread in the community that this disciple would not die" (John 21:23, NRSV). The rumor was given credence because of Jesus' love for John. There is some conjecture that John may have been a cousin to Jesus. Adding to the disciples' misunderstanding is the apparent expectation that Jesus would come back for them before they died. In Jesus' promise to prepare a place for them, some of the disciples heard an implicit promise to return soon, not understanding that Jesus had not stated an exact time for His return. They may have forgotten Jesus' teaching that no one knows the time of His return except the Father alone (see Mark 13:32). John therefore corrected the insinuation made by some believers that he would not die. Interestingly, Jesus' last words recorded by John refer to His return, although He gives no timeline.

John declares that Jesus performed many additional miracles and acts that were not reported, exclaiming that it would be impossible to chronicle all of His deeds. Remember, these Gospels were written many years *after* the period. This is why they do not contain all of the deeds of Jesus. The building and maintaining of a personal relationship with the Lord will help to fill in the blanks of our understanding.

THE LESSON APPLIED

When Jesus reveals to Peter that he would one day lose his youth and be led by someone else, it was a prediction of Peter's arrest and death. However, this lesson can be applied literally in our contemporary lives. Taken from this perspective, Jesus is teaching that our lives are finite and someone else will eventually have to be in a position to take care of us. Have you ever studied the life cycle? To some extent, as people age, they become babies again. Peter is told that someone else will lead him and someone else will gird him. This is akin to someone else feeding and clothing us when we are no longer able to complete those simple tasks alone. While we are able, we should depend on Jesus for all of our wants and needs.

LET'S TALK ABOUT IT

1. What does the phrase "Follow me" mean?

When Jesus speaks about following Him, there are many facets to what initially seems to be a simple command. First, and most basically: To where are we to follow Him? The short answer to this question is: wherever He leads us. In conjunction with the command to follow, we are told to take up our cross. This suggests that we are to follow Him even to the point of death. Taking all of this into consideration, today's lesson is not speaking of a destination *per se*, but rather commanding a specific lifestyle. In following Jesus, we take on a role of servanthood and holy living for the rest of our days. We grow in grace through His mercy, which allows us to deny the trappings of the world in both our thoughts and deeds. Eventually, following Him leads us to eternal life with Him.

HOME DAILY DEVOTIONAL READINGS
APRIL 16–22, 2018

MONDAY	TUESDAY	WEDNESDAY	THURSDAY	FRIDAY	SATURDAY	SUNDAY
God Promises Mercy to All People	Job's Pain Determined in Heavenly Court	Moses Summoned by God	Jesus, Our Example on the Throne	Vision of Four Living Creatures	Elders Worship and Praise God Together	Heavenly Worship
Genesis 9:8–17	Job 1:6–12	Exodus 19:20–25	Hebrews 12:1–6	Ezekiel 1:5–14	Revelation 19:1–8	Revelation 4:1–6, 8–11

THE LORD GOD THE ALMIGHTY

REVELATION 4:1–6, 8–11

King James Version	*New Revised Standard Version*
AFTER this I looked, and, behold, a door was opened in heaven: and the first voice which I heard was as it were of a trumpet talking with me; which said, Come up hither, and I will shew thee things which must be hereafter.	AFTER this I looked, and there in heaven a door stood open! And the first voice, which I had heard speaking to me like a trumpet, said, "Come up here, and I will show you what must take place after this."
2 And immediately I was in the spirit: and, behold, a throne was set in heaven, and one sat on the throne.	2 At once I was in the spirit, and there in heaven stood a throne, with one seated on the throne!
3 And he that sat was to look upon like a jasper and a sardine stone: and there was a rainbow round about the throne, in sight like unto an emerald.	3 And the one seated there looks like jasper and carnelian, and around the throne is a rainbow that looks like an emerald.
4 And round about the throne were four and twenty seats: and upon the seats I saw four and twenty elders sitting, clothed in white raiment; and they had on their heads crowns of gold.	4 Around the throne are twenty-four thrones, and seated on the thrones are twenty-four elders, dressed in white robes, with golden crowns on their heads.
5 And out of the throne proceeded lightnings and thunderings and voices: and there were seven lamps of fire burning before the throne, which are the seven Spirits of God.	5 Coming from the throne are flashes of lightning, and rumblings and peals of thunder, and in front of the throne burn seven flaming torches, which are the seven spirits of God;
6 And before the throne there was a sea of glass like unto crystal: and in the midst of the throne, and round about the throne, were four beasts full of eyes before and behind.	6 and in front of the throne there is something like a sea of glass, like crystal. Around the throne, and on each side of the throne, are four living creatures, full of eyes in front and behind.
• • • • • •	• • • • • •
8 And the four beasts had each of them six wings about him; and they were full of eyes within: and they rest not day and night, saying, Holy, holy, holy, Lord God Almighty, which was, and is, and is to come.	8 And the four living creatures, each of them with six wings, are full of eyes all around and inside. Day and night without ceasing they sing, "Holy, holy, holy, the Lord God the Almighty, who was and is and is to come."

MAIN THOUGHT: Thou art worthy, O Lord, to receive glory and honour and power: for thou hast created all things, and for thy pleasure they are and were created. (Revelation 4:11, KJV)

REVELATION 4:1–6, 8–11

King James Version

9 And when those beasts give glory and honour and thanks to him that sat on the throne, who liveth for ever and ever,

10 The four and twenty elders fall down before him that sat on the throne, and worship him that liveth for ever and ever, and cast their crowns before the throne, saying,

11 Thou art worthy, O Lord, to receive glory and honour and power: for thou hast created all things, and for thy pleasure they are and were created.

New Revised Standard Version

9 And whenever the living creatures give glory and honor and thanks to the one who is seated on the throne, who lives forever and ever,

10 the twenty-four elders fall before the one who is seated on the throne and worship the one who lives forever and ever; they cast their crowns before the throne, singing,

11 "You are worthy, our Lord and God, to receive glory and honor and power, for you created all things, and by your will they existed and were created."

LESSON SETTING
Time: A.D. 90s
Place: Patmos

LESSON OUTLINE
I. **The Throne of God**
(Revelation 4:1–3)
II. **The Attendants of the Throne**
(Revelation 4:4–6)
III. **The Worship**
(Revelation 4:8–11)

UNIFYING PRINCIPLE

People wonder to whom they should give ultimate allegiance. Who deserves to be worshiped and praised? Revelation teaches that God alone is worthy of all praise, wonder, and awe.

INTRODUCTION

One of the most misunderstood books of Scripture, the Apocalypse (Revelation) of John was one of the last books to be received into the canon. Filled with metaphorical images, this book cannot be read literally. As a continuation of the Gospel of John, the Apocalypse reveals the special relationship John had with Jesus. In today's text, John has the honor of being invited into heaven where he witnesses God, seated high and exalted on His throne, surrounded by twenty-four elders and four creatures worshiping God while waiting for the arrival of Jesus. Writing in exile on the island of Patmos (see Rev. 1:9), John was in a unique position that allowed him to compose while being "in the Spirit" (v. 10, NRSV). The focus of the entire book is Jesus Christ.

EXPOSITION

I. THE THRONE OF GOD (REVELATION 4:1–3)

John was permitted to witness some of the inner workings around the heavenly throne. With the days of his youth behind him, John might have reminisced about the times he spent with Jesus in the flesh. He was with Him at the ascension. By now, many of the things that Jesus had said had come to pass. Jesus, in His glory, was now revealed to John, the last of the original Twelve. He, unlike the other Evangelists, had a special perspective on Jesus as both fully human and fully divine.

In this vision, John is invited to approach an open door in order to witness events in preparation for Jesus' Second Coming.

The invitation that John received concerned the future: "'Come up here, and I will show you what must take place after this'" (v. 1, NRSV). While this verse indicates that events will take place later, the importance of this statement is that these events *must* occur.

The door was perhaps an opening in the sky or in the clouds that would give John clear sight into the heavenly realm. The voice that spoke to John was powerful "like a trumpet" (v. 1, NRSV). Used on the battlefield before the days of radios, trumpets signaled charges or retreats and could be heard over great noise. Additionally, these instruments had a ceremonial role in announcing the arrival of a powerful figure. John says, "At once I was in the spirit, and there in heaven stood a throne, with one seated on the throne!" (v. 2, NRSV).

The first voice is that of Jesus. In trying to parse out the images here—and to determine an exact progression of events—some have asked why John's statement that he was "in the Spirit" (v. 2, NRSV) does not come at the beginning of verse one, "since the vision of the open door in heaven presupposes a condition of ecstasy" (G.R. Beasley-Murray, *The Book of Revelation*, Reprint Ed. [Eugene: Wipf and Stock, 2010], 112). As Beasley-Murray points out, there are no necessary "inconsistencies" here: "It is more likely that verse 1 indicates the beginning of a new section in the Revelation and verse 2 emphasizes the Spirit's inspiration of the prophet" (112).

The throne John saw was not empty. God is the "one seated on the throne" that John describes (v. 2, NRSV). Whatever John's physical condition, he understood what he saw. As John was ushered into the throne room, he surely must have been overwhelmed. He was given the unique privilege of being in the presence of the Lord. John joins the prophets and the apocalyptic seers in hearing the voice of God. One such seer was Ezekiel, who warned the people against building houses that would not protect them from the Babylonians. Ezekiel wrote that "the spirit lifted me up and brought me to the east gate of the house of the LORD, which faces east" (Ezek. 11:1, NRSV). Amos also certifies God's gift of discovery to a visionary: "Surely the Lord GOD does nothing, without revealing his secret to his servants the prophets" (Amos 3:7, NRSV).

Notice the appearance of the One who was sitting on the throne: the description is one of sheer beauty and majesty. Recall Isaiah in awe of the breathtaking splendor and grandeur of seeing the Lord on the throne (see Isa. 6:1–8). The reference to the jewels in today's text emphasizes the beauty of God's presence. One form of jasper is a clear stone that resembles a diamond. Sardius is akin to a ruby, while emerald is a brilliant green. John does not say that God was the *color* of these stones; instead, as light passed through them, the colors yielded an indescribably radiant appearance.

Jasper and carnelian were among the gemstones found on the breastplate of the high priest. Jasper occurs again in the description of the New Jerusalem, which will shine with the glory of God (see Rev.

21:11). The entire scene is complemented by a rainbow that contains all the colors of the spectrum.

II. THE ATTENDANTS OF THE THRONE (REVELATION 4:4–6)

There is much debate as to the identity of the twenty-four elders. The basis of the differing opinions begins with the description of them: they were "dressed in white robes, with golden crowns on their heads" (v. 4, NRSV). Those who argue that the elders are human beings state that angels are never called elders, nor do they wear crowns or sit on thrones anywhere else in Scripture. Moreover, white clothing in the book of Revelation is always worn by the saints (see, e.g., Rev. 3:4). Within this position, several views could be posited: The twenty-four elders could be (1) the twelve patriarchs (OT) and the twelve apostles (NT), symbolic of the whole people of God; (2) the great saints of the OT seen as preceding the NT saints; (3) the whole community built on the twenty-four orders of the priesthood outlined in 1 Chronicles 24:4–5; (4) the Church as the true Israel; or (5) a heavenly court sitting on thrones of judgment. Since there are no other human beings in this scene, there are others who argue that these figures are angels, perhaps "the council of the holy ones" (Ps. 89:7, NRSV). Whatever the case, much more important than the identification of these beings is their key function: worship.

The throne of God emits flashes of lightning and the sounds of thunder (see v. 5). Recall that when Jesus spoke during a festival in Jerusalem, the crowd reacted to the voice: "The crowd standing there heard it and said that it was thunder" (John 12:29, NRSV). The power of the thunder and lightning, including a great earthquake, was again observed by John after the seventh angel poured out his bowl (see Rev. 16:17–18).

Of the numbers that carry symbolic significance, seven is the most important. The command to write to seven churches is the first instance of this emphasis in Revelation. In today's text, John then speaks of "seven flaming torches, which are the seven spirits of God" (4:5, NRSV). At times, this passage has been misread as if the lamps and spirits are separate, when they are actually one and the same. There are not seven lamps *and* seven spirits, but seven lamps *which are* the seven spirits.

Finally, John describes the expanse of the area by saying that there was before the throne "something like a sea of glass, like crystal" (v. 6, NRSV). More than likely, John is describing the great floor that led up to the throne, which reflected all the brilliance and majesty of the hall. In addition, there are some creatures who are in the middle of the gathering. They are described as having eyes in both the front and back of their bodies, signifying that they are all-seeing creatures. These beings are sometimes understood as a representation of Christ, as revealed in the four Gospels: in Matthew, the lion of the tribe of Judah; in Mark, the ox as the servant of Yahweh; in Luke, the incarnate human Jesus; and in John, the eagle as the divine Son of God.

III. THE WORSHIP (REVELATION 4:8–11)

The creatures were constantly praising God: "day and night without ceasing they sing" (v. 8, NRSV). The theme of their constant praise is God, the One who is, who was, and who is to come. The song of praise sung by these creatures is another from the pantheon of praises to God. It ranks with the prayer of Solomon (see 2 Chron. 6:12–42), as well as the Magnificat of Mary (see Luke 1:46–55). The creatures constantly praise God. They are speaking of Jesus, the Word: "In the beginning was the Word, and the Word was with God, and the Word was God…And the Word became flesh and lived among us, and we have seen his glory" (John 1:1, 14, NRSV). The third part of the praise is that He is yet to come. This praise anthem again points to the fact that these things will soon occur (see Rev. 4:1).

The creatures give thanks to God, who is seated on the throne, praising Him as One who is eternal. Nonetheless, the focus of their praise continues to be in preparation for receiving the Lamb of God. Notice that the creatures give thanks to God. The creatures obviously know what God has done for those who love Him. They know what God is doing for the saved, who will live with Him for eternity.

Not to be outdone by the creatures, the elders later fall down before God's throne and worship Him with a chant of praise that echoes that of the creatures. The elders acknowledge that God "'created all things'" (4:11, NRSV). They cast down their crowns (see v. 10), symbolizing the honor that would be given to the victor at the athletic games so popular in the ancient world. Like Paul, who used the language of victory celebrations in sports (see 2 Tim. 4:7), John invokes this athletic metaphor to describe God's victory over Satan.

THE LESSON APPLIED

This lesson lifts many images from the book that are readily explained, while others seem problematic because they are not clarified. In Revelation, we see an old man (John), who has never left his position as an apostle and who continues his work faithfully. Old age will eventually sap the strength of every Christian because of the deterioration of our bodies. Some things we used to do, we will no longer be able to do. But as we move into the elder years of our lives, we have an opportunity to transform our continued relationship with the Lord. The focus of this lesson is on God, of course. The images and the storyline are part of the understanding of what is yet to be revealed. However, we must not lose sight of the special reward and honor given to John, not because of his age but due to his faithfulness.

What will be said of us in our old age? How will we (or others) look back upon our lives? Will we be focused on all the time we have wasted, or will we be able to look back at all the years we have spent faithfully serving the Lord? The Apostle John lived a full life in service to the Lord. According to tradition, he was the only one of the Twelve to die in old age of (apparently) natural causes. He spent much of his time in the city of Ephesus in Asia Minor, and a number of stories about him survive in the oral tradition of the early Church. While he did not die in the spectacular manner of a Peter or a Stephen, his legacy is with us in the form of his writings: Gospel, a set of letters, and the Revelation, all of which focus powerfully on the meaning of Jesus and of the lives we live in and through Him. Whatever else might be said about John, he was active in service to the Lord, always alert to threats to the Gospel and not merely awaiting death. Will the same be said of us? What have we done in the Kingdom beside occupy a pew every Sunday? Have we cared for the needy? Have we shared the Gospel? Have we strengthened a brother or sister in Christ? None of this, of course, has to be on a grand scale. Surely John did not think of his day-to-day service in such terms. What was important for him—and for us—is that he devoted himself to the task every day.

LET'S TALK ABOUT IT

1. What happens when we allow our worship to grow tired and cold?

Believers place God at the center of their worship, as today's text clearly shows. However, what happens when we allow our worship to become stagnant or inconsistent? When that happens, we lose all our focus on and connection with the Lord. It is ironic that we have trouble with consistent praise to God, given that He is our never-failing Source of blessing and mercy. It is sad that God would have to listen to inanimate objects (such as rocks) cry out their praise, or to have a donkey worship Him (Luke 19:40; Num.. 22:23–33). In today's lesson, we learn that there are creatures worshiping God constantly, irrespective of our actions. Although the description of these creatures is strange, the imagery should not frighten but reassure us that God is worthy of all praise. Consider your own heart. Is it ready for worship (see Matt. 5:23–25)? Is it pure and receptive to hearing and obeying the Word as proclaimed in preaching, music, and the Lord's Supper? What's more, how do you prepare for worship? Do you prepare at all? Take stock of these questions this week. Have you checked your praise meter lately?

Today's lesson provides us with an opportunity to see the worship of God in its fullness. It reminds us that it is not us alone in our respective church buildings who gather to worship God from week to week. In worship we join together with all of the saints, living and dead, and with the heavenly hosts in praise to God. It is tempting to get lost in the details of our worship assemblies (matters of style, for example) and to thereby lose sight of the cosmic significance of our worship. It is well for us to remember it, though, because when we forget, worship has a tendency to turn into a self-indulgent experience designed and executed for our own pleasure rather than God's.

HOME DAILY DEVOTIONAL READINGS
APRIL 23–29, 2018

MONDAY	TUESDAY	WEDNESDAY	THURSDAY	FRIDAY	SATURDAY	SUNDAY
Rejoice! Your Salvation Is in Christ	All Subject to God Through Christ	Sanctified by Lambs Sacrificed Daily	Christ, Our Suffering, and Salvation	Eat the Scroll, Speak My Words	Only One Can Open the Scroll	All Creatures Worship the Lamb
1 Peter 1:3–9	1 Corinthians 15:20–28	Exodus 29:38–46	Romans 8:31–39	Ezekiel 2:8–3:11	Revelation 5:1–5	Revelation 5:6–14

Blessing, Glory, Honor Forever

Revelation 5:6—14

King James Version

AND I beheld, and, lo, in the midst of the throne and of the four beasts, and in the midst of the elders, stood a Lamb as it had been slain, having seven horns and seven eyes, which are the seven Spirits of God sent forth into all the earth.

7 And he came and took the book out of the right hand of him that sat upon the throne.

8 And when he had taken the book, the four beasts and four and twenty elders fell down before the Lamb, having every one of them harps, and golden vials full of odours, which are the prayers of saints.

9 And they sung a new song, saying, Thou art worthy to take the book, and to open the seals thereof: for thou wast slain, and hast redeemed us to God by thy blood out of every kindred, and tongue, and people, and nation;

10 And hast made us unto our God kings and priests: and we shall reign on the earth.

11 And I beheld, and I heard the voice of many angels round about the throne and the beasts and the elders: and the number of them was ten thousand times ten thousand, and thousands of thousands;

12 Saying with a loud voice, Worthy is the Lamb that was slain to receive power, and riches, and wisdom, and strength, and honour, and glory, and blessing.

13 And every creature which is in heaven, and on the earth, and under the earth, and such as are in the sea, and all that are in them, heard

New Revised Standard Version

THEN I saw between the throne and the four living creatures and among the elders a Lamb standing as if it had been slaughtered, having seven horns and seven eyes, which are the seven spirits of God sent out into all the earth.

7 He went and took the scroll from the right hand of the one who was seated on the throne.

8 When he had taken the scroll, the four living creatures and the twenty-four elders fell before the Lamb, each holding a harp and golden bowls full of incense, which are the prayers of the saints.

9 They sing a new song: "You are worthy to take the scroll and to open its seals, for you were slaughtered and by your blood you ransomed for God saints from every tribe and language and people and nation;

10 you have made them to be a kingdom and priests serving our God, and they will reign on earth."

11 Then I looked, and I heard the voice of many angels surrounding the throne and the living creatures and the elders; they numbered myriads of myriads and thousands of thousands,

12 singing with full voice, "Worthy is the Lamb that was slaughtered to receive power and wealth and wisdom and might and honor and glory and blessing!"

13 Then I heard every creature in heaven and on earth and under the earth and in the sea, and all that is in them, singing,

MAIN THOUGHT: Saying with a loud voice, Worthy is the Lamb that was slain to receive power, and riches, and wisdom, and strength, and honour, and glory, and blessing. (Revelation 5:12, KJV)

REVELATION 5:6—14

King James Version | *New Revised Standard Version*

I saying, Blessing, and honour, and glory, and power, be unto him that sitteth upon the throne, and unto the Lamb for ever and ever.
14 And the four beasts said, Amen. And the four and twenty elders fell down and worshipped him that liveth for ever and ever.

"To the one seated on the throne and to the Lamb be blessing and honor and glory and might forever and ever!"
14 And the four living creatures said, "Amen!" And the elders fell down and worshiped.

LESSON SETTING
Time: ca. A.D. 95
Place: Patmos

LESSON OUTLINE
I. **The Identification of the Lamb (Revelation 5:6–7)**
II. **The Power of Song (Revelation 5:8–10)**
III. **Exaltation of the Multitude (Revelation 5:11–14)**

UNIFYING PRINCIPLE
People find it difficult to find a source of allegiance that is permanent and lasting. What type of response do they give when they find this lasting allegiance? Revelation speaks of joyful praise and eternal worship of God.

INTRODUCTION
Our narrative for today begins where last week's lesson ended. John prepares the reader for the One who is worthy to open the sealed scrolls. Chapter five will serve as a prelude to chapter six—which, unfortunately, we will not cover in this quarter's lessons—where the Lamb will begin to break the seals. In this chapter, both the One who is seated on the throne and the Lamb are worshiped *prior* to the breaking of the seals, and the focus of the narrative is on the worthiness of the One and the Lamb. Their worth is not exclusive to the events described herein; their worth is from eternity. Although the emphasis in Revelation is on the end times, there is a cosmic line that connects the praise at creation, bisecting the life of the world, to the end times. The scene is an enormous throne room filled with the creatures and elders, with the addition of angels and all of creation, proclaiming the worthiness of the One and the Lamb.

EXPOSITION
I. THE IDENTIFICATION OF THE LAMB (REVELATION 5:6–7)
In our last lesson, we witnessed the creatures with eyes in the front and back of their bodies (see Rev. 4:6). The Scriptures do not elaborate on the placement of the eyes. Rather the point is the abundance of their eyes, symbolizing their ability to see everything at all times. The twenty-four elders are a more complex representation. It is disputed as to whether these elders were patriarchs or saints from the Old Testament, apostles, or a gathering of priests. Whatever the case may be, they represent those whom God has placed on lesser thrones, in a position of honor surrounding Him.

The function of both the creatures and the elders is to praise God. They do not compete with each other. The Scriptures highlight the individual worship of each (see Rev. 4:8–11).

John introduces a new entity into the narrative, "a Lamb standing as if it had been slaughtered, having seven horns and seven eyes" (5:6, NRSV). The position of the Lamb is striking; it stands between the throne of God and the elders and creatures. The center of attention is the Lamb. The Lamb was not processed as though for human consumption. John uses the Greek verb *sphazō*, meaning "to butcher or to violently slaughter." Although this seems to indicate that the Lamb is in a position of weakness, nothing could be further from the truth. The Lamb is standing in a position of power.

Our initial impression of a defeated lamb is erroneous: the Lamb is not vanquished but victorious. First, John has already introduced this figure as "'the Lion of the tribe of Judah, the Root of David, [who] has conquered'" (v. 5, NRSV). One of the most powerful creatures, the lion represents strength and might. Secondly, the lamb is said to have seven horns (see v. 6). "The horn," G.B. Caird observes, "is the symbol of strength, the eye of wisdom. Christ possesses in all their fulness the omnipotence and omniscience of God; he is 'the power of God and the wisdom of God' (1 Cor. i.24)" (*The Revelation of Saint John* [London: A&C Black, 1966], 75). Recall the Passover Lamb could not have any broken bones; therefore, even the specter of the cross reveals the upright or standing Lamb in a position of power. Additionally, the seven eyes represent the Spirit of God, which completes the gathering in this worship assembly of God the Father, Jesus the Son, and the Holy Spirit.

Recall that John begins to weep because it seems as if no one is worthy enough to open the seals to the scroll of the Book of Life. One of the elders, however, will speak up in song and say that there is One, springing from the Root of David, who is worthy to open the Book. There is some interesting interplay between the One on the throne and the Lamb: "[The Lamb] went and took the scroll from the right hand of the one who was seated on the throne" (v. 7, NRSV). The scroll was not available for just anyone to take; only the One who was worthy could do so. The imagery of the Lamb taking the scroll may invoke a negative connotation due to the verb used (Grk. *lambanō*), which can mean "to take." However, in keeping with the meek yet powerful attributes of the Lamb, we should focus in on a secondary meaning "to receive." The Lamb was the only one who was worthy to receive the scroll. Whereas the taking of the scroll could seem overly aggressive as the actions of an unruly king, the Lamb's worthiness to receive the scroll indicates the permanence of ownership. The scroll belonged to the Lamb from the foundations of time, from all eternity.

For believers, an interesting example of this same concept can be found when Jesus asks God, "'Let this cup pass from me; yet not what I want but what you want'" (Matt. 26:39, NRSV). What did God say to His Son in reply to cause Him to stay the course? We are not told directly, but undoubtedly their celestial conversation illuminates the interplay between the two in today's text.

II. THE POWER OF SONG (REVELATION 5:8–10)

In last week's lesson, the elders cast the golden crowns toward the throne in a posture of worship (see Rev. 4:10). The scene now shifts to the elders holding harps and golden bowls filled with incense. Only the harp and the trumpet are mentioned as musical instruments in heavenly worship in Revelation. They indicate that the elders continue to worship the One on the throne and the Lamb. However, the focus of the worship now shifts to the Lamb. The twenty-four elders fall down before the Lamb with their harps and their golden bowls filled with incense. These bowls were open plates upon which the incense could be openly burned. The bowls, we are told, are "the prayers of the saints" (5:8, NRSV). As Caird notes, "Along with their own worship the elders present the prayers of God's people, because this is the moment to which all those prayers have been directed" (76). The elders and creatures are those who acknowledge the One who is worthy of worship.

The angelic worship from the elders and creatures breaks into a new song in the worship of the One who is able to break the seals and thus reveal the contents of the scroll. John proclaims that this is a "new song" (v. 9, NRSV). John introduces the chants of the previous chapter during which the creatures say, "'Holy, holy, holy, the Lord God the Almighty'" (Rev. 4:8, NRSV), while the elders say, "'You are worthy....'" (Rev. 4:11, NRSV).

The first verse of the song is divided into three distinct parts. The first part is "'You are worthy to take the scroll and to open its seals'" (5:9, NRSV). This segment proclaims that there is only One capable of breaking the seals. This part announces the subject of the song, and it is obvious that this honor is given by the Lord. The next lines tell us that the Lamb is worthy because "'[He was] slaughtered'" and because "'by [His] blood [He] ransomed for God saints from every… nation'" (v. 9, NRSV). Although the Lamb was slain, He prevailed. The worship of the Lamb in this song reinforces the resurrection and glory of the One who was slain. This second part proclaims the reason for the Lamb's worthiness. Lastly, the third part indicates the purpose of the Lamb's great and final sacrifice.

The song concludes: "'You have made them to be a kingdom and priests serving our God'" (v. 10, NRSV). "Them" refers to all who have kept the faith and have been rewarded with eternal life. Because of the Lamb's death, we have been positioned as a kingdom of priests before God, with a promise of reigning on earth in the future. The final phrase, "'and they will reign on earth'" (v. 10, NRSV), establishes the reward of those faithful to the Lord. In this case, the saints will be a kingdom. The saints are corporately a "kingdom" and individually "priests." As priests, they serve Him in worship and witness. The saints belong to God and thus serve Him by participating in the universal mission to the nations. John has previously confirmed the status of these saints: "[He] made us to be a kingdom, priests serving his God and Father…." (Rev. 1:6, NRSV). The wording of this verse further confirms their status. The elders could be singing of their own redemption in either the first or third person.

III. EXALTATION OF THE MULTITUDE (REVELATION 5:11–14)

Just when it seems that the celestial celebration has reached its zenith, John looks, and hears a multitude of voices emanating from around the throne. At first glance, the syntax is confusing. John does not say that he saw the gathering, but that he "heard the voice" (v. 11, NRSV). To provide further description, John notes that they sang "with full voice" (v. 12, NRSV; Grk. *phonē megalē*). In music, the immediate result of singing in unison is a noticeable increase in volume. John realized that the number of the group was huge: "myriads of myriads and thousands of thousands" (v. 11, NRSV).

The multitude declares in a new chant, "'Worthy is the Lamb that was slaughtered to receive power and wealth and wisdom and might and honor and glory and blessing'" (v. 12, NRSV). Many of these are things that all kings seek. Unfortunately, earthly kings often do not seek wisdom or honor. In many instances, earthly kings and rulers seek power and riches in a dishonorable manner. The Scriptures are filled with examples of unjust rulers. Solomon, however, was an example of one who sought wisdom as opposed to wealth, and God rewarded him immensely. Here, the blessings have been given to One who is worthy to enjoy them.

Now, all of creation joins in the celebration and worship. The language is a reminder of the creation story of Genesis. The culmination of creation was the completion of the heavens and earth and the population of them. All of creation is involved here—the heavens, the earth (including the land and seas) and even the area *under* the earth. Notice that the sea is mentioned last, possibly due to the symbolism of the book, in which the sea represents evil and chaos. Therefore, it is placed with the underworld rather than with the earth.

Returning to the singers, we come to the climax of the celebration. With salutations of grandeur and majesty, the gathering praises the One on the throne and the Lamb. Listening to their praise, John notes that the elders "fell down and worshiped" (v. 14, NRSV). Again, all of creation is gathered here, and the praise is contagious. The four living creatures pronounce the "Amen." The term *amēn* signifies trustworthiness or reliability. In a liturgical setting such as this one, the meaning of the term is "so be it." The worshipers acknowledge that the Lord is satisfied with their praise and worship.

THE LESSON APPLIED

In today's text, both the Father and the Son are on display. God is identified as the One who sits upon the throne, and Jesus is the Lamb. However, we must not miss the Holy Spirit, who is introduced with language that might be unfamiliar. The worthiness of the Triune God is unlimited and cannot be described by the faltering speech of humanity. All of creation reveals that Christ's mission was for the salvation of all nations, regardless of culture or identity. All of creation will one day bow down in worship. As Paul wrote in his letter to the Philippians, "So that at the name of Jesus every knee should bend, in heaven and on earth and under the earth" (Phil. 2:10, NRSV). It is difficult for us to imagine this, given the world in which we live. As we look around, we see a society—and a world at large—that is in rebellion against the rule, the government, of God. Wars rage, poverty and disease take the lives of so many, marriages and families are torn apart, everywhere faith seems to be in retreat. At the root of all of this is the prevalence of sin in our world. Jesus came to deal with humanity's sin problem, but that problem will not receive its ultimate solution until the day when Jesus returns. We look forward to that day as a time when we will leave all of the pain and struggles of this life behind to dwell with God, to gather around His throne with the countless others in worship and praise to His name.

LET'S TALK ABOUT IT

1. Will we be a part of the heavenly assembly?

As the author of Hebrews wrote, "Jesus Christ is the same yesterday and today and forever" (Heb. 13:8, NRSV). The forms of worship that we have available to us today are unlimited. We are limited only by our indifference, obstinacy, or apathy. Today's text reminds us that all of creation worships the Lord. Are we included in this gathering? Or will we be among those who have been banished to the abyss, only to watch in horror from a distance the expansive, eternal praise taking place around the throne of God? In our walk with the Lord, we must make each day count toward our position as part of that congregation that has the ability and knowledge to take part in the new song about the worthiness of the Lamb. If we are to receive His promise to reign with Him, we cannot wait.

2. How can song affect our understanding of God?

One of the headings in today's lesson is "The Power of Song." The worship scenes in Revelation 4–5 very helpfully remind us of the centrality of song in the worship of God. You may recall from lesson three how the people recited a portion of Psalm 136 at the dedication of the temple: "For he is good, for his steadfast love endures forever" (2 Chron. 7:3, NRSV). Remember, too, how the seraphim continually sang in the presence of God: "'Holy, holy, holy is the LORD of hosts; the whole earth is full of his glory'" (Isa. 6:3, NRSV). Singing expresses central truths about God with feeling and directs our hearts toward Him in a way that few other expressions can match. How do you approach singing in worship? Do you let the choir or the instrumentalists handle the music while you sit back and observe (as though worship were a performance)? Or do you fully participate, joining in musical praise to our Lord and Savior?

Giving from a Generous Heart

Adult Topic:	Background Scriptures:
Sowing and Reaping	Exod. 25:1–7; 35:4–29; Lev. 27:30–33; 2 Cor. 9:6–8

Exodus 35:20–29; 2 Corinthians 9:6–8

King James Version

AND all the congregation of the children of Israel departed from the presence of Moses.

21 And they came, every one whose heart stirred him up, and every one whom his spirit made willing, and they brought the Lord's offering to the work of the tabernacle of the congregation, and for all his service, and for the holy garments.

22 And they came, both men and women, as many as were willing hearted, and brought bracelets, and earrings, and rings, and tablets, all jewels of gold: and every man that offered offered an offering of gold unto the Lord.

23 And every man, with whom was found blue, and purple, and scarlet, and fine linen, and goats' hair, and red skins of rams, and badgers' skins, brought them.

24 Every one that did offer an offering of silver and brass brought the Lord's offering: and every man, with whom was found shittim wood for any work of the service, brought it.

25 And all the women that were wise hearted did spin with their hands, and brought that which they had spun, both of blue, and of purple, and of scarlet, and of fine linen.

26 And all the women whose heart stirred them up in wisdom spun goats' hair.

27 And the rulers brought onyx stones, and stones to be set, for the ephod, and for the breastplate;

28 And spice, and oil for the light, and for the anointing oil, and for the sweet incense.

New Revised Standard Version

THEN all the congregation of the Israelites withdrew from the presence of Moses.

21 And they came, everyone whose heart was stirred, and everyone whose spirit was willing, and brought the Lord's offering to be used for the tent of meeting, and for all its service, and for the sacred vestments.

22 So they came, both men and women; all who were of a willing heart brought brooches and earrings and signet rings and pendants, all sorts of gold objects, everyone bringing an offering of gold to the Lord.

23 And everyone who possessed blue or purple or crimson yarn or fine linen or goats' hair or tanned rams' skins or fine leather, brought them.

24 Everyone who could make an offering of silver or bronze brought it as the Lord's offering; and everyone who possessed acacia wood of any use in the work, brought it.

25 All the skillful women spun with their hands, and brought what they had spun in blue and purple and crimson yarns and fine linen;

26 all the women whose hearts moved them to use their skill spun the goats' hair.

27 And the leaders brought onyx stones and gems to be set in the ephod and the breastpiece,

28 and spices and oil for the light, and for the anointing oil, and for the fragrant incense.

MAIN THOUGHT: But this I say, He which soweth sparingly shall reap also sparingly; and he which soweth bountifully shall reap also bountifully. (2 Corinthians 9:6, KJV)

EXODUS 35:20-29; 2 CORINTHIANS 9:6-8

King James Version

29 The children of Israel brought a willing offering unto the LORD, every man and woman, whose heart made them willing to bring for all manner of work, which the LORD had commanded to be made by the hand of Moses.

• • • 2 Corinthians 9:6–8 • • •

BUT this I say, He which soweth sparingly shall reap also sparingly; and he which soweth bountifully shall reap also bountifully.

7 Every man according as he purposeth in his heart, so let him give; not grudgingly, or of necessity: for God loveth a cheerful giver.

8 And God is able to make all grace abound toward you; that ye, always having all sufficiency in all things, may abound to every good work.

New Revised Standard Version

29 All the Israelite men and women whose hearts made them willing to bring anything for the work that the LORD had commanded by Moses to be done, brought it as a freewill offering to the LORD.

• • • 2 Corinthians 9:6–8 • • •

THE point is this: the one who sows sparingly will also reap sparingly, and the one who sows bountifully will also reap bountifully.

7 Each of you must give as you have made up your mind, not reluctantly or under compulsion, for God loves a cheerful giver.

8 And God is able to provide you with every blessing in abundance, so that by always having enough of everything, you may share abundantly in every good work.

LESSON SETTING

Time: 15th c. B.C.
(Exodus);
A.D. 50s
(2 Corinthians)
Place: Sinai (Exodus);
Macedonia
(2 Corinthians)

LESSON OUTLINE

I. The People Bring
Their Offerings
(Exodus 35:20–21)
II. The Offerings
(Exodus 35:22–29)
III. The Grace of Givers
(2 Corinthians 9:6–8)

UNIFYING PRINCIPLE

People want to live lives of gratitude. How can they express their thankfulness properly? God welcomes the offerings of those who will give with generous and cheerful hearts.

INTRODUCTION

The central theme of today's lesson is that "God loves a cheerful giver" (2 Cor. 9:7, NRSV). The setting of today's text from Exodus is the gathering of provisions for the construction of the tabernacle. We might think that the nation of Israel would be incapable of supplying these goods for construction. After all, they had only recently been freed from forced bondage. They were, however, allowed to take some of the spoils of Egypt. The focus of today's narrative is on the people who willingly gave of their possessions and their skills. We must not lose sight of the ones who might have refused to participate because they did not have willing hearts. The account in Exodus is supported by Paul's encouragement to the church in Corinth, which emphasizes the continual need for this teaching.

EXPOSITION

I. THE PEOPLE BRING THEIR OFFERINGS (EXODUS 35:20–21)

Moses had previously assembled the entire congregation of the people of Israel and commanded them to begin the construction of the tabernacle. On this occasion, Moses begins by encouraging Israel to provide labor and material for the project: "These are the things that the LORD has commanded you to do…Take from among you an offering to the LORD; let whoever is of a generous heart bring the LORD's offering…All who are skillful among you shall come and make all that the LORD has commanded: the tabernacle, its tent and its covering" (Exod. 35:1, 5, 10, NRSV). Moreso than the mind, the heart is the center of this call. Moses invites only those who have a willing or passionate heart. From those who are willing, Moses requests precious metals, such as gold, silver, and bronze, and also fine linens, oils, incense, precious stones, and other materials that will be needed to construct the tabernacle. Additionally, items for the priestly garments worn by Aaron and his sons were included in the inventory.

Notice the emphasis on willingness in the narrative. Verse 21 recounts that "they came, everyone whose heart was stirred, and everyone whose spirit was willing, and brought the LORD's offering to be used for the tent of meeting" (NRSV). The text does not indicate who spurned the invitation. It does say, however, that those of the community who were willing brought their contribution to the Lord. Unfortunately, there were probably some whose lack of faith or whose greed prevented their participation.

The Lord blessed the people who freely gave. Recall, it was not that long ago that they had been captives in Egypt, and it was the Lord who had brought them out of bondage. There has been some discussion as to where the people obtained goods such as gold, precious jewels, and dyed cloth. Remember though that the Lord had favored Israel during her departure from Egypt, causing the Egyptians to give them whatsoever they wanted (see Exod. 12:35–36). These blessings of God are a reminder of how God cares for His people.

II. THE OFFERINGS (EXODUS 35:22–29)

The text now becomes more specific about the kind of gifts that were brought "All who were of a willing heart brought brooches and earrings and signet rings and pendants, all sorts of gold objects, everyone bringing an offering of gold to the LORD" (v. 22, NRSV). In this moment, we see a reversal of the moment when men and women tore off their gold to be melted down to make a golden calf (see Exod. 32). God had forgiven this act of extremely poor judgment and defiance. On this occasion, they had no control over how the jewelry would be used. The negative act of providing the gold for making the golden calf was now offset by the positive joy of constructing an edifice dedicated to God Now, all could joyfully present their wealth as an offering to the Lord.

Notice that besides the linens that were used, additional materials included animal skins or hides, which were dyed red after the tanning procedure. Some interpreters find no inherent significance in the colors found in the Scripture. But that is not always the case. Consider a few examples. The color black was traditionally worn during periods of mourning. This is still true today, but it was certainly moreso in the ancient world. Purple was also a significant color, featuring prominently in the construction of both the tabernacle and the temple. Purple was a color that only the rich could afford. The significance of its use is that nothing of finery was to be withheld from God. The color red was a symbol of authority and royalty and could be interpreted as a sign of God's power and authority. The color red also symbolizes blood, the foundation of sacrificial worship.

Animal skins were used because only the best of materials were rendered unto God in the construction of the tabernacle. The skins were an important aspect in construction. The wooden framework of the tabernacle had three coverings: first, the immediate covering of the tabernacle; second, the tent covering of goat hair; and third, a protective covering of rams' skins cast over the whole.

Everything that was used in the construction of the tabernacle was special yet practical. All of it, though, was a sign that the people were giving God their best. The Israelites chose to use acacia wood (see v. 24) because it was the only kind of wood available in the Sinai desert. It had a high tolerance for heat and was heavier and harder than other kinds of wood. Moreover, it was durable and not easily damaged by insects. Acacia was an excellent material that could also be used in other types of woodworking, such as the making of cabinets, storage bins, and other containers.

Verses 25 and 26 focus on the women who contributed to the project. In addition to their normal domestic duties, the women here, whose hearts were stirred, gave from a willing heart. Those who gave out of a willing heart were blessed because the abundance of their provisions reflected God's grace. The women spun fabrics and participated in the dying of the skins, although a tanner would have been involved in the treatment of the skins.

The "leaders" (v. 27, NRSV) who brought the onyx and stones for setting the ephod and breastplate are best identified as the leaders of their respective tribes. These men were in a position to contribute these precious stones either from their own personal collection or from those of their tribesmen. The ephod was a sleeveless garment held to the body by a skillfully woven band (see Exod. 28:8). On the straps were placed two onyx stones, with the names of six tribes on each stone.

The "breastpiece" (v. 27, NRSV) of judgment was a square piece of beautiful material, folded in half, that opens at the top like a pouch and is placed over the front of the ephod. It was adorned with twelve precious stones (in four rows), on which were engraved the names of the twelve tribes. Recall that John would later refer to the brilliance and significance of these stones when he first viewed the throne room of God (see Rev. 4:3). Of the precious stones seen in that heavenly encounter, jasper, carnelian, sardius, and emeralds were affixed to the vestments of the high priest.

Also included in the inventory were "spices and oil for the light, and for the anointing oil, and for the fragrant incense"

(Exod. 35:28, NRSV). Obviously, oil was needed for fuel to burn in the lamps, but it was also needed for anointing. The oil for the light was olive oil, and was to be used in the lamps for the lampstand (see 25:37). Olive oil was also used in the recipe of sweet smelling spices to be mixed with incense for the anointing oil for ordaining the priests (see 30:24). Incense was also needed to keep the aroma of the tabernacle from becoming offensive. The smell of the animals used for both work and sacrifice would have been overpowering. The people wanted to present a sweet smell to the Lord.

The end of today's text repeats the fundamental idea: "All [those] whose hearts made them willing to bring anything for the work that the LORD had commanded by Moses to be done, brought it as a freewill offering to the LORD" (35:29, NRSV). There were likely some who did not participate. Moses served as an overseer and probably did not necessarily perform any of the tasks himself. Instead, he served as the vessel through which the Lord gave His instructions. The freewill offering was provided voluntarily and was urged by the movement of the Spirit in their hearts.

III. THE GRACE OF GIVERS (2 CORINTHIANS 9:6–8)

We will now turn to a New Testament text that pushes this same point. Paul encouraged the church at Corinth. He knew the blessings that were to be gained from a willingness to serve the Lord. The metaphor he uses here is simple yet powerful: "The one who sows sparingly will also reap sparingly, and the one who sows bountifully will also reap bountifully" (2 Cor. 9:6, NRSV). Many similar statements are found in the Scriptures. Consider the following: "Some give freely, yet grow all the richer; others withhold what is due, and only suffer want" (Prov. 11:24, NRSV). Elsewhere, Luke quotes Jesus: "'Give, and it will be given to you. A good measure pressed down, shaken together, running over, will be put into your lap; for the measure you give will be the measure you get back'" (Luke 6:38, NRSV). Our liberality should be like that. The Greek term translated "sparingly" in 2 Corinthians 9:6 is *pheidomenōs*. It has an even stronger connotation—*stingy*. Stingy people are cheap and do everything cheaply, which reflect their cheap love for the Lord. In contrast, being bountiful is a reflection of one who is well thought of. The Greek term *eulogia* means "generous gift" or "bounty." The one who gives "bountifully" (Grk *ep' eulogiais*) therefore benefits from the bounty of heaven. One who demonstrates generosity of heart and substance is usually very well-received in the community.

"God loves a cheerful giver" (2 Cor. 9:7, NRSV), not one who gives because he or she is forced, made to feel guilty or coerced. Paul places the urge to give at the center of the heart. We can readily think of all sorts of reasons why one might feel compelled to give: out of a sense that everyone else is doing so, or in order to maintain a certain status in the church. Paul teaches that if the people give from any other perspective than that of reflecting God's gifts, they are committing financial suicide. God does not want the gifts of the stingy or the cheap, because those gifts are given "reluctantly or under compulsion" (v. 7, NRSV). "Reluctantly" (Grk *ek lupēs*) means to be sad or filled with grief. When we give from this perspective, we are grieved or saddened because we *have* to give, which puts us in a sorrowful or grudging mood. It is impossible for our gifts to be blessed, or to be a blessing, when we give from this position. God sees the heart, and He also knows that our true feelings are revealed in the heart. Paul is declaring that even the act of giving is a gift of the Holy Spirit.

By way of conclusion, Paul reminds the church at Corinth that "God is able to provide you with every blessing in abundance" (v. 8, NRSV). God is able to spread His grace into every facet of our lives. We become an extension of His blessings. Having an abundance is a blessing from the hand of God. God provides believers with a profusion of blessings to be used and enjoyed in every circumstance. The Greek verb *perisseuō* is used to indicate that God provides a *superabundant* bounty that is both superior in quality and beyond measure.

The Lesson Applied

Believers find a sense of joy and satisfaction in giving, especially to their churches and other institutions. The confidence that Christians possess is described in the exhortations of Exodus and 2 Corinthians. We can be thankful for a God who replenishes our possessions. We can thank God for our vocations that allow us to care for our families and to provide for our churches. Fish fries, dinners, and raffle sales are not a part of God's plan for giving. If we treat God in this manner, our financial obligations to Him will yield desultory results. The people who followed the will of God were blessed to continue to follow the will of God.

Let's Talk About It

1. What is your attitude toward giving?

Have you ever noticed that the people who give to the Church always have it to give, whereas the ones who do not never seem to get out of the hole? If you spoke to the people who give, they would share their stories with you, letting you know that they have not always had it together like they do now. Almost always, though, they will tell you that once they started tithing and giving back to God, they had it to give. These people have found the secret of heavenly wealth in an earthly reality. God loves a cheerful giver, and the ones who give back to God receive much more from Him. Remember, the one with a tight fist closes his or her hand, not allowing anything to come out. But the one with an open hand gives freely, allowing God to replenish what was once there.

HOME DAILY DEVOTIONAL READINGS
MAY 7–13, 2018

MONDAY	TUESDAY	WEDNESDAY	THURSDAY	FRIDAY	SATURDAY	SUNDAY
Honor God with Your First Fruits	Martyrs, First Fruits for God	Gifts, a Pleasing Sacrifice to God	Preparing Grain Offerings	Acceptable Offerings Are Without Blemish	Observing the Sabbaths and the Festivals	Present Your Fruits to God First
Proverbs 3:1–10	Revelation 14:1–5	Philippians 4:15–20	Leviticus 2:1–10, 14	Leviticus 22:17–20	Leviticus 23:1–8	Leviticus 23:9–14, 22

Bringing First Fruits

Adult Topic:	Background Scriptures:
Reasons to Give	Leviticus 2:14; 23:9–22

Leviticus 23:9–14, 22

King James Version

AND the Lord spake unto Moses, saying,

10 Speak unto the children of Israel, and say unto them, When ye be come into the land which I give unto you, and shall reap the harvest thereof, then ye shall bring a sheaf of the firstfruits of your harvest unto the priest:

11 And he shall wave the sheaf before the Lord, to be accepted for you: on the morrow after the sabbath the priest shall wave it.

12 And ye shall offer that day when ye wave the sheaf an he lamb without blemish of the first year for a burnt offering unto the Lord.

13 And the meat offering thereof shall be two tenth deals of fine flour mingled with oil, an offering made by fire unto the Lord for a sweet savour: and the drink offering thereof shall be of wine, the fourth part of an hin.

14 And ye shall eat neither bread, nor parched corn, nor green ears, until the selfsame day that ye have brought an offering unto your God: it shall be a statute for ever throughout your generations in all your dwellings.

• • • • • •

22 And when ye reap the harvest of your land, thou shalt not make clean riddance of the corners of thy field when thou reapest, neither shalt thou gather any gleaning of thy harvest: thou shalt leave them unto the poor, and to the stranger: I am the Lord your God.

New Revised Standard Version

THE Lord spoke to Moses:

10 Speak to the people of Israel and say t them: When you enter the land that I am gi ing you and you reap its harvest, you sha bring the sheaf of the first fruits of you harvest to the priest.

11 He shall raise the sheaf before the Lor that you may find acceptance; on the day afte the sabbath the priest shall raise it.

12 On the day when you raise the sheaf, yo shall offer a lamb a year old, without blemisl as a burnt offering to the Lord.

13 And the grain offering with it shall be two tenths of an ephah of choice flour mixed wit oil, an offering by fire of pleasing odor to th Lord; and the drink offering with it shall be wine, one-fourth of a hin.

14 You shall eat no bread or parched grain fresh ears until that very day, until you hav brought the offering of your God: it is a sta ute forever throughout your generations in a your settlements.

• • • • • •

22 When you reap the harvest of your lan you shall not reap to the very edges of you field, or gather the gleanings of your harves you shall leave them for the poor and for th alien: I am the Lord your God.

MAIN THOUGHT: Speak unto the children of Israel, and say unto them, Whe ye be come into the land which I give unto you, and shall reap the harvest thereof then ye shall bring a sheaf of the firstfruits of your harvest unto the priest. (Leviticus 23:10, KJV)

LESSON SETTING
Time: Unknown
Place: Region of Sinai

LESSON OUTLINE
I. **God Speaks to Moses**
   (Leviticus 23:9–11)
II. **The Offerings**
   (Leviticus 23:12–14)
III. **The Provision for Gleaning**
   (Leviticus 23:22)

UNIFYING PRINCIPLE
In a culture of scarcity, people acquire and hoard the best they can afford. How can they live less fearfully and more joyfully during difficult economic times? God called His people to worship Him with the first and best of their lives.

INTRODUCTION
Today's lesson deals with the criteria for observance of the Festival of First Fruits. This particular celebration followed the Passover and the Festival of Unleavened Bread but linked them to Pentecost. While at Sinai, God provided guidelines designed for the people to enact once they settled in Canaan. First Fruits was not observed at Sinai and would not be practiced until they reached their destination. Israel would not begin their journey to Kadesh-Barnea until the second year after their arrival at Sinai, as it would take Israel a year to erect the tabernacle. Consequently, these observances would begin two years after Israel was delivered from bondage.

Leviticus means "pertaining to the Levites," the designated priests of Israel. The laws found therein relate to all of Israel, not just the priests. Today's lesson is about expressing gratitude to the Lord for His provisions, but it also highlights the holiness of God and His care for Israel. Outside of the specific requirements of the sacrifices, God made provisions for strangers and those who are in need. Lastly, we will see how these laws point us to Jesus' ultimate and final act of sacrifice.

EXPOSITION
I. GOD SPEAKS TO MOSES (LEVITICUS 23:9–11)
In today's text, we find Moses at Mount Sinai following the construction of the tabernacle. All of the people who had willing hearts gave of their possessions and of their skills in order to construct the Tent of Meeting. On this occasion, God again spoke to Moses, outlining a set of commandments concerning the observance of several festivals: Passover, Unleavened Bread, First Fruits, and Pentecost. Today's lesson focuses on First Fruits.

Israel was preparing to enter into the Promised Land, a blessing and a fulfillment of the promise that God had made to Abraham (see Gen. 12:1–3). The nation consisted of those who were dedicated followers of God. There were those, however, who continued to live on the fringe of the faithful. But those who willingly obeyed received the blessing of their own land.

God had Moses speak to the nation of Israel *en masse*. Moses served as God's voice to the people. Notice that God reminded Moses that Israel would be entering the land "that I am giving you" (Lev. 23:10, NRSV). God reminds His people that it is He who is in command of their destiny and that the Promised Land was not obtainable without Him as their

Provider. The land, however, was not unoccupied. There were inhabitants who would resist the Israelite intruders moving into their land. God constantly reminded Israel: "You shall not follow the practices of the nation that I am driving out before you. Because they did all these things, I abhorred them" (Lev. 20:23, NRSV). Israel would have to fight for the land. But because the land belonged to God, the battle would be won.

Through Moses, God said to the people, "You shall inherit their land, and I will give it to you to possess, a land flowing with milk and honey" (v. 24, NRSV). It was not their own might, but God who would achieve this victory. The metaphor of a land flowing with milk and honey elicits images of a lush and fertile terrain. We are reminded of Eden, but a significant difference is that Israel would have to work the land. However, following the fruits of their labor, God promised that there would be a great harvest in the land.

The purpose of First Fruits was to praise God for the harvest and to dedicate the bounty of the crops. Israel would give God the first portion of the crops (see Lev. 23:10). This was not a totally new idea. Israel was commanded to offer the *first* of the crop and not what was left over. The history of humanity was stained because of the attitude of Cain in offering his crops to the Lord. Israel knew that history and was directed to follow the commandment. With regard to the crop, it is most likely the barley harvest that is in mind because it was harvested during March–April, the time of year that this feast was celebrated. (Wheat was not ready for harvesting until

later, in June–July. Moreover, wheat wa normally only available for the wealthy whereas barley was more freely availabl for everyone. God required the gift from the barley crop, symbolizing His care fo both rich and poor.)

The sheaf is a bundle of the harveste grain before the grains are separate from the stalks. The reading "you shal bring the sheaf of the first fruits of you harvest to the priest" (v. 10, NSRV) als indicates the *measure* of the kernels i the sheaf. The word *sheaf* may presen a problem in some cultures where th practice of tying grain into bundles i unknown. Some might interpret it as "th first bunch of grain you tie together. The Hebrew term *omer,* though, is a dr measure of a tenth of an ephah (abou two liters) and is translated as "sheaf. The size of the sheaf would be the sam for everyone to present to the priest t wave before the Lord.

After the barley offering was brough to the priest, he lifted it above his hea and waved it before God and befor the people. This was a sign that it wa being offered to God, while the peopl acknowledged that God would receiv the submission. This was not to be take as an empty gesture; the people woul know that their gifts were acceptabl under the conditions outlined in th commandment. They understood tha God would reward their faithfulness Remember, God had to accept both th offering and the hearts of the people.

First Fruits was celebrated on th day after the sabbath, which mean that when Israel arrived in the Lan they would participate in this specia ceremony on the sixteenth day of the month. No work of any kind would be performed on the sabbath.

II. THE OFFERINGS
(LEVITICUS 23:12–14)

The barley offering was not the only provision offered to God. Each person also had to include a one-year-old male lamb to be sacrificed as a burnt offering to the Lord (see v. 12). The age of the ram could be symbolic in that Israel would be at Sinai for almost a year. Another aspect of the animal's age was that it was to be new. Like the offering commandment, the age of the animal was important because the animal would not have had any time to mate or be spoiled by human use. Moreover, the age of the lamb harkened to the original set of specifications found in the preparations for Passover: "your lamb shall be without blemish, a year-old male" (Exod. 12:5, NRSV). The lamb was to be without defect or blemish because God does not want something His people would not want for themselves. Again, Abel's offering of the best of his lambs to God should remind the people that God wants the best of their provisions and the best of themselves.

It may seem interesting that God issues instructions for the grain and drink offerings but does not give any instructions for the sacrifice of the animal. This is not something that God had overlooked. They had just celebrated Passover, and the requirements for the sacrifice of the lamb on this occasion would have been the same. The sacrificial lamb would not have had any of its bones broken. Likewise, the sacrificial Lamb that would conquer Calvary would also share these characteristics. Moses had no idea what God's objectives were in issuing this decree; God was preparing the nation for worship and for an existence of peace and provision.

The final lot of the items offered to the Lord was "an ephah of choice flour mixed with oil ... and the drink offering with it shall be of wine" (Lev. 23:13, NRSV). The wording for this verse might be better read as an offering made by fire as an appeasing fragrance for Yahweh, along with a drink offering of a fourth of a hin of wine. The grain offering is to be processed into a fine flour measuring two-tenths of an ephah. (This would have been about four dry quarts of flour.) The oil is significant for two reasons. First, the oil would assist in the burning of the flour and provide an aromatic fragrance. Remember, these are commands from God that have not yet been executed; God already knows the recipe for a sweet fragrance. Second, the oil served to anoint the altar and the sacrifice. The symbolism is important here, whether the anointing is for priests or kings, in that it will forever be an integral part of God's design. In keeping with this, wine represents the lifeblood of humanity, and most importantly, the shed blood of our Savior. The drink offering of wine was to be a fourth of a hin (a hin being roughly equivalent to a gallon) and poured on the altar. Finally, it is helpful to remember that the wine offering and all other facets of the offering were related to the offering of the grain crop. They were all produced from the land that God gave to His people.

At the conclusion of the terms of this observance, God reminded Israel that they would live in a land that was provided by Him. As such, following His commandments would ensure their blessings and livelihood. They were not to eat or drink of their crops until they offered the first of their bounties to the Lord. Remember, the most important provision was the land that He gave them, the land where He had chosen their fathers and promised to bless them. First Fruits would serve as a dedication to God and an offering of thanks to Him for the bountiful blessings that they would receive. Again, the people were not to indulge in the grain of the land until God had received His first due. This was God's harvest; He was the Owner of the land, and its produce was His to do with as He pleased. He had graciously shared the land and its harvests with the people. The perpetual observance of this festival created a seamless flow from Passover to Unleavened Bread to First Fruits to Pentecost. The term "forever" (Heb. ʿolam) indicates an eternal or continuous existence (see v. 14). God did not want Israel to forget His gift of the Land and His role as their supreme Provider. He constantly reminded them of who was responsible for their blessings.

III. THE PROVISION FOR GLEANING (LEVITICUS 23:22)

As a capstone to the commandment, God included a proviso that illustrates His concern for the stranger and the destitute. This last stipulation is that when the people gathered in the harvest, they were not to reap the corners of the fields or gather the gleanings or leftover stubble of grains from the general harvest. Initially, it seems as though God were commanding the farmers to allow part of their crop to rot in the fields. However, their crops would be so blessed by God that their barns would overflow. God's concern for those who were not a part of His covenant people, and for the destitute, shows clearly His love. He used this overflow to bless the needy. This reminds us of contemporary calls to conserve food, whether it originates in restaurants, churches, or our individual homes, because there still exist the needy and the stranger.

One of the most well-known accounts of how this concept worked is found in the account of Ruth, who was blessed to meet Boaz because she was allowed to glean in his field. The gleanings not only provided for the needy (like Ruth and Naomi) but also served as a reminder of Israel's former situation and of the God who is the Father of all blessings. God has always been a Friend to those in need and a Protector of those we sometimes label as "foreigners." However, God does not view anyone as an alien because He created the whole of humanity. In Him, there is no such concept by which anyone would be distant from Him, except through the separation that sin causes. The proviso regarding gleaning continues through Jesus, in that we are aliens or foreigners living in a strange land and heaven is our eternal home. And we are all needy; we all depend on the blessings of the Lord and His provisions that are received unmerited.

THE LESSON APPLIED

Although the instruction in today's lesson seems to be specific to the items required by the Lord for the observance of this festival, there exists a much deeper, more theological background. Jesus Himself was a fulfillment of the meaning of First Fruits. Paul tells us that on the third day, when our Lord rose from the dead, He was the first fruits of God's harvest: "But in fact Christ has been raised from the dead, the first fruits of those who have died. For since death came through a human being, the resurrection of the dead has also come through a human being; for as all die in Adam, so all will be made alive in Christ. But each in his own order: Christ the first fruits, then at his coming those who belong to Christ" (1 Cor. 15:20–23, NRSV). The image of Christ as the first fruits is evocative of Christ's role in the larger scheme of redemption. Just as the Festival of the First Fruits conceived of the offering of the first fruits as a promise, a down payment of sorts, on the rest of the crop, so the resurrection of Jesus is a promise, a down payment, on the general resurrection of the dead at His return. Because He was raised, we as faithful believers can anticipate our own resurrection at His coming.

Let's Talk About It

1. Believers are convinced of the benefits and joys of sharing. Are we only found in a giving spirit at Christmas?

Our God is a year-round Provider. Too often, though, we are not. But whether we are willing or not, the opportunities for us to share our resources remain. As Jesus Himself promised, "The poor you will always have with you, but you will not always have me" (Matt. 26:11, NIV). Because this is true, we should be spurred to greater generosity. Consider the words of Deuteronomy 15: "Since there will never cease to be some in need on the earth, I therefore command you, 'Open your hand to the poor and needy neighbor in your land'" (v. 11, NRSV). Let us notice just one example. The conservation of food is so important because there are so many who experience hunger. But how many households today throw away food because they don't like leftovers? How many churches throw away food because there was so much that it could not all be eaten? In some ways, we are all guilty of dishonoring God's gleaning code. Some agencies, schools, and churches have plans in place because they are moved to eradicate hunger. This is not a new movement: the hungry have always needed food. In America, one of the most prosperous nations in human history, we would think hunger would not exist. We have to do our part, though, because it indeed exists. May we allow God to use us to bless others through His blessings to us.

Home Daily Devotional Readings
May 14–20, 2018

Monday	Tuesday	Wednesday	Thursday	Friday	Saturday	Sunday
Keeping the Sabbath Yields Good Crops	Lands and Houses Shared with All	Bear Each Other's Burdens	I Will Maintain Covenant with You	Fairness in Buying and Selling Property	Helping One Another Face Difficulties	Sabbatical Year and Year of Jubilee
Leviticus 26:3–6	Acts 4:32–37	Galatians 6:1–5	Leviticus 26:9–13	Leviticus 25:13–17	Leviticus 25:35–38	Leviticus 25:1–12

REMEMBERING WITH JOY

ADULT TOPIC: CREATING AN EQUITABLE ECONOMY	BACKGROUND SCRIPTURE: LEVITICUS 25

LEVITICUS 25:1–12

King James Version

AND the LORD spake unto Moses in mount Sinai, saying,

2 Speak unto the children of Israel, and say unto them, When ye come into the land which I give you, then shall the land keep a sabbath unto the LORD.

3 Six years thou shalt sow thy field, and six years thou shalt prune thy vineyard, and gather in the fruit thereof;

4 But in the seventh year shall be a sabbath of rest unto the land, a sabbath for the LORD: thou shalt neither sow thy field, nor prune thy vineyard.

5 That which groweth of its own accord of thy harvest thou shalt not reap, neither gather the grapes of thy vine undressed: for it is a year of rest unto the land.

6 And the sabbath of the land shall be meat for you; for thee, and for thy servant, and for thy maid, and for thy hired servant, and for thy stranger that sojourneth with thee,

7 And for thy cattle, and for the beast that are in thy land, shall all the increase thereof be meat.

8 And thou shalt number seven sabbaths of years unto thee, seven times seven years; and the space of the seven sabbaths of years shall be unto thee forty and nine years.

9 Then shalt thou cause the trumpet of the jubile to sound on the tenth day of the seventh month, in the day of atonement shall ye make the trumpet sound throughout all your land.

New Revised Standard Version

THE LORD spoke to Moses on Mount Sinai, saying:

2 Speak to the people of Israel and say to them: When you enter the land that I am giving you, the land shall observe a sabbath for the LORD.

3 Six years you shall sow your field, and six years you shall prune your vineyard, and gather in their yield;

4 but in the seventh year there shall be a sabbath of complete rest for the land, a sabbath for the LORD: you shall not sow your field or prune your vineyard.

5 You shall not reap the aftergrowth of your harvest or gather the grapes of your unpruned vine: it shall be a year of complete rest for the land.

6 You may eat what the land yields during its sabbath—you, your male and female slaves, your hired and your bound laborers who live with you;

7 for your livestock also, and for the wild animals in your land all its yield shall be for food.

8 You shall count off seven weeks of years, seven times seven years, so that the period of seven weeks of years gives forty-nine years.

9 Then you shall have the trumpet sounded loud; on the tenth day of the seventh month—on the day of atonement—you shall have the trumpet sounded throughout all your land.

MAIN THOUGHT: And ye shall hallow the fiftieth year, and proclaim liberty throughout all the land unto all the inhabitants thereof: it shall be a jubile unto you; and ye shall return every man unto his possession, and ye shall return every man unto his family. (Leviticus 25:10, KJV)

LEVITICUS 25:1–12

King James Version

10 And ye shall hallow the fiftieth year, and proclaim liberty throughout all the land unto all the inhabitants thereof: it shall be a jubile unto you; and ye shall return every man unto his possession, and ye shall return every man unto his family.

11 A jubile shall that fiftieth year be unto you: ye shall not sow, neither reap that which groweth of itself in it, nor gather the grapes in it of thy vine undressed.

12 For it is the jubile; it shall be holy unto you: ye shall eat the increase thereof out of the field.

New Revised Standard Version

10 And you shall hallow the fiftieth year and you shall proclaim liberty throughout the land to all its inhabitants. It shall be a jubilee for you: you shall return, every one of you, to your property and every one of you to your family.

11 That fiftieth year shall be a jubilee for you: you shall not sow, or reap the aftergrowth, or harvest the unpruned vines.

12 For it is a jubilee; it shall be holy to you: you shall eat only what the field itself produces.

LESSON SETTING
Time: Unknown
Place: Mount Sinai

LESSON OUTLINE
I. **The Sabbath Year (Leviticus 25:1–7)**
II. **The Year of Jubilee (Leviticus 25:8–12)**

UNIFYING PRINCIPLE

People hold a sense of entitlement when it comes to their wealth, possessions, and land. How can they be freed from their possessions possessing them? God called the covenant people to active, responsible, and joyful stewardship of all He had given them.

INTRODUCTION

Today's lesson continues upon last week's lesson. Moses continues to have a conference with God on Mount Sinai, where God instructs Moses on the laws that will guide the people. This mountain was such a holy place that when the people first arrived there, only Moses could ascend. There was a perimeter placed around the mountain that prohibited the people from ascending or even touching the borders of it, on pain of certain death (see Exod. 19:12–13). God instructed Moses in the observance of many celebrations—Passover and First Fruits among them—but our focus today will be upon the Year of Jubilee.

EXPOSITION

I. THE SABBATH YEAR (LEVITICUS 25:1–7)

God's vision for His people was that by living within the grace of His Law, they would prosper. The giving of the Law preceded Israel's arrival in the land. As today's text indicates, it was important that the people be constantly reminded who was giving the land. That is the frame for Moses' remarks to the people on this occasion: "When you enter the land that I am giving you, the land shall observe a sabbath for the LORD" (Lev. 25:2, NRSV).

We are familiar with the sabbath as the day that God rested following creation, the day that is set aside to abstain from work, and the day that is solely reserved for the purpose of worshiping God.

The land, of course, was not literally to keep the sabbath. Rather, the people must stop their normal practice of cultivation and allow the land to rest in order to honor the Lord. The purpose of this was a renewed focus on the restoration and healing of the land.

Verse three might initially be confusing because it may seem as if God is telling Moses that "six years you shall sow your field, and [for an additional] six years you shall prune your vineyard" (NRSV). This would imply a period of twelve years. This should be understood as a single six-year period, though. The Hebrew terms *shaneh* meaning "year" and *shesh* meaning "six" are repeated twice in the original language. It is likely that they are structured this way for emphasis on each action.

The second part of this command is that during the seventh year, the land will be rested from planting and cultivation. Again, this sabbath is to honor the Lord and, by extension, serve as a benefit to the people. This part of the ordinance states that they are forbidden to work the land (see vv. 4–5). This sabbath to the Lord was based on a complete year in which no agricultural activity took place. Farmers would more than likely turn to other forms of commerce and trade, but God planned for the potential lack of provision. It may seem as if this proviso would cause harm and suffering for Israel. The point, though, was to teach them that God would provide.

God goes further, forbidding the gathering of crops that might well rot on the vine and in the fields. Moreover, there was to be no organized harvest and no selling of the produce to others. God tells Moses, "You may eat what the land yields during its sabbath—you, your male and female slaves, your hired and your bound laborers who live with you" (v. 6, NRSV). God was concerned for the animals used in the farming community, which were covered in His provision for rest. Again, the sabbatical year brought a cessation of all normal agricultural activity.

Hence, there would be an abundance that would be provided by the Lord. At face value, this does not seem feasible. Who would be able to foresee the yield of each field or the needs of the landowners? Additionally, could Moses or Aaron predict the consumption rate of individual families or anticipate the collective desires of the tribes? The obvious answer is that only the Lord who provides has foresight into future events. This type of situation was not a new phenomenon in the history of Israel.

The provisions of God are so extensive and far-reaching that even the animals were not forgotten in this equation. Healthy animals would be needed to produce dairy products such as milk; they would be used as beasts of burden and in transport but not for plowing, due to the prohibition. In verse seven, both wild and domesticated animals are included. The point of this verse is that there will be enough crops to feed both domesticated and wild animals. In this period, meat was a rare commodity; animals could be killed for meat, but it was not common. Lastly, not to be omitted is the fact that the animals normally used for sacrifice would continue to be used in this fashion. Honoring God and keeping the terms of the celebrations and feasts, even during the seventh year, would continue as usual.

II. The Year of Jubilee (Leviticus 25:8–12)

Verse eight can initially be confusing, counting seven sabbath years and multiplying these years by seven, to reach a total of forty-nine years. However, God makes sure that Moses understands that each sabbath year is important. The association of fifty with liberty, as well as rest, emerges in God's establishment of the Year of Jubilee. Every seventh year was to be a sabbath year, in which the land lies fallow (see Lev. 25:4). But after seven sabbath years had passed, Israel was to observe the fiftieth year as a second sabbath year, a Year of Jubilee (see Lev. 25:11–12).

The seventh month in the Hebrew calendar was Ethanim (later called Tishri). This month is equal to our months of September–October, which would occur at the completion of the agricultural cycle. On the tenth day, shofars (ram's horns) would be sounded throughout the land to signal the Day of Atonement. This horn would be used to make an announcement that would be heard and understood by everyone. The term *yobel,* translated "jubilee," referred to the ram's horn.

In this year, on the Day of Atonement, a trumpet blast signals the return to its original owner of any land sold and the freedom of any Israelites in the land who have been sold as servants (see vv. 28, 40–41). Ideally, a Jubilee year would occur at least once in the lifetime of every Israelite. The greatest significance of this event was its association with sabbath rest and liberty.

The English word *atonement* was formed by combining the two words *at* and *one* and denotes a state of togetherness and reconciliation between two people. Atonement presupposes that two parties have been estranged, and are in need of being reconciled and restored to a state of harmony. The Day of Atonement is also known as a day of "covering over" or propitiation. Known as Yom Kippur, it was the most important annual fast. Although God provided these instructions prior to the actual events, He was still in the act of reconciling Israel to Him.

The release mentioned in verse ten is in both the freeing of servants or slaves and the return of property. In this verse, all of the people were to return to their own properties and to their own families: "In this year of jubilee you shall return, every one of you, to your property" (Lev. 25:13, NRSV). With the expansion of the nation and the passage of time, trade and bartering would occur, and God provided this system of equity on the basis of landownership.

God's provisions would sustain the nation. Land, at this juncture, was the most precious commodity in Israel's possession. Therefore, the command was that the land be returned, without any costs involved, to the original owners or to the one who sold it. God also foresaw that men with expansionist mindsets would acquire the lands of their neighbors who were under duress. In this system, however, God steers Israel away from the temptations of greed and exploitation. The only caveat is that a house within a walled city, if sold and not repurchased within a year, became the permanent possession of the buyer. There was an exception that the houses in the cities that belonged to any Levites would revert to the original owners. The "return to families" is not meant to convey the image of people returning to their original homes but is focused on the release of the servants or slaves. In Israel, there were indentured servants, who served for a period of seven years, and there were also slaves. Nevertheless, all labor contracts were torn up in this fiftieth year of jubilee.

During the fiftieth year of jubilee, the land would rest. It is important to remember that the land would actually rest during the forty-ninth *and* the fiftieth year, which means that the land would rest for two whole years. The requirements for the observations and the sabbath were not to be altered and would not change. In the Jubilee year, there would be enough crops in store to sustain the entire nation, its animals, the needy, and the aliens. God reminds Moses, "The land shall not be sold in perpetuity, for the land is mine; with me you are but aliens and tenants" (Lev. 25:23, NRSV). This indicates that the people were also foreigners, except for the blessings and provisions of the Lord, and they were to be good stewards of that which He was entrusting to them.

THE LESSON APPLIED

Israel was initiated into one of the key standards of modern agriculture, crop rotation, which is still today integral to the overall health of arable land. Rotating crops is a practice of growing different crops in different seasons, in order to prevent the crops from sapping nutrients from the soil. Rotation allows nutrients, depleted from the previous year's cycle, to replenish themselves. One only has to recall the destruction caused by cotton during the antebellum period to understand its value. Due to greed and the intense demand for the crop, especially in European markets, the landowners stripped the land of its nourishing qualities and destroyed the ability of the land to produce the crop.

LET'S TALK ABOUT IT

1. **What lessons could Israel learn from the practice of Jubilee?**

Today's lesson deals with a set of requirements that would sustain the nation if they chose to adhere to those requirements. Although the celebration of Jubilee resulted in a return of land to the families who originally owned it, the ultimate Owner was God. The nation of Israel (regardless of the family) was the current tenant. God provides, and God also supplies. For Israel, Jubilee was a reminder that they were dependent on God for everything. He was the Source of everything they called their own. In light of that, it mattered a great deal how they treated each other.

HOME DAILY DEVOTIONAL READINGS
MAY 21–27, 2018

MONDAY	TUESDAY	WEDNESDAY	THURSDAY	FRIDAY	SATURDAY	SUNDAY
The Atoning Sacrifice for the People	The Lord Hears the Righteous Cry	Jesus Tasted Death for Everyone	Jesus Brings Salvation Through Suffering	Jesus Destroys the Devil's Power	Jesus, the People's High Priest Forever	Jesus, Our Redeemer and Deliverer
Leviticus 16:15–19	Psalm 34:11–18	Hebrews 2:5–9	Hebrews 2:10–13	Hebrews 2:14–16	Hebrews 7:18–28	Psalm 34:1–10; Hebrews 2:17–18

REJOICING IN RESTORATION

ADULT TOPIC:	BACKGROUND SCRIPTURES:
MORE THAN GOOD	LEVITICUS 16; PSALM 34; HEBREWS 2:5–18

PSALM 34:1–10; HEBREWS 2:17–18

King James Version

I WILL bless the LORD at all times: his praise shall continually be in my mouth.

2 My soul shall make her boast in the LORD: the humble shall hear thereof, and be glad.

3 O magnify the LORD with me, and let us exalt his name together.

4 I sought the LORD, and he heard me, and delivered me from all my fears.

5 They looked unto him, and were lightened: and their faces were not ashamed.

6 This poor man cried, and the LORD heard him, and saved him out of all his troubles.

7 The angel of the LORD encampeth round about them that fear him, and delivereth them.

8 O taste and see that the LORD is good: blessed is the man that trusteth in him.

9 O fear the LORD, ye his saints: for there is no want to them that fear him.

10 The young lions do lack, and suffer hunger: but they that seek the LORD shall not want any good thing.

• • • Hebrews 2:17–18 • • •

WHEREFORE in all things it behoved him to be made like unto his brethren, that he might be a merciful and faithful high priest in things pertaining to God, to make reconciliation for the sins of the people.

18 For in that he himself hath suffered being tempted, he is able to succour them that are tempted.

New Revised Standard Version

I WILL bless the LORD at all times; his praise shall continually be in my mouth.

2 My soul makes its boast in the LORD; let the humble hear and be glad.

3 O magnify the LORD with me, and let us exalt his name together.

4 I sought the LORD, and he answered me, and delivered me from all my fears.

5 Look to him, and be radiant; so your faces shall never be ashamed.

6 This poor soul cried, and was heard by the LORD, and was saved from every trouble.

7 The angel of the LORD encamps around those who fear him, and delivers them.

8 O taste and see that the LORD is good; happy are those who take refuge in him.

9 O fear the LORD, you his holy ones, for those who fear him have no want.

10 The young lions suffer want and hunger, but those who seek the LORD lack no good thing.

• • • Hebrews 2:17–18 • • •

THEREFORE he had to become like his brothers and sisters in every respect, so that he might be a merciful and faithful high priest in the service of God, to make a sacrifice of atonement for the sins of the people.

18 Because he himself was tested by what he suffered, he is able to help those who are being tested.

MAIN THOUGHT: O taste and see that the Lord is good: blessed is the man that trusteth in him. (Psalm 34:8, KJV)

LESSON SETTING

Time: Unknown
Place: Unknown

LESSON OUTLINE

I. **Blessings to the Lord (Psalm 34:1–3)**

II. **God, My Deliverer (Psalm 34:4–7)**

III. **Pointing to Jesus (Psalm 34:8–9; Hebrews 2:17–18)**

UNIFYING PRINCIPLE

People want relief from their fears and brokenness. Where does such hope come from? Hope for restoration is found through God's gift of Jesus and His sacrifice.

INTRODUCTION

Some of the most beautiful songs and poems are written in times of despair. Songs, however, are often a reminder that God is a Deliverer from oppression at the hands of our enemies. To understand today's psalm, we must look at a life-and-death situation that David faced (see 1 Sam. 21). In the midst of depression, David composed a soothing song that praised God for protecting him through all his troubles. Psalm 34 is an acrostic, with the first letter of each successive verse beginning with the successive letters of the Hebrew alphabet. Our companion text from the Letter to the Hebrews reminds us of how Jesus became like us, and identified with our suffering so as to be the Savior we needed.

EXPOSITION

I. BLESSINGS TO THE LORD (PSALM 34:1–3)

David was being pursued by Saul, whose insane jealously had driven him to put David to death. Saul wanted to kill David because David had become the national hero of Israel. The young shepherd boy who killed Goliath had captured the imaginations of both his people and his enemies. The people danced and praised David with a song, "Saul has killed his thousands, and David his ten thousands" (1 Sam. 21:11, NRSV). This was a tribute to David's skills as a warrior. Saul was incredibly jealous and worked to ensure that David would never ascend to his throne. What Saul forgot is that it was the Lord who would choose who would rule Israel.

As David fled the assassins of Saul, he found himself in the small city of Nob, located northeast of Bethlehem and south of Ramah (see 1 Sam. 21:1). David sought refuge there from a priest named Abimelech (note that Abimelech is spelled Ahimelech in 1 Sam. 21), seeking food and shelter. There was an issue, though. Abimelech did not have any regular bread available but only the Bread of the Presence, which was restricted to consumption by the priests (see v. 4). The bread was a symbol that Israel recognized God as the Provider of her daily bread, and the twelve loaves represented the twelve tribes. David was not a priest and was not permitted to eat the sacred bread. Nonetheless, Abimelech provided shelter and offered the bread as sustenance.

Additionally, Abimelech gave David the sword of Goliath, which was a possession of the priest (see vv. 8–9). Abimelech's recognition of his moral obligation to preserve David's life by providing bread superseded the ceremonial regulation concerning who could eat the Bread of the Presence. Christ, when questioned by some Pharisees concerning His perceived disrespect for sabbath laws, would later refer to this event by posing it as a challenge and asking who actually broke the law by eating the bread, the priests or David (see Matt. 12:3–4). In this example, Jesus taught that compassion for the needs of people was more important than the regulations of the Pharisees.

David then fled to Philistine territory and sought refuge from Achish, king of Gath (see 1 Sam. 21:10). (Achish is referred to as Abimelech in the superscription of Psalm 34.) Although Achish seemed to protect David, David was not convinced and plotted a way of escape; he pretended to be insane and was allowed to flee from Achish. One might surmise that David's cleverness had allowed him to escape the wrath of Saul and the plotting of Achish, but David knew that it was the Lord who was his Protector.

At some point, David sat down and composed this song of thanks to God. He begins by saying, "I will bless the LORD at all times" (Ps. 34:1, NRSV), which is a tribute to the God who protects David *all of the time*. David's praise for God is continually a part of his speech and conversation, and he makes it known that his entire being is involved in praise and adoration: "his praise shall continually be in my mouth" (v. 1, NRSV). David speaks of praise emanating from his soul, the deep wellspring of human emotion. Recall Jesus' description of how one is to love the Lord with one's heart, soul, mind, and strength (see Mark 12:30). For David, this phrase points to his pride in the joy of being a recipient of God's protection.

The next phrase— "let the humble hear and be glad" (Ps. 39:2, NRSV)—could be interpreted to mean that if those in need (i.e., those who have been marginalized by the powers of the world) could hear his declaration, and rejoice in God as their Deliverer, their situations would improve.

Continuing his song of praise, David extends the invitation by encouraging all who will to join him to magnify the Lord. David realizes that God is omnipotent and that what has been extended to him is but a fraction of God's power. Although David was alone when he composed this song, he was thinking of the people his words would encourage. "Let *us* exalt his name together" (v. 3, NRSV; emphasis added) calls for a unified effort from those who need the provisions of the Lord. David's encouragement to exalt God's name is symbolic of giving Him high praise that exceeds the boundaries of both the tabernacle and heaven. Exalting the name of God is centered in the soul and can only be accomplished by a contrite people.

II. GOD, MY DELIVERER (PSALM 34:4–7)

It is then that David reminisces and recalls the situation that inspired him to compose this song. A better understanding of this stanza is to imagine David looking for and being granted the protection and deliverance of the Lord. Location plays an integral part in understanding this stanza. We have spoken of the situation that he experienced in Nob and Gath; however, David's thanks for being delivered extended to every place. David was in the presence of his enemies. When he looked for the Lord, it was at a time when he desperately needed to be rescued. God's response to David was an answer, an immediate release. A closer meaning than the term *fear* here would be the word *terror* (see v. 4). Someone about to lose his life would doubtless undergo sheer fright, which would be physically and mentally debilitating. David, however, gives thanks to God for His response.

David exclaims that all who seek Him will find Him, and the radiance of their countenance would be revealed. Sadness and terror would be replaced by expressions of joy (see v. 5). Because of their relationship with the Lord, they will never be ashamed or return to their previous state.

David continues by saying, "This poor soul cried, and was heard by the LORD" (v. 6, NRSV). The poor man is David himself. David completely humbles himself, noting that he is powerless in his own defense and captive in enemy territory. David further extends this to all who are helpless and in trouble. What is important is David's declaration that we are saved from all our troubles or challenging situations.

Referring to the pantheon of heavenly hosts, David continues to take pride in the power of the Lord by further acknowledging another aspect of God's protection. The "angel of the LORD" (v. 7, NRSV) spoken of in this psalm "encamps around" the believer. This invokes images of God's power resting on those who respect or fear Him. As in other occurrences of this phrase, it could be referring to one of the angels, or perhaps to God Himself. Regardless, the angel encamps around those who love God, and they are constantly guarded and protected by Him.

III. POINTING TO JESUS (PSALM 34:8–9; HEBREWS 2:17–18)

David asserts that those who take refuge in the Lord will be blessed in their own right. "Those who take refuge in [God]" (v. 8, NRSV) connects verses seven and eight: those who are blessed take refuge in the camp of the Lord. To "taste" God is to experience Him, and those who experience Him see and know His goodness. Recall the language God used for each aspect of His creation: all of His works were "good."

All who are considered His saints ("holy ones," v. 9, NRSV) are commanded to live with the Lord. It is to be understood that this encouragement is for the saved only, those who are looking forward to the day when God removes all vestiges of deprivation. Verse nine speaks of fear, not so much in the sense of being afraid of God (although this may be applicable in certain situations), but in the sense of revering or being in awe of the majesty of the Lord. Those who live in reverence of the Lord will never experience the pangs of want or feel estranged from Him.

We now move to the New Testament and to the fulfillment of the promises of God to protect those who love Him and are called according to His purpose. God sent His Son to experience a physical existence (i.e., the need for food and shelter and the desire for companionship, etc.). As the One who was sent to redeem humanity, He was the Giver of grace and mercy and served as a Beacon for the lost. Jesus "had to become like" us (Heb. 2:17, NRSV) while retaining the glory of heaven. He never absconded His role in the hierarchy of earth and heaven because His role was to be the supreme Sacrifice for all who believed on Him. The "sacrifice of atonement" (v. 17, NRSV) points to God's wrath being satisfied by the death of Christ (see Rom. 3:25; 1 John 2:2). Sin interrupts normal relations with God; expiation removes sin and restores the relationship.

Jesus Christ, who is the subject of this text, was tempted not only by the trials that generally befall humans but also by those that were designed to sidetrack Him in the purpose of His coming to earth. This should produce hope in us: Jesus's mission will be fulfilled and we are part of that promise. We face trials and temptations daily. Although our enticements vary, we share a common distraction: we are all tempted to turn away from God. Assistance from heaven will come in various ways; we must simply believe and serve as witnesses that it will come.

David concludes Psalm 34 with these words: "The young lions suffer want and hunger, but those who seek the LORD lack no good thing" (v. 10, NRSV). Young lions are fearless because they have not yet reached maturity. They rely on brute strength and their own physicality to hunt their enemies. However, they also fight for recognition as the next king of the pride. While it seems as if they have everything going for them, David realizes that they, too, have weaknesses. He mentions the lions because they are thought of as the strongest of all animals. But even they suffer want and hunger. People "who seek the LORD lack no good thing" (v. 10, NRSV).

THE LESSON APPLIED

We face discouraging challenges throughout our lives. We must, however, realize that God did not bring us this far to leave us in the midst of our enemies, without protection or any resource. A songwriter once said that to be a great songwriter, one must go through some hurt and pain. David expresses deep joy in the midst of his trials. How could he experience both sadness and joy? It is because the emotion of terror was replaced by the ecstasy of delight, regardless of his present situation.

LET'S TALK ABOUT IT

1. How do Psalms 34 and 23 compare?

Psalm 34 contains twenty-two verses. However, the superscription that reads, "Of David, when he feigned madness before Abimelech, so that he drove him out, and he went away" is verse one in the Hebrew text. This song of praise is one of David's best efforts and is connected to Psalm 23. Among many other similarities we can see a shared emphasis between the two on deliverances from enemies.

HOME DAILY DEVOTIONAL READINGS
MAY 28–JUNE 3, 2018

MONDAY	TUESDAY	WEDNESDAY	THURSDAY	FRIDAY	SATURDAY	SUNDAY
David Eats the Bread of Presence	Lord Desires Mercy Not Sacrifice	Plucking Grain	The Sabbath Is for Merciful Acts	The Father and I Are Working	Deliver Justice for the Oppressed	Meet Human Need on the Sabbath
1 Samuel 21:1–6	Hosea 6:1–6	Leviticus 19:9–10; Deuteronomy 23:25	Luke 14:1–6	John 5:9–18	Psalm 10:12–18	Matthew 12:1–14

FOURTH QUARTER

Lesson material is based on International Sunday School Lessons and International Bible Lessons for Christian Teaching. Copyrighted by the International Council of Religious Education, and is used by its permission.

JUNE, JULY, AUGUST 2018

WRITER: DR. BERNARD WILLIAMS

SUGGESTED OPENING EXERCISES

1. **Usual Signal for Beginning**
2. **Prayer (Closing with the Lord's Prayer)**
3. **Singing (Song to Be Selected)**
4. **Scripture Reading:**
   Psalm 1:1–6 (KJV)

Director: Blessed is the man that walketh not in the counsel of the ungodly, nor standeth in the way of sinners, nor sitteth in the seat of the scornful.

School: But his delight is in the law of the LORD; and in his law doth he meditate day and night.

Director: And he shall be like a tree planted by the rivers of water, that bringeth forth his fruit in his season; his leaf also shall not wither; and whatsoever he doeth shall prosper.

School: The ungodly are not so: but are like the chaff which the wind driveth away.

Director: Therefore the ungodly shall not stand in the judgment, nor sinners in the congregation of the righteous.

All: For the LORD knoweth the way of the righteous: but the way of the ungodly shall perish.

Recitation in Concert:

Joshua 1:6–8 (KJV)

6 Be strong and of a good courage: for unto this people shalt thou divide for an inheritance the land, which I sware unto their fathers to give them.

7 Only be thou strong and very courageous, that thou mayest observe to do according to all the law, which Moses my servant commanded thee: turn not from it to the right hand or to the left, that thou mayest prosper withersoever thou goest.

8 This book of the law shall not depart out of thy mouth; but thou shalt meditate therein day and night, that thou mayest observe to do according to all that is written therein: for then thou shalt make thy way prosperous, and then thou shalt have good success.

CLOSING WORK

1. **Singing**
2. **Sentences:**

James 4:6–10 (KJV)

6 But he giveth more grace. Wherefore he saith, God resisteth the proud, but giveth grace unto the humble.

7 Submit yourselves therefore to God. Resist the devil, and he will flee from you.

8 Draw nigh to God, and he will draw nigh to you. Cleanse your hands, ye sinners; and purify your hearts, ye double minded.

9 Be afflicted, and mourn, and weep: let your laughter be turned to mourning, and your joy to heaviness.

10 Humble yourselves in the sight of the Lord, and he shall lift you up.

3. **Dismissal with Prayer**

JUSTICE AND SABBATH LAWS

MATTHEW 12:1–14

King James Version

AT that time Jesus went on the sabbath day through the corn; and his disciples were an hungred, and began to pluck the ears of corn, and to eat.

2 But when the Pharisees saw it, they said unto him, Behold, thy disciples do that which is not lawful to do upon the sabbath day.

3 But he said unto them, Have ye not read what David did, when he was an hungred, and they that were with him;

4 How he entered into the house of God, and did eat the shewbread, which was not lawful for him to eat, neither for them which were with him, but only for the priests?

5 Or have ye not read in the law, how that on the sabbath days the priests in the temple profane the sabbath, and are blameless?

6 But I say unto you, That in this place is one greater than the temple.

7 But if ye had known what this meaneth, I will have mercy, and not sacrifice, ye would not have condemned the guiltless.

8 For the Son of man is Lord even of the sabbath day.

9 And when he was departed thence, he went into their synagogue:

10 And, behold, there was a man which had his hand withered. And they asked him, saying, Is it lawful to heal on the sabbath days? that they might accuse him.

11 And he said unto them, What man shall there be among you, that shall have one sheep, and if it fall into a pit on the sabbath day, will he not lay hold on it, and lift it out?

New Revised Standard Version

AT that time Jesus went through the grainfields on the sabbath; his disciples were hungry, and they began to pluck heads of grain and to eat.

2 When the Pharisees saw it, they said to him, "Look, your disciples are doing what is not lawful to do on the sabbath."

3 He said to them, "Have you not read what David did when he and his companions were hungry?

4 He entered the house of God and ate the bread of the Presence, which it was not lawful for him or his companions to eat, but only for the priests.

5 Or have you not read in the law that on the sabbath the priests in the temple break the sabbath and yet are guiltless?

6 I tell you, something greater than the temple is here.

7 But if you had known what this means, 'I desire mercy and not sacrifice,' you would not have condemned the guiltless.

8 For the Son of Man is lord of the sabbath."

9 He left that place and entered their synagogue;

10 a man was there with a withered hand, and they asked him, "Is it lawful to cure on the sabbath?" so that they might accuse him.

11 He said to them, "Suppose one of you has only one sheep and it falls into a pit on the sabbath; will you not lay hold of it and lift it out?

MAIN THOUGHT: But if ye had known what this meaneth, I will have mercy, and not sacrifice, ye would not have condemned the guiltless. (Matthew 12:7, KJV)

MATTHEW 12:1–14

King James Version	*New Revised Standard Version*
12 How much then is a man better than a sheep? Wherefore it is lawful to do well on the sabbath days.	12 How much more valuable is a human being than a sheep! So it is lawful to do good on the sabbath."
13 Then saith he to the man, Stretch forth thine hand. And he stretched it forth; and it was restored whole, like as the other.	13 Then he said to the man, "Stretch out your hand." He stretched it out, and it was restored, as sound as the other.
14 Then the Pharisees went out, and held a council against him, how they might destroy him.	14 But the Pharisees went out and conspired against him, how to destroy him.

LESSON SETTING

Time: Probably A.D. 27, the first year of Jesus' public ministry

Place: The northern edge of the Sea of Galilee, near Bethsaida (Bethesda) and Capernaum

LESSON OUTLINE

I. Jesus Breaks the Rules (Matthew 12:1–2)

II. Pharisees Condemn Jesus for Breaking the Rules (Matthew 12:3–5, 9–11)

III. Justification for Rule-breaking (Matthew 12:6–8, 12–14)

UNIFYING PRINCIPLE

Our justice system was established to provide equity. What should we do when certain interpretations of the law interfere with responding to human need? Two events in Jesus' life, plucking grain and healing a man with a withered hand on the sabbath, illustrate the priority of responding to human need.

INTRODUCTION

The events portrayed in Matthew 12:1–14 occurred fairly early in Jesus' public ministry. According to Matthew's placement of the story, Jesus had performed some miracles, preached the Sermon on the Mount and called His Twelve Disciples, yet was still ministering in the region around the northern edge of the Sea of Galilee, not far from Capernaum.

The prelude to this chapter, Matthew 11, recorded His pronouncement of woe upon three particular cities, all of which sat at the northern edge of the Sea of Galilee: Bethsaida, Capernaum, and Chorazin. Bethsaida, the home of Peter, John, and Andrew, lay slightly to the east, while Capernaum was at the very northern tip of the Sea, and Chorazin was just a few kilometers north of Capernaum. It was in and around these three cities that Jesus found His disciples.

Matthew did not record exactly where Jesus and His followers had been staying, nor did he tell us why they were on their way through grain fields, but it is probable that they had been encamped outside one of these cities and had risen early on the Sabbath to head into town for worship at the synagogue. The miracles that Jesus had begun to do had drawn crowds around Him, so staying away from town would have afforded the disciples and Jesus some quiet time. Also, it may well have left them with scant provisions so that, as they began their journey to town, they needed to restock their food supply. Both situations provided Jesus with teaching moments during which He enlightened the Pharisees, the disciples, and the others who were witnesses to the encounter.

EXPOSITION

I. JESUS BREAKS THE RULES (MATTHEW 12:1–2)

As Jesus and His disciples set out, they chose to walk through the fields of grain that lay outside the city. The King James Version interprets the Greek as ears of corn, but the actual Greek word (stachys) is a general word for any grain that grows from a stalk. It is more likely that the grain in question was either wheat or barley, both of which were more commonly grown in and around the Sea of Galilee. For whatever reason, since the disciples were hungry, they began to pick grain from the stalks, rub them in their hands to rub off the chaff, and eat them. That the disciples were willing to eat uncooked kernels of grain is an indication that the hunger they felt was acute.

According to Deuteronomy 23:25, the act itself was expressly permitted, except that it was "servile work." On any other day of the week, picking grain off the stalk and eating it would not have been objectionable, but on the Sabbath it was prohibited work and, therefore, sinful. Exodus 20:10 records one of the Ten Commandments, which prohibited work on the Sabbath, but it did not define what should be classified as "work." As people tend to do, the Jewish religious leaders began to wrestle with the concept of work

and what it meant to work on the Sabbath. For example, was it okay to cook a meal? Their answer: no, cooking was prohibited on the Sabbath. Was it okay to walk? Their answer to that question was more complex. People needed to walk to get to the synagogue, so some walking must be permitted, but walking to the store to sell an item was not permitted and was severely frowned upon.

Gradually, the concept of "servile work" was developed. Simply put, if one's work was self-serving or menial, it was prohibited. If one's work was holy, or noble, as would be the case with walking to synagogue, it was permitted, but only up to a maximum of two thousand paces. Feeding oneself by plucking grain, in the minds of the Pharisees, who prided themselves on their rigorous adherence to the smallest details of Sabbath rules, fell clearly into the category of prohibited menial and self-serving work.

Additionally, Matthew does not tell us why the Pharisees happened to be in the grain fields as Jesus and His disciples walked by. However, we can imagine that they were keeping an eye on Jesus. He had already gained a significant following and was therefore probably the hot topic of conversation due to the incredible success of His early miracles. Initially, they may have been simply curious, but it did not take long for them to realize that Jesus did not fit their preconceived ideas of what a good, observant Jewish man should be. He ate with sinners, called a tax collector to be one of His special inner-circle disciples, and challenged the traditional understanding of God's purposes in His Sermon on the Mount. He was, as they were beginning to think, a troublemaker and a threat to their own power, and, as such, merited very close scrutiny.

Having arrived at the synagogue, Jesus' challenge to the Pharisees and how they interpreted the Sabbath rules continued. The Pharisees, having already seen Jesus and His followers break the rules, were just waiting to see what He might do next. One of them challenged Jesus to see if He would continue to disregard the rules. Matthew noted they asked Him a question about healing on the Sabbath with the intention of gathering evidence upon which to base an accusation against Him as being a Sabbath-breaker.

Jesus again did not disappoint them. After asking a question in return about how the Pharisees themselves interpreted the Sabbath rules, Jesus proceeded to heal the man with the withered hand. Twice in one morning, Jesus had broken the Sabbath rules, as interpreted by the Pharisees. Matthew records that the Pharisees left the synagogue and began to discuss strategies by which they might obtain a death sentence against Jesus, which was the prescribed penalty for willful disobedience against the Sabbath laws. On the surface, it seemed they had a clear case against Him and that Jesus' ministry would end in tragedy before it got started.

II. PHARISEES CONDEMN JESUS FOR BREAKING THE RULES (MATTHEW 12:3–5, 9–11)

In response to the two challenges from the Pharisees, Jesus offered several examples in defense of both His disciples' plucking grain and His direct healing of the man with the withered hand. First, He said that such activity had been permitted in the past, as evidenced both by Scripture and current practices of the priests.

1 Samuel 21:6 records the instance Jesus refers to, where David entered the tabernacle and ate the showbread. David, on the run for his life and nearly starved, was given the showbread by the priest, Ahimelech, in apparent violation of the rules governing that bread. The Pharisees certainly had read this passage of Scripture but did not question the correctness of Ahimelech's decision, yet now they questioned Jesus for permitting His disciples to satisfy their own hunger.

Another objection which the Pharisees must have had in mind was that plucking grain was classified as "servile work." And yet, Jesus retorted, the priests in the temple do servile work on the Sabbath and no one objects. Sacrifices were offered on the Sabbath, and those sacrifices required work. Some of the work, such as actually burning the sacrifice on the altar, would have been classified as "holy" work and been beyond question. But the priests also cleaned up the altar after the sacrifices, gathered wood for the fire which could have easily been done the evening before the Sabbath, and performed other auxiliary tasks that would not have met the criteria to be called "holy." Those tasks were servile work and, by the measure of the Pharisees, should have been forbidden. Yet the Pharisees offered no objection to those duties.

Jesus had pointed out that the greatest of all the kings of Israel, David, from whose line they knew the Messiah was to come, had broken the Sabbath rules. Also, He pointed out that the priests who served in the temple regularly broke the Sabbath rules. Finally, as the Pharisees challenged Jesus about whether it was lawful to heal on the Sabbath, Jesus bluntly stated that they themselves would gladly break the letter of the law in order to save a sheep that had fallen into a pit. Their economic concerns would evidently overrule their theological prohibitions. Thus, Jesus insinuated that the accusers of the disciples' hands were indeed less than clean in this matter, and that their motives were suspect.

The Pharisees were hypocritical. What David had done, they'd found perfectly acceptable. What the priests did every Sabbath, they found blameless. What they themselves would do if the occasion demanded, they reasoned was appropriate given the economic loss. Yet what Jesus' disciples had done in plucking the grain to satisfy their hunger and what Jesus did in healing a man's withered hand, they condemned. Jesus said first that God desires mercy above sacrificial obedience to rules. Then He concluded that it was perfectly lawful to do good on the Sabbath, and the Pharisees knew it was lawful as well. They had a list of rules that they expected everyone else to obey, but they conveniently made their own exceptions when it suited them to do so.

III. Justification for Rule-Breaking
(Matthew 12:6–8, 12–14)

Jesus was under no illusion that the Pharisees would respond to His words with a total change of heart. They already knew the truth of what He had told them, but they understood as well that to relax the rules, to put the Sabbath back into its proper place as a gift from God to serve the people's need for rest and spiritual renewal, would undermine their own status as strict interpreters of the law.

It was not for their benefit that Jesus made His defense of the disciples and of His healing work. Rather, it was for the disciples that Jesus stood strong in the face of the Pharisees' condemnation. The old ways were beginning to be swept away in the light of the newness of the Gospel of the coming Kingdom of God, and the freedom of the new ways was beginning to dawn. No longer would the Sabbath be a day when people must obey a stringent and merciless code of behavior. The Sabbath was given by God to serve humanity, not the other way around (Mark 2:27).

Jesus rebuked the Pharisees for condemning the disciples for rubbing a few ears of grain, which the Pharisees would never have done had they truly understood and followed the word and will of God, who preferred acts of compassion and mercy to the observance of rites and ceremonies. They had twisted the intention of the commandment to honor the Sabbath until the Sabbath had become more important than the people it was given to serve.

The same was true with the Pharisees' take on Jesus healing the withered hand. There sat a poor human being suffering with a hand that had, presumably, once been strong and useful, but which throughout his life had grown weak and deformed. Jesus was there for the day; this was not His home synagogue and so there might not have been another opportunity for Him to heal this man. Even after questioning the Pharisees about their own willingness to rescue a sheep in trouble, Jesus did not expect them to rejoice at the healing they were about to witness. Again, as with His comments about the grain, Jesus was speaking to His disciples and to those gathered that morning at the synagogue hoping to draw closer to God. It was a moment ripe for teaching and redirection. Therefore, He asserted that people are more valuable than sheep and that no good work is forbidden on the Sabbath.

Effectively, Jesus was helping to save lives. By contrast, the Pharisees were looking for ways to condemn and to take life away. To the Pharisees, the law was something to be enforced and to which people must blindly submit. To Jesus, the law was a gift from God to help people live more peaceful and happy lives. It was never to be construed to prohibit either doing good or meeting one's basic life needs. God wants compliance for our own good, not because He is a despotic tyrant looking to lord His authority over humanity. And, when the choice arises between compliance and compassion, God wants His people to choose compassion.

THE LESSON APPLIED

Jesus confronted the Pharisees, who used the law to maintain their life of privilege and their authority over the community of believers. Their interpretation of the law was self-serving. When they manipulated the law in this way, they stripped it of its God-given purpose as a response to human need.

Paul spoke of not knowing what it meant to covet until he became aware of the law against coveting (Rom. 7:7). Within all of us is that original sin that rebels against God's Law. We, like the Pharisees, are prone to put on the face of Christianity while harboring within ourselves a rebellious, self-serving spirit.

But as Jesus said, God desires mercy, and not simply the outward actions of our religious practice. A Pharisee could bring a bull to the temple for sacrifice but retain his proud spirit. We, likewise, can attend every church service, give our tithes and offerings, read our Bibles, and even offer our prayers, but still harbor a spirit that refuses to show mercy to those who are hurting, cast aside, or in desperate need. Let us not neglect the outward practices of our faith, but let us always strive to do them with the proper spirit.

LET'S TALK ABOUT IT

1. When is it permissible to break a rule?

This text reminds us that Jesus came to save others. Alleviating human need—not only spiritual but also physical—was His concern and propelled Jesus to action. It is always right to save others or respond to human need. By doing so, we model Jesus' behavior.

HOME DAILY DEVOTIONAL READINGS
JUNE 4–10, 2018

MONDAY	TUESDAY	WEDNESDAY	THURSDAY	FRIDAY	SATURDAY	SUNDAY
Rehearse the Deeds of the Lord	God's Tree of Justice for All	Jesus Affirmed As Son of Man	Jesus Not Believed in Hometown	Will Son of Man Find Faith?	Jesus Explains Parable of the Weeds	Defer Judgment until the Final Day
Psalm 78:1–8	Ezekiel 17:22–24	Matthew 16:13–20	Matthew 13:54–58	Luke 18:1–8	Matthew 13:34–43	Matthew 13:24–33

PARABLES OF GOD'S JUST KINGDOM

ADULT TOPIC:	BACKGROUND SCRIPTURE:
YOU REAP WHAT YOU SOW	MATTHEW 13:24–43

MATTHEW 13:24–33

King James Version

ANOTHER parable put he forth unto them, saying, The kingdom of heaven is likened unto a man which sowed good seed in his field:

25 But while men slept, his enemy came and sowed tares among the wheat, and went his way.

26 But when the blade was sprung up, and brought forth fruit, then appeared the tares also.

27 So the servants of the householder came and said unto him, Sir, didst not thou sow good seed in thy field? from whence then hath it tares?

28 He said unto them, An enemy hath done this. The servants said unto him, Wilt thou then that we go and gather them up?

29 But he said, Nay; lest while ye gather up the tares, ye root up also the wheat with them.

30 Let both grow together until the harvest: and in the time of harvest I will say to the reapers, Gather ye together first the tares, and bind them in bundles to burn them: but gather the wheat into my barn.

31 Another parable put he forth unto them, saying, The kingdom of heaven is like to a grain of mustard seed, which a man took, and sowed in his field:

32 Which indeed is the least of all seeds: but when it is grown, it is the greatest among herbs, and becometh a tree, so that the birds of the air come and lodge in the branches thereof.

New Revised Standard Version

HE put before them another parable: "The kingdom of heaven may be compared to someone who sowed good seed in his field;

25 but while everybody was asleep, an enemy came and sowed weeds among the wheat, and then went away.

26 So when the plants came up and bore grain, then the weeds appeared as well.

27 And the slaves of the householder came and said to him, 'Master, did you not sow good seed in your field? Where, then, did these weeds come from?'

28 He answered, 'An enemy has done this.' The slaves said to him, 'Then do you want us to go and gather them?'

29 But he replied, 'No; for in gathering the weeds you would uproot the wheat along with them.

30 Let both of them grow together until the harvest; and at harvest time I will tell the reapers, Collect the weeds first and bind them in bundles to be burned, but gather the wheat into my barn.'"

31 He put before them another parable: "The kingdom of heaven is like a mustard seed that someone took and sowed in his field;

32 it is the smallest of all the seeds, but when it has grown it is the greatest of shrubs and becomes a tree, so that the birds of the air come and make nests in its branches."

MAIN THOUGHT: Let both grow together until the harvest: and in the time of harvest I will say to the reapers, Gather ye together first the tares, and bind them in bundles to burn them: but gather the wheat into my barn. (Matthew 13:30, KJV)

MATTHEW 13:24–33

King James Version

33 Another parable spake he unto them; The kingdom of heaven is like unto leaven, which a woman took, and hid in three measures of meal, till the whole was leavened.

New Revised Standard Version

33 He told them another parable: "The kingdom of heaven is like yeast that a woman took and mixed in with three measures of flour until all of it was leavened."

LESSON SETTING

> **Time:** A.D. 27
> **Place:** Galilee, probably near Capernaum

LESSON OUTLINE

   I. **Accept Those Who Struggle (Matthew 13:23–30)**

  II. **Tend Your Own Garden (Matthew 13:31–32)**

 III. **Let Your Light Shine (Matthew 13:33)**

UNIFYING PRINCIPLE

People want to experience living in a world filled with justice. Where can we find justice? Jesus' parables describe the Kingdom of Heaven, where God's justice is merciful, pervasive, and certain.

INTRODUCTION

Jesus spoke these three parables early in his ministry, shortly after He had called the Twelve to be His inner circle of followers. These men were still trying to figure out exactly who Jesus was and the extent of His ministry. Was Jesus the Messiah many expected, a military deliverer who would command the armies of Israel to throw off Roman oppression so that the glory of Israel might be re-established? Was Jesus a great prophet, like Elijah, calling the people to repent and return to the pure practice of the covenant faith given to Moses?

To help His followers begin to understand what was happening as He led them around Galilee and, eventually, to Jerusalem, Jesus told them parables of the Kingdom of Heaven. As was His custom, He chose metaphors that drew on objects with which His followers were familiar. .

From these parables, or illustrations, Jesus taught that the Kingdom of Heaven was to be a Kingdom where justice reigned, to a growing extent now and into perfect fullness as time progressed.

EXPOSITION

I. ACCEPT THOSE WHO STRUGGLE (MATTHEW 13:24–30)

To understand these parables properly, it is essential to know what Jesus meant by "the kingdom of heaven." The disciples thought they understood because it was a term commonly used in apocalyptic discussions during the time of Jesus' ministry.

Most Jews accepted that the Kingdom of Heaven consisted of the Promised Land, that portion of earth given by God first to Abraham, and then to Jacob and his offspring through God's covenant with Moses. The Kingdom of Heaven, in their minds, was the specific land on which they lived, but restored to its full scope and glory, as it had been when David and Solomon ruled. Jews of Jesus' day mostly believed that the Messiah would be the king who would restore this kingdom, and that he would rule as God's anointed. It would be, quite literally, heaven on earth.

Two millennia later, we know that Jesus was not speaking of the restoration of Israel, at least not in the way the Jews understood it. We understand that the Kingdom of Heaven is a present reality in the Church and will only become fully present upon Christ's return. At that time, creation will be made new and Christ will reign in eternal glory as the King of kings. For now, however, the Kingdom of Heaven is imperfectly realized in the lives of the believers who acknowledge Christ as Lord. It is this Kingdom, present among humanity but not yet perfected, about which Jesus tells.

The Kingdom, Jesus pointed out, is like a field of wheat. A plant known as "false wheat," also called darnel, looks strikingly similar to wheat. If planted next to wheat, one would be hard pressed to tell them apart. The Jews of Jesus' day referred to it this imitator as *zizanion* or *zanin*. Regular wheat berries are the wonderful golden color normally associated with the plant. The berries of *zanin,* however, are black and slightly poisonous, if eaten. In Jesus' day the seeds of *zanin* often intermingled with true wheat and the two plants would grow together in the field. Were the planter to rush out and try to yank up all the *zanin*, the true wheat would likely also be uprooted and the harvest lessened.

The key was to wait until the "plants came up and bore grain, then the [*zanin* (described in the text as tares or weeds)] appeared as well" (13:26, NRSV). The farmer could then see clearly which plants bore golden grain, and separate them.

Just as the careless grain merchant peddling true wheat mixed with *zanin* was the enemy of the grain farmer, so had an enemy of the Kingdom of Heaven planted false believers amid the true. He may well have had Satan in mind, but the word He chose for "enemy" is more generally applied to anyone who seeks to corrupt or ruin. He also may have had the Pharisees in mind. They had corrupted Judaism into a religion of strict obedience to an ever-expanding list of rule rather than a fellowship of joy with their covenant God and others who praised His name.

Jesus sought to impress upon His disciples (and upon us) was that *zanin* can only be safely uprooted at harvest. For now, as the wheat of the Kingdom grows, we are to leave the *zanin* alone because we are not able to accurately tell the true wheat from the false wheat. If we attempt to label some as false believers and make them so uncomfortable that they withdraw from our midst, we also risk driving away some true believers who are merely struggling to learn how to live in obedience to the King. When Jesus returns, He will separate the true wheat from the false wheat.

Allowing false wheat to grow in our midst does not mean we must tolerate the proliferation of weeds bearing no resemblance to wheat. However, in a just community, we must strive to err on the side of mercy and acceptance. The Kingdom of Heaven is gradual, not just in how it grows in the world but also in how it develops in each of our hearts.

II. Tend Your Own Garden (Matthew 13:31–32)

Jesus' next parable compared the Kingdom of Heaven to a mustard shrub. In warmer climates, the mustard shrub grows exceptionally large, though in cooler climates it grows relatively small, reaching a height of only three or four feet. He likely chose this plant because the size proportion of the mature plant to the tiny seed from which it grows makes it one of the most remarkable of all plants.

The "someone" (13:31) who sowed the seed is Jesus who, at that moment, was sowing the seed of the Kingdom into the hearts and minds of His disciples. People have marveled throughout the centuries that Jesus entrusted the purposes of God to a mere handful of disciples. It was indeed an inauspicious start, similar in size to a mustard seed, but Jesus knew how it would grow. Today, the number of lives that have been saved by that small start is incalculable, and still growing.

The key phrase in this parable is "'when it has grown'" (v. 32, NRSV). Not only does the overall magnitude of the Kingdom of Heaven grow greater each year, but the maturity of the individual believer's faith should also grow consistently. When the first stalk of a mustard plant emerges from the ground, it is green and tender. Easily broken or crushed, it draws nourishment from the ground in which it is planted and gradually becomes more solid and strong, able to withstand forces that would have destroyed it when it first emerged.

Each believer is like a blossoming shoot of the mustard shrub. Our primary concern is not what others are doing. Instead, we do well to pay attention to our own growth. While encouraging the growth of others, we should tend to ourselves and develop into strong, solid branches capable of bearing fruit and broadcasting the faith appropriately. As we tend to our own growth, we can respond to life's bumps and bruises with faith and hope, in humility and strength, as Jesus did. And as Christians stand together, the greatness of what has grown from the tiny seed planted in Galilee through Jesus gradually becomes more apparent.

III. LET YOUR LIGHT SHINE (MATTHEW 13:33)

Jesus' shortest parable compared the Kingdom of Heaven to a batch of dough. While many modern translations use the word "yeast" in Matthew 13:33, the actual Greek word is more correctly translated as "leaven." Anyone familiar with bread baking knows the difference. Leaven is dough that has already been through the rising process. It contains yeast, which is what causes it to rise, but it also contains flour, water, and various other ingredients.

Before the advent of modern packaging, the only way for the average person to make bread was to use a small lump of dough from a previous batch that had been allowed to rise. Yeast was not commercially available in those days. All they had was dough, handed from family to family, swapped with neighbors, and even sold in the markets.

On the day for baking bread, one measured amounts of flour and water, oil, salt, and other ingredients, and then, into the resulting dough ball, added a small lump of leftover dough from a previous batch, which was the leaven that would cause the new batch to rise. The leaven would then to spread throughout the new dough. Then, before baking, they separated a small chunk of the now-risen dough to provide the leaven for the next loaf.

As the small amount of leaven spread through the lump of dough, so would the small Kingdom of Jesus spread through the world. Hence, the process of evangelism. But the Kingdom also spreads within congregations as individual believers live within the context of community. The more mature believers become examples to newer converts, who learn how to live for Christ largely by observing others.

The leaven of the Kingdom is the Holy Spirit working in the hearts of believers in such that they grow in grace and present ever more mature representations of faith. Preaching the Gospel is the essential first step into the Kingdom of Heaven, but in order for the bread of life to rise properly, Christians need to be living testimonies to the justice and mercy of God.

Justice, as illustrated by these three parables, involves accepting those whose lives may not show the full measure of God's grace at a particular moment; making sure our own lives demonstrate justice; and allowing ourselves to be taught by those who have greater wisdom, and in turn teaching those who are not as far along as we are.

THE LESSON APPLIED

The way Christians live among one another should also be the way we live among the people of the world—in complete humility, kindness and justice. When we treat one another with justice but fail to treat non-Christians with justice, we make it seem as if the beauty of living for Christ is only for the initiated. We risk putting off the very people we are trying to reach for Christ.

Part of behaving justly with non-Christians is not expecting them to know the Bible and how to live like Christians. Those of us who have surrendered to the lordship of Christ may be in agreement about moral issues, but we must be careful not to be condemning if non-Christians do not embrace the same morality. That is not to suggest that we ignore immoral behavior, but rather to suggest that we be careful about how we present our moral positions so that we do not come off as being judgmental.

A simple way to do that is to live what we believe before the world around us. We should make the right choices so that we stand for Kingdom principles, while at the same time treating those who violate those principles with mercy and respect.

LET'S TALK ABOUT IT

1. What is a tare?

Tares are weeds that resemble young wheat. Metaphorically, tares are persons whose verbal utterances and actions mirror those of persons of the community of faith, but whose motives are not to please God or to be an example of Jesus' lordship over their lives.

HOME DAILY DEVOTIONAL READINGS
JUNE 11–17, 2018

MONDAY	TUESDAY	WEDNESDAY	THURSDAY	FRIDAY	SATURDAY	SUNDAY
Wash Away Your Evil Ways	Let Justice Roll Like Water	Honor Your Father and Mother	The Spirit Gives Life	Call No One Profane or Unclean	What Defiles Comes from the Heart	Treat Your Parents Justly
Isaiah 1:12–17	Amos 5:18–24	Exodus 20:12; Deuteronomy 5:16	2 Corinthians 3:1–6	Acts 10:23–33	Mark 7:14–23	Matthew 15:1–9

JESUS TEACHES ABOUT JUSTICE

ADULT TOPIC:	BACKGROUND SCRIPTURES:
MORE THAN LIP SERVICE	MATTHEW 15:1–9; MARK 7:1–13

MATTHEW 15:1—9

King James Version

THEN came to Jesus scribes and Pharisees, which were of Jerusalem, saying,

2 Why do thy disciples transgress the tradition of the elders? for they wash not their hands when they eat bread.

3 But he answered and said unto them, Why do ye also transgress the commandment of God by your tradition?

4 For God commanded, saying, Honour thy father and mother: and, He that curseth father or mother, let him die the death.

5 But ye say, Whosoever shall say to his father or his mother, It is a gift, by whatsoever thou mightest be profited by me;

6 And honour not his father or his mother, he shall be free. Thus have ye made the commandment of God of none effect by your tradition.

7 Ye hypocrites, well did Esaias prophesy of you, saying,

8 This people draweth nigh unto me with their mouth, and honoureth me with their lips; but their heart is far from me.

9 But in vain they do worship me, teaching for doctrines the commandments of men.

New Revised Standard Version

THEN Pharisees and scribes came to Jesus from Jerusalem and said,

2 "Why do your disciples break the tradition of the elders? For they do not wash their hands before they eat."

3 He answered them, "And why do you break the commandment of God for the sake of your tradition?

4 For God said, 'Honor your father and your mother,' and, 'Whoever speaks evil of father or mother must surely die.'

5 But you say that whoever tells father or mother, 'Whatever support you might have had from me is given to God,' then that person need not honor the father.

6 So, for the sake of your tradition, you make void the word of God.

7 You hypocrites! Isaiah prophesied rightly about you when he said:

8 'This people honors me with their lips, but their hearts are far from me;

9 in vain do they worship me, teaching human precepts as doctrines.'"

MAIN THOUGHT: This people draweth nigh unto me with their mouth, and honoureth me with their lips; but their heart is far from me. (Matthew 15:8, KJV)

LESSON SETTING

Time: A.D. 27

Place: Gennesaret on the shore of the Sea of Galilee

LESSON OUTLINE

I. Jesus Accused
(Matthew 15:1–2)

II. Jesus Turns the Tables
(Matthew 15:3–6)

III. The Injustice of Lip Service
(Matthew 15:7–9)

UNIFYING PRINCIPLE

Sometimes things we do out of tradition are not fair to others. How do we act with true fairness and justice? When the Pharisees confronted Jesus on a question of ritual observance, he challenged them to do what is truly fair and just and not merely talk about it.

INTRODUCTION

Things were beginning to get out of hand. Jesus had embarrassed the Pharisees at Capernaum by rebuking their protestations when He allowed His disciples to pluck grain on the Sabbath and then when He healed a man on the Sabbath. The Pharisees began to plot among themselves how to do away with this man they considered a troublemaker (see Matt. 12:14).

Large crowds were following Jesus. Those crowds were amazed to witness Jesus cast a demon from a blind and mute man (see Matt. 12:22–23). The people began to wonder if Jesus might be the Son of David, a title reserved for the long-awaited Messiah. Later, He astounded the citizens of Nazareth, among whom He had grown up, though they refused to believe in Him (see Matt. 13:54–58).

Hard on the heels of that confrontation came word that Herod feared Jesus might be John the Baptist, whom Herod had killed, risen from the dead (see Matt. 14:1–2). Even when Jesus tried to get away from the crowds, they followed Him (see Matt. 14:13–14). To their astonishment, Jesus fed them from a basket containing a meager meal of five small loaves of bread and two fish (see Matt. 14:19).

The culmination of this groundswell of popularity came at Gennesaret, where the crowds flocked to Jesus from the entire region, bringing their sick for Him to heal. The people begged that they might simply touch the hem of Jesus' garment and Matthew recorded that "all who touched it were healed" (14:36, NRSV). His popularity with the crowds set the scene for conflict with the religious leaders, who were not impressed with Him.

EXPOSITION

I. JESUS ACCUSED (MATTHEW 15:1–2)

In response to all this tumult, a delegation of Pharisees and scribes was dispatched from Jerusalem. Of the scribes, Merrill Unger writes that from the time of Ezra and the return of the Jews from exile in Babylon, "the scribes appeared as the zealous guardians of the law. . . . They were the *teachers* of the people, over whose life they bore complete sway. In [New Testament] times the scribes formed a finely compacted class, holding undisputed supremacy over the people" (*The New Unger's Bible Dictionary* [Chicago: The Moody Bible Institute of Chicago, 1957], 1544; italics original). The Pharisees were a subset of the scribes who had rejected all involvement with the government of the populace in favor of advocating for strict adherence to even the minutest details of the scribal laws governing daily behavior. In short, the two groups were the keepers of Jewish propriety.

This legalistic delegation was sent from the capital expressly to watch and report on Jesus' activities. What they observed gave them ample reason to believe that their mission was well-founded. There sat Jesus and His disciples preparing to eat a meal without first washing their hands! It was a violation of the law of Moses that the scribes and Pharisees were charged with maintaining among the citizenry.

Originally, handwashing was required only for priests (see Exod. 30:17–21), but the practice was widely adopted for the people's ritual cleanness by the time of Jesus' ministry. Washing hands was a symbolic cleansing as well as general sanitation. It was presumed that as people went about their daily business, they would come in contact with something or someone considered unclean, especially in the areas outside Jerusalem where the Jews lived in close proximity to pagan nations. The crowd that gathered around Jesus came in part from Tyre and Sidon, pagan cities along the coast of the Mediterranean. The disciples had been involved in crowd control, trying to keep the multitudes from crushing Jesus in their eagerness to receive what Jesus was offering. There was no way the disciples and Jesus had not become ceremonially unclean.

One can almost hear the self-righteous triumph in the accusation they hurled at Jesus: "'Why do your disciples break the tradition of the elders? For they do not wash their hands before they eat'" (Matt. 15:2, NRSV). The scribes and Pharisees felt sure they had Jesus right where they wanted Him, breaking the Law. In the minds of the scribes and Pharisees, Jesus and His disciples were only paying lip service to being observant Jews while their actions showed them to be hypocrites. Justice demanded that the scribes and Pharisees protect the letter of the Law as well as the well-being of the Jews there. They did so by calling Jesus out for His disregard of proper observance of the law and of their authority to determine disciplinary action for the transgressors thereof.

II. JESUS TURNS THE TABLES (MATTHEW 15:3–6)

Had Jesus chosen to respond directly to the scribes and Pharisees, He could have offered one of three possible answers. First, He might have replied that He had not been paying attention and that, if He had been watching, He would have insisted that His disciples wash. That would have opened Him up to the charge of letting things get out of control, and He could have been discredited in the eyes of the crowd. Yet on the other hand, He would have appeased the scribes and the Pharisees, who were seeking to gain power over Him before the people.

A second possible answer might have been that the rule about washing one's hands was unimportant. That answer would have been false, and likely would have resulted in a more intense confrontation. The scribes and Pharisees could have accused Him immediately of heresy and whipped the crowd into a frenzy. That day would come, but this day was not yet the fullness of time and Jesus knew it.

The third possible response could have been that the tradition was wrongly interpreted by the scribes and Pharisees. In fact, this is the answer He gave when He explained what had happened to the crowd (see Matt. 15:10–11). He did not question that defilement was possible. Rather, He questioned how defilement came about. This answer was a direct challenge to the scribes and Pharisees, but one that they would have delighted to debate had not Jesus prefaced His answer by turning the tables on them.

Essentially, Jesus took their point that He was paying lip service to being a good Jew and turned the situation to show that the scribes and Pharisees were the hypocrites. Exodus 20:12 records God's command to honor one's father and mother. Giving honor to parents begins in a person's heart, but it always translates into actions. One chooses the words used to describe one's mother and father based upon the attitudes of one's heart. If someone despises her father, she will not lift a finger when he needs help. Likewise, if that person honors her mother, she will rush to provide help should the need arise.

But not so with the scribes and the Pharisees. They had developed a tradition that made it possible to claim to be honoring parents but treat those very same parents with disdain. The tradition of "corban" indicated something had been dedicated to the work and ministry of God. A man could avoid spending money on his parents if he declared that his wealth was "corban." It was like writing a will leaving everything to the church with the exception that the church had no jurisdiction over how the money was to be spent.

Once a person declared his wealth as corban, he could claim that he would be robbing God to spend it on his parents. Yet he would retain the right to spend that same money on his own needs. It was tantamount to legal trickery to keep one's funds for personal use yet claim to be serving God while neglecting elderly parents.

Jesus challenged the scribes and Pharisees, in the clear hearing of the crowd. They were accusing His followers of being hypocrites for breaking a relatively minor rule. At the same time, they advocated for a rule that led others to break one of the Ten Commandments and disregard aged and ill parents. "Who are the real hypocrites here?" Jesus essentially asked them.

Jesus said the scribes and Pharisees needed to pluck the log out of their own eyes before condemning the speck they perceived in Jesus and His disciples. The real sin and filth lay within the religious leaders' hearts of deceit and selfishness.

Such traditions not only caused people to misunderstand the law, but stopped them from doing the more important things that the law required. Elsewhere, Jesus rebuked the scribes and Pharisees for tying heavy burdens around the necks of others that they were unwilling to bear themselves (see Matt. 23:4). By portraying rules as being essential to the practice of a vibrant faith and then privately excusing their own violation of those very same rules, the scribes and Pharisees had become false teachers, hypocrites, and workers of injustice. Their practice nullified their teachings.

III. THE INJUSTICE OF LIP SERVICE (MATTHEW 15:7–9)

In His rebuke of their practices, Jesus told the scribes and Pharisees that Isaiah was speaking of them when he prophesied hundreds of years earlier that "this people" were only paying lip service to their obedience to God and the Law of Moses (see Isa. 29:13). As a result of their two-faced concept of ministry, Jesus commented that their hearts were far from God and their worship was in vain. The idea of vain worship is that which fails to honor God and please Him. Because the scribes and Pharisees were leading people to violate

God's express command to honor their parents, the emotion with which they offered their worship was meaningless. All that they might have hoped to gain from worship, the good will of their God and the inward benefit of God's favor, were forfeited.

Jesus remarked in His Sermon on the Mount that "'You will know them by their fruits'" (Matt. 7:20, NRSV). A good tree cannot bear bad fruit nor a bad tree bear good fruit. One's actions bear testimony to what is truly going on in that person's heart. When one claims to be of stalwart faith but then behaves as if he is exempt from observing the rules of faithful practice, that person is only offering God lip service. When a person claims to honor God but then twists God's commands to excuse himself from obeying, that person is a hypocrite. Selective compliance to God's will and way is never an option available to Jesus' followers.

THE LESSON APPLIED

Jesus was not kind to hypocrites. His condemnation of those who failed to walk their talk should give each of us pause. There are so many ways in which we fail to live out the faith we profess that it pays to take stock of our behavior often.

For some, protestations that God is first in their lives are shown to be false when the sermon goes a bit too long and they grow concerned that they may miss the start of the big game. For others, offering a few dollars to the poor excuses their disregard for a homeless beggar on the street later that day. Still others claim to love their brothers and sisters in Christ yet are quick to judge and criticize when they see them acting in a manner that may be unlike Christ. Such actions expose hearts that are far from God, as were the hearts of the scribes and Pharisees who confronted Jesus. Living justly honors God not only with our lips but also with the actions we take.

LET'S TALK ABOUT IT

1. **Did Jesus mean to suggest that all religious traditions are unimportant?**

The short answer is no. In the case of the confrontation recorded in Matthew 15:1–9, He did not even suggest that it was wrong to wash before eating. His point was not to condemn the tradition but rather to put it in its proper relationship to the direct commandment of God and the need to practice justice by the way we live. The Pharisees and scribes compromised their faith traditions by adding rules to it that gave them unjust and unfair exemptions. However, their advantage was short-lived as Jesus examined their motives and held them accountable.

HOME DAILY DEVOTIONAL READINGS
JUNE 18–24, 2018

MONDAY	TUESDAY	WEDNESDAY	THURSDAY	FRIDAY	SATURDAY	SUNDAY
The Folly of Riches	Oppressing the Poor Leads to Loss	Both Oppressors and Righteous Receive Justice	Blessed Are the Poor	Two Responses to the Light	Entry into the Kingdom of Heaven	Lazarus Cannot Help the Rich Man
Psalm 49:1–4, 16–20	Proverbs 22:1–2, 7–9, 16	James 5:1–5	Luke 6:20–26	John 3:16–21	Matthew 19:23–30	Luke 16:19–31

REAPING GOD'S JUSTICE

ADULT TOPIC:	BACKGROUND SCRIPTURES:
THE TABLES ARE TURNED	LUKE 16:19–31; JOHN 5:24–30

LUKE 16:19–31

King James Version

'HERE was a certain rich man, which was lothed in purple and fine linen, and fared umptuously every day:

0 And there was a certain beggar named azarus, which was laid at his gate, full of ores,

1 And desiring to be fed with the crumbs vhich fell from the rich man's table: moreover e dogs came and licked his sores.

2 And it came to pass, that the beggar died, nd was carried by the angels into Abraham's osom: the rich man also died, and was buried;

3 And in hell he lift up his eyes, being in orments, and seeth Abraham afar off, and azarus in his bosom.

4 And he cried and said, Father Abraham, ave mercy on me, and send Lazarus, that he ugust dip the tip of his finger in water, and ool my tongue; for I am tormented in this ame.

5 But Abraham said, Son, remember that nou in thy lifetime receivedst thy good things, nd likewise Lazarus evil things: but now he is omforted, and thou art tormented.

6 And beside all this, between us and you nere is a great gulf fixed: so that they which vould pass from hence to you cannot; neither an they pass to us, that would come from nence.

7 Then he said, I pray thee therefore, father, nat thou wouldest send him to my father's ouse:

New Revised Standard Version

"THERE was a rich man who was dressed in purple and fine linen and who feasted sumptuously every day.

20 And at his gate lay a poor man named Lazarus, covered with sores,

21 who longed to satisfy his hunger with what fell from the rich man's table; even the dogs would come and lick his sores.

22 The poor man died and was carried away by the angels to be with Abraham. The rich man also died and was buried.

23 In Hades, where he was being tormented, he looked up and saw Abraham far away with Lazarus by his side.

24 He called out, 'Father Abraham, have mercy on me, and send Lazarus to dip the tip of his finger in water and cool my tongue; for I am in agony in these flames.'

25 But Abraham said, 'Child, remember that during your lifetime you received your good things, and Lazarus in like manner evil things; but now he is comforted here, and you are in agony.

26 Besides all this, between you and us a great chasm has been fixed, so that those who might want to pass from here to you cannot do so, and no one can cross from there to us.'

27 He said, 'Then, father, I beg you to send him to my father's house—

MAIN THOUGHT: But Abraham said, Son, remember that thou in thy lifetime eceivedst thy good things, and likewise Lazarus evil things: but now he is comorted, and thou art tormented. (Luke 16:25, KJV)

LUKE 16:19–31

King James Version

28 For I have five brethren; that he may testify unto them, lest they also come into this place of torment.

29 Abraham saith unto him, They have Moses and the prophets; let them hear them.

30 And he said, Nay, father Abraham: but if one went unto them from the dead, they will repent.

31 And he said unto him, If they hear not Moses and the prophets, neither will they be persuaded, though one rose from the dead.

New Revised Standard Version

28 for I have five brothers—that he may warn them, so that they will not also come into this place of torment.'

29 Abraham replied, 'They have Moses and the prophets; they should listen to them.'

30 He said, 'No, father Abraham; but if someone goes to them from the dead, they will repent.'

31 He said to him, 'If they do not listen to Moses and the prophets, neither will they be convinced even if someone rises from the dead.'"

LESSON SETTING
Time: A.D. 29
Place: Judea

LESSON OUTLINE
I. The Rich Man's Comfort
(Luke 16:19–21)
II. The Rich Man's Torment
(Luke 16:22–26)
III. Prophets and Signs
(Luke 16:27–31)

UNIFYING PRINCIPLE

There is great concern for the inequities in the lives of the poor versus the rich. How will these inequities be resolved? The story of the rich man and Lazarus tells us that the poor will receive their reward.

INTRODUCTION

Luke recounted a confrontation between Jesus and the religious leaders who were always lurking nearby listening to what He was telling the crowds who followed Him. According to Luke 15, the conflict began when the scribes and Pharisees grumbled that Jesus and His disciples ate with "sinners" (v. 2, NRSV). These sinners were people the scribes and Pharisees did not approve of and would not associate with

themselves. In response to their complaint Jesus told a series of parables about God' desire to seek and save those who were ir the most desperate need of it.

The first was of a shepherd who rejoiced after finding his lost sheep. Next He spoke of a woman who lost one of her ten coin and turned her house upside down in orde to find it. Following these examples is the parable of the prodigal, Jesus' accoun of a young man who took his father' goods and wasted them on riotous living All three stories were intended to be an explanation as to why Jesus associated with those marginalized by society, but the religious leaders did not appear to ge the point. They failed to understand Jesus priorities.

Seeing the Pharisees' hard hearts and self-congratulatory pride, Jesus next tol His disciples about the corrupting influ ence of riches ending with the principle "'No one can serve two masters.... You cannot serve God and wealth'" (Luke 16:13, NRSV). He drew a clear line in the sand concerning being rich in the things o this material world. One makes a choice either to pursue wealth or a relationship with God, but Jesus emphasized that no one can honestly seek both equally.

The response of the scribes and Pharisees to what Jesus had to say and to which they listened carefully was to ridicule Jesus (see Luke 16:14). They presumed that their wealth was a sign of God's favor and thought Jesus was ridiculous for challenging the accepted wisdom of the day. After a brief retort to those who listened but who refused to understand His words, Jesus turned to His disciples and to the crowd who waited anxiously for what He might say next, and told the story of the rich man and Lazarus. It was a story of the haves versus the have-nots which left the latter justified before their Creator.

EXPOSITION

I. THE RICH MAN'S COMFORT (LUKE 16:19–21)

Through the centuries scholars have debated whether the story of the rich man and Lazarus was based on real events and people or was another parable. Most parables did not name any of their characters. This is the only one of Jesus' parables in which one of the characters has a name: Lazarus, or Eleazar as it would be transliterated from Hebrew. Naming one character but not the other was likely a way to create contrast between two of the parable's actors. This Lazurus is evidently not the same person who was personally associated with Jesus noted in John 11. We do know it was a popular name meaning "God does help." The fact that the tide eventually turns in Lazarus' favor bears out this meaning.

It seems the rich man was not simply rich but also powerful and popular. He dressed in purple and fine linen. Purple was the rarest and most expensive color of cloth of the day, normally worn only by the very rich. Even fairly wealthy merchants could not afford such an extravagant luxury, leaving the reader to conclude this rich man was in the very upper strata of the wealthy of his day. The text reveals that he also feasted sumptuously every day. These feasts would have been more than private extravagant meals. Feasts involved inviting important guests and providing entertainment. The man knew people and those people came regularly to the parties he threw. It may have been that he was a powerful political figure, a top religious leader, or one of the most successful businessmen of his day. Whoever he was, real or imaginary, he had it all, and the people who assumed that his wealth proved that he was blessed by God lined up to be associated with him.

The estate of this rich man had a gate, much like the most exclusive mansions today. At this gate, where guests passed on their way to the rich man's parties, lay Lazarus. Lazarus was covered in sores, and those sores must have been exposed for all to see because Jesus noted that dogs would come by and lick them. All Lazarus wanted was to be given a few of the scraps that fell on the floor as the rich man and his guests stuffed themselves. Sick and starving, Lazarus is illustrated as a miserable person who deserved some form of help or mercy, but no one, least of all the rich man at whose gate he lay, seemed to care. The poverty and sickness from which Lazarus suffered were viewed by the elite of the day as signs of God's curse just as wealth was believed to be a sign of God's favor. Lazarus, they believed, was accursed and rejected by God. In fact his condition was seen as evidence of sin. Job underwent a similar accusation from Bildad who believed Job's suffering was caused by some secret sin Job had committed (see Job 8).

Had the scribes and Pharisees who overheard Jesus begin His story listened with open ears to the parables Jesus had told earlier, they might have understood that it was people like Lazarus whom God viewed with compassion and mercy that Jesus had come to seek and save. Yet their ears were stuck in the selfish mode of hearing only those things that bore out their error-prone beliefs. Jesus' previous teachings were totally rejected by them because they considered Jesus a trouble-maker and a rabble-rouser. In the minds of the religious elite, the rich man had it all and Lazarus was getting what he deserved, punishment for his sin.

II. THE RICH MAN'S TORMENT
(LUKE 16:22–26)

The turning of the tables in Jesus' story began when both men died. Jesus' prophecy that spoke of the great reversal that the first shall be last and the last shall be first is revealed here (see Matt. 19:30). Lazarus was released from his earthly misery and carried by angels to the very bosom of Abraham. This was an image that would have been very evocative to all who listened to Jesus. The bosom of Abraham was equivalent to paradise. Abraham is depicted in Scripture as a friend of God, and it was through him that the promise of divine blessings was established (see Gen. 12; Rom. 4). Thus the Jewish people styled paradise as the place where the souls of good people rested from death to the resurrection and were comforted by the father of the faith. It was not the place where the religious leaders would have expected Lazarus to be carried. Jesus' point here is that God initiated a reversal of fortunes.

Then the rich man died too. Jesus simply says he was buried, but one can imagine the pomp and lavish pageantry of this man's funeral. When he awoke to his final fate, to the surprise of the listeners, Jesus revealed the unbelievable reversal of fortunes for the rich man; he was in Hades being tormented. Donald Fleming says, "The rich man had been so concerned with building his wealth and enjoying it that he had forgotten God and no longer noticed the needs of others" (*Bridgeway Bible Commentary* [Brisbane: Bridgeway Publications, 2005], 468).

The commonly held belief of Jews in Jesus' day was that, when a person died, he or she went to one of two places: either to abide in Abraham's bosom where one awaited their final salvation or to Hades (sometimes called Sheol or simply the grave) where their everlasting torment began. Hades was not the final resting place of the wicked dead; that place was Gehenna, or hell, the lake of fire described in the book of Revelation. Paradise and Hades were two distinct places separated by an enormous gulf which made it impossible for people placed on one side to cross over to the other. However, those being tormented in Hades were able to look in agony across that gulf and see the blessed dead in Paradise.

As an aside, when Jesus hung on the cross and told the one thief, "Today you will be with me in Paradise" (Luke 23:43, NRSV), it was this Paradise to which he referred, not to heaven, the final abode of the righteous dead. It is also possible that the verse about Jesus preaching to the "spirits in prison" during the days when he was dead is a reference to those awaiting the final fulfillment though there is much disagreement and no certainty about to whom that refers (1 Pet. 3:19, NRSV).

Resting in the arms of Abraham, Lazarus was comforted. Across the gulf, the rich man saw this and cried out to Abraham to allow Lazarus to dip his finger in water and cool the rich man's tongue. What the rich man refused to do for Lazarus during life he now cried out for Lazarus to do for him. Just a scrap of food from the table was all Lazarus had wanted. Just a drop of cool water was what the rich man sought. Yet he did not get what he so desperately desired. The gulf could not be crossed and, anyway, said Abraham, "'During your lifetime you received your good things'" (Luke 16:25, NRSV).

Jesus' point is quite emphatic here. Just because one lives the life here on earth does not mean that it will yield eternal life or vice-versa. Eternal life is not predicated on human wealth, education, or other measures of affluence. Salvation comes about according to one's response to God's offer to accept Jesus Christ as one's Lord and personal Savior. In his life the rich man had refused to pattern his life according to God's desire to establish mercy to others and was thus suffering for his disobedience (see Matt. 5:1–9, NRSV).

Jesus has nothing more to say about Lazarus, who has been given all that anyone could hope for after a lifetime of suffering. He was in Paradise and, when the final resurrection arrives, will be welcomed to heaven to spend all eternity in bliss. The text implies that the evil things that drove him to seek and find consolation in life beyond the grave has ended and he has been ushered into eternity with the tables turned in his favor.

III. PROPHETS AND SIGNS (LUKE 16:27–31)

There is much more to be said about the suffering to be endured by the rich man who was ill-inspired to lend a helping hand to Lazarus. Abraham informed the tormented man that the good things he enjoyed during his earthly life had ended. From this point on, the rich man would remain in agony because the tables had been turned against him. The opportunity to create a change in his final destination had ended. His choice against being benevolent revoked the hope of benevolence to him. He became the recipient of what he gave. Paul reminded his readers in Galatians 6:7, "Do not be deceived; God is not mocked, for you reap whatever you sow" (NRSV). The rich man was reaping what he had sown.

He finally understood the terrible, awful choices he had made in his treatment of Lazarus. The rich man begged Abraham to send Lazarus to the home of his five brothers tell them what they were in store for if they did not repent. To this request, Abraham responded simply that they had Moses and the prophets to whom they could listen. Knowing that these brothers had paid no more attention to them than he himself had paid, the rich man suggested that Lazarus' coming back from the dead would accomplish faithfulness in his brothers that Moses and the prophets could not. Abraham rightly replied that the problem was not with the messengers but rather with the closed ears of those to whom the message was sent. This was the major point to which Jesus' story was driving. The scribes and Pharisees had everything going for them now, but that wealth, power, and position in life had worked to their disadvantage because it caused them to close their ears to any suggestion that God might not be delighted with them. Moses could come, the prophets could come, and even the Son of God could come Himself and rise from the dead, yet these blind guides would never hear what they said or taught.

Jesus had spoken in His explanation of the parable of the soils of those who heard the word but in whom the thorns of worldliness and wealth choked the word so that it produced no fruit (see Mark 4:18–19). James would later write that the rich should weep and howl at the terrible calamities that were going to come down upon them (see James 5:1–6). Paul warned Timothy about those who desire to get rich and how they pierce themselves with countless sorrows (see 1 Tim. 6:10). The rich man in Jesus' story paid no attention to the warnings in Scripture and paid the price for his failure to listen.

THE LESSON APPLIED

For those of us who are not wealthy, there is a temptation to read the story of the rich man and Lazarus and excuse ourselves because we do not believe the message applies to us. However, to think that Jesus was only speaking to the richest and poorest among us is to be in danger of closing our ears to the message of the Gospel just as surely as did the rich man in the story. Many of us have enough. Probably, truth be told, most of us have more than enough. There are, however, some among us who lack enough. Some lack greatly and others lack only a little. Jesus told the person with two coats to give one coat to the person with none and the person with enough food to share with the person who lacks enough food (see Luke 3:11). For those of us who have more than enough, whether we are vastly rich like the man in the story or only slightly well-off, the question hangs in the balance as to what we will do with what we have.

LET'S TALK ABOUT IT

1. Is it a sin to be rich?

No; all of God's gifts are blessings to use to further His ministry of salvation. It is when we use any of our gifts inappropriately and hold them only for ourselves that they become our god and therefore sinful.

HOME DAILY DEVOTIONAL READINGS
JUNE 25–JULY 1, 2018

MONDAY	TUESDAY	WEDNESDAY	THURSDAY	FRIDAY	SATURDAY	SUNDAY
Joseph Forgives His Brothers	Forgiveness and Healing of the Land	Forgiving and Consoling the Offender	Forgive Each Other's Complaints	Keep Forgiving Each Other	God's Forgiveness Depends on Us	Offer Mercy and Forgiveness Freely
Genesis 50:15–21	2 Chronicles 7:12–16	2 Corinthians 2:5–11	Colossians 3:12–17	Luke 17:1–4	Matthew 6:9–15	Matthew 18:21–35

PARABLE OF THE UNFORGIVING SERVANT

ADULT TOPIC: TO FORGIVE AND BE FORGIVEN	BACKGROUND SCRIPTURE: MATTHEW 18:21–35

MATTHEW 18:21–35

King James Version

THEN came Peter to him, and said, Lord, how oft shall my brother sin against me, and I forgive him? till seven times?

22 Jesus saith unto him, I say not unto thee, Until seven times: but, Until seventy times seven.

23 Therefore is the kingdom of heaven likened unto a certain king, which would take account of his servants.

24 And when he had begun to reckon, one was brought unto him, which owed him ten thousand talents.

25 But forasmuch as he had not to pay, his lord commanded him to be sold, and his wife, and children, and all that he had, and payment to be made.

26 The servant therefore fell down, and worshipped him, saying, Lord, have patience with me, and I will pay thee all.

27 Then the lord of that servant was moved with compassion, and loosed him, and forgave him the debt.

28 But the same servant went out, and found one of his fellowservants, which owed him an hundred pence: and he laid hands on him, and took him by the throat, saying, Pay me that thou owest.

29 And his fellowservant fell down at his feet, and besought him, saying, Have patience with me, and I will pay thee all.

30 And he would not: but went and cast him into prison, till he should pay the debt.

New Revised Standard Version

THEN Peter came and said to him, "Lord, if another member of the church sins against me, how often should I forgive? As many as seven times?"

22 Jesus said to him, "Not seven times, but, I tell you, seventy-seven times.

23 "For this reason the kingdom of heaven may be compared to a king who wished to settle accounts with his slaves.

24 When he began the reckoning, one who owed him ten thousand talents was brought to him;

25 and, as he could not pay, his lord ordered him to be sold, together with his wife and children and all his possessions, and payment to be made.

26 So the slave fell on his knees before him, saying, 'Have patience with me, and I will pay you everything.'

27 And out of pity for him, the lord of that slave released him and forgave him the debt.

28 But that same slave, as he went out, came upon one of his fellow slaves who owed him a hundred denarii; and seizing him by the throat, he said, 'Pay what you owe.'

29 Then his fellow slave fell down and pleaded with him, 'Have patience with me, and I will pay you.'

30 But he refused; then he went and threw him into prison until he would pay the debt.

MAIN THOUGHT: Shouldest not thou also have had compassion on thy fellowservant, even as I had pity on thee? (Matthew 18:33, KJV)

MATTHEW 18:21–35

King James Version

31 So when his fellowservants saw what was done, they were very sorry, and came and told unto their lord all that was done.

32 Then his lord, after that he had called him, said unto him, O thou wicked servant, I forgave thee all that debt, because thou desiredst me:

33 Shouldest not thou also have had compassion on thy fellowservant, even as I had pity on thee?

34 And his lord was wroth, and delivered him to the tormentors, till he should pay all that was due unto him.

35 So likewise shall my heavenly Father do also unto you, if ye from your hearts forgive not every one his brother their trespasses.

New Revised Standard Version

31 When his fellow slaves saw what had happened, they were greatly distressed, and they went and reported to their lord all that had taken place.

32 Then his lord summoned him and said to him, 'You wicked slave! I forgave you all that debt because you pleaded with me.

33 Should you not have had mercy on your fellow slave, as I had mercy on you?'

34 And in anger his lord handed him over to be tortured until he would pay his entire debt.

35 So my heavenly Father will also do to every one of you, if you do not forgive your brother or sister from your heart."

LESSON SETTING
Time: A.D. 29
Place: Near Capernaum

LESSON OUTLINE
I. Peter Sets the Stage
(Matthew 18:21–22)
II. The King and the Servants
(Matthew 18:23–27)
III. The King's Response
(Matthew 18:28–35)

UNIFYING PRINCIPLE

People desire forgiveness even though they refuse to forgive. What are consequences of an unforgiving heart? The parable of the unforgiving servant teaches us to forgive as we have been forgiven.

INTRODUCTION

Jesus had just laid out for His disciples the process by which offenses were to be handled in the Kingdom. Recorded in Matthew 18:15–20, His instructions were precise. When a Kingdom believer has been the victim of an offense by another Kingdom believer, the one offended is to go first to the offender and point out exactly what the offender has done to cause the offense (18:15). Should the offender repent at that moment, it is a cause for rejoicing because the two have been reconciled to one another.

Should, however, the offender not repent, then the one against whom the offense was committed is to return with two or three other believers and repeat the process. This, Jesus taught (18:16), was to be done so that there would be two or three witnesses to the entire process, including the claim of offense and the reaction by the accused offender. These witnesses, it would appear, were to add their viewpoint to the discussion as well, in hopes that the offender would, this time, repent.

If there was still no repentance, the situation was to be presented to the church (18:17). By this we should understand the entire assembled body of believers that regularly meet together. This public airing of the offense was so that everyone understood why, should there still be no repentance, the offenders were to be asked to remove themselves from the church, at least until such time repentance took place.

Jesus closed this teaching by saying that whatever the church agreed to do (binding a punishment or loosing the same) to discipline an unrepentant believer would be honored by God, who, Jesus said, would be in their midst as they considered what to do about the issue.

This teaching was a new concept to the disciples. There was no Jewish teaching of similar character about how to deal with those who offended their fellow believers. And, of course, given the newness, Peter had questions, either spoken on his own or spoken on behalf of the entire group for whom he generally served as spokesman.

EXPOSITION

I. PETER SETS THE STAGE (MATTHEW 18:21–22)

Before we begin to look at the specifics of what Jesus had to say, we should stop to ask what, precisely, one believer might do that would be considered a sin against another believer. Of course, someone might commit an obvious sin, such as stealing from a fellow believer. One might gossip or speak evil of a fellow believer, either to their face or behind their back to others. But, more generally, a believer is enjoined by Christ to love their fellow believers, not simply with good feelings but in actions as well. 1 John 3:17 tells us that if we see our fellow believer in need and we have the ability to meet that need but do not do so, God's love does not abide in us. Anytime one believer fails to treat another believer with genuine Christian love and charity, that believer has sinned against the one he or she has mistreated.

In the immediate aftermath of Jesus' presentation of the process for discipline within the new body of believers, Peter wondered how many times one person was required to go through this process with another. Jesus had laid out a clear, linear process. Step one was to confront the offender one-on-one. Step two was to go back with two or three others. Step three was to take the unresolved issue before the church, and step four was to remove the offenders from the body and treat them as if they were non-believers. So, Peter kept thinking in terms of process. What if the same person kept doing the same thing over and over again? Where was the limit on how many times that person should be put through the discipline process?

Jewish tradition generally required one Jew to forgive another Jew three times. Peter apparently decided, based upon his experience that Jesus always seemed to go beyond what Jewish traditions required, that he would suggest a larger number. Seven, the number associated with fullness, completion, and perfection, seemed like the right number to throw out, and Peter said, "'As many as seven times?'" (v. 21, NRSV). Jesus replied with a number likely drawn from the story of Cain and Lamech from Genesis 4. Some Bible versions present this number as seventy and seven, while other versions suggest seventy times seven. Either number conveys the point Jesus was making, that God's expectation is that forgiveness be offered without limit.

To drive home the point that forgiveness was to be offered freely and limitlessly, Jesus told the disciples a parable about a servant who sought forgiveness for massive debt, but was unwilling to forgive a fellow servant for a much smaller debt.

II. THE KING AND THE SERVANTS (MATTHEW 18:23–27)

There was a king. This king, said Jesus, decided the time had come to settle up with his servants. Matthew's account allegorizes the story so that the characters involved in it represent God, the disciples, and all the others who would yield their lives in service to God's Kingdom.

The king began with, presumably, the one who owed him the most, a sum of 10,000 talents. This amount is indicative of an incredible sum that the servant is unable to pay back. Working at average wages of the day (one denarius for ten hours of labor), it would take approximately nine years to earn a talent. In simple terms, this servant owed the king 90,000 years of wages! This poor servant owed the king more than he could ever have hoped to repay, much as you and I owe God more, as forgiven sinners, than we could ever hope to repay. This is precisely Jesus' point in choosing such a sum to illustrate to Peter the unlimited boundaries of forgiveness.

The servant, in an impossible situation, prostrated himself before the king and made a promise he had no way of keeping. "Give me some time! I'll pay it all back!" He was afraid that he and his wife and children were about to be sold into indentured service, from which they could not be freed for fifty years, until the year of Jubilee (see Lev. 25:39–41). The debt one owed a creditor was real and was often used to the creditor's advantage. However, the Scripture strictly forbade Israelites from abusing one another in this manner. They were to observe a sense of brotherhood between the tribes that distinguished them from the neighboring nations.

The servant's appeal for leniency was so pathetic that the king's heart was filled with compassion and pity. In an amazing act of kindness and generosity, the king cancelled the debt and released the servant from his awesome financial obligation.

Faced with a similar situation, in which the servant now found himself in the king's place, even if his fellow servant owed only a small fraction of what he himself had been forgiven, the first servant refused to adopt the generosity of the king. For his failure to pay even a small debt, the second servant would be called to account.

In both situations there were similar circumstances. First, there was a debt owed, and that debt was both real and significant. Even one hundred denarii represented four months' wages, or about $15,000 in today's American economy. The first servant's debt was beyond comprehension, but even the second servant, remanded to prison by the first servant, could never have hoped to come up with four months' wages while locked up in prison. So, there were two debts, neither of which was going to be repaid.

Also in each situation, the debtor expressed repentance and sorrow over the accumulation of such a significant debt. Each debtor prostrated himself before the one to whom he owed the debt and begged for mercy. Their pleas were identical cries for patience and forbearance. That, however, is where the similarities end. It is hard to imagine how a servant who had just been forgiven a debt of the magnitude of 10,000 talents could turn so harshly on a fellow servant who owed only a fraction of that huge sum, but that is what happened. Jesus was making a point that those who have been forgiven so much by God often find it difficult to forgive even the most minor offenses done to them by others.

Where the king had reacted to the first servant with pity and compassion, with mercy beyond measure, the first servant reacted to the second with harsh intolerance and pitiless cruelty. Jesus' point is that is not how believers are to treat one another. One good turn deserves another. Forgiveness received is not forgiveness until it is passed forward. God's forbearance, patience, and kindness toward us in our sin is meant to bring us to the point where we see our sin and seek to correct it in light of His grace and mercy. This automatically carries with it an attitude of repentance and forgiveness, reminding us that as God forgives us, we must be forgiving to others for their infractions against us (see Rom. 2:4). That is the ultimate goal of the discipline Jesus had outlined before starting His parable. It is exactly another way of expressing the need to practice the Golden Rule.

III. THE KING'S RESPONSE (MATTHEW 18:28–35)

Upon hearing of the way the first servant treated the second when faced with the same kind of debt for which the king had forgiven him, the king summoned the first servant back before him. The debt which had been freely forgiven was reinstated and the unforgiving servant was not simply jailed as he had done to the second servant, but was remanded for torture. Since the debt was so large as to be impossible to repay, this torture was going to last forever. This passage reveals that forgiveness is cyclical. In order for the initial offer of forgiveness to be effective, the one being forgiven must forgive others. Passing it forward satisfies and affirms the initial offer of forgiveness. What the Lord had just described was what His Father would do to anyone who failed to forgive a brother or sister.

No matter how you explain what Jesus had to say, it is clear that God takes very seriously our obligation to treat one another with merciful justice. Nowhere does Jesus suggest we have to like it, though the spiritual blessings we receive by forgiving others are wonderful. Forgiveness is hard. It is more than verbalization. It is a heartfelt initiative that pulls at the very core of our emotions, yet it is something that we must do. Our model is Jesus, who forgave His enemies for crucifying Him (Luke 23:34). Whether we like it or not, however, we are still commanded to forgive and keep on forgiving without end.

THE LESSON APPLIED

The text requires us to ask several "what if" questions. What if Adam and Eve had simply asked for forgiveness rather than blame God and one another for their sin in the Garden? What if Cain had inquired of his brother how to please God? If these motifs of forgiveness had been invoked, the mishap of human sin might have been averted. Jesus' point here is that reconciliation and restoration to one another are not optional. Forgiveness is something God takes quite seriously. Notice Matthew 6:14–15 concludes the periscope of the Model Prayer with a conditional blessing or curse. The person hearing the directive on how to pray is left to decide whether or not he or she will exercise forgiveness. Hence, the first servant was not forgiven because he refused to forgive the servant who owed him. This means that divine forgiveness is predicated on the human willingness to forgive others.

All the emphasis in the parable of the wicked servant and the king was on the attitudes of those against whom an offense has been committed. When offended, we are to forgive. But what about when we ourselves are the offenders? What can we learn from this parable about the right attitude and actions when we have offended a brother or sister?

First of all, obviously enough, we should strive with all our might to avoid giving offense, especially when the other person is new to the faith (see Matt. 18:6). But if the occasion does arise where we offend another, let us note that the first servant was forgiven because of how he approached the king initially.

He acknowledged the legitimacy of the debt or offense. He did not try to persuade the king that the debt was a minor matter or that it was unfair or undeserved. He said, "I'll pay you." The admission of the debt owed or the offense given is the starting point for reconciliation—no minimizing, no excuses of how the offended party ought to forgive, just the starting point of owning up to what we have done or not done.

From that point, an expression of godly sorrow, or repentance, is needed. This is not simply saying, "I'm sorry." Instead, it is a recognition of what one has done to cause the offense and a firm resolve to avoid a repetition. "I know I did it, I am sorry I hurt you, myself, and others. I am sorry I ruptured our relationship, and I promise you I will not do that again" are the kind of repentant responses that will go a long way toward resolving the offense.

Finally, a plea for mercy and forgiveness is appropriate. Simply to ask, "Please forgive me" will let the offended party know that you wish to reconcile with them. After that, it is up to them to behave like the king and not like the first servant. In other words, the text requires something from the offender and the one offended to move swiftly toward resolving the issue.

LET'S TALK ABOUT IT

1. Why is the Golden Rule so important for Christians to believe and practice?

It is important because it is the way of God. He looks out for us. He treats us with love, respect, and kindness, even though we don't deserve it. He even placed Himself in our stead to atone for human sin. Essentially, the Lord God did for us as believers what we could not do for ourselves.

HOME DAILY DEVOTIONAL READINGS
JULY 2–8, 2018

MONDAY	TUESDAY	WEDNESDAY	THURSDAY	FRIDAY	SATURDAY	SUNDAY
Visual Reminder of the Commandments	Jesus Fulfills the Law and Prophets	Craving Attention While Cheating Widows	Doing Is More Important than Speaking	Keeping People Away from the Kingdom	Blind Guides Confuse Meaning of Oaths	Jesus Critical of Scribes and Pharisees
Numbers 15:37–41	Matthew 5:17–20	Luke 20:45–47	Matthew 23:5–12	Matthew 23:13–15	Matthew 23:16–22	Matthew 23:1–4, 23–26

JESUS CRITICIZES UNJUST LEADERS

ADULT TOPIC: HYPOCRITES!	BACKGROUND SCRIPTURE: MATTHEW 23

MATTHEW 23:1–8, 23–26

King James Version

THEN spake Jesus to the multitude, and to his disciples,

2 Saying, The scribes and the Pharisees sit in Moses' seat:

3 All therefore whatsoever they bid you observe, that observe and do; but do not ye after their works: for they say, and do not.

4 For they bind heavy burdens and grievous to be borne, and lay them on men's shoulders; but they themselves will not move them with one of their fingers.

5 But all their works they do for to be seen of men: they make broad their phylacteries, and enlarge the borders of their garments,

6 And love the uppermost rooms at feasts, and the chief seats in the synagogues,

7 And greetings in the markets, and to be called of men, Rabbi, Rabbi.

8 But be not ye called Rabbi: for one is your Master, even Christ; and all ye are brethren.

• • • • •

23 Woe unto you, scribes and Pharisees, hypocrites! for ye pay tithe of mint and anise and cummin, and have omitted the weightier matters of the law, judgment, mercy, and faith: these ought ye to have done, and not to leave the other undone.

24 Ye blind guides, which strain at a gnat, and swallow a camel.

25 Woe unto you, scribes and Pharisees, hypocrites! for ye make clean the outside of the cup and of the platter, but within they are full of extortion and excess.

New Revised Standard Version

THEN Jesus said to the crowds and to his disciples,

2 "The scribes and the Pharisees sit on Moses' seat;

3 therefore, do whatever they teach you and follow it; but do not do as they do, for they do not practice what they teach.

4 They tie up heavy burdens, hard to bear, and lay them on the shoulders of others; but they themselves are unwilling to lift a finger to move them.

5 They do all their deeds to be seen by others; for they make their phylacteries broad and their fringes long.

6 They love to have the place of honor at banquets and the best seats in the synagogues,

7 and to be greeted with respect in the marketplaces, and to have people call them rabbi.

8 But you are not to be called rabbi, for you have one teacher, and you are all students.

• • • • •

23 "Woe to you, scribes and Pharisees, hypocrites! For you tithe mint, dill, and cummin, and have neglected the weightier matters of the law: justice and mercy and faith. It is these you ought to have practiced without neglecting the others.

24 You blind guides! You strain out a gnat but swallow a camel!

25 "Woe to you, scribes and Pharisees, hypocrites! For you clean the outside of the cup and of the plate, but inside they are full of greed and self-indulgence.

MAIN THOUGHT: The scribes and the Pharisees sit in Moses' seat: All therefore whatsoever they bid you observe, that observe and do; but do not ye after their works: for they say, and do not. (Matthew 23:2–3, KJV)

MATTHEW 23:1–8, 23–26

King James Version	*New Revised Standard Version*
26 Thou blind Pharisee, cleanse first that which is within the cup and platter, that the outside of them may be clean also.	26 You blind Pharisee! First clean the inside of the cup, so that the outside also may become clean.

LESSON SETTING
Time: A.D. 30s
Place: Jerusalem

LESSON OUTLINE
I. Jewish Religious Leadership
   (Matthew 23:1–2)
II. The Way of the Jewish Leaders
   (Matthew 23:3–8, 23–25)
III. Jesus Presents a Better Way
   (Matthew 23:26)

UNIFYING PRINCIPLE
We encounter leaders who expect people to do one thing while they do something else. Is there a fair response to such an expectation? Jesus challenges unjust leaders to change or experience destruction.

INTRODUCTION
The final drama of Jesus' earthly ministry was unfolding, and if anyone thought Jesus might try to make nice with the religious leaders in Jerusalem, they were sorely mistaken. Matthew records (21:9) that Jesus entered Jerusalem in preparation for the Passover to the thunderous cheers of a large crowd, shouting "Hosanna" and calling Jesus the Son of David, a Messianic title (see 21:9). The city was in an uproar over the One whose miracles and teachings had caught everyone's attention (see 21:10). Jesus, however, very quickly began to act quite differently than the people had expected, and the religious leaders bore the brunt of His confrontations.

He cleansed the temple area of those who made their livings overcharging the worshipers for the animals required for sacrifice (see 21:15). The next day, as he taught in the Temple courtyard, the chief priest, Caiaphas, and the elders of the Sanhedrin council challenged him. Rebuking their veiled motives, Jesus told the most important leaders of Judaism that tax collectors and prostitutes would enter the Kingdom of heaven ahead of them (see 21:31) and then proceeded to tell these powerful men that their power was going to be taken from them (see 21:43). Needless to say, they were not pleased. It was one thing to argue in Galilee on a hillside where few would overhear. It was an entirely different matter to criticize the leaders of the Jewish community during the Passover when Jerusalem was teeming with observant Jews there to celebrate the Passover feast.

Matthew 22 recounts the repeated attempts by the religious establishment to trap Jesus into saying something that would turn the crowd against Him so that He could be arrested without causing a riot. At every turn, Jesus stood his ground and won the crowds with wisdom and insight. But His days were numbered and He knew it. He was to have only one last opportunity to speak to the people. Matthew 23 records that last sermon.

EXPOSITION

I. JEWISH RELIGIOUS LEADERSHIP (MATTHEW 23:1–2)

Before beginning to examine what Jesus said to these leaders, let us examine to whom His comments were addressed. Matthew mentions chief priests and scribes, Pharisees and elders. Who were these people?

To understand the hierarchy of the Jewish religion in Jesus' day, one needs to keep in mind that there were offices and there were also groups of like-minded religious thinkers.

The highest official position in the Jewish religious hierarchy was that of chief priest. He was appointed by the Romans for however long they wished to leave him in power, but once in place, he largely oversaw matters pertaining to the Jewish people and their faith. During the last week of Jesus' ministry, Caiaphas was the high priest, though his father, Annas, had served as such in the recent past and still wielded influence among the Jewish leadership and community.

The governing body of Judaism, under the headship of the high priest, was the Sanhedrin. They heard matters of Jewish law and passed down decisions based upon their deliberations. Members of the Sanhedrin came from three main groups: the high priests, scribes, and elders. These men were Sadducees and Pharisees.

The Pharisees were more liberal in their acceptance of oral tradition and honored the oral laws as equal to the written Mosaic laws of the Torah (Genesis–Deuteronomy). The Sadducees were the ones who conservatively honored only the Mosaic Law. The Pharisees were, by far, the larger and more popular group of religious leaders, but Sadducees were the majority on the Sanhedrin and controlled it.

When a case was brought before the Sanhedrin, it was the scribes who presented the Law. They were students of the minutest details of the Law, capable of arguing on any matter that might come before the Sanhedrin. Scribes could be Pharisees or Sadducees, though the majority were Pharisees.

Rabbis and elders were positions related to the synagogues; The elders ran the synagogues and the rabbis did the teaching, either on the Sabbath at the synagogues or during the week in and around town. One could go to the temple on any given day and find a collection of rabbis holding forth on this or that in the courtyards, just as Jesus, often called rabbi by His followers, did (see Matt. 21:23).

There were other positions of power, such as the temple guards and the priests, but these groups did not figure directly into the final conflict between Jesus and the religious leaders.

Jesus did not single out the Pharisees because they were any worse or better than the Sadducees. They were simply more numerous and more likely to want to argue about the Law, since they considered themselves the ultimate experts of it. The scribes would have sought out Jesus from a desire to ensure He was teaching according to the accepted interpretations and to challenge anything they felt might be heretical. The Sadducees confronted Jesus on occasion, mostly about resurrection, in which they emphatically did not believe.

II. THE WAY OF THE JEWISH LEADERS
(MATTHEW 23:3–8, 23–25)

Knowing the purpose for the Law, Jesus interpreted it quite differently than His Jewish contemporaries. There is no doubt that what Jesus observed with the scribes and Pharisees, the elders and teachers, broke His heart. His lament over Jerusalem at the end of Matthew 23 clearly shows how desperately in need the people were for solid religious leadership that truly focused their attention on God rather on the persons delivering it. Jesus' observance of the leaders' actions was the basis of His critique.

His first observation was about the hypocrisy of the way the leaders acted. They sat "on Moses' seat," which meant that they occupied positions within the religious structure that gave them the authority to dictate how the people were to observe life as Jews (23:2, NRSV). Jesus told those listening to Him to do what these leaders said. They were the authority and Jesus never suggested that the people did not need leaders. However, He also told the people not to follow the example of their leaders, who did not practice what they preached. The people were to observe actions of the Jewish leaders. They restricted the behavior of the people with stringent rules without providing any guidance to the people about how they were supposed to live their lives under those rules. In fact, they likely had no idea how to live under the rules since they did not adhere to the rules themselves.

The leaders were enthralled with their own importance. The scribes made their phylacteries and tassels extra-large to impress people with their devotion to the Law. They always sought the places of honor at banquets and the best seats at the synagogues so that people would know how important they were. They loved to be approached with awe in the marketplace, much like a sports or movie celebrity might enjoy being recognized and asked for an autograph. It was a huge ego trip, born of pride and self-righteousness.

Not content to lord it over everyone else, these leaders made sure the common people knew how much lower on the totem pole they were. The leaders "lock[ed] people out of the kingdom of heaven" (23:13, NRSV). They kept reminding the people how unworthy they were as Jews because they could not keep all the rules put upon them by the Pharisees. These leaders went on mission trips to convert proselytes, and then having won them to Judaism, led them astray and crushed their spirits with accusations that they were not correctly practicing their new religion.

They had developed a clever way of allowing themselves to get around the promises they made before God when they took their positions. If they took an oath in the name of the Holy of Holies, they were not required to keep it. Only if the oath was taken on the Corban gold, money dedicated to the temple's operations was the oath binding. The Pharisees felt because they were the models and enforcers of the Law that it did not apply to them. They saw nothing wrong with twisting it to their advantage.

Jesus' next complaint was about how they practiced tithing. They gave to God the insignificant products of the earth and entirely neglected the principles behind the Law: justice, mercy, and faith. For this, Jesus called them blind guides, whitewashed tombs, and a family of snakes. They were dead inside but considered themselves even better than their ancestors, who had killed the prophets sent to warn Israel to repent.

For all of this and more, Jesus told these high and mighty pretenders that they would not "escape being sentenced to hell" (23:33, NRSV). In a few days, Jesus would be crucified, but He would rise. These blind guides, still alive but already dead, were without hope. Jesus would reign for all eternity, but the power and position of the Jewish religious leaders was going to come to an end soon.

III. Jesus Presents a Better Way (Matthew 23:26)

Sandwiched in among all the woes and criticisms which Jesus heaped upon the religious leaders, He gave the crowds listening to Him that day some clues about a better way to live than what they observed in their leaders.

In verse 3, Jesus told the people to be obedient to those in authority over them even while not mimicking those same leaders practice of the messages they preached. They regarded the Law with high esteem. Jesus did also and wanted the people to do the same. However, the Jewish leaders used the Law to control and entrap people. Their hearts were not right, which is why Jesus commanded them to clean themselves on the inside.

In verse 8, He warned the people against seeking honor from people. Such seeking almost always comes from a heart of pride and vanity, and should that honor be gained, it brings with it the temptation of self-righteousness. According to the text it is better to remain a humble servant than to gain a misguided sense of one's own importance to God and to other people.

In verses 20–22, reacting to the sleight-of-hand used by the Pharisees to negate their vows, Jesus told the people to honor their vows and commitments. Elsewhere He said, "Do not swear by your head, for you cannot make one hair white or black. Let your word be 'Yes, Yes' or 'No, No'; anything more than this comes from the evil one" (Matt. 5:36–37, NRSV). It should not require some sort of formal oath for people to do what they have said they will do. Neither should people invent excuses for failing to do as they have said and think that they are thereby excused. That is how the Pharisees lived and Jesus wanted better for his listeners.

Lastly, Jesus, by implication, redirected the entire focus of religion away from keeping rules. The rules should be kept, but not at the expense of things that are most basic. He listed justice, mercy and faith. Justice ensured that people were not cheated or relegated to being unimportant. Mercy ensured that people were given a second chance just as we, ourselves, want a second chance when we stumble. And faith always looked for the good in people.

Rather than tying up burdens on people as the Pharisees did, Jesus taught that justice, mercy, and faith would form the foundation of a redeemed society in which everyone could live with a sense of being an important and vital part of society.

The Lesson Applied

People in modern American society, especially if they are poor or from a marginalized group, often crave significance. The culture around us suggests that we can find significance by being popular or by achieving celebrity status. Many of us seek to draw attention to ourselves in one way or another.

Some dress outlandishly or choose a wild hair style or color. Others cover their bodies with tattoos and piercings. People buy attention-getting cars to drive, seek to live in fancy homes, buy the latest trendy items and love attending concerts by the latest and most popular musicians. Facebook, Twitter, and Instagram are filled with prideful photos, showing material gain.

In church, those who consider themselves important seek the best seats just like the Pharisees did, while others try to outdo everyone else when it comes to shouting and clapping and swaying to the music. We run to snap a picture with television preachers, put clever bumper stickers on our cars, and always want to have something insightful to add during Bible study.

The pharisaical spirit lives on. It is anathema to the humble servant spirit that Jesus urged his listeners to cultivate. Those of us who are in leadership positions do well to discourage this self-promoting behavior in ourselves and others and encourage all who claim to follow Christ to put first things first: to live with justice, mercy and faith. As Micah 6:8 says, "What does the LORD require of you but to do justice, and to love kindness, and to walk humbly with your God?" (NRSV).

That is not to say we do not need rules. Rules are necessary and can prevent great harm when they are followed accordingly. However, rules cannot be so burdensome that they lose their focus. The goal is for people to live in harmony with God's love and with one another. When those same rules do more harm than good, they lose their purpose. The Pharisee knew this to be true and their actions indicate it. The Pharisees failed to keep the laws by developing ways to subvert their adherence to it.

LET'S TALK ABOUT IT

1. **What does this passage have to say to those who feel the need to confront those in power?**

Jesus' crucifixion did not come only because of this final sermon, but the sermon encapsulated all that He had to say about the evil being done by those charged with leading the people. People in power tend to get used to their power and will often react quite negatively to challenge. When we confront the abuse of power, we should not expect a welcome mat to be placed before us. For Jesus the confrontation meant death.

HOME DAILY DEVOTIONAL READINGS
JULY 9–15, 2018

MONDAY	TUESDAY	WEDNESDAY	THURSDAY	FRIDAY	SATURDAY	SUNDAY
Ask, God Will Respond	I Always Remember You in Prayer	Unceasing Prayer, Essential in Church Ministries	God's Justice for the Widow	Take Care of Widows Now	The Lord Watches His People	Keep Insisting until Justice Comes
Luke 11:5–13	Romans 1:7–15	1 Thessalonians 5:12–18	Deuteronomy 10:17–21	Acts 6:1–6	Psalm 33:18–22	Luke 18:1–8

THE WIDOW AND THE UNJUST JUDGE

| ADULT TOPIC:
PERSISTENCE PAYS OFF | BACKGROUND SCRIPTURE:
LUKE 18:1–8 |

LUKE 18:1–8

King James Version

AND he spake a parable unto them to this end, that men ought always to pray, and not to faint;

2 Saying, There was in a city a judge, which feared not God, neither regarded man:

3 And there was a widow in that city; and she came unto him, saying, Avenge me of mine adversary.

4 And he would not for a while: but afterward he said within himself, Though I fear not God, nor regard man;

5 Yet because this widow troubleth me, I will avenge her, lest by her continual coming she weary me.

6 And the Lord said, Hear what the unjust judge saith.

7 And shall not God avenge his own elect, which cry day and night unto him, though he bear long with them?

8 I tell you that he will avenge them speedily. Nevertheless when the Son of man cometh, shall he find faith on the earth?

New Revised Standard Version

THEN Jesus told them a parable about their need to pray always and not to lose heart.

2 He said, "In a certain city there was a judge who neither feared God nor had respect for people.

3 In that city there was a widow who kept coming to him and saying, 'Grant me justice against my opponent.'

4 For a while he refused; but later he said to himself, 'Though I have no fear of God and no respect for anyone,

5 yet because this widow keeps bothering me, I will grant her justice, so that she may not wear me out by continually coming.'"

6 And the Lord said, "Listen to what the unjust judge says.

7 And will not God grant justice to his chosen ones who cry to him day and night? Will he delay long in helping them?

8 I tell you, he will quickly grant justice to them. And yet, when the Son of Man comes, will he find faith on earth?"

MAIN THOUGHT: And shall not God avenge his own elect, which cry day and night unto him, though he bear long with them? (Luke 18:7, KJV)

LESSON SETTING

Time: A.D. 30

Place: On the way to Jerusalem, between Samaria and Galilee

LESSON OUTLINE

I. The Unjust Judge and the Widow (Luke 18:1–5)

II. The Unjust Judge and God (Luke 18:6–7)

III. Let's Get Real (Luke 18:8)

UNIFYING PRINCIPLE

People become discouraged when their requests for relief seem to go unanswered. Why should we persist? Jesus promises justice to those who persistently request relief from unjust treatment.

INTRODUCTION

Jesus had spoken of the Kingdom of God, first to the Pharisees in response to another one of their challenges (see Luke 17:20) and then, immediately thereafter, to the disciples. He told them, "The days are coming when you will long to see one of the days of the Son of Man, and you will not see it" (v. 22, NRSV). He knew exactly what was coming, and He knew that the disciples would need to be strong in prayer if they hoped to keep their faith alive in the face of what lay ahead for all of them.

These men, save Judas, of course, were going to be hounded to the ends of the earth, arrested again and again by both the Jewish leaders and the Romans, persecuted, driven from their homes, tortured, beaten, and in many cases, martyred—all because they followed Jesus and desired to serve God in whatever ways He might call them to serve. They were about to see their Leader executed and be accused by angry mobs and religious zealots for participating in a blasphemous heresy against Judaism. And, with the exception of a few precious moments, they would have to face it all without Jesus' personal presence to comfort and direct them.

It was going to get rough. The injustice that they would have to face would tempt them to give up if they were left to their own resources. To prepare and show them how to find the strength and courage to face what Jesus knew was to come upon them, He told them a parable about a little old widow and a heartless judge. In this parable He hoped they would see the necessity of a constant and deliberate prayer life.

EXPOSITION

I. THE UNJUST JUDGE AND THE WIDOW (Luke 18:1-5)

Jesus gave this parable to help the disciples better understand the kind of prayer that would be necessary if they wished God to help them deal with the difficult times that lay ahead of them.

In a "certain city" (v. 2) there was a judge sitting in his courtroom. This man, according to Jesus, had absolutely no reverence for God, nor any sense of shame concerning the cruel and heartless way in which he treated the poor and helpless, who came before him with their issues. People in Jesus' day, as now, often believed wealth, power, and position to be signs of God's favor. It is possible this judge automatically presumed that the opponent of this widow was in the right simply because he or she was more powerful and wealthier than the poor widow.

Widows had it tough. There was no social security, and typically women were not permitted to inherit property, so when a woman's husband died, she was either left to the good graces of her children and extended family or thrown into begging for alms. The temple had funds with which to provide for widows, but those funds would not have been available to help her settle a legal claim. She was on her own, subject to the whims of the judge who, according to Jesus, had absolutely no regard for her. She was the epitome of a helpless individual at the mercy of an uncaring and unjust system.

What she did have was persistence. The scene Jesus portrayed might be comical if the stakes for this poor woman were not so high. Imagine the scene. Court is gaveled into session and, through the door at the rear of the courtroom, for the umpteenth time, comes a little old lady, stooped from the hard life of widowhood, but with a determined expression on her face. Approaching the bench, just as she had the day before and the day before that, or as far back as anyone in the courtroom could remember, she looked up at the judge and uttered the same words she had spoken for as long as she had been coming to him. "Your honor, grant me relief from the unjust demands of my opponent." Then she simply stands there awaiting a response, knowing from her endless attempts exactly what the merciless judge will say, and yet forcing him to say it again. "Denied. Now, away with you, and stop bothering this court!" And so, off she goes with not another word. Watching her exit, the judge knows one thing for sure—she will be back tomorrow, and the day after that, and the day after that until she gains justice. He has the power to deny her request, but he cannot deny her the right to make that request.

And so, the judge finally relents. His attitude toward the widow is unchanged. He has not suddenly decided that she is deserving of his mercy; he is simply tired of seeing the door to the court open and this troublesome old lady trudge, once again, up to his bench. The judge has not changed his mind about God and the justice of God's Kingdom either. He decides to grant her request for one reason alone: she has beaten him into submission.

The next day, the scene repeats, right up to the moment when the courtroom waits to hear, once again, the word, "Denied." This time, however, the judge grants her request. She must have been overjoyed. The courtroom is amazed. The judge merely slumps in exhausted relief. He will not have to listen to this annoying old lady again. Her persistence has paid off. ✠

II. THE UNJUST JUDGE AND GOD (Luke 18:6–7)

The question Jesus presented in this drama was, "Why did the judge not simply grant her request sooner?" He caused himself a lot of unnecessary grief by postponing the inevitable.

With that thought in their minds, Jesus asked the disciples to consider how God might respond in a similar situation. A judge with absolutely no respect for God or compassion for those with no power and prestige had given in and done what he did not want to do. He responded favorably and justly to the widow's request only after her constant pleading. God, on the other hand, has the utmost compassion for those wronged by life's injustices and has promised to right the wrongs done to His beloved children who cry out in anguish to Him day after day. Their persistent cry touches the deep corridors of God's loving heart and compels Him to act decisively on His children's behalf.

In the Sermon on the Mount (Matt. 7:11), Jesus had taught that if we, who are far from perfect, know how to give good gifts to those who ask, how much more does God wish to give good gifts to those who ask Him? This parable is an illustration of God doing exactly what Jesus had taught He would do.

The people of God to whom Jesus made reference in Luke 18:7–8 cry out day and night seeking relief from the evils that befall them. Whereas the judge made the poor widow wait and wait, Jesus told the disciples that God would never delay their blessing because of selfishness. Jesus asked a rhetorical question, "'Will [God] delay long in helping them?'" (v. 7, NRSV). The answer is, of course, no! God is not inconsiderate, nor is He only concerned about His image or about pleasing those in power or those with wealth. Jesus pointed out that God will "quickly" grant justice to those who seek it of Him.

Donald Fleming, in the *Bridgeway Bible Commentary*, remarked, "If an ungodly judge will give a just judgment to a helpless widow solely to be rid of her ceaseless pleading, how much more will the holy God answer the cries of his persecuted people?" ([Brisbane: Bridgeway Publications, 2005], 468). To God, we are not like this widow, the object of indifference and contempt, but dear to Him as the apple of His eye. Neither is He like the judge, an abusive and inconsiderate authority concerned only for himself.

III. Let's Get Real (Luke 18:8)

Why do so many of us suffer injustice that seems to go on and on with no relief? Let us even get more specific and talk about the evil and injustice of systemic racism. American society has been plagued by this evil since its birth as a nation. People of color have been forced to labor as slaves and sharecroppers, while others served toiling on railroad development, or doing laundry with little or no wages to help keep the wheels of modern industrial and post-industrial society turning. But racism remains a strong and negative force that hampers the progress of American society, and the question comes, "Where is God's answer? When will it ever end?"

God does not immediately put an end to the wrongs of the wicked or to human suffering. There is a difference between quick and immediate. When one prays about injustice, or about any evil, God may tarry longer than we would prefer. Sometimes He uses these things to accomplish His holy and righteous purpose. Yet we can be sure God's answer will come in His own time and way.

Let us distinguish between prayer for relief from the general evil of racism, as compared to prayer about a specific personal experience with racism. We live in a fallen world populated by sinful people. While a prayer that God will bring an end to racism is certainly not a wrong prayer, we must understand that racism, war, poverty, and the other evils of this world will never completely end until the Kingdom of God comes in all its fullness. On the other hand, this does not mean that God will not help us to overcome specific issues of evil that take place in our own lives.

When we encounter a personal experience that seems to us to be racist (or any other injustice), the first question we do well to ask is whether or not it is truly an injustice. Just because another person got the job you thought you should get does not, in and of itself, mean the decision was racist. It is easy to play the race card, but when someone throws racism out without a serious and prayerful consideration of whether or not there might be other factors, that person does an injustice to those who suffer genuine racism. People who claim to love and follow God owe it to one another to be as certain as humanly possible that a true injustice has occurred.

Another consideration is to ask oneself if what one initially reacted to as injustice might simply be that one did not get what one wanted and is now upset. If something costs thirty dollars and a person only has twenty, it is not unjust that he or she cannot buy the item. Or if a person didn't get the job because he or she lacked a specific qualification, this candidate was not passed over because of racism. This person simply wasn't qualified. One must learn to accept it and, if it is important to the person seeking employment, go get qualified. However, if the rules change in the middle of the game, there is cause for concern and may be a veritable case of injustice.

God responds to persistent prayer. Though we may be upset for a while over an instance of injustice, we often simply don't care enough to put the kind of persistence into our prayers that will bring a response from God. We offer up a few quick prayers about it then get distracted by the grind of daily life and forget to persevere. It is not God's problem if we just don't care enough to wrestle with Him in persistent prayer.

Some people, too, doubt that God will truly answer. That is why Jesus made the comment at the close of His parable about finding faith. It may be that we don't think we are worthy of God's answer, or it may be that we assume what we read in the Bible no longer works in the modern world. We can put on a good Christian front for the world around us, but God is not fooled by our posturing. If one truly believes that God hears and answers prayer, then one should grab hold of Him and not let go until He answers. The example of Jacob's wrestling with God in Genesis 32:22–32 is there to help us see the benefit of such a struggle with the Lord. Jacob refused to let go of the divine presence until he was blessed.

Finally, some say they want relief from injustice, be it racism or any other injustice, but what they truly want is for God to punish the person who mistreated them. James wrote about those who do not get what they seek because they ask out of wrong motives (James 4:3). Those who practice injustice often do so from hearts filled with deep woundedness. God may answer your prayer for justice by blessing the person who inflicted the injustice upon you so that his or her heart is changed and that person's own wounds healed. If that thought is upsetting, then you might want to check your motives.

Dedicated and persistent prayer in the face of injustice will bring about an answer from God. We have Jesus' promise of that, but that promise will not be realized if it is haphazardly composed and offered. We will not find fulfillment from prayers offered for the wrong motives or those that seek to manipulate God into giving us what we want, nor will we find relief in prayers offered in doubt as to whether God cares enough or is even still up there listening. Dedicated, persistent and faithful prayers are the ones God will always answer, but be mindful that God will answer in His own time and in His own way.

THE LESSON APPLIED

We Americans live in an instant society. We want to be entertained, so we turn on the TV and, instantly, we are entertained. We want to be fed, so we go to a nearby restaurant and, almost instantly, food is presented to us. We desire something, so we pull out our credit card and, in the blink of an eye, that something is ours.

Our prayers often reflect our demand for instant gratification. When we face a crisis or an injustice, we want to hurl up to God a quick prayer, claim a promise, and conclude we have done all that is required for God to respond. Then, when God fails to respond, we blame Him. Or we get discouraged and sad, as if maybe we are not good enough to merit an answer from God.

The real problem is that most of us don't have much experience with perseverance in prayer. Perhaps, every morning, we ask God to bless us and our families, but to prevail in sincere and persistent prayer about a situation that, at least at first, does not seem to change, is foreign to many of us.

The kind of prayer that Jesus said would quickly get a response from God must be earnest. Not haphazard or poorly thought out, but honest and deeply focused on crying out to God from the depths of our being—then doing it again, and again, and yet again, until God becomes assured of our willingness to cling to Him. It won't take long in the grand scheme of things, but it is going to take longer and require more emotional effort than most of us are usually prepared to spend.

LET'S TALK ABOUT IT

1. Aren't we bothering God when we keep repeating the same prayer day after day?

The judge in the parable was bothered by the widow because he had no concern or compassion for her. God is not like that. He always wants to hear from us about the things we have to talk over with Him. It is not the way a parent feels when a child keeps asking for a cookie. God does not roll his eyes and think, "Oh, no, here comes so-and-so again." We are more precious to God when we come to Him earnestly and repeatedly, and He will always welcome us with compassion and love.

2. Do prayers for relief from injustice have to follow some sort of pattern?

God is not interested in the packaging. He's interested in the content. One need not use big "prayer" words, nor pepper the prayer with Scripture. A heartfelt prayer of a single simple sentence voicing our request serves to focus God's attention on our needs. The widow's prayer was simple, "Grant me relief from the injustice of my oppressor." It worked for her and will work for you.

HOME DAILY DEVOTIONAL READINGS
JULY 16–22, 2018

MONDAY	TUESDAY	WEDNESDAY	THURSDAY	FRIDAY	SATURDAY	SUNDAY
Enter by the Narrow Gate	Jesus, Gate of Salvation	Stay Connected to Jesus	By Their Fruits You Will Know	Hear and Act on the Word	Abundant Life Today and Eternally	Strive to Enter God's Kingdom
Matthew 7:13–14	John 10:1–10	John 15:1–11	Matthew 7:15–23	Matthew 7:24–29	Mark 10:28–31	Luke 13:22–30

ENTERING GOD'S KINGDOM

ADULT TOPIC: COME IN	BACKGROUND SCRIPTURES: MATTHEW 7:15–23; LUKE 13:22–30

LUKE 13:22–30

King James Version

AND he went through the cities and villages, teaching, and journeying toward Jerusalem.

23 Then said one unto him, Lord, are there few that be saved? And he said unto them,

24 Strive to enter in at the strait gate: for many, I say unto you, will seek to enter in, and shall not be able.

25 When once the master of the house is risen up, and hath shut to the door, and ye begin to stand without, and to knock at the door, saying, Lord, Lord, open unto us; and he shall answer and say unto you, I know you not whence ye are:

26 Then shall ye begin to say, We have eaten and drunk in thy presence, and thou hast taught in our streets.

27 But he shall say, I tell you, I know you not whence ye are; depart from me, all ye workers of iniquity.

28 There shall be weeping and gnashing of teeth, when ye shall see Abraham, and Isaac, and Jacob, and all the prophets, in the kingdom of God, and you yourselves thrust out.

29 And they shall come from the east, and from the west, and from the north, and from the south, and shall sit down in the kingdom of God.

30 And, behold, there are last which shall be first, and there are first which shall be last.

New Revised Standard Version

JESUS went through one town and village after another, teaching as he made his way to Jerusalem.

23 Someone asked him, "Lord, will only a few be saved?" He said to them,

24 "Strive to enter through the narrow door; for many, I tell you, will try to enter and will not be able.

25 When once the owner of the house has got up and shut the door, and you begin to stand outside and to knock at the door, saying, 'Lord, open to us,' then in reply he will say to you, 'I do not know where you come from.'

26 Then you will begin to say, 'We ate and drank with you, and you taught in our streets.'

27 But he will say, 'I do not know where you come from; go away from me, all you evildoers!'

28 There will be weeping and gnashing of teeth when you see Abraham and Isaac and Jacob and all the prophets in the kingdom of God, and you yourselves thrown out.

29 Then people will come from east and west, from north and south, and will eat in the kingdom of God.

30 Indeed, some are last who will be first, and some are first who will be last."

MAIN THOUGHT: Strive to enter in at the strait gate: for many, I say unto you, will seek to enter in, and shall not be able. (Luke 13:24, KJV)

LESSON SETTING

Time: A.D. 30 (Luke)
A.D. 28 (Matthew)
Place: Galilee, on the way to

Jerusalem (Luke);
Beside the Sea
of Galilee, near
Capernaum (Matthew)

UNIFYING PRINCIPLE

People desire to be rewarded for what they consider acceptable behavior. What kind of behavior is acceptable? Jesus taught that we must bear good fruit and come to Him through a narrow way.

INTRODUCTION

The question of who is going to heaven and who is not has always been at the center of faith. Jeremiah voiced the question to God, as recorded in Jeremiah 12:1–2, "Why does the way of the guilty prosper? Why do all who are treacherous thrive? You plant them, and they take root; they grow and bring forth fruit; you are near in their mouths yet far from their hearts" (NRSV). It seemed to him, as it has to countless others over the centuries, that God blesses people who do not deserve it and neglects those who deserve better from God.

By the day of Jesus, the accepted wisdom among the Jewish teachers was that the Jews were "in" and the Gentiles were "out." A Jew might be in trouble if he or she made little serious attempt to follow the Law of Moses, but few Jews were so cavalier about their religion. Most made at least a fitful attempt to follow the Law, and the teachers generally held that to be good enough. What really mattered, these teachers said, was that one had been circumcised and that one made the obligatory sacrificial offerings, including, of course, giving generously to the temple ministry.

As Jesus began to teach, those listening to him heard what sounded like a different message. Jesus called the teachers "a brood of vipers" and "blind guides" (Matt. 23:33, 16, NRSV). As He began His Sermon on the Mount, He spoke of God's blessings falling not upon those who kept the requirements of the Law, but on those who were of a certain character—the weak, the humble, the persecuted, and the merciful. He spoke of a "narrow gate" (7:13) or a "narrow doorway" (Luke 13:24), implying that entering the Kingdom of Heaven was far more difficult than the teachers made it sound.

EXPOSITION

I. RAVENOUS WOLVES—
FALSE TEACHERS
(Matthew 7:15–20)

Immediately after speaking to the crowd on the shore of the Sea of Galilee about the gate to heaven being narrow and the gate to destruction being broad, Jesus spoke about the two primary ways in which people might miss the narrow gate. The first of those, listed in our background Scripture in Matthew 7:15–20, was to become the victim of a false teacher. An analysis of the background text will help us to understand the real significance of the printed text of Luke 13:22–30.

There were among the people, Jesus said, false prophets. Here He was not talking about men who claimed to be tellers of the future destiny of Israel, as had been the great prophets like Isaiah, Ezekiel, and Jeremiah, but about men who claimed to have an inside track to God, who knew things not made clear to the common people. They were, in short, men who claimed to have a "word from God," special stuff they would tell to those whom they thought worthy. This was exactly the attitude demonstrated by the scribes and Pharisees, who generally had contempt for the common folks and who lorded it over them as if they were specially favored by God with understanding that everyone else lacked.

These false teachers were like ravenous wolves, frothing at the mouth in anticipation of feasting on the flesh of their victims. They appeared, Jesus said, to be sheep, devout followers of God, but were in reality phonies who sought only to advance their own agendas by using God and the things of God. These devourers, as Jesus said elsewhere (Matt. 23:6), loved the places of honor at banquets and the best seats in the synagogues. Clearly He is speaking of the scribes and Pharisees and the other self-important leaders of the Jews, but the same type of folks are with us today. Their power and prestige, their titles and the respect they believe they have earned, are of utmost importance to the "wolves" of today, just as they were in Jesus' day.

Such people may be recognized by the fruit they bring forth. John Wesley called this "a short, plain, easy rule, whereby to know true prophet from false prophets" (*New Testament Commentary* [Grand Rapids: Baker Book House, 1957], 10). This fruit refers to converts who, just like their mentors, fail to truly follow the will of God, but it also refers to the methods that the false prophets use, which reveal their self-serving motives. These motives might include a focus on money, adopting a superior attitude towards those over whom the person has influence, a love of status and prestige, self-promotion, and the desire to build for oneself an empire.

People who produce such evil fruit will be treated just as a tree might be if it produced rotten fruit—they will be cut down and burned, a reference to the final judgment when these false prophets will find themselves cast into the lake of fire reserved for unrepentant sinners.

II. MIRACLE WORKERS— FALSE DISCIPLES (Matthew 7:21–23)

The second way Jesus spoke of by which a person might be left out of the Kingdom of Heaven was to be a false disciple. This is a person who exhibits the outward signs of being a disciple but who, on the inside, is unchanged by the Gospel. These people are, Jesus said, those who may cry "Lord, Lord" in loud exclamation of their submission to Christ, yet despite those loud protestations, they are who Paul described as "lovers of themselves, lovers of money, boasters, arrogant, abusive, disobedient to their parents, ungrateful, unholy, inhuman, implacable, slanderers, profligates, brutes, haters of good, treacherous, reckless, swollen with conceit, lovers of pleasure rather than lovers of God, holding to the outward form of godliness but denying its power" (2 Tim. 3:2–5).

Looking at the character traits Paul describes, it might seem that such a person would clearly be disqualified from participation in God's Kingdom, but Jesus adds some things that make the situation, at least to the casual observer, a bit trickier. These same people Paul described will claim to Jesus that they have prophesied in His name, that they have cast out demons and done works of great power in the name of Christ. They will be like the Jews who denied the heart of their faith and still felt they were safe because they had been circumcised and offered sacrifices.

Albert Barnes remarks, "The power of working miracles had no necessary connection with piety. God may well, if He chooses, give the power of raising the dead to a wicked man" (*Barnes' Notes on the New Testament* [Grand Rapids: Kregel Publications, 1962], 334). Such workers of amazing signs know nothing of the true will of God, which 1 Peter 4:2 says is not about fulfilling one's human desires. Paul writes in 1 Thessalonians 4:3, that it is God's will that people be sanctified, meaning that their hearts are evermore turned from the things of the world to the things of God. We are told in 1 Thessalonians 5:18 that those who do God's will give thanks in every circumstance. Romans 12:2 adds that those who follow the will of God do what is good and acceptable and perfect.

And so, Jesus says in Matthew 7:23, those workers of great miracles who have no inward sanctification and no godly character will hear Jesus say to them, "Get out of here, you worker of iniquity. I have never so much as made your acquaintance." The language of His reaction is forceful, as if these pretenders to discipleship would be kicked out of heaven like someone being forcibly removed from an event by the police for inappropriate behavior and unbecoming conduct.

III. THE NARROW DOOR—
THE TRUE WAY
(LUKE 13:22–30)

It is possible that the "someone" (Luke 13:23) who asked Jesus a question as He made His way slowly from Galilee to Jerusalem had heard Jesus' Sermon on the Mount. Certainly, the teachings of Jesus about the narrow gate and how hard it was to find it had caused an uproar in the crowds, who were wondering why Jesus seemed to be suggesting that the teaching of the Pharisees that all Jews were good was actually incorrect. This someone likely voiced the question that was on many minds that day: "Will only a few be saved?"

Jesus was not interested in responding to that question by discussing numbers. How many or how few might make it was of no particular consequence to the one who asked the question. The only thing that mattered to the questioner was whether or not he or she would make the cut. And so Jesus returned to the image of the narrow door or gate.

The word translated as "narrow" is a Greek word, *stenos*, that is used to describe situations where strain or great effort is required. To strive is also indicative of something that demands hard work, and it is a present tense verb that implies continued ongoing action. Jesus is telling the questioner and everyone else listening that getting through the tight squeeze of the door to the Kingdom of Heaven will demand an ongoing effort against all the forces in the world that pull one away from the door.

Many will try to enter but will not make it through the narrow door. The word "try" means that, though one may have made a serious attempt, at some point the person gave up. Those who wish to make it through the narrow door are required to keep striving, not giving up even when it seems that they are not making progress. There are those who "try" Christ for a while but feel that they just aren't getting from this Christian thing what they expected, and so they quit trying and all efforts cease.

Some may say such a person has fallen away. Others may say that person was never truly on the way. Either way, the result is the same. The Owner of the house will eventually shut the door, and those who have quit trying will be left outside. Leon Morris, a noted evangelical scholar, in his commentary on Luke, says, "Neither here nor elsewhere is there any indication that genuine seekers find themselves excluded from the kingdom, but there is inevitably a time-limit on the offer of salvation. When the door of opportunity is finally shut it will be too late. People must strive to enter now" (*Luke: An Introduction and Commentary* [Grand Rapids: William B. Eerdmans Publishing Company, 1988], 247).

On the day when the door is shut, those who think they should have made it through the door will be standing on the outside, pounding on the door in the hopes that it will again be opened and that they will be welcomed in. They will trot out their list of works done: "We ate and drank with you," and, "You were among us teaching in our streets." To these cries Jesus will reply, "I have no idea where you are from, now get out of here." He will turn them away.

Then these people, suddenly faced with the reality that they are excluded, will cry in horror and howl in outraged defiance. Their true nature will burst forth when faced with the final truth, and they will act like the ravenous wolves Jesus described in Matthew 7. They will look through the windows, see Abraham, Isaac, and Jacob, and all the prophets inside, and understand that what they thought would be enough for them, their Jewish heritage, was not going to be enough after all.

As a final affront, those who counted upon their Jewish credentials would gaze in horror as the Gentiles poured into the Kingdom from every direction while they, the "chosen people," were locked out. The last, the lowest, the scum would come in while the first, the chosen, the descendants of Abraham, were left outside.

Jesus' answer to the question, "Will only a few be saved?" is that it depends upon how one defines "few." Not everyone who thinks they deserve heaven will get in, but the Kingdom will be overflowing with those willing to submit to the will of God, to deny their fleshly cravings, and to keep on striving to find the way through the "narrow door" (Luke 13:24, NRSV).

THE LESSON APPLIED

One of the beauties of the local church is that the people know one another, including those in leadership. It is easy to observe uncommitted ministers who promise this or that, and much of it may be perfectly harmless. The problem is that they live ragged lives and do not present the Gospel message from converted hearts.

Many of them are about building an empire that glorifies them rather than the Lord God. They are ravenous wolves that seek to enrich themselves at the expense of poor, innocent people whose only desire is to find favor with God. No matter how many miracle services or claims that this person or that person was healed from cancer, the fruits of self-aggrandizement bear witness to evil desires at work. One even wonders about churches where it can seem that the minister and the staff are more interested in building an empire than about the welfare of the flock.

There is probably good reason why the early Christians met in small groups, in homes, where the people knew one another intimately and knew their leaders just as intimately. Christians must come to know who their leaders are and respect them only when the needs of the poor, the disenfranchised, the spiritually depressed, and those stifled in sin are met.

Fruit is much easier to judge the closer one gets to an intimate relationship. Our relationship with the Lord should help keep us focused on doing ministry so that those outside the gate may hear His voice and seek His salvation.

LET'S TALK ABOUT IT

1. Does this passage teach salvation by works?

With words like "strive" and "try to enter" and talk of finding one's way through a narrow door, it may seem like Jesus is emphasizing works over faith. However, faith is the soil from which the works of righteousness grow. Even the evildoers to whom Jesus referred did good works, but they did those works from faithless hearts. Those who find the narrow door and get through must begin their journey at the starting point of faith in Christ. James tells us faith is the foundation upon which we build our ministry (James 2).

2. Can an unconverted sinner truly perform miracles?

John Wesley famously remarked, after journeying to the American colonies to preach to the Native American tribes, "I went to America, to convert the Indians, but oh! Who shall convert me?" He had preached to and brought to Christ a large number of his listeners but found to his dismay that his own heart was cold and unconverted. God can choose anyone to accomplish His purposes, so do not let your good works be a substitute for an unconverted heart.

3. If God is love, why won't He save everyone?

God made us free moral agents with the ability to choose our own path or way of life. God respects us enough to allow us to decide to accept or reject His love for us. It is a matter of our faith. We can either decide that God has no jurisdiction over us as our Creator and Benefactor, or we can choose to honor Him and repent of our transgression against His holy will and standard for living. The choice is ours. We can either serve Him or the gods we have created for ourselves. His love allows us to make our own choices, and it saddens His heart when we do not choose Him.

HOME DAILY DEVOTIONAL READINGS
JULY 23–29, 2018

MONDAY	TUESDAY	WEDNESDAY	THURSDAY	FRIDAY	SATURDAY	SUNDAY
Exemptions from Military Service	The Wealthy and Kingdom Membership	Take Up the Cross and Follow	My True Mother and Siblings	The Gentiles Will Listen	Count the Cost, then Follow Me	Everyone Invited to the Great Dinner
Deuteronomy 20:5–8	Luke 18:18–25	Matthew 16:24–28	Mark 3:31–35	Acts 28:23–28	Luke 14:25–33	Luke 14:15–24

PARABLE OF THE GREAT DINNER

ADULT TOPIC:	BACKGROUND SCRIPTURE:
JOIN THE PARTY	LUKE 14:15–24

LUKE 14:15–24

King James Version

ND when one of them that sat at meat with im heard these things, he said unto him, lessed is he that shall eat bread in the kingom of God.

6 Then said he unto him, A certain man made great supper, and bade many:

7 And sent his servant at supper time to say them that were bidden, Come; for all things re now ready.

8 And they all with one consent began to make excuse. The first said unto him, I have ought a piece of ground, and I must needs go nd see it: I pray thee have me excused.

9 And another said, I have bought five yoke of xen, and I go to prove them: I pray thee have e excused.

0 And another said, I have married a wife, nd therefore I cannot come.

1 So that servant came, and shewed his lord ese things. Then the master of the house eing angry said to his servant, Go out quickly to the streets and lanes of the city, and bring hither the poor, and the maimed, and the alt, and the blind.

2 And the servant said, Lord, it is done as ou hast commanded, and yet there is room.

3 And the lord said unto the servant, Go out to the highways and hedges, and compel em to come in, that my house may be filled.

4 For I say unto you, That none of those men hich were bidden shall taste of my supper.

New Revised Standard Version

ONE of the dinner guests, on hearing this, said to him, "Blessed is anyone who will eat bread in the kingdom of God!"

16 Then Jesus said to him, "Someone gave a great dinner and invited many.

17 At the time for the dinner he sent his slave to say to those who had been invited, 'Come; for everything is ready now.'

18 But they all alike began to make excuses. The first said to him, 'I have bought a piece of land, and I must go out and see it; please accept my regrets.'

19 Another said, 'I have bought five yoke of oxen, and I am going to try them out; please accept my regrets.'

20 Another said, 'I have just been married, and therefore I cannot come.'

21 So the slave returned and reported this to his master. Then the owner of the house became angry and said to his slave, 'Go out at once into the streets and lanes of the town and bring in the poor, the crippled, the blind, and the lame.'

22 And the slave said, 'Sir, what you ordered has been done, and there is still room.'

23 Then the master said to the slave, 'Go out into the roads and lanes, and compel people to come in, so that my house may be filled.

24 For I tell you, none of those who were invited will taste my dinner.'"

MAIN THOUGHT: So that servant came, and shewed his lord these things. Then he master of the house being angry said to his servant, Go out quickly into the treets and lanes of the city, and bring in hither the poor, and the maimed, and the alt, and the blind. (Luke 14:21, KJV)

LESSON SETTING

Time: A.D. 30
Place: On the way to Jerusalem, at the home of a Pharisee

LESSON OUTLINE

   I. **Jesus Attends a Banquet (Luke 14:15–17)**
   II. **A Guest Makes a Comment (Luke 14:18–20)**
   III. **Jesus Responds to the Comment (Luke 14:21–24)**

UNIFYING PRINCIPLE

Some people eagerly accept invitations to important events while others feel that they have better things to do. What are the consequences of rejecting such invitations? Jesus declares that those who reject His invitation will not be allowed in His Kingdom.

INTRODUCTION

By the time the events of Luke 14 occurred, Jesus was at the very height of His public popularity. He was on the way to Jerusalem to join the multitudes in celebrating the Passover. He would find Himself welcomed in Jerusalem by a cheering throng shouting "Hosanna!" and "Blessed is He who comes in the name of Yahweh!"

As He slowly made His way toward that riotous welcome and the passion that would follow hard on its heels, Jesus was likely accompanied by many followers, including, of course, His disciples. Some of those would have rushed ahead to the next town to shout up and down the streets that Jesus, the famous miracle-worker and potential Messiah, was coming.

Being in a town where He had no relatives or home, Jesus would have been welcomed by the town leaders, invited to

synagogue and, perhaps, offered an opportunity to read the Scriptures and expound upon them. It would also have been typical for one of the important people in town to hold a banquet to which all the important personages would be invited to eat with and hear from their highly celebrated Guest. Three things are important in this text. First, the text examines the parable from the perspective of an invitation to a divine banquet. Second, the text analyzes the various excuses used by the invited not to come to the banquet. Third, the excuses are revealed for what they are.

EXPOSITION

I. JESUS ATTENDS A BANQUET (Luke 14:15–17)

In the town to which Jesus arrived on this particular Sabbath lived one of the members of the Sanhedrin, a Pharisee and a leader of the people (14:1). This man had been the one to prepare the banquet welcoming Jesus, and it is very likely he did so in order to give the Jewish religious leaders an up-close and personal opportunity to try to get Jesus to say or do something for which they might accuse Him before the Sanhedrin. At any rate, they were watching Jesus closely as He entered the home of the Pharisee.

Luke says only that a man with dropsy, a water-retention problem that is often incurable and can be life-threatening, was there in front of Jesus. Perhaps the man was a plant, invited there by the Pharisee to test Jesus, or perhaps he just showed up after hearing that Jesus was in town. Either way, Jesus knew that if He just healed the man, the Pharisee and his accomplices would claim He had broken the Sabbath aw. So, to disarm them, Jesus made them take a side first. "Is it lawful to heal on the Sabbath, or not?" He asked. The right answer was that it was perfectly lawful, as He had proven in previous encounters. But Jesus was going to force the Pharisee to either lie or admit that healing was lawful. The Pharisee and his guests were in a bind. They chose to simply keep silent, hoping they could still trap Jesus. So, Jesus simply healed the man and then asked them if they would treat their animals better than a needy human being. They said nothing, but the tone for the banquet had been set.

Leon Morris, in his commentary on Luke, observes, "At this particular feast there was an undignified scramble for the places of highest honor and Jesus commented on it" (*Luke* [Downers Grove: InterVarsity Press, 1988], 249). Banquet seating in those days was very formal, with a U-shaped arrangement of couches, each of which held three diners. The place of highest honor was the couch at the base of the U, the center seat of the three. Next were those to that guest's left and right, then, in turn, the couches moving down the arms of the U away from the center. Apparently, the guests were rushing to get as close as possible to the base of the U. Jesus upbraided everyone for their unseemly behavior, but in a way that took some of the sting out of His remarks, by making the story about a wedding feast so He did not appear to be embarrassing any of the guests by singling them out.

Turning, at this point, to the host, Jesus suggested that when he gave banquets, he might consider inviting those who could not repay him with a counter-invitation, rather than inviting all the usual relatives, friends, and power-brokers. Doing so, Jesus suggested, would reap for the host a great reward at the Messianic resurrection feast, a feast that every devout Jew expected to attend. In effect, Jesus was suggesting that to invite the poor now might make it possible for the host to occupy one of the seats of honor at the most important banquet ever held. Again, Jesus showed tact and good manners by turning His comments about bad behavior into a lesson on how to get an even better seat at an even more wonderful feast.

II. A GUEST MAKES A COMMENT (LUKE 14:18–20)

As heads nodded at Jesus' wisdom about the Messianic banquet, one of the guests offered a comment. "Oh, yes, it will be a great blessing to be at that feast," the speaker said, as if he was confident of his own place at that table. Luke makes no mention of it, but it is easy to imagine many of the other guests uttering a hearty "amen" at their pleasure in the idea of what they all believed to be their birthright as good Jews.

Some Jews, most notably the Sadducees, who did not believe in a resurrection, thought this banquet would occur in the immediate aftermath of the Messiah's driving out of the Roman occupiers and the reestablishment of the full glory of Israel. Others believed this banquet would not occur until the day when all the righteous deceased Jews, including Abraham, Moses, Elijah, King David, and the Prophets would be raised and seated around the table. To have a place of honor at such a banquet would be the ultimate dream of any Pharisee. It would be an honor one could not refuse.

Donald Fleming, in the *Bridgeway Bible Commentary*, says of this guest's comment, "One of the guests, hearing Jesus' illustrations about feasting, tried to impress him with a comment concerning the coming great feast in the kingdom of God" ([Brisbane: Bridgeway Publications, 2005], 466). Rather than impress Jesus, however, the man's comment led Jesus to tell a story.

III. JESUS RESPONDS TO THE COMMENT (LUKE 14:21–24)

Though Jesus only referred to the host in His story as "someone," all the listeners would have understood that this story was going to make a point about the Messianic banquet. This someone was, they knew, the Messiah Himself. The host, said Jesus, invited many, which everyone would have understood in their own minds to be the entirety of all the righteous Jews who had ever lived, including, of course, themselves and their special friends.

Once the meal was prepared, the host sent his servant out to inform the guests that it was time to eat. In a culture with no clocks and a somewhat relaxed sense of punctuality, it was common for guests to be given a second invitation once everything was ready. Having accepted the initial invitation, the guests, it was assumed, only needed to be told that the moment had arrived. They all should have known that the banquet was being held that day and made no plans that would interfere with their attendance since they had already indicated they would attend. In Jesus' story, however, the guests began to trot out excuses. It was these excuses that troubled Jesus the most.

The first cancellation was based upon the excuse that the individual had just purchased property and must go examine it. But who buys property without examining it before the purchase, not after? If the person truly did not examine the property before buying it, he was a fool. If he had already examined it, then taking another look could wait. The land was not going anywhere, and he ought to have honored his commitment to come to the feast. Instead, he trotted out a lame and self embarrassing excuse.

The second cancellation was even more ridiculous than the first. This man said that he had just purchased five pairs (yokes) of oxen and he was on his way to try them out. Again, who buys oxen without taking a close look at them to be sure they are healthy and capable of doing the work oxen were expected to do? This man wanted the host to believe that he had bought five yoke of oxen, sight unseen, and must immediately go to make sure he got good oxen. It was foolish. The oxen were what they were at this point. Waiting until after the banquet to check them out would cause no harm. The truth was, the man just did not want to come, and so he invented an excuse that fooled no one.

These two, however, pale in comparison to the silliness of the third excuse. This man said that he could not come because he had just gotten married. If the wedding had been that day, then why did he ever accept the invitation to begin with? Surely he knew it was to be held on his wedding day. If he had been married for a short time, then there was absolutely nothing about now being married that would make it improper for him to attend the banquet

This excuse did not even have a ring of truth to it. This guest apparently cared not one bit about whether or not he might offend the host; he just wanted not to have to go.

Of these three excuses, Robert Jamieson states, "Nobody is represented as saying, I will not come; nay, all the answers imply that but for certain things they would come, and when these are out of the way they will come" (*Commentary on the Whole Bible* [Harrington: Delmarva Publications, 2013], 3007). That would not have been lost on the host, who was now faced with the prospect of invited guests snubbing him but showing up late and expecting to be welcomed with open arms.

The host was furious. He told his servant to leave immediately, go to the streets where the poor, the sick, the lame, and the blind hung out, and bring as many as wished to come to the banquet to take the places of the impudent men who had canceled for such transparently feeble reasons. Having done so, the servant then reported that there were still seats available, at which point the host instructed the servant to leave the town, go out into the countryside and the main highways, where Gentiles and heathens would be passing by, and convince as many as necessary to come to the feast so that all the places were occupied. The host summed up his displeasure by remarking that "none of those who were invited will taste my dinner" (v. 24, NRSV).

Luke makes no record of how the guests responded to Jesus' story. If they had become incensed, realizing that He was telling them that they were not going to be among those blessed to eat bread in the Kingdom of God, Luke would likely have noted it. This time, the point Jesus made must have gone right over their heads. He had been among them for nearly three years now, performing one miracle after another as proof of God's anointing, teaching anyone who would stop to listen and claiming repeatedly to be the Messiah. Jesus had spent three years speaking of the Kingdom of Heaven and inviting all who would to come. All the while, these proud, self-satisfied men were too busy being good Pharisees, guardians of righteousness and Judaism, to come. They had their excuses—Jesus heals on the Sabbath, He lets His followers pick grain on the Sabbath, He hangs out with sinners, etc. But those excuses were even sillier and more insulting than the excuses offered in the parable Jesus told.

These poor, wretched men had been invited to the greatest banquet that would ever be. They were convinced that they would be welcome later, despite the excuses they offered for rejecting Jesus now, but they were to be sadly surprised as the Gentiles, the poor, the blind, and the tax collectors gathered around the banquet table while they, guardians of self-righteousness, were shut out.

THE LESSON APPLIED

We all likely know of non-Christians who, when invited to surrender their lives to the King of kings, made excuses for why they were not ready at the moment. Those are sad folks who may never get another chance, but it is not those folks that Jesus' story is aimed at. Instead, it is we who call ourselves "children of God" who would do well to take heed of what Jesus had to say. Once we receive Christ and commit to a life of discipleship, the rest of our days in this life will be comprised of one test after another, one learning experience after another, one opportunity for greater sanctification after another. We are being transformed, shaped, pruned like a vine, made fit for heaven and conformed to the image of our Lord, Jesus Christ.

If we receive good, God waits to see what we will do with it, whether we will spend it on our own ease and pleasure or use it to help others. If we receive illness, God watches to see whether or not we will accept it in faith, trust Him to guide us through, and find in the test greater strength and perseverance in our faith.

At any point in this ongoing testing, we may find ourselves tempted to offer up an excuse as to why we no longer wish for God's work to proceed in our lives. We want to stay invited, but we do not wish to suffer the refiner's fires. When those moments come, let us remember those poor banquet guests and how the host reacted to their begging to be excused.

LET'S TALK ABOUT IT

1. **What is it about the Pharisees that made it so hard for them to accept Jesus as the Messiah?**

With all their faults that the Gospels point out, the Pharisees were, after all, just people. The problem they had was that Jesus threatened their livelihood and their positions as leaders. Some of them certainly were so convinced of their own righteousness that they could not imagine a Kingdom of Heaven where they did not retain a prominent place. Many simply could not get their heads around the idea that the religious structure they had constructed might not be God's perfect will for His people. They felt threatened by Jesus rather than embraced by Him.

2. **Does God really care more for the poor and marginalized that He does for the rich and powerful?**

God loves every one of us equally. Being rich is a temptation to pride and self-satisfaction. Whatever temptations the poor and marginalized face, pride and self-satisfaction are not usually among them. The poor and marginalized have nowhere to go but up and, usually, nothing of much significance to lose by surrendering their lives to Jesus. Instead, the poor and marginalized more often wonder what exactly God might see in them that everyone else seems to be missing. It is this humility of stature that makes it easier for the poor and marginalized to find favor in God's sight. And the justice of God is always turned toward those who have been cast aside by others.

HOME DAILY DEVOTIONAL READINGS
JULY 30–AUGUST 5, 2018

MONDAY	TUESDAY	WEDNESDAY	THURSDAY	FRIDAY	SATURDAY	SUNDAY
The Power of the Gospel	Bear Fruits of Repentance	Genuine Christian Behavior	Gentiles Experience Repentance	Paul's Joy at Corinthians' Repentance	Doers of the Law Are Justified	God's Righteous, Impartial Judgment
Romans 1:16–17	Luke 3:7–14	Romans 12:14–21	Acts 11:15–18	2 Corinthians 7:9–11	Romans 2:12–16	Romans 2:1–12

GOD'S JUSTICE

| ADULT TOPIC:
EQUITY FOR ALL | BACKGROUND SCRIPTURE:
ROMANS 2:1–16 |

ROMANS 2:1–12

King James Version

THEREFORE thou art inexcusable, O man, whosoever thou art that judgest: for wherein thou judgest another, thou condemnest thyself; for thou that judgest doest the same things.

2 But we are sure that the judgment of God is according to truth against them which commit such things.

3 And thinkest thou this, O man, that judgest them which do such things, and doest the same, that thou shalt escape the judgment of God?

4 Or despisest thou the riches of his goodness and forbearance and longsuffering; not knowing that the goodness of God leadeth thee to repentance?

5 But after thy hardness and impenitent heart treasurest up unto thyself wrath against the day of wrath and revelation of the righteous judgment of God;

6 Who will render to every man according to his deeds:

7 To them who by patient continuance in well doing seek for glory and honour and immortality, eternal life:

8 But unto them that are contentious, and do not obey the truth, but obey unrighteousness, indignation and wrath,

9 Tribulation and anguish, upon every soul of man that doeth evil, of the Jew first, and also of the Gentile;

10 But glory, honour, and peace, to every man that worketh good, to the Jew first, and also to the Gentile:

New Revised Standard Version

THEREFORE you have no excuse, whoever you are, when you judge others; for in passing judgment on another you condemn yourself, because you, the judge, are doing the very same things.

2 You say, "We know that God's judgment on those who do such things is in accordance with truth."

3 Do you imagine, whoever you are, that when you judge those who do such things and yet do them yourself, you will escape the judgment of God?

4 Or do you despise the riches of his kindness and forbearance and patience? Do you not realize that God's kindness is meant to lead you to repentance?

5 But by your hard and impenitent heart you are storing up wrath for yourself on the day of wrath, when God's righteous judgment will be revealed.

6 For he will repay according to each one's deeds:

7 to those who by patiently doing good seek for glory and honor and immortality, he will give eternal life;

8 while for those who are self-seeking and who obey not the truth but wickedness, there will be wrath and fury.

9 There will be anguish and distress for everyone who does evil, the Jew first and also the Greek,

10 but glory and honor and peace for everyone who does good, the Jew first and also the Greek.

MAIN THOUGHT: But glory, honour, and peace, to every man that worketh good, to the Jew first, and also to the Gentile: For there is no respect of persons with God. (Romans 2:10–11, KJV)

ROMANS 2:1–12

King James Version	*New Revised Standard Version*
11 For there is no respect of persons with God.	11 For God shows no partiality.
12 For as many as have sinned without law shall also perish without law: and as many as have sinned in the law shall be judged by the law;	12 All who have sinned apart from the law will also perish apart from the law, and all who have sinned under the law will be judged by the law.

LESSON SETTING

    Time: ca. A.D. 55
    Place: Likely written from Corinth near the end of Paul's second missionary journey

LESSON OUTLINE

  I. The Situation in Rome (Historical Background)
 II. Judging One Another (Romans 2:1–4)
III. Judged by God (Romans 2:5–12)

UNIFYING PRINCIPLE

It is very easy to judge others, condemning them for doing the same thing we have done. How can we avoid being judgmental? Paul teaches that God's kindness, forbearance, and patience lead us to repentance and new life.

INTRODUCTION

Paul had plans, which he laid out in Romans 15:22–33. He was probably in Corinth at the time he wrote his letter to the church at Rome, on his way to Jerusalem to bring the suffering Christians there an offering given to him by the churches he had visited on his second missionary journey.

He was somewhat concerned that when he arrived in Jerusalem he might be charged with breaking the Jewish law by preaching freedom and by opening up "The Way to Gentiles." He asked for prayer from his Roman Christian audience that he might somehow be delivered from that peril (see 15:31).

His ultimate goal, according to his letter, was to pass through Rome on his way to Spain. He would make that journey by ship, and Rome was a very reasonable half-way point in what would be a voyage of several months. Paul always hoped to get to Rome to meet the believers there, but now there was an issue of immediate concern that required him to write a letter to them instead of waiting to handle it at a later time when he would be there in person.

EXPOSITION

I. THE SITUATION IN ROME (HISTORICAL BACKGROUND)

In A.D. 49, the Roman Emperor Claudius had banished all Christians from Rome for activity that he felt was a threat to the public order in the city. The historian Suetonius records that there was a group of troublesome people who refused to remain silent about a man he called "Chrestus." Part of what alarmed Claudius was that this group was succeeding in making converts among a broad cross-section of the people.

Some Roman officials had become Christians. Some servants from the palace of Claudius himself professed this faith, as did a significant number of soldiers in the Roman army. The educated of the city were among the converts. The poor were converted in great numbers. There were Jews, of course, who may have been the nucleus of the early church, but by the time Claudius issued his banishment decree, the vast majority of Roman Christians were from Gentile backgrounds.

This mixture of backgrounds sparked dissention. Albert Barnes writes, "[The Jews] were in the habit of accusing and condemning the Gentiles as wicked and abandoned; while they excused themselves on the ground that they possessed the law and oracles of God, and were his favorite people" (*Notes, Explanatory and Practical, on the Epistle to the Romans* [New York: Leavitt, Lord & Company, 1834], 49).

Rome was, by this time, a very immoral city where one could find just about any vice one cared to seek out. The Gentile Christians were not inclined to engage in the most egregious of these vices, but they still attended the gladiator spectacles, bet on the chariot races, paraded naked at the public baths, and followed other customs of the day which were perfectly acceptable in Roman society, but highly offensive to the Jewish believers.

The Gentiles, responding to the scorn of the Jewish believers, ridiculed them for practicing strict obedience to a set of rules that were no longer binding on Christians. The church at Rome had likely received a copy of the letter sent from Jerusalem requiring only that believers abstain from meat sacrificed to idols and from fornication (see Acts 15:28–29), and the Gentile believers could not fathom why the Jewish believers continued to insist on circumcision, to shun certain other readily available foods, and to practice the other facets of Jewish faith.

Claudius had banished the Christians for publicly proclaiming Christ and for being a threat to the public order. It does not take much imagination to picture a group of Gentile Christians speaking with other pagan Romans about Jesus, only to have a group of Jewish Christians disrupt the conversation by saying that the Gentiles had it wrong, or vice versa.

Various house churches that comprised the life of the greater church of Rome had probably come under contention. By the time Paul sat down to write them a letter, they were divided into Jewish home groups and Gentile home groups, thus institutionalizing in the life of the church their disagreement over the Gospel. The reports Paul was getting about the accusations flying back and forth between the Jewish and the Gentile believers alarmed him. The Gospel of Jesus Christ was coming into disrepute among the Roman citizenry and the Roman Emperor because the two sides were at each other's throat over whose Gospel was the *true* Gospel.

II. JUDGING ONE ANOTHER (ROMANS 2:1–4)

After introducing the impact on the lives of people who paid no respect to God in Romans 1, Paul summarized his point in 1:32 by saying, "They know God's decree, that those who practice such things deserve to die—yet they not only do them but even applaud others who practice them" (NRSV). People who live in antipathy to God will face God's judgment, he concluded. He begins chapter 2 with the word "therefore," meaning that what he is now going to say is in application of this conclusion.

Both sides in the Roman church dispute would have heartily agreed with that conclusion, but each would have thought that it only applied to the other side in the dispute. What they failed to appreciate was that in setting themselves up as judges of those with whom they disagreed, they were, in effect, usurping God's role as Judge. What was even worse, as Paul points out in 2:1, the people hurling the accusations were guilty of the very same kinds of contact of which they were accusing the others. In short, both sides were being hypocritical and outlandish.

Verses 3 and 4 expose a terrible reality among the Roman believers. Paul asked them a rhetorical question about whether or not they think that if they commit the kinds of sins for which they accuse others, they themselves will escape God's wrath. The obvious answer should be "no," but it seems that some of the people had actually convinced themselves that because they had not been judged to date, their behavior was acceptable to God. Paul had to remind them that the forbearance and patience of God in delaying judgment is meant not to show approval of the behavior, but to give offenders time to come to their senses and repent. Of this reality, Donald Fleming, in the *Bridgestone Bible Commentary*, observes, "[People] know that God is just and that he punishes sin. Therefore, when they suffer no immediate punishment for their behaviour, they think that God approves of them and will not punish them" (*https://www.studylight.org/commentaries/bbc/romans-2.html*). It is an example of exactly the kind of darkened minds Paul had written about earlier in Romans 1:21. This kind of dangerous attitude of self-justification without repentance was, as Paul wrote in 2:5, "storing up wrath" for the day of God's judgment (NRSV). Jesus had taught that it was good to store up treasures in heaven by doing good deeds here on earth (Matt. 6:19–21). Instead of storing up treasures, these Roman Christians were piling up great storehouses of wrath that would be waiting for them when the Day of Judgment would come to fruition.

III. JUDGED BY GOD (ROMANS 2:5–12)

John Wesley observed in his commentary on Romans, "knowledge without practice only increases guilt" (*http://www.sacred-texts.com/bib/cmt/wesley/rom002.htm*). The Romans had the Gospel calling them to unity in the faith and to submission to the Lord. Yet they were fighting with each other, not only accusing each other of the very same kinds of sins they themselves were committing but also treating the other side as if they were not truly believers. God, whose judgment both sides agreed was just and true, was not holding off that judgment because the way the two sides were acting was acceptable. Rather, God wanted to give them time to repent.

Yet, Paul said, eventually the righteous judgment of God would be revealed. At that time it would not be the theological niceties of the disagreement that would be God's focus, but rather the way the two sides had lived their own individual lives. God would "repay according to each one's deeds" (2:6, NRSV).

Each individual would, at that time of God's true judgment, fall into one of two camps. Paul is addressing not unbelievers who would all be judged for their failure to bow before God, but rather believers. These believers would, Paul points out, be either those who "by patiently doing good seek for glory and honor and immortality" (2:7, NRSV), or they would be those who "are self-seeking and who obey not the truth but wickedness" (2:8, NRSV).

Those who seek to do good, Paul says, will receive good from God. They will be given eternal life, while the ones who obey wickedness will be given wrath and fury. The good will receive the reward of glory and honor and peace, exactly what they had dedicated their lives to pursuing. Anguish and distress await those who gave their lives over to wickedness, which does not necessarily mean licentious behavior alone. The strife and accusations being hurled by the two sides at one another was wickedness because it was harming the furtherance of the Gospel as well as rupturing the relationships within the church body and fellowship.

Paul concludes that at this final judgment, it will not matter whether one was a Jew or a Gentile. It would not matter whether one had come from a rich background or a poor one, from power or humble origin. What would matter is the way one lived as a follower of Christ, and the Roman Christians were failing the test.

John R. W. Stott summarizes this passage by saying, "[Gentiles] will perish because of their sin, not because of their ignorance of the law (*Reading Romans with John Stott*, Vol. 1 [Downers Grove: InterVarsity Press, 2016], 44). The Jews, on the other hand, who have been given the Law, are expected to keep it and will be judged based on their sin against the Law. The way people have sinned (in knowledge or ignorance of the Law) will be the way they will be judged.

Paul would later in his letter write, "The faith that you have, have as your own conviction before God.... But those who have doubts are condemned if they eat, because they do not act from faith; for whatever does not proceed from faith is sin" (14:22–23, NRSV). In order to store up reward and not wrath, the key is to live by what you know to be right and true and let the other person do the same.

THE LESSON APPLIED

So, where do we draw the line? Are Christians supposed to simply let other Christians engage in behavior that they feel is clearly sinful? If a believer sincerely thinks his or her actions are acceptable, does that make it okay for that individual? Most of us do not wish to be like the judgmental believers to whom Paul addressed his comments in today's lesson, but neither do we want to sit idly by and watch a fellow Christian destroy his or her life by ignoring blatant sin.

To get somewhat of an understanding, let us first notice that Paul does not say that the difference of opinion among the Roman Christians was not a significant issue. In fact, much of his ministry among the churches was in opposition to the idea that Gentile converts must be required to obey the Jewish law. The problem with the Romans was not the issue that they were disagreeing over; it was the hypocritical and condemning way in which they carried out their disagreement.

Before we confront another believer, let us make sure our own house is in order.

Then, let us remember that God waits, even in the face of open sin, giving the sinner every opportunity to repent. Finally, if it becomes, in our minds, essential that we speak up, let us do so gently with compassion and the understanding that we may someday find ourselves in the same position, and with the only intention being to turn the individual toward repentance.

LET'S TALK ABOUT IT

1. Why does Paul address his comments to someone, "whoever you are" (2:1)?

The form of address Paul used here is what is known as a diatribe. It was a very popular way for philosophers in the Roman Empire to make a pointed and challenging argument without making it seem as if they were singling out specific individuals. Paul most likely knew enough of what had been going on in Rome to have named names, but, in the interest of courtesy and politeness, he chose to use a more impersonal way, familiar to all who heard the letter, to address the problem he had to address. His goal was not to inflict pain on anyone, but to extend them an opportunity to come to true faith in Christ Jesus. We as Christians should adopt this method of gentle confrontation with the goal in mind to move the persons to repentance without embarrassing them.

2. Will some believers experience anguish and distress when they face God?

In 1 Corinthians 3:10–15, Paul speaks of builders who build upon the foundation of the Gospel. Those who build using gold and stone will see their work survive the judging fire of God. Those who build using wood, hay, and stubble will see their work burned up, though they themselves will be saved. While genuine believers will not be condemned to hell, those whose works are of bad quality may well see their rewards evaporate in the fire of God's judgment, leaving those believers to feel anguish and distress.

3. What is the purpose of the book of Romans?

The Apostle Paul goes to great lengths in this book to show the path of salvation as coming through faith in Jesus Christ. The key verse and theme of Romans are Romans 1:17–18 and justification by faith, respectively.

This faith is that Jesus is the Son of God and has fulfilled the divine standard of God through His perfect life. Because He satisfied God's commandment, God raised Him to new life. Those who believe in Him have the righteousness of God imputed into them and are therefore saved from sin.

HOME DAILY DEVOTIONAL READINGS
AUGUST 6–12, 2018

MONDAY	TUESDAY	WEDNESDAY	THURSDAY	FRIDAY	SATURDAY	SUNDAY
God Provides Food to the People	The Widow's Generosity	Generous Self–Giving of Jesus	Excel in Generosity	Generosity Results in Mutual Thanksgiving	Support the Ministry of Church Leaders	Balance Need and Abundance Fairly
Exodus 16:13–17	Mark 12:38–44	Philippians 2:5–11	2 Corinthians 8:1–6	2 Corinthians 9:11–15	2 Corinthians 8:16–24	2 Corinthians 8:7–15

GLOBAL ECONOMIC JUSTICE

ADULT TOPIC:	BACKGROUND SCRIPTURES:
CHARITABLE EQUITY FOR ALL	2 CORINTHIANS 8; 9

2 CORINTHIANS 8:7–15

King James Version

THEREFORE, as ye abound in every thing, in faith, and utterance, and knowledge, and in all diligence, and in your love to us, see that ye abound in this grace also.

8 I speak not by commandment, but by occasion of the forwardness of others, and to prove the sincerity of your love.

9 For ye know the grace of our Lord Jesus Christ, that, though he was rich, yet for your sakes he became poor, that ye through his poverty might be rich.

10 And herein I give my advice: for this is expedient for you, who have begun before, not only to do, but also to be forward a year ago.

11 Now therefore perform the doing of it; that as there was a readiness to will, so there may be a performance also out of that which ye have.

12 For if there be first a willing mind, it is accepted according to that a man hath, and not according to that he hath not.

13 For I mean not that other men be eased, and ye burdened:

14 But by an equality, that now at this time your abundance may be a supply for their want, that their abundance also may be a supply for your want: that there may be equality:

15 As it is written, He that had gathered much had nothing over; and he that had gathered little had no lack.

New Revised Standard Version

NOW as you excel in everything—in faith, in speech, in knowledge, in utmost eagerness, and in our love for you—so we want you to excel also in this generous undertaking.

8 I do not say this as a command, but I am testing the genuineness of your love against the earnestness of others.

9 For you know the generous act of our Lord Jesus Christ, that though he was rich, yet for your sakes he became poor, so that by his poverty you might become rich.

10 And in this matter I am giving my advice: it is appropriate for you who began last year not only to do something but even to desire to do something—

11 now finish doing it, so that your eagerness may be matched by completing it according to your means.

12 For if the eagerness is there, the gift is acceptable according to what one has—not according to what one does not have.

13 I do not mean that there should be relief for others and pressure on you, but it is a question of a fair balance between

14 your present abundance and their need, so that their abundance may be for your need, in order that there may be a fair balance.

15 As it is written, "The one who had much did not have too much, and the one who had little did not have too little."

MAIN THOUGHT: For ye know the grace of our Lord Jesus Christ, that, though he was rich, yet for your sakes he became poor, that ye through his poverty might be rich. (2 Corinthians 8:9, KJV)

LESSON SETTING
Time: A.D. 50s
Place: Corinth

LESSON OUTLINE
I. **Paul's Plea to the Corinthians (2 Corinthians 8:7–14)**
II. **Paul's Thanks for Titus (2 Corinthians 8:15)**

UNIFYING PRINCIPLE

We want to be generous to those in need. What motivates true generosity when the needs seem so overwhelming? Paul encouraged the Corinthians' generosity in response to God's generous gifts to them.

INTRODUCTION

In 2 Corinthians 7, Paul describes how Titus came to Macedonia and reported to Paul that the church in Corinth was doing well. Paul and his companions had anxiously awaited Titus' report and were consoled by his arrival. Paul demonstrates his love and care for the Corinthian congregation throughout his description of Titus' arrival and report. Paul discloses that he does and does not regret the letter he sent to the Corinthians. He does regret the letter because it grieved them. Knowing that this grief has brought the Corinthians to repentance, however, has put Paul's mind at ease (7:8–9). Paul also shares that he is joyful about the way Titus was received because it confirms Paul's boasting about them. Paul now turns his request to the Corinthians to give.

He builds on the encouragement he has given to the Corinthians in the previous section in attempting to elicit the response of giving from the Corinthians. In order to encourage the practice of giving in the Corinthian church, Paul drew on the experience of the Macedonian churches. Paul described the Macedonians' generosity in light of their suffering. He wrote, "During a severe ordeal of affliction, their abundant joy and their extreme poverty have overflowed in a wealth of generosity on their part" (8:2, NRSV). The Macedonians' giving was paradoxical.

In spite of their "affliction," the Macedonians still had "abundant joy." Through their abundant joy and in "their extreme poverty," they were able to give in a "wealth of generosity." Paul used extreme opposites here to demonstrate that it was through God's grace that the Macedonians were able to respond in ways that seemed to run counter to their situation. Paul wrote of "the grace of God that has been granted to the churches of Macedonia" (v. 1, NRSV). The Macedonians' generosity was an example for the Corinthians to follow. The generosity of the Macedonians and the gift of the Corinthians was for the need in the Jerusalem church (see 1 Cor. 16:3). Today in 2 Corinthians 8, we learn about Paul's teaching to the Corinthians on the equality and gift of giving and receiving.

EXPOSITION

I. PAUL'S PLEA TO THE CORINTHIANS (2 CORINTHIANS 8:7–14)

Following up on the work of Titus, Paul made an appeal to the Corinthian church concerning giving. He builds on the foundation of what has happened in the Macedonian churches and goes on to note that the Corinthians "excel in everything—in faith, in speech, in knowledge, in utmost eagerness, and in our love for ou—so we want [the Corinthians] to xcel also in this generous undertaking" 2 Cor. 8:7, NRSV). It may be confusing to understand how the Corinthians could xcel in Paul's love for them. However, what Paul meant was that the love that the Corinthians had was from Paul because he inspired them to have it by the care he exhibited. So in other words, Paul wanted the Corinthians to excel in the love in them that was inspired by him and his companions. This builds on Paul's earlier boast to Titus concerning the nature of the Corinthians' hospitality.

In Paul's plea for the Corinthians, he does not command them to give. Instead, he builds upon the experience of the Macedonians and the hospitable nature of the Corinthians in making his plea— I do not say this as a command, but I am testing the genuineness of your love against the earnestness of others" (v. 8, NRSV). Paul must tread lightly with the Corinthians in this new letter if he wants to recover his relationship from the grief his last letter caused. His approach must be balanced and appeal to the Corinthians' good nature.

Additionally, Paul does not command the Corinthians to give, because genuine giving must be a choice. If we look back to the beginning of this epistle, we can see that Paul has been testing the Corinthians in their faithfulness. In the past, he was testing them in their ability to address the one who was causing strife in the church (see 2 Cor. 2:5–11), and now he is testing their love in the matter of giving. This should not be understood as an attempt by Paul to manipulate in a sinister way the life of the Corinthian church. Paul is instead at work to help form their character in their ability to address conflicts in the church in a way that builds the church up instead of destroying it. Likewise, he is at work here to form their character into that of a giving congregation motivated by their love for the Church universal.

In 2 Corinthians 8:8–13, Paul teaches the aspect of sacrificial giving based upon Christ's sacrifice for humankind. In verse 9, the Greek term charis can be rendered as "grace." Paul contextualizes the notion of giving by pointing to Jesus. There is a connection between this point in 2 Corinthians and Philippians regarding the self-giving nature of love. Paul writes in Philippians, "Let the same mind be in you that was in Christ Jesus, who … emptied himself" (2:5–7, NRSV). Jesus gave up His place in heaven to become human and further humbled Himself to the point of dying on a Roman cross. He, who was wealthy in all senses of the word, "became poor, so that by his poverty [believers] might become rich" (2 Cor. 8:9, NRSV). Make no mistake about it, Christ does not make us all rich economically. However, Christ does offer rich new relationships, new families, a sense of belonging, shared resources, and eternal life (see Mark 10:29–30).

Paul reminds the Corinthian church of Christ's sacrifice in verse 9. It is appropriate for the Corinthians to give back to members of the Body of Christ, the community of faith that Christ brought together through His sacrifice. Christ gave of Himself, and Paul calls for the Corinthians to give of themselves.

In 2 Corinthians, Paul uses the same concept of giving of one's self from

Philippians but frames it in economic terms. This re-framing is appropriate because Paul is building on the example of the Macedonians—and in doing so, connecting the kenosis (self-emptying) of Christ Jesus to the self-giving of the Macedonians—in making his appeal for the Corinthians to give financially.

Paul now makes it clear that he is not commanding the Corinthians to give but exhorting them to reclaim their previous desire to do so—"it is appropriate for you who began last year not only to do something but even to desire to do something—now finish doing it, so that your eagerness may be matched by completing it according to your means" (2 Cor. 8:10–11, NRSV). Paul is pointing out that the conflicts that have arisen in the recent past have distracted the Corinthians from their promise and desire to give. However, he uses the examples of the Macedonians and Jesus to help rekindle the generous spirit they once had.

Paul also makes it clear that he does not desire giving to become a burden for the Corinthians. He desires that they should give according to their means. Paul sees, and wants the Corinthians to see, that while a congregation has a responsibility to those in the congregation, the congregation also has a responsibility to attend to the material and spiritual needs of those in the Church universal.

In verse fifteen, Paul alludes to an Old Testament story (see Exod. 16:18). When the children of Israel were wandering in the wilderness, God gave them bread from heaven called manna. They were instructed to take as much as they needed. Some gathered a lot but did not have much leftover after consumption. Other gathered small amounts of manna bu still had a little leftover. Each group ha just enough—no matter their need, bi or small. All shared fair access and fai distribution of needed resources.

Fair does not mean equal. If large fami lies received the same amount of manna a small families, then large families woul experience lack. If small families receive that same amount allotted to large fami lies, then the small families would be a an advantage because they would hav surplus. So fair access and distribution i about equitable access and distribution Paul's point is about fairness.

Paul expects the churches to do the part according to their ability, and t help each other in times of need. Th Corinthians had great prosperity becaus of their social location as a bustlin economic trade center. However, ther might come a time when they may be i need. Their generosity in the Jerusaler collection would be reciprocated in th future. In the letter to the Romans, Pau talks about the reciprocity related to th Jerusalem collection. The Jewish believ ers had shared their spiritual wealth wit the Gentiles, so the Gentile believer should reciprocate by ministering to th material needs of the Jewish believers (se Rom. 15:27).

II. PAUL'S THANKS FOR TITUS (2 CORINTHIANS 8:15)

Paul gave thanks for Titus' role i promoting and collecting the Jerusaler offering. Paul notes Titus' passio and excitement about this task. It seem as though Titus was self-motivated an took initiative to make the campaig successful. Paul knew he himself could not do this work alone. He enlisted the help of Titus and others to collect the offering for the Jerusalem church. Effective leaders recognize the talents and passions of others and allow them to put those things to work. Not only do effective leaders delegate to others, but they also praise and formally acknowledge the work of their co-laborers. This is what Paul did in 2 Corinthians. Offering praise can encourage continued commitment and growth from ministry workers.

Paul told the Corinthians that three men were being sent to them to collect their offering. They already knew Titus, who had been among them before. Paul does not name the other two men. One of them was appointed by the churches to assist with the collection, according to verse 19. Paul also does not say which churches appointed him; however, it could have been those in Macedonia or Asia Minor or Galatia. Nevertheless, he has a widespread, good reputation. It is also unclear whose idea it was to elect him to this receiving delegation. Was it Paul's or the churches'? We do not know, but it does seem like this first unnamed brother is a part of the team to ensure the integrity of the team.

The other team member is closely affiliated with Paul. The elected member is independent of Paul. Paul had faced accusations of greed in Thessalonica and would again later in Corinth. Having an independent member protected Paul's reputation and removed the potential for abuse of the churches' generosity. Paul explicitly alludes to this protection: "We intend that no one should blame us about this generous gift that we are administering, for we intend to do what is right not only in the Lord's sight but also in the sight of others" (2 Cor. 8:20–21).

THE LESSON APPLIED

Throughout 2 Corinthians, Paul is at work to develop the character of the Corinthian church. He does this by pointing to their previous good works and desires. Paul knows that there is within the Corinthian church the ability to live communally in a life of faithful discipleship. This ability, of course, does not come from the Corinthians, but from the grace of God. In his appeal to the story of the Macedonians, Paul describes a people who are living in a way that runs counter to their circumstances. He describes this as grace as well. Far too often, grace is only thought about in terms of justification. Paul, however, is discussing grace as something that forms character.

God meets His people in their actions with His grace to form them to be the people He intends for the life of the world. Although Paul praised the Macedonians for giving out of their poverty, God is to be praised ultimately and above all. The Macedonians' giving is a result of God's nature, character, and likeness being formed in them. When we allow ourselves to conform to the image of God, then we will do things that He does. God gave of Himself for the world. As we recognize that sacrifice, we will be willing to give of ourselves to our community and to the world beyond it.

LET'S TALK ABOUT IT

1. **Paul made arrangements for the Corinthians to give. How should we**

be intentional today about providing opportunities to give?

The traditional way of giving in church typically happens during Sunday morning service. The majority of churches' operating budgets are funded by what is collected in the offering plates on Sunday. This model of giving may have been successful when church attendance was high in our society decades ago when people who identified as Christians would faithfully attend church. Nowadays the church competes for people's commitment in the area of time and money and unfortunately, too often the church does not sustain people's commitment.

People go on vacations, attend social events, or stay home for a break from church. The church must be intentional about reaching these people despite their absence. Churches can provide opportunities for them to give online—through the church's website or an app. We must ask ourselves, if one of our church members woke up in the middle of the night inspired to give to the work of the Lord, is there a way to facilitate that desire to give?

We also should think about estate planning—asking members to include the church or one of its ministries in their wills or insurance policies.

Churches can hold annual drives to create legacy giving. Host workshops with estate lawyers to help members draft wills and set up financial trusts.

2. How do you motivate people to do ministry?

It is common with any cause—in or outside of the church—for people to be excited in the initial stages. However, as the mission takes time, money, and effort, people's commitment can wane. Such was the case with the Jerusalem offering. Initially, the Corinthians were committed to giving, but within a year's time, they had become unmotivated.

In order to boost their participation, Paul took three basic steps. First he reminded them of their commitment. Sometimes people will only follow through with a vow when they are held accountable. Don't be afraid to remind someone of what they committed to do in ministry. Secondly, Paul gave them an example of another church's participation ministry. It was a church with fewer resources than the Corinthians, but through determination and effort they had done more. Lastly, Paul pointed to Jesus as the ultimate Sacrifice. We must keep Christ at the center of all ministry endeavors. Remind others that the church's service to the community is about glorifying our risen Savior.

HOME DAILY DEVOTIONAL READINGS
AUGUST 13–19, 2018

MONDAY	TUESDAY	WEDNESDAY	THURSDAY	FRIDAY	SATURDAY	SUNDAY
Many Members in One Body	Aim to Live by the Spirit	Respond to Abuse with a Blessing	Treat Enemies with Love and Mercy	Don't Act by Human Standards	New Life in Christian Community	Behavioral Action Goals of Christians
1 Corinthians 12:12–26	Galatians 5:16–26	1 Peter 3:8–12	Luke 6:27–36	2 Corinthians 10:1–5	Romans 12:1–8	Romans 12:9–21

LOVING AND JUST BEHAVIOR

ADULT TOPIC: EQUITY IN CONDUCT	BACKGROUND SCRIPTURE: ROMANS 12:9–21

ROMANS 12:9–21

King James Version

LET love be without dissimulation. Abhor that which is evil; cleave to that which is good.

10 Be kindly affectioned one to another with brotherly love; in honour preferring one another;

11 Not slothful in business; fervent in spirit; serving the Lord;

12 Rejoicing in hope; patient in tribulation; continuing instant in prayer;

13 Distributing to the necessity of saints; given to hospitality.

14 Bless them which persecute you: bless, and curse not.

15 Rejoice with them that do rejoice, and weep with them that weep.

16 Be of the same mind one toward another. Mind not high things, but condescend to men of low estate. Be not wise in your own conceits.

17 Recompense to no man evil for evil. Provide things honest in the sight of all men.

18 If it be possible, as much as lieth in you, live peaceably with all men.

19 Dearly beloved, avenge not yourselves, but rather give place unto wrath: for it is written, Vengeance is mine; I will repay, saith the Lord.

20 Therefore if thine enemy hunger, feed him; if he thirst, give him drink: for in so doing thou shalt heap coals of fire on his head.

21 Be not overcome of evil, but overcome evil with good.

New Revised Standard Version

LET love be genuine; hate what is evil, hold fast to what is good;

10 love one another with mutual affection; outdo one another in showing honor.

11 Do not lag in zeal, be ardent in spirit, serve the Lord.

12 Rejoice in hope, be patient in suffering, persevere in prayer.

13 Contribute to the needs of the saints; extend hospitality to strangers.

14 Bless those who persecute you; bless and do not curse them.

15 Rejoice with those who rejoice, weep with those who weep.

16 Live in harmony with one another; do not be haughty, but associate with the lowly; do not claim to be wiser than you are.

17 Do not repay anyone evil for evil, but take thought for what is noble in the sight of all.

18 If it is possible, so far as it depends on you, live peaceably with all.

19 Beloved, never avenge yourselves, but leave room for the wrath of God; for it is written, "Vengeance is mine, I will repay, says the Lord."

20 No, "if your enemies are hungry, feed them; if they are thirsty, give them something to drink; for by doing this you will heap burning coals on their heads."

21 Do not be overcome by evil, but overcome evil with good.

MAIN THOUGHT: Let love be without dissimulation. Abhor that which is evil; cleave to that which is good. (Romans 12:9, KJV)

LESSON SETTING
     Time: ca. A.D. 55–57
     Place: Rome

LESSON OUTLINE
  I. **The Character of a Christian
     (Romans 12:9–13)**
 II. **The Treatment of Enemies
     (Romans 12:14–21)**

UNIFYING PRINCIPLE

We want to be loving persons. What makes for genuine love in the world? Paul offers the marks of true love that are to be lived by the faithful.

INTRODUCTION

There is broad scholarly consensus that the Apostle Paul wrote this letter from the city of Corinth, most likely some time during the winter of A.D. 55–56 or 56–57. (You may recall that Acts 18:1–17 contains an account of his stay in Corinth.) What is less clear is the exact purpose of the letter to the church in Rome. Several reasons for writing have been discerned from the text of the letter, and there is much debate among commentators about these reasons. Michael Gorman describes a few of the reasons: "Most scholars agree that there is a variety of reasons for Romans. For instance, the letter serves as a splendid introduction to the apostle and his teaching so that the Romans will both accept him when he comes (whether or not there were already some critics of Paul in Rome) and, he no doubt hopes, for their support in his mission work, especially as he heads for Spain. In the meantime, he also wants support for the collection for the poor Jewish believers in Jerusalem, and he undoubtedly desires a positive reception of his gospel and ministry when he actually goes to Jerusalem. The moral support of the Roman church would certainly help him in that regard" (*Apostle of the Crucified Lord: A Theological Introduction to Paul and His Letters* [Grand Rapids: Eerdmans, 2004], 342–343). All of these can be clearly derived from the text.

Finally, we can discuss the place of today's text in the larger context of the letter. Of course, there are as many possible outlines of this letter as there are scholars and commentators who have written on it. As valuable as some (or even all) of those may be, there is one key division in this letter—the one that comes between 11:36 and 12:1—that is of particular importance for us. It is at this point that Paul transitions from the doctrinal discussion of the first eleven chapters to the ethical emphasis of the final chapters. C. K. Barrett captures the significance of this division, and cautions us not to overplay it even as we recognize its importance: "It is pointed out in most commentaries that a major division of the epistle falls between chs. xi and xii; chs. i–xi form the dogmatic part of the epistle, chs. xii and xii (or xii–xv) the ethical. There is, of course, a measure of truth in this observation; but it is a serious mistake to treat the two parts of the epistle as distinct from each other. Paul's dogmatic teaching is misunderstood if it is not seen to require ethical action, and his ethical teaching cannot be grasped if it is not recognized that it rests at every point upon the dogmatics. So far from its being a contradiction of the doctrine of justification by faith (good works returning, as it were, by a back door after their formal expulsion) [the ethical teaching] is best understood as an exposition of the obedience which is n essential element in faith (i. 5), and of he gratitude which redeemed and justified man is bound to feel towards the merciful God" (*The Epistle to the Romans* [New York: Harper & Brothers, 1957], 230; emphasis added). Put in another way, we cannot understand Romans 12–15 apart from Romans 1–11. So, despite what we might be tempted to think, Paul was not contradicting himself when he gave the instructions listed in Romans 12. With that in mind, let us turn to today's text.

EXPOSITION

I. THE CHARACTER OF A CHRISTIAN (ROMANS 12:9–13)

As we just pointed out, Paul's appeals to the Romans to live in a manner that is worthy of Christ are based on the doctrinal teaching of the first eleven chapters of the letter. We see that explicitly at the beginning of chapter 12: "I appeal to you therefore, brothers and sisters, by the mercies of God…" (v. 1, NRSV). Paul's "therefore" indicates that everything he is about to say is based upon everything he has just said.

Paul begins, "Let love be genuine; hate what is evil, hold fast to what is good" (v. 9, NRSV). The command to love comes first. As Barrett notes, everything that follows this "illustrate[s] various aspects of the general command of love" (240). Paul specifically enjoined that love be "genuine" (Grk. *anypokritos*), not insincere, and without hypocrisy. Those of us who have been Christians for many years have no doubt seen this tendency in ourselves or in others. Paul warns us against it—a more difficult call than we might sometimes think. What follows—"hate what is evil, hold fast to what is good"—might seem to diverge from the exhortation to love. We

should instead see it as a definition of love: love entails the pursuit of the good and the utter rejection of evil. One can see similar language in the Prophets: "hate evil and love good" (Amos 5:15, NRSV). Michael F. Bird notes that the "emotive language of 'hate' and 'cling'" can be found throughout the Jewish tradition, as well as in the Fathers: "According to Origen, 'A person who does not hate the vices cannot love and preserve the virtues'" (*Romans* [Grand Rapids: Zondervan, 2016], 431).

With the next set of commands, Paul turns his focus to the mutual character of love: "love one another with mutual affection; outdo one another in showing honor" (Rom. 12:10, NRSV). This mutuality is emphasized by the appearance of *allēlous* (Grk. "one another") in both phrases. There is considerable variation in how the first clause is rendered. The NIV (2011) reads, "Be devoted to one another in love," which is weak and doesn't fully capture the force of what Paul is saying. The fundamental issue is how best to understand the force of *philadelphia* in this clause. Barrett's rendering, "with love that befits a brotherhood be affectionate to one another" (240), on the other hand, puts more load-bearing weight on *philadelphia* than we can rightly expect it to support. The NRSV's "love one another with mutual affection" and the ESV's "love one another with brotherly affection" strike a fair middle ground, so long as we remember the familial connotations behind *philadelphia* and *philostorgos*.

Verse eleven turns to a more general exhortation: "do not lag in zeal, be ardent in spirit, serve the Lord" (NRSV). Bird's comments here are apt: "The first part of the command is that Christians should not become complacent in their divine service. They should not allow their diligence to dwindle. In contrast, they should serve the Lord with a fiery fervency. Several translations miss out on the metaphor of fire that stands behind the word *zeō* as it means to be emotionally stirred up, to boil over, and be on fire.... The [Common English Bible] is preferable with 'be on fire in the Spirit as you serve the Lord!' Instead of letting the flame of love fade, believers need to keep the spiritual fire in their bellies freshly kindled!" (431–32).

The final two verses in this portion of the text contain a series of exhortations that suggests that they were addressed to a group of persecuted believers. Paul writes, "Rejoice in hope, be patient in suffering, persevere in prayer" (v. 12, NRSV). The exhortations in verse twelve encourage the believers in Rome not to be discouraged, but to look beyond their circumstances (whatever those might be exactly) to the reward that is to come.

Paul then reminds them to renew their concern and care for one another and for the stranger in their midst: "Contribute to the needs of the saints; extend hospitality to strangers" (v. 13, NRSV). Here, as elsewhere, Paul exhorts churches to give priority to the needs of their own so that the community of believers might be strengthened. This was certainly not a call to ignore needy pagans, as Paul's very next words concerning hospitality toward strangers make clear, but taken as a whole Paul's words on the subject establish a clear priority. The Church's care for her own is a demonstration of God's love and a reaffirmation of an idea that Paul states

more clearly elsewhere: "Whoever does not provide for relatives, and especially for family members, has denied the faith and is worse than an unbeliever" (1 Tim 5:8, NRSV).

II. THE TREATMENT OF ENEMIES (ROMANS 12:14–21)

The second portion of today's text changes direction, focusing our attention more directly on the realities of life as a persecuted minority. As we read these lines, we should recall the words of Jesus in the Sermon on the Mount: "Blessed are you when people revile you and persecute you and utter all kinds of evil against you falsely on my account.... You have heard that it was said, 'You shall love your neighbor and hate your enemy.' But I say to you, Love your enemies and pray for those who persecute you, so that you may be children of your Father in heaven" (Matt. 5:11, 43–45, NRSV).

It is easy for us to forget that the Christian faith took root in a world, a society, that was hostile to its claims. The earliest churches begun and nurtured by the apostles faced mistrust and hostility from both pagans and Jews. We see a good deal of evidence of this in the New Testament itself, as well as instruction given to the disciples regarding how to deal with the challenge of persecution. First-century persecution, we should recall, did not entail rounding up hundreds or thousands of believers at a time and imprisoning or executing them. (Systematic empire-wide persecution only commenced in the third century A.D.) Far more often it entailed social ostracism or economic pressure or similar methods. Compared to more extreme forms of persecution, these were relatively mild. Mild, though, is not the same thing as inconsequential or meaningless. On either end of the spectrum of persecution, being a Christian carried a significant cost with it.

But with the reality of persecution, there also came a new way of dealing with it, outlined by Paul. The common ethic in such a situation, accepted by both pagans and Jews, was to seek revenge either individually or perhaps at the hands of the ruling authorities. Paul's words, though, are a total rejection of this (quite natural) impulse: "Bless those who persecute you; bless and do not curse them.... If it is possible, so far as it depends on you, live peaceably with all" (Rom. 12:14, 18, NRSV).

The final verses are even more explicit; they totally upend our expectations for how we should treat our enemies: "No, 'if your enemies are hungry, feed them; if they are thirsty, give them something to drink; for by doing this you will heap burning coals on their heads.' Do not be overcome by evil, but overcome evil with good" (vv. 20–21, NRSV; citing Prov. 25:21–22 [LXX]).

THE LESSON APPLIED

Many of the things that Paul urges on his readers in today's text may seem obvious to us. That may be true, of course, but all of us periodically need the reminders that this passage offers. After faith in Christ, Christian community is founded first and foremost on genuine love and concern for our brothers and sisters. That love is not merely abstract or theoretical; it calls upon each of us not to seek retribution but to make sacrifices for one another, to "outdo one another in showing honor" (v. 10, NRSV).

LET'S TALK ABOUT IT

1. **Do Paul's words about enemies apply to the Church today?**

Before we can talk about just how applicable these words are, we must acknowledge another reality. Sometimes we as American Christians are tempted to believe that we have no enemies. We enjoy the freedom of religion. We live in a society that is comprised of a majority of (at least nominal) Christians. Most of us, though, have lived long enough to know that the proclamation of the Gospel elicits hostility on the part of many. Whatever their motivations, they oppose the Gospel standard by which we seek to live our lives. How are we called to interact with them? In precisely the manner suggested to us by the Apostle Paul, we are to love and not revile them. We are to serve and do good to them. We are to model the character of our Lord Jesus.

HOME DAILY DEVOTIONAL READINGS
AUGUST 20–26, 2018

MONDAY	TUESDAY	WEDNESDAY	THURSDAY	FRIDAY	SATURDAY	SUNDAY
Buried in Baptism; Raised with Christ	God's Example in All Relationships	Life with Christ in the World	Life in the Spirit	Speak Truthfully Always	Replace Anger with Forgiveness	Live the New Life in Christ
Colossians 2:6–12	Matthew 5:43–48	John 17:14–19	Romans 8:1–11	Ephesians 4:25–30	Ephesians 4:31–5:2	Colossians 3:1–17

PRACTICING JUSTICE

ADULT TOPIC: EQUITY IN CHARACTER	BACKGROUND SCRIPTURES: EPHESIANS 4:25–5:2; COLOSSIANS 3:1–17

COLOSSIANS 3:5–17

King James Version

MORTIFY therefore your members which are upon the earth; fornication, uncleanness, inordinate affection, evil concupiscence, and covetousness, which is idolatry:

6 For which things' sake the wrath of God cometh on the children of disobedience:

7 In the which ye also walked some time, when ye lived in them.

8 But now ye also put off all these; anger, wrath, malice, blasphemy, filthy communication out of your mouth.

9 Lie not one to another, seeing that ye have put off the old man with his deeds;

10 And have put on the new man, which is renewed in knowledge after the image of him that created him:

11 Where there is neither Greek nor Jew, circumcision nor uncircumcision, Barbarian, Scythian, bond nor free: but Christ is all, and in all.

12 Put on therefore, as the elect of God, holy and beloved, bowels of mercies, kindness, humbleness of mind, meekness, longsuffering;

13 Forbearing one another, and forgiving one another, if any man have a quarrel against any: even as Christ forgave you, so also do ye.

14 And above all these things put on charity, which is the bond of perfectness.

15 And let the peace of God rule in your hearts, to the which also ye are called in one body; and be ye thankful.

New Revised Standard Version

PUT to death, therefore, whatever in you is earthly: fornication, impurity, passion, evil desire, and greed (which is idolatry).

6 On account of these the wrath of God is coming on those who are disobedient.

7 These are the ways you also once followed, when you were living that life.

8 But now you must get rid of all such things—anger, wrath, malice, slander, and abusive language from your mouth.

9 Do not lie to one another, seeing that you have stripped off the old self with its practices

10 and have clothed yourselves with the new self, which is being renewed in knowledge according to the image of its creator.

11 In that renewal there is no longer Greek and Jew, circumcised and uncircumcised, barbarian, Scythian, slave and free; but Christ is all and in all!

12 As God's chosen ones, holy and beloved, clothe yourselves with compassion, kindness, humility, meekness, and patience.

13 Bear with one another and, if anyone has a complaint against another, forgive each other; just as the Lord has forgiven you, so you also must forgive.

14 Above all, clothe yourselves with love, which binds everything together in perfect harmony.

15 And let the peace of Christ rule in your hearts, to which indeed you were called in the one body. And be thankful.

MAIN THOUGHT: Put on therefore, as the elect of God, holy and beloved, bowels of mercies, kindness, humbleness of mind, meekness, longsuffering. (Colossians 3:12, KJV)

COLOSSIANS 3:5—17

King James Version	*New Revised Standard Version*
16 Let the word of Christ dwell in you richly in all wisdom; teaching and admonishing one another in psalms and hymns and spiritual songs, singing with grace in your hearts to the Lord.	16 Let the word of Christ dwell in you richly; teach and admonish one another in all wisdom; and with gratitude in your hearts sing psalms, hymns, and spiritual songs to God.
17 And whatsoever ye do in word or deed, do all in the name of the Lord Jesus, giving thanks to God and the Father by him.	17 And whatever you do, in word or deed, do everything in the name of the Lord Jesus, giving thanks to God the Father through him.

LESSON SETTING
Time: A.D. 50s
Place: Colossae

LESSON OUTLINE
  I. **Paul's Ethical Exhortations (Colossians 3:5–11)**
  II. **Paul's Exhortations for Virtuous Living (Colossians 3:12–17)**

UNIFYING PRINCIPLE
People want to live lives that make a difference. What makes for living justly in the world? Paul encourages the faithful to clothe themselves with the love of Christ and let the peace of Christ rule in their hearts.

INTRODUCTION
This letter to the Colossian Christians was written to dissuade them from a particular philosophy of the time. Biblical scholars have debated the nature and origin of this philosophy. Some have claimed that it was a Jewish form of Gnosticism or from a Jewish mystic cult. Others have speculated the philosophy was of Hellenistic origins. Lastly, there are others who believe that it is a syncretistic combination of Jewish and Hellenistic thought and practice. Whatever its origin, the writer of Colossians exhorts his audience not to embrace the philosophy but rather good works. Major features of this philosophy included practices such as worship of angels, preoccupation with visions, and strict self-denial and abstention (see 2:8, 18, 23). Paul argues that adherence to these beliefs and practices is a result of being caught up in "philosophy and empty deceit, according to human tradition, according to the elemental spirits of the universe, and not according to Christ" (Col. 2:8, NRSV). Paul pleads with the Colossians to strongly reconsider their decision to go back to these rudimentary elements.

EXPOSITION

I. PAUL'S ETHICAL EXHORTATIONS (COLOSSIANS 3:5–11)
Beginning in verse five, Paul makes a shift from the affirmations about heavenly mindedness in verses one through four. Now Paul addresses ethical exhortations that concern one's behavior on earth. This shift does not indicate departure or contradiction of the previous exhortations. Rather, Paul's instructions in verses five through eleven are embodied in practical living by the person who has heaven in mind. In other words, our future glory in

heaven has implications for the way we live in the present.

The teachers of the erroneous philosophy were also concerned about how the Colossians lived on earth, particularly about what they did with their physical bodies in the earthly realm. Paul takes up this same notion, but from a totally different perspective. The false teachers were strict about what one did with one's body with superficial regulations: "'Do not handle, Do not taste, Do not touch'" (Col. 2:21, NRSV). To these regulations Paul says, "All these regulations refer to things that perish with use; they are simply human commands and teachings" (v. 22, NRSV). Here in 3:5–11, Paul does not give restrictions for a list of body parts as the false teachers would. Rather, Paul gives a list of vices, which the Colossians are encouraged to "put to death" (v. 5, NRSV). Putting to death these vices is dying with Christ. In Paul's mind, we have not only died with Christ at the moment of our conversion, but continue to die with Christ as we reject and turn away from evil behavior on a daily basis.

The first five vices that Paul lists in verse five start off explicitly sexual and then become more general. In verse eight, Paul lists five more general vices. The first vice is fornication (Greek *porneia*); it is a broad term used for sexual immorality but closely associated with temple prostitution. Impurity also associated with sexual sin is typically linked to fornication in the Pauline epistles (see 2 Cor. 12:21; Gal. 5:19; 1 Thess. 4:3, 7). Passion, which also could be translated as lust, probably refers to uninhibited sexual desire. Evil desire begins the list of more general vices.

Greed is next and can be also translated as covetousness. Paul links it to idolatry. This kind of greed sees things and people as existing only for personal pleasure and use. Greed does not appreciate, respect, or acknowledge God as Creator, but rather elevates creation to the center of life, which is idolatrous.

Those who do not heed the apostle will face the wrath of God. In the beginning of chapter three, Paul had encouraged the Colossians to set their minds on things above. This heavenly mindset should encourage righteous living on earth. Now in verse six, Paul warns them of impending punishment if they do not put off sinful living. This should not be taken as Paul trying to guilt the Colossians into following the right path, but rather to give them full knowledge of their choices.

Paul reminds his audience that these vices are how they once lived. They should not be current habits. Paul encourages the Colossians to completely stop practicing the five vices listed in verse five and then adds five more vices to the list in verse eight. Anger begins the list. Wrath follows and is almost synonymous with anger. However, as Andrew Lincoln points out, "Stoic writers sometimes distinguished them, with rage denoting the initial explosion of anger" (*The New Interpreter's Bible* Vol. XI [Nashville: Abingdon Press, 2000], 643). Malice denotes any intent to cause harm to another person. Slander (Greek *blasphēmia*) is when a person's reputation is maligned and falsely accused. Abusive language is the use of foul and obscene language. These vices also should not be found among the community of believers.

Paul's list of vices moves from sexual to more general and from general to more specific vices of speech. He concludes his lists of vices with one last speech vice: lying. Lying, just like the other vices, not only damages an individual's reputation as a follower of Christ but also destroys the community of faith. Paul is concerned about these believers as individuals and as a body of believers. He wants to preserve the integrity of each believer and that of the community. These vices break down communication, destroy trust, and breed division in the community.

In verse nine, the Greek terms *apkeduo* and *enduo* refer to putting off and putting on clothing. Again, Paul takes up a notion that would be similar to the erroneous philosophy. The act of stripping the body might have been an ascetic practice. However, Paul adds his own ethical twist to the concept of stripping one's self: stripping off the old person and its old behavior. This figurative language is connected to the baptism, which is a theme used throughout the passage. Throughout this letter to the Colossians, Paul has been alluding to baptism and particularly its symbolism of dying with Christ to one's old self and being raised with Him to new life. Paul's analogy of putting off the "old self" and putting on the "new self" is also found in Romans 6.

In verse 11, the term "Greek" refers to all Gentiles as contrasted with Jews. The Scythian in verse 11 refers to an uncultured person mainly from around the Black Sea. The demographic descriptors indicate the entire world in its sections. This is contrasted with Christ as the only Reconciler for all.

II. PAUL'S EXHORTATIONS FOR VIRTUOUS LIVING (COLOSSIANS 3:12–17)

Paul now moves to talking about virtues that would benefit the community and promote harmony among them. Just as he has encouraged the Colossians to put off certain vices, he now encourages them to put on specific virtues. This is an important step because if Paul does not give his readers something to work towards, it would be easy for them to fall back into their old habits. Learning new positive behavior will leave less time for picking up old negative behavior. Paul understood this about human nature.

Paul declares the Colossians to be "God's chosen ones, holy and beloved" (v. 12, NRSV), which were titles commonly given to the children of Israel, God's first chosen people. Paul's declaration must have had a powerful effect on his readers. The Jews, although socially marginalized at the time, had a sense of pride because of their relation to the Creator. They were proud to be God's chosen people, His beloved, and set apart for Himself. Paul sees his Gentile readers in the same light. It was through God's grace and initiative that the Gentiles became a part of God's people. As newly adopted children of God, they had to learn a new way of living.

Paul admonished the Colossians to put on compassion and kindness. It is impossible to have a unified community without community members having genuine concern and care for each other. Jesus told His disciples on one occasion, "'By this everyone will know that you are my disciples, if you have love for one another'" (John 13:35, NRSV).

This expectation is not for everyone, but only for those who have accepted God's invitation to be God's own chosen people through Jesus Christ.

Love creates the perfect bond of peace within the community. Love is the greatest virtue we can possess, which is similar to what Paul says in 1 Corinthians 13. Lincoln characterizes love in these texts this way: "In 1 Corinthians love is a personified power of the new ages; here it is like a garment to be put on or appropriated by believers. In Colossians, it is more explicitly the peace of Christ that is personified and sees, as ruling the new order" (648).

God is concerned about us being faithful members of the Body of Christ who display God's love. Love continues to be the greatest virtue that we can possess. God is concerned about both our words and our deeds being done in the name of the Lord Jesus. God is praised and thanked when Jesus is lifted up in our lives.

THE LESSON APPLIED

We have new life in Christ. Because He died and was raised from the dead, we die to sin and are raised to righteous living. The same Spirit that brought Him from the dead lives inside of us and empowers us to live virtuous and holy lives. As believers, we are able to do good works not only individually but collectively as communities of faith. When we exhibit holy living, our communities are unified. They are not uniform in the sense that all members think, act, speak, and look alike. Our unity is the bringing together of diverse people through a shared principle of loving God and loving each other. Our good works are experienced first within the community of faith and then abroad. With greater unity within, we are able to have greater impact on the world.

LET'S TALK ABOUT IT

1. What is the importance of baptism for the Christian?

As Baptists, we do not believe that baptism has the power to save us. Jesus' sacrifice is the only thing that provides salvation for the sinful nature of humanity. Our sins are washed away in the blood of Jesus, not the waters of baptism. Therefore, baptism is a sign—solemn and beautiful—of our faith in the crucified, buried, and risen Savior, Jesus Christ. Baptism shows our identification with Christ and the effect of His death and resurrection—that we, too, are dead to sin and resurrected to a new life. Baptism is an outward marker of this experience, but the true evidence of this experience is that we live new lives. We put off old sinful habits and put on virtuous living.

MONDAY	TUESDAY	WEDNESDAY	THURSDAY	FRIDAY	SATURDAY	SUNDAY
David Eats the Bread of Presence	Lord Desires Mercy Not Sacrifice	Plucking Grain	The Sabbath Is for Merciful Acts	The Father and I Are Working	Deliver Justice for the Oppressed	Meet Human Need on the Sabbath
1 Samuel 21:1–6	Hosea 6:1–6	Leviticus 19:9–10; Deuteronomy 23:25	Luke 14:1–6	John 5:9–18	Psalm 10:12–18	Matthew 12:1–14

Notes

Notes